ENTREPRENEURIAL
MANAGEMENT IN
SMALL FIRMS

Ian Chaston

Los Angeles | London | New Delhi
Singapore | Washington DC

SAGE Publications Ltd
1 Oliver's Yard
55 City Road
London EC1Y 1SP

SAGE Publications Inc.
2455 Teller Road
Thousand Oaks, California 91320

SAGE Publications India Pvt Ltd
B 1/I 1 Mohan Cooperative Industrial Area
Mathura Road
New Delhi 110 044

SAGE Publications Asia-Pacific Pte Ltd
33 Pekin Street #02-01
Far East Square
Singapore 048763

Library of Congress Control Number: 2009922029

British Library Cataloguing in Publication data

A catalogue record for this book is available from
the British Library

ISBN 978-1-84860-024-9
ISBN 978-1-84860-025-6 (pbk)

Typeset by C&M Digitals Pvt Ltd, Chennai, India
Printed by MPG Books Group, Bodmin, Cornwall
Printed on paper from sustainable resources

Mixed Sources
Product group from well-managed
forests and other controlled sources
www.fsc.org Cert no. SA-COC-1565
© 1996 Forest Stewardship Council
FSC

Contents

Guided Tour   vi
Preface   vii

1   Entrepreneurs   1

2   Planning   20

3   Opportunity Research   35

4   Growth, Chasms and Money   53

5   Market Assessment   73

6   Internal Capability   92

7   Strategy and Culture   109

8   Entrepreneurial Innovation   126

9   Entrepreneurial Promotion   144

10 Pricing and Distribution   162

11 Family and Social Entrepreneurship   183

12 Twenty-first-century Entrepreneurs   200

Glossary   221

References   241

Index   258

Guided Tour

Chapter Objectives: A clear set of bullet pointed learning objectives are provided at the beginning of each chapter.

Case Study and Case Aims: Each chapter includes boxed cases, together with case aims that outline what the case illustrates and how.

Summary Learning Points: Useful concluding points reiterate and summarise the main issues raised.

Additional Information Sources: A selection of further readings and websites, arranged according to their topic relevance.

Glossary: A detailed glossary of terms provided at the end of the book.

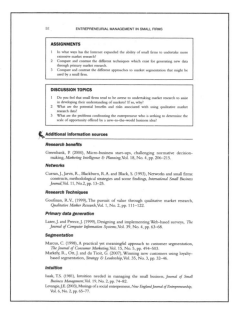

Assignments: Suggestions for practical assignments to enable students to put their learning to work.

Discussion Topics: A range of questions provide a starting point for further discussion and debate of issues raised.

Companion Website

Be sure to visit the companion website at www.sagepub.co.uk/chaston to find a range of teaching and learning materials.

For instructors:

- An **instructors' manual** offering further information about the chapter coverage, as well as guidance on the chapter assignments and discussion topics.
- Detailed **PowerPoint** slides for each chapter.

For students:

- Extensive **online journal readings** – *over 200* full-text journal articles.
- **Links to relevent websites** are provided and will help with research and assignments.
- An **online glossary** that covers all the relevant terms in the book.

Preface

In the provision of undergraduate and postgraduate programmes, business schools recognise their success is dependent on the provision of courses which can enhance the employability of their students. Until very recently, most students were interested in acquiring the educational qualifications which would increase the probability of obtaining a managerial post in a large private or public sector organisation. Given both the research orientation of academics and the career aspirations of students, syllabus content has remained dominated by theories associated with the effective management of large organisations.

During the 1980s industrial restructuring led to the Small and Medium-size (SME) sector becoming the primary source of new job creation in many Western nation economies. Governments who had traditionally focused their economic policies on assisting large firms, redirected resources into the provision of support programmes to assist existing small firms and to increase the rate of new small business start-ups. This change in public sector policy caused more academics to begin researching the small firm sector. From these studies it became apparent that business practices in many small firms are very different from those previously identified in relation to the large firm sector.

By the 1990s, students entering further and higher education were expressing interest in programmes which contained modules about small business management. This trend could be attributed to factors such as the declining employment opportunities in large firms, observing the impact on their parents' generation of companies 'downsizing' and concerns about working in the anonymous, inflexible environments that can exist in a very large corporation. Many colleges now offer small business courses at certificate, undergraduate or postgraduate level. The standard content of these courses and topic coverage in the supporting textbooks includes issues such as the personal characteristics of owner/managers, small business start-ups, causes of business failure, alternative small firm structures, business planning, financial management, sources of finance, human resource management, business law, organisational change and small business life cycle theory.

Although this growing interest in small business has resulted in an expansion of programme provision, many of these courses still continue to present small business management and entrepreneurship as synonymous concepts. Acceptance of this concept has been accelerated by actions such as Governments and academic researchers using data on the number of business start-ups as a measurement of the level of entrepreneurship within a country. In reality, however, small business is a typology which defines the size of a firm. This is in contrast to entrepreneurship which is the terminology to define a specific form of managerial behaviour. The behavioural trait, which involves a risk taking, innovative, proactive orientation to achieve business growth, can be exhibited by both individuals and entire organisations.

The need to separate the two concepts of small business and entrepreneurship is critical because the vast majority of small firms are run by non-innovative individuals and the businesses have no growth potential. These operations can be considered as non-entrepreneurial. Although any introductory programme about small business management should provide an understanding of the characteristics of small firms, students seeking to deepen their knowledge of small firm management issues and acquire an understanding of how small firms identify and implement a growth strategy, do need to be provided with knowledge about successful entrepreneurial management strategies within the SME sector.

The importance of understanding entrepreneurs and their role in the small firm is critical because the outcome of SME sector growth in developed nations is the generation of new sources of employment and a significant added contribution to a country's gross national product (GNP). Examination of growth strategies reveals most entrepreneurs' success is achieved by building totally new market demand which has yet to be recognised by large firms as a significant source of future opportunity. In the majority of these cases, pre-emption of market opportunity is achieved by an entrepreneur recognising that changing customer needs are creating a significant opportunity to move into a new market sector well ahead of their more ponderous, reactive counterparts in the large firms sector. Somewhat more rarely, an outstanding small firm entrepreneur will achieve above average growth by developing a new product or operational process that is superior to any other offering in the market. The outcome of this latter scenario is the firm will defeat even incumbent, large firm competitors and becomes the new market leader within an industrial sector.

The usual reason why large firms do not exhibit an entrepreneurial orientation is that over the years senior management have determined that within their industrial sector, there are well established conventions that define the products and production processes that will permit the retention of market dominance. This often leads to large firms ignoring the implications of fundamental change in customer needs or the potential impact of new technology. Instead the large firms exhibit a somewhat myopic orientation and continue to utilise very similar managerial philosophies in relation to issues such as selecting customer targets and strategies to sustain future performance. This scenario was exemplified in the late twentieth century by Steve Jobs whose launch of the Apple Personal Computer had a dramatic impact on computer firms such as IBM who had perceived the future as one totally dominated by mainframe computers. Then at the beginning of the twenty-first century, as large companies in the IT and telecommunications sectors sought to determine how technological convergence could be exploited, Steve Jobs again demonstrated his entrepreneurial flair by launching his solution to exploiting the Internet to access music; namely the amazing iPod™ product.

In recent years, the increasingly competitive nature of the job market is causing more students to require syllabus coverage relevant and transferable into the world of work. Although some academics may decry what they perceive is a trend in reducing academic rigour in order to deliver more vocationally orientated courses, business studies students increasingly expect to be provided with evidence that theoretical concepts to which they are being exposed actually are utilised by industry. This issue is critically important in the case of entrepreneurship courses because academics need to appreciate the existence of certain small firm management realities. Firstly, the complex theories originally developed for use in the large firm sector often prove ineffective when transferred into the SME sector. Secondly, owner/managers rarely accept a new business theory without being provided with supporting evidence of applicability to small firms. Fortunately, however, successful owner/managers intuitively seem to know when a theory is relevant or what major modifications they will need to make to a concept before it becomes suitable for adoption within their organisation. Thirdly, many owner/managers, due to their entrepreneurial orientation, tend to prefer immediate action over lengthy reflection. This means that although owner/managers appreciate being shown new planning and decision-making analysis tools, their preference is for techniques (a) simple enough to be understood by themselves and their employees and (b) that do not require massive quantities of expensive market research before they can be applied.

The need to ensure theoretical concepts presented in the text are compatible with real world managerial practice has been a critical issue throughout the development of the materials covered in this text. Chapter 1 provides an introduction to the small firms sector, small firm classification, defines entrepreneurs and examines both the motivation and personality traits of these individuals, entrepreneurship as an evolving theory, examines how small firms grow by exploiting opportunities ahead of large firms and suggests a simple process model for assessing entrepreneurial opportunities.

The destiny of small firms is determined by factors in the external environment over which the owner/manager has little control. There is, however, a tendency for entrepreneurs to be action orientated and a preference to avoid spending a long period of time developing a detailed business plan. Research evidence in relation to the benefits of planning in the small firms sector is somewhat contradictory. Chapter 2 examines these contradictions and presents some alternative perspectives about formal planning which will be encountered amongst entrepreneurs. In addition to an adversity to develop detailed business plans, many owner/managers are somewhat sceptical about using the market research techniques described in standard marketing texts or proposed by market research firms. In part this is because research procedures are often complex or perceived as being too unaffordable. Nevertheless information can be invaluable in gaining a better understanding of issues such as the scale of opportunity offered by changing market conditions, evidence of customer dissatisfaction or the potential impact of a new technology. Hence entrepreneurial owner/managers do need to drop their aversion to market research. Chapter 3 attempts to achieve this aim by presenting a variety of proven, low cost techniques which are capable of fulfilling the research needs of small firms seeking to identify ways of achieving entrepreneurial growth.

Given the often quoted, but probably erroneous, statements about the high failure rate among small firms, Chapter 4 provides a review of the issues which can create obstacles in both the creation and ongoing operations of small firms. Coverage is provided on key influencing factors such as the effective management of cash flow and succession planning. There is also consideration of the sources of support available to the small firm and the degree to which such inputs are perceived as beneficial by owner/managers.

Few markets contain customers who exhibit entirely homogeneous product needs. This means small firms need to assess the nature of their external business environments when seeking to identify new opportunities. Hence Chapter 5 covers the processes associated with gaining an understanding of how key external variables can support or obstruct the implementation of a successful growth strategy. Some marketing purists feel it should only be customer need which should determine a firm's strategy. Available evidence suggests, however, that success is more probable when small firms develop and exploit an internal competence which is superior to that of their competitors. Chapter 6 presents the concept of competence assessment, the resource-based view of the firm and how identified internal strengths or weaknesses can influence development of a successful business plan.

As stated above, few markets contain customers who exhibit entirely homogeneous product needs. Having assessed the external and internal environments in which the small firm is operating and determined the degree of customer diversity, the small firm is only then in a position to define a growth strategy. Chapter 7 demonstrates how data on the external business climate and internal competencies of the firm can be combined to create an entrepreneurial marketing strategy. In the SME sector, leadership style will dominate company culture and strongly influence business performance. Hence this chapter also covers the critical issue of ensuring the selected strategy is compatible with leadership and culture which exists within the small firm.

Entrance into a new market or exploiting changing customer needs often demands a revision in the small firm's current products or internal processes. Chapter 8 examines the managerial processes associated with identifying and implementing an effective innovation plan. Building awareness in a new market is an important objective, but small firms often lack the resources to invest in large scale promotion campaigns. Chapter 9 reviews the various options that exist which permit the delivery of cost effective promotional campaigns. Among small firms there is a tendency to believe the only critical issue when determining their pricing policy is the degree to which discounts should be offered to customers. Chapter 10 examines a somewhat more sophisticated approach to selecting an optimal pricing strategy. This chapter also reviews how the identification of appropriate distribution channels can sometimes dramatically enhance market performance.

A very large number of small firms are created and managed by families. Hence Chapter 11 examines how certain unique characteristics of family firms will influence the performance of these organisations and how poor succession planning can lead to decline or business failure. Another emerging trend among small firm entrepreneurs is their increasing willingness to apply their skills in assisting disadvantaged communities. Consequently Chapter 11 also provides coverage of social entrepreneurship and examines how this philosophy can be especially effective in assisting disadvantaged peoples in developing nations. The pace of technological change which provided numerous opportunities to challenge incumbent larger organisations in the last century is unlikely to slacken during the twenty-first century. Chapter 12 provides coverage of assessing how certain variables can impact the potential success of a new technology. There is also coverage of the opportunities presented by three major areas of business and social change; namely global warming, healthcare and nanotechnology.

The standard structure of each chapter is to introduce managerial concepts and models supported by 'real world' case materials to demonstrate the practical validity of the ideas about how entrepreneurs can exploit innovation as the basis for implementing successful growth strategies in SME sector organisations. The intended primary readership target for this text are undergraduate and postgraduate students enrolled in a small business management programme who having gained an understanding of the basic principles of small firm management, now wish to expand their knowledge to include exploiting entrepreneurship to achieve significant business growth within a smaller organisation. The materials are also of relevance to individuals from public sector support agencies and owner/managers seeking to enhance their knowledge of how entrepreneurship can provide an effective platform through which to achieve faster business growth in the SME sector.

1

Entrepreneurs

Chapter objectives

The aims of this chapter are to assist the reader to:

- be aware of the role of the small business sector in relation to job creation in industrial nations
- comprehend some of the alternative ways of classifying small firms
- understand the concepts and alternative definitions of entrepreneurs
- be aware of the growth opportunities confronting entrepreneurial firms
- comprehend the motivation and personality traits of entrepreneurs.

Small business

Sector importance

At the end of the Second World War, as American industry moved to exploit mass production as the basis on which to stimulate a consumer-led economic recovery and Western Europe used the Marshall Plan to rebuild industrial infrastructure, the large firm sector was the dominant source of wealth generation and employment in developed nation economies. As a consequence Governments' economic policies tended to be biased towards sustaining the existence of large corporations. By the 1970s, however, large firms in key sectors such as steel, cars and electrical goods in the Western democracies were beginning to perform poorly in both domestic and overseas markets. Various economists have offered alternative views about the causes of this decline (McIntye 1989). Their conclusions include variables such as inflexible labour practices, myopic behaviour of managers or misguided economic policy decisions by incumbent political parties. Whichever of these economic theories is correct, during the 1970s events such the OPEC oil crisis, funding ever growing welfare budgets, the power of the unions to obstruct the introduction of more flexible working practices and an upward spiral in the rate of inflation, all combined to erode large firm profitability.

In the face of declining productivity and rising costs, the number of jobs within many large Western manufacturers began to decline as firms lost market share to newly emerging lower cost producers within the Pacific Rim such as Japan and Taiwan. Further pressure on employment levels was created by some major Western corporations, in an attempt to stabilise operating costs, relocating their manufacturing operations to lower wage rate nations elsewhere around the globe.

By the 1980s, the combined impact of these adverse economic trends was that the Small and Medium-size Enterprise (SME) sector in both the USA and Western

Europe had become an increasingly important source of employment and a significant contributor to Gross Domestic Product (GDP) (Ayyagari et al. 2007). In the UK, for example, by the end of the twentieth century the small firm sector was providing 55 per cent of all employment and contributing over a quarter of the nation's total GDP. Elsewhere within the European Union (EU), small firms have an even more important economic role, generating over 65 per cent of total employment.

This situation was not just confined to the original member states of the EU. The fall of communism within the former Eastern Bloc countries who subsequently became members of the EU, resulted in small firms playing an important role in compensating for the rising unemployment caused by the closure or privatisation of large, state-owned enterprises. In Poland, for example, with unemployment in the region of 20 per cent of the population, economic recovery has been attributed to the impact of the number of small businesses rising from approximately 1 million in the 1990s, to almost 4.5 million by 2004 (Kornecki 2006).

Job creation

The apparent importance of the SME sector as a source of jobs has not been lost upon politicians in the major industrial nations. Since the 1980s, many Governments have invested heavily in schemes aimed at promoting higher rates of small business creation through actions such as the provision of grants, offering free or subsidised training and creating a vast array of advisory services. Whether these initiatives have achieved the desired outcome of increased creation of long term permanent jobs is, however, a somewhat contentious issue. During the 1980s, for example, the UK Government focused support on persuading young, unemployed people in economically depressed regions of the country to become self-employed. Recent analysis of the impact of these support initiatives indicates that the long term outcome was that they had a negative impact on employment levels. Van Stel and Storey (2004), who undertook this research, suggest that once grant assistance came to an end, those people with limited human capital or financial resources having been 'press ganged into starting a small business', ceased trading and again became unemployed. The researchers contrast this situation with the 1990s, where the UK Government focused their attention on providing support for existing, growth orientated small firms. This change in support emphasis was accompanied by an increased level of job creation in the SME sector.

The view that Governments should focus their job creation efforts on supporting only those small firms with potential for significant business growth is echoed in Cervantes' (1996) review of economic development initiatives in a number of developed economies. He concluded that the most successful schemes in terms of real, long term job creation were those which targeted newer industries by assisting the adoption of new technologies or assisting firms in these sectors to gain access to venture capital.

In those cases where researchers have attempted a closer examination of the claims made by both politicians and certain academics about the job creation capability of the small firms sector, actual data rarely seem to support such claims (Bennett 1994). For example, an analysis of the 245,000 American companies started up in 1985 found that 75 per cent of the employment gains generated by 1988 occurred in those firms that had more than 100 employees at time of launch. Yet this group of firms only represented 1 per cent of the total firms in the sample. Similarly, in the UK an assessment of 560,000 firms which initially started with less than 20 employees, only about 10 per cent showed any evidence of new job creation over time and less than 1 per cent ever grew into enterprises with more than 100 employees.

The issue of the limited capability of small firms to be an important source of new jobs has recently been further validated across a large number of other countries around the world. Using cross-sectional data on the 37 countries participating in the Global Entrepreneurship Monitor (GEM) 2002 study, Wong et al. (2005) compared the different types of entrepreneurial activity as measured using the GEM project's typology of Total Entrepreneurial Activity (TEA) rates – High Growth Potential TEA, Necessity TEA, Opportunity TEA and Overall TEA. Across these different types of entrepreneurship the researchers determined that only firms in the High Growth Potential TEA group had a significant impact on nations' economic growth. This result caused the researchers to conclude that fast growing new entrepreneurial small firms, not new small conventional one person start-up businesses, accounted for most of the new job creation by the SME sector in the majority of nations included in the GEM study.

A further contribution to the job creation debate was made by Van Praag and Versloot (2007) who analysed the results from 87 different studies. They concluded these studies indicate that the question of whether small firms make a significant contribution to increasing the number of new, permanent jobs in a country remains an ambiguous issue. This is because in many cases the number of new jobs created by business start-ups is often accompanied by a very similar reduction in the number of jobs caused by newly established small firms failing to survive for any significant period of time. Where there does seem to be agreement across the various research studies which were reviewed is that new small firms which are very successful and survive, are likely to create more new jobs than older, more established companies in the same industrial sector.

The view that only a select few new small firms will generate new, permanent jobs is echoed in an earlier study by Audretsch (2002 p. 16). This researcher posited that 'those new firms that are successful will grow, whereas those that are not will remain small and may ultimately exit from the industry if operating at a suboptimal scale of output'. In Audretsch's opinion, there is evidence to suggest that the success of a new small firm will to a certain degree be determined by the fact that 'the underlying technological regime influences the process of firm selection and therefore the type of firm with a higher propensity to exit'. In his view one cannot merely examine the situation at a single point in time, but instead need to assess the business case for job creation in relation to the point in the life cycle for each specific industrial sector. In those cases where the industry sector is relatively new and highly innovative, small firms will be a major new source of job creation. During the growth stage of the sector life cycle, large firms will tend to become the innovative force and these organisations will be the primary source of new job creation. In maturity of the life cycle, the large firms will remain the dominant force. However, because the level of innovation within the sector will have fallen, this will be reflected in job creation becoming minimal within the sector.

The other issue about the benefits of economic policies aimed as stimulating job creation in the small firms sector which is frequently ignored by the politicians is the quality of the jobs being created and their per capita contribution to GNP. The Austrian economist, and recognised leading authority in the field of entrepreneurship, Schumpeter (1942) concluded that large firms will usually outperform smaller firms in relation to the commercialisation and successful exploitation of innovation.

Davis et al. (1994) supported this perspective and concluded that with certain exceptions, the available evidence would suggest that on average, large firms offer higher quality employment in terms of wages, fringe benefits, working conditions, opportunities for skill enhancement and overall job security. Their opinion is supported by numerous other studies comparing the earning and working conditions in the large versus the small firm sector. Van Praag and Versloot (2007 p. 376), for example, from their review of SME sector research studies concluded that small firms 'pay their workers lower base wages and offer fewer benefits'. They posit that this situation is not attributed to a desire by owner/managers to exploit their workforce but instead is reflective of the reality that the average productivity of employees is usually found to be much lower than that achieved within equivalent large firm operations in the same industrial sector. The available evidence also suggests that in many cases the owner/manager's personal earnings are somewhat lower than their managerial counterparts in the large firm sector. Certainly this perspective is shared by owner/managers in many Western nations who will confirm that running their business involves long hours in return for an income usually much lower than the average wage paid to those in employment within the same country. Furthermore in the UK, for example, unemployed individuals enrolled in Government schemes to help the unemployed frequently discover the income from self-employment is lower than the money they would have received by remaining in receipt of unemployment benefit.

Analysing small firms

Small firm definitions

In the same way that for much of the twentieth century Governments have traditionally concentrated on economic policies aimed at assisting the large firm sector, the majority of academics have also tended to focus on large organisations when undertaking research and the generation of new management theories. It was only in the 1980s that small firms began to be recognised as a sector of the economy which deserved special attention. The need for this special focus is because small firms operate across very different, highly variable business environments which demand that their owner/managers exhibit somewhat unique managerial skills.

A major problem confronting the early researchers was to define what is a small business (Ayyagari et al. 2007). To minimise sample variance caused by differences in sales, size, production or industrial sector, the solution in the large firms sector is to access detailed information on individual firms. These data are available from a diversity of public and private sector sources. Equivalent data sets rarely exist for SME sector firms. One reason for this situation in the UK, for example, is that unlike limited companies, sole traders and partnerships are not required to file statements of financial performance with any Government body which would then cause them to be accessible to researchers. Hence many researchers, in seeking to identify different types of firm are often forced to rely heavily on whatever public sector statistics are available. In many cases the only statistics available are the number of firms within a country classified in relation to the number of employees within each type of firm (O'Reagan and Ghobdian 2004).

Unfortunately there are significant differences across these statistics both between and within countries in relation to the definition of employee count used to classify a business as a small firm. In the USA, for example, the Federal Government uses the definition that small firms are those organisations with less than 500 employees (Peterson et al. 1996). This contrasts with the American Small Business Administration (SBA) which in determining which firms might qualify for certain types of grant aid, uses the criteria for small manufacturing firms as employing up to 1,500 employees depending upon the industry sector and in the case of service firms, businesses with annual sales not exceeding $23 million. Further variations are then found at State level in the USA. Georgia, for example, defines a small firm as a business with sales less than $500,000 and makes no specification in relation to the number of employees.

Within the EU since 1996, the SME sector has been defined as being constituted of organisations employing less than 250 people. This definition is then disaggregated into '*micro enterprises*' employing up to 9 individuals, '*small businesses*' employing between 10 and 49 individuals and '*medium businesses*' which employ between 50 and 249 staff. Even within the EU, however, confusion is created by the European Commission altering this definition when announcing new support schemes (Anon. 2003). What occurs in this situation is the EU may add other criteria to the definition of number of employees to include variables such as (1) maximum annual sales of €40 million, (2) maximum €27 million on the balance sheet, (3) minimum 75 per cent of the company owned by the management or the business is run by an owner/manager plus their family.

Small firm growth

A complication which has emerged in seeking to understand business practices in the SME sector is that as researchers began to focus on the factors influencing the growth rate of small firms, some realised that the most important factor is often not the size of firm, but the motivation of the owner/manager (Storey and Sykes 1996). Some owner/managers run their business to generate an adequate income, whereas others exploit innovation and change as the basis for achieving significant business growth. These latter firms are usually considered to have adopted an entrepreneurial business orientation.

Within non-entrepreneurial small firms, Storey and Sykes proposed there are two types of business; namely '*lifestyle firms*' and '*operationally constrained businesses*'. The former are operations created to provide their owner/managers with an income sufficient to finance their desired lifestyle. Examples are artists creating a craft business, retirees affording to relocate to a warmer climate by establishing a holiday rentals business and individuals operating a small firm in a way that permits them sufficient freedom to regularly enjoy a hobby such as golf or boating (Morrison and Teixeira 2004).

Most operationally constrained small firms are based in market sectors where it is difficult to be different, supply may exceed demand, competition is intense and market entry by new unskilled people is not uncommon (Hitt et al. 1982). Under these circumstances, profitability tends to be very low and opportunities to generate a scale of profit sufficient to fund business expansion are virtually non-existent. Scenarios of this nature are to be found in most abundance in highly fragmented service industries such as retailing and catering.

Entrepreneurial growth firms can also be subdivided in two types; namely '*sectoral specialists*' and the '*giant killers*'. Most sectoral specialist firms operate in markets also partially served by large firms. What occurs is an owner/manager identifies an emerging need among certain customer segments that currently remains unsatisfied. By exploiting the flexibility and speed of response that is a characteristic of the SME sector, the entrepreneurial small firm is able to establish a strong, highly defendable, market presence long before their counterparts in the large firm sector have even become aware of the new opportunities available through responding to changing customer needs.

Most giant killer propositions are founded by one or more individuals who have identified an opportunity which can be exploited by developing a new technology or introducing a new form of business process. At the outset, some of these entrepreneurs do have expectations that because large firms appear to be ignoring a potentially massive opportunity, their new enterprise will eventually achieve market leadership. In other cases, the new business may be launched without the founder having any idea of the huge potential of the business proposition which they have created. Recent examples of this latter scenario in the IT industry are provided by Dell Computers in the marketing of personal computers (PCs) and Yahoo! and Google™, whose search engines now dominate the Internet industry. In none of these cases did the founders, when first identifying their new business idea, have any expectations about the huge scale of personal wealth that they would eventually enjoy.

It is not always the case that the new entrepreneurial firm will achieve and then retain market leadership. There will be instances where an existing large firm decides to respond to the emerging threat and moves to destroy the new upstart. Another possible outcome in terms of the long term destiny of a rapidly growing entrepreneurial firm is that a large company recognises the huge market potential of the concept, but lacks the internal capabilities to rapidly develop and launch their own competitive offering. The large company may, therefore, decide to acquire the entrepreneurial smaller firm. This latter outcome is demonstrated by YouTube, the on-line video streaming business. Once this firm began to exhibit market success in terms of the number of visitors to their Website, the company was acquired by the market leader search engine, Google™.

CASE STUDY

Large firm retaliation

Case aims: To illustrate that (a) an entrepreneurial idea, as well as involving a new product, can also be about a new business process and (b) lacking adequate financial resources may mean the new business is vulnerable to a counter attack by existing larger firms in the market.

Many successful entrepreneurs would not consider a new invention is their most probable route to success. More typically they tend to be individuals who, having identified an unsatisfied customer need or market problem, concentrate on the creation of a new business model. In the 1980s, the UK entrepreneur Freddy Laker was aware few people in Britain could afford to fly across the Atlantic to the USA. At that time most of the major airlines faced high operating costs because of their strategy of maintaining a huge fleet of aircraft in order to offer travellers a diversity of international and domestic destinations.

Laker's new business model was to establish a low cost airline operation, called Skytrain, using a small number of aircraft, initially only flying on a single route. To further reduce operating costs, he decided to operate a 'walk-on walk-off' operation that did not require the passengers to make an advanced reservation. Instead, seats were sold on a 'first come, first served' basis to potential passengers arriving at the airport. The first route he chose to open for Skytrain was the one with the highest number of travellers; namely London to New York. The savings in operational costs created by his business model were passed along to the customer in the form of ticket prices that undercut companies such as TWA and British Airways.

Before Skytrain even started operations, the major elephants in the airline industry, recognising the financial damage that Laker could inflict on their business, applied pressure on the UK and US authorities to refuse approval for the new airline to operate across the Atlantic. After lengthy legal actions, approval was granted and the first flights began in 1977. The huge success of the business caused Laker to add new routes and buy new aircraft.

The major airlines realised that the company's expansion plan was undercapitalised and that Skytrain was vulnerable to any competition which weakened the firm's cash flow. Hence a number of the major airlines conspired together and agreed to match Laker's prices even though this meant incurring operating losses. Eventually their actions, combined with some poor financial decisions by Laker, forced his business into bankruptcy in 1982. Subsequently Laker brought to court the largest aviation anti-trust case in history.

Entrepreneurs

Defining the entrepreneur

In the early nineteenth century, the French economist J.B. Say defined entrepreneurship (i.e. the practice of the entrepreneur) as a process involving the shifting of economic resources from an area of low productivity into an area of higher productivity and greater yield. One of the first British economists to use the term – J.S. Mill – perceived entrepreneurs as individuals engaged in giving direction, supervising, controlling and risk taking. As most of Mill's identified activities can also be attributed to most managers, he concluded that the key difference was entrepreneurs were prepared to take greater risks.

Another economist, the Austrian Joseph Schumpeter (1934), also concerned himself with the role of the entrepreneur. He perceived entrepreneurship to be a 'meta-economic event' such as the introduction of a new technology which causes a major market change. In the Schumpeterian model of economics, managers in large firms typically continue to use traditional conventional approaches where demand is stable and they remain confident about having an accurate understanding of customer needs. In contrast, Schumpeter posited that entrepreneurship is the process most likely to prevail in those circumstances where the market is in disequilibrium and customers have needs which are not being fulfilled. An example would be the impact of the aeroplane on the world's ocean going, passenger liner industry.

Schumpeter considered the distinguishing attribute of the entrepreneur was not that of risk taking, but the willingness to exploit innovation as a path through which to succeed when competing with existing firms. He proposed that innovation could cover a range of possible alternative actions. These include: (1) developing a new product or service, (2) creating a new production process, (3) identifying new markets, (4) discovering new sources of supply and (5) creating new organisational forms.

Since the Second World War, a somewhat broader view of entrepreneurship and the characteristics which define the entrepreneur has emerged amongst management theorists. Entrepreneurship has been redefined as the process of 'creating something different by devoting the necessary time and effort, assuming the accompanying financial, psychological, and social risks and receiving the resulting rewards of monetary and personal satisfaction' (Hisrich and Peters 1992 p.9). Miller (1983) proposed that the entrepreneurial orientation of a firm is demonstrated by the extent to which top managers take risks, favour change and exploit innovation to achieve a competitive advantage. This definition is echoed by Hills and LaForge (1992) who, on the basis of a review of research published to date, concluded that being a successful entrepreneur requires the presence of certain attributes; namely an ability to create a new organisation which exploits innovation and develops a unique operation that supports business growth.

CASE STUDY

Entrepreneurial philosophy

Case aims: To illustrate (a) the orientation of entrepreneurs towards the creation of new products, (b) the difficulty of gaining acceptance of a new idea among major incumbents within an industrial sector and (c) the need for persistence.

Many successful new small businesses are created because an individual identifies an unsatisfied customer need or an unresolved customer problem. This business philosophy was very apparent even in the early years of the Industrial Revolution. Exemplars are provided by astute inventors such as Abraham Darby (iron smelting), James Hargreaves (the spinning jenny) and Thomas Newcomen (the atmospheric steam engine). A more recent example of this entrepreneurial problem/solution approach to business is provided by the UK inventor Trevor Baylis. He knew that market expansion for portable radios in poorer parts of the world was limited by the costs associated with replacing the radio's batteries. He ignored the conventional view that there was a need for lower cost batteries. Instead he had the idea of creating a clockwork radio. Having been faced with both Marconi and Philips rejecting his concept as completely unfeasible, he decided to establish his own manufacturing operation in South Africa. From this base he successfully introduced the clockwork radio into developing nations across the world.

Entrepreneurial attributes

Despite the extensive writings about how entrepreneurs differ from other individuals in the SME sector, there continues to be a tendency for both politicians and some academics to treat small business and entrepreneurship as synonymous, freely interchangeable terms. In part this is due to entrepreneurship being a more appealing title than small business. Hence both politicians and Universities seeking to publicise their interest in small business tend to refer to their activities as being concerned with supporting entrepreneurship. Acceptance of the two terms being interchangeable has increased due to the Babson/London Business School Global Entrepreneurship

Monitor (GEM) (Sternberg and Wennekers 2005). This project, which seeks to measure the importance of small business across different nations, uses 'the number of people considering starting a small business in the next 12 months' as a measurement of entrepreneurial activity (www.gemconsortium.org).

In contrast, Gartner (1988) argued that entrepreneurship should be considered as a unique managerial process which is defined in terms of innovative behaviour traits allied to a strategic orientation concerning the pursuit of profitability and growth. There have been a number of empirically based efforts to measure the attributes of the entrepreneur in terms of personality traits, attitudes, and management behaviours. For reasons of ease of measurement, the trait-based perspective has dominated and continues to be the most widely utilised. The approach is exemplified by Utsch et al.'s (1999) investigation of the differences between entrepreneurs and managers in East Germany. They observed that entrepreneurs exhibited greater levels of self-efficacy, higher order need, readiness to change, interest in innovation, a Machiavellian attitude (or 'competitive aggression'), and desire for achievement than individuals who are employed as managers.

Gartner has drawn a clear distinction between entrepreneurs and owner/managers in small business. His perspective is supported by Stewart et al. (1998) who found that many small business owners were more comparable to managers in larger firms than to entrepreneurs. These researchers found entrepreneurs achieved higher ratings for variables such as a desire for achievement, risk taking and involvement in innovation. Hyrsky (2000), in a study of small business managers in Europe, North America and Australia, identified work commitment, energy, innovativeness, risk taking, ambition, achievement and egotistic features as dimensions of entrepreneurship. Georgelli et al. (2000) described 'being entrepreneurial' as a willingness to take risks, being innovative, and an ambition to grow. These latter researchers went on to suggest that the core competencies for entrepreneurship are a capacity for changing business processes, the launching of new products or services and a planning capacity. They noted that not all small businesses are equipped with these capabilities, nor are all owner/managers necessarily predisposed towards them.

Covin and Slevin (1988 p. 224) defined an entrepreneurial style in terms of the extent to which 'managers are inclined to take business-related risks (a risk-taking dimension), favour change and innovation (an innovation dimension), and compete aggressively with other firms (a proactiveness dimension).' A non-entrepreneurial style in their terms is characterised as being risk-averse, non-innovative, passive, and reactive. They developed a measure of entrepreneurial style based upon previous theorising and research by Khandwalla (1977) and Miller and Friesen (1982). Their research led to the development of one of the first fully validated tools for empirically measuring entrepreneurial orientation.

Although there is widespread agreement that entrepreneurs engage in innovative activities, one area of ongoing debate within the literature is the degree to which entrepreneurs can also be characterised as risk takers. Brockhaus (1987), for example, confirmed the findings of some other researchers by being unable to identify any statistically significant difference between the risk taking propensity of a group of entrepreneurs and a group of managers working in the large firm sector. In his view many researchers had reached an erroneous conclusion about risk taking either because of reliance on anecdotal information or because they failed to recognise that risk taking is influenced by a multitude of factors. He proposed that these include variables such as the nature of the industry, prevailing economic conditions, the age of the business, the size of the firm and the educational/experience levels of the respondents.

CASE STUDY

Entrepreneurs are not infallible

Case aims: To illustrate that (a) even successful entrepreneurs can make mistakes and (b) repetition of the same entrepreneurial concept in a different market sector may not always be a wise move.

The 'ups and downs' entrepreneurs face over their lifetime does mean they need a certain degree of faith in their skills as innovators. Unfortunately there is a tendency for the media to present successful entrepreneurs as having the 'Midas Touch'. Such adulation may cause the feted individual to possibly rush into new ventures without totally assessing the potential for failure. Some people might attribute this trait to Stelios Haji-Ionnou. This ebullient individual, assisted by being from a wealthy family, was the founder of the UK budget airline, EasyJet. Lionised by regular appearances in television documentaries, he then created EasyGroup as a platform through which to launch a whole range of firms based around the concept of offering lower priced propositions to consumers. Some ideas, like his chain of internet cafes, have been successful. The jury is still out for his cruise ship business. For some other ventures, such as his low-cost cinema idea Easycinema, the curtain has already fallen and the business has been closed.

The importance of entrepreneurs

The issue of entrepreneurship may also be linked to the wider agenda of regional or national economic growth. For example, Kuratko and Hodgetts (1998) noted the importance of new and smaller firms to the United States' economy and in particular of the job creating capability of fast-growing businesses versus lifestyle businesses. The former type of firm, referred to as 'gazelles' in Birch's (1979) terminology, are identified by Kuratko and Hodgetts as being leaders in innovation. They cited evidence of total number of innovations, innovations per employees, and numbers of patents in support of this assertion. Olsen et al. (2000) argued that most employment growth is attributable to the minority of firms that grow quickly. They also noted that business owners' motives for growth are not homogeneous and 'appear to reflect experiential and situational differences'.

Hamal and Prahalad (1996), commenting upon the difference between innovation in the large firms sector versus the outcome associated with entrepreneurial behaviour, proposed that the latter activity will lead to the emergence of a completely new concept. An example of this type of scenario is provided by the impact on the retail sector caused by the launch of the on-line bookseller www.Amazon.com. Hamel and Prahalad used examples of significant change to propose the influence of unsatisfied market needs will frequently result in entrepreneurial firms breaking with convention and exploiting this emerging opportunity through the provision of a new, more innovative, solution. These writers have concluded that major changes in industrial sectors have typically occurred because a company 'has changed the rules of the game'. In their view 'to create the future, a company must (1) change in some fundamental way the rules of engagement, (2) redraw the boundaries between industries and/or (3) create entirely new industries'.

On the basis of such perspectives, Chaston (2000a) proposed an alternative definition for entrepreneurship; namely:

> The behaviour exhibited by an individual and/or organisation which adopts a philosophy of challenging established market conventions during the process of developing new solutions.

This definition provides a simple method to assess whether an observed market innovation can be classified as entrepreneurial. If the observed change is based upon a logical extension of current, well established practices such as those utilised to develop a new improved version of an existing national brand of detergent, then the outcome can be classified as conventional innovation. Whereas, should the change clearly break with convention (e.g. the introduction of washing technology which does not involve the use of water) then the observed outcome can be considered as entrepreneurial.

A useful secondary advantage offered by the proposed definition is that it permits the classification of entrepreneurial versus non-entrepreneurial activities at any level within the organisation (e.g. a new approach to decision-making within a department), between organisations, between industrial sectors and between different countries. Within any of these comparisons, one is testing whether the solution is an extension of existing industry practices or represents a genuine break with convention.

CASE STUDY

The benefit of convention challenging

Case aims: To demonstrate that by challenging conventions an entrepreneur can totally alter the nature of a major industry.

Possibly the most outstanding modern day story of achievement through challenging conventional thinking is provided by one of the world's richest men, Bill Gates. At a time when other members of the computer industry were competing to launch new improved hardware, Bill Gates broke with convention by adopting the view that the future profitability in the IT industry would be owned by whoever achieved dominance in the supply of software. He founded Microsoft which focused on becoming the world standard for personal computer operating systems and applications software. The first breakthrough came when IBM adopted Microsoft's MS:DOS operating system for their next generation of PCs. This contract had the huge benefit that the Microsoft product would automatically gain distribution on a global scale because it would be installed in every IBM PC to be manufactured. The success of the operating system was followed by Microsoft's launch of the Windows suite of word processing, spreadsheet and database packages. At this juncture Microsoft was able to persuade virtually every PC manufacturer to install the Windows product as a standard software system on their respective machines. The outcome is a company which has become the industry standard for many areas of software and consequently enjoys a virtual global monopoly in the software installed on PCs.

The entrepreneurship option

Self-employment traits

Consideration of the option to become self-employed may arise at any point in a person's life, from immediately after leaving college, at an optimal point during their career or as a lifestyle change following retirement (Kane and Spizman 1988). In some sectors of industry such as the pure arts or graphic design, the very limited job opportunities relative to the number of college leavers virtually mandates that most individuals will have no option but to become self-employed. Within the professions such as accountancy and law, it is quite usual for individuals wishing to have greater control over their earnings or lifestyle to resign from a large organisation in order to open their own practice. Some people upon retirement perceive starting their own business as an opportunity to become more immersed in something of great personal interest such as an existing hobby. Others become self-employed because their pension or savings will not cover their living costs.

The growing interest in the creation and successful management of small firms over the last 20 years has caused researchers and management experts to attempt to identify the managerial traits which are exhibited by owner/managers and the entrepreneur (Beugelssdijk and Noordaven 2005). A common aspiration is to identify a universal theory that can be applied to all scenarios. This aim exists despite the fact that an examination of the real world soon reveals owner/managers and entrepreneurs come in numerous 'different shapes and sizes'. Hence caution is advisable when reading certain academic writings or watching television programmes about small business. This is because in many cases the generalisations that are presented are often somewhat removed from reality.

Certain projects concerning the identification of the characteristics exhibited by owner/managers have been undertaken using an adequate, well validated research methodology. Consequently these studies offer useful insights about some of the characteristics exhibited by owner/managers in relation to motivation and behaviour. One extremely large scale study was that undertaken by Professor Schein at the Massachusetts Institute of Technology (MIT) in America (Schein 1996). As an occupational psychologist his aim was to determine whether people exhibit differences in relation to their career preferences and their chosen career paths. Based upon an assessment of values, needs and abilities he evolved a model in which he posits that people can be classified into five career types (or 'anchors'). These are: (1) *technical/functional*, (2) *managerial*, (3) *security and stability*, (4) *autonomy and independence* and (5) *entrepreneurial creativity*. His research indicates that people are most satisfied in their working life if they follow a career path compatible with their dominant career anchor.

In seeking to understand career motivations and career paths in the small business sector, Feldman and Bolino (2000) used the Schein typology to assess which career anchors are evident among the self-employed in the USA. The results indicated that the most dominant career anchor (46 per cent of respondents) was the desire for autonomy and independence. The second most important career anchor (33 per cent of respondents) was the desire for entrepreneurial creativity. Scales used in their study which indicate the attitudes of these two career anchor types are shown in Table 1.1. In terms of job satisfaction and psychological well-being, those anchored by entrepreneurial creativity reported a higher level of overall life satisfaction than individuals seeking autonomy.

Table 1.1   *Dominant career anchors of self-employed persons*

Autonomy
1   The chance to pursue my own lifestyle and not be constrained by rules
2   A career free from organisational restriction
3   A career which permits maximum freedom to choose my own work environment
4   Being able to retain a sense of freedom and autonomy
5   Not constrained by organisations of the business world in general.

Entrepreneurial creativity
1   Able to create or build something that is entirely my idea
2   Using my skills to build a new business
3   I am motivated by the number of ideas which are totally mine
4   To invent or create something of my own is very important
5   I have always wanted to be my own boss.

Source: adapted from Feldman and Bolino (2000)

To gain further understanding of respondent attitudes, the researchers also implemented interviews to generate qualitative data. A major theme which emerged from these interviews was most self-employed persons have a desire to escape or avoid the bureaucracies which they perceive exist in large organisations. By starting their own business this permitted them to either have greater control over their future destinies or to have greater freedom to be creative. Their greatest frustration has been the discovery that running a small business often involves spending hours on administrative tasks such as dealing with paperwork, taxes and Government legislation.

Entrepreneurial traits

A number of academics have sought to identify a typology which defines the traits and the motivations which are specific to entrepreneurs. In many cases their aim has been to use the typology to then assess the degree to which certain traits can be associated with the business performance of small firms. The drawback in many of these proposed models is they are often based upon the researcher's own perceptions of what makes a successful entrepreneur and insufficient attention is given to validating the accuracy of the measurement scales which have been developed. As a result when other researchers have attempted to use these scales, the outcome has often been that of being unable to establish a statistically meaningful relationship between the measurement tool and business performance (Gartner 1988).

One recent exception to this generalisation about scale validity is the work undertaken by Robichaud et al. (2001). These researchers initially drew upon in-depth interviews with small business owners which, when linked to frameworks from other research studies, were used to develop a measurement tool based upon 18 questions. The tool formed the basis of a mail survey sent to almost 600 Canadian small business owner/managers. The large database that was generated permitted factor analysis to be applied to the results. The outcome, as shown in Table 1.2, was that the 18 questions could be assigned to one of four specific factors which are typically exhibited by entrepreneurs; namely (1) *independence/autonomy*, (2) *intrinsic reward*, (3) *extrinsic reward* and (4) *security*.

Table 1.2   *Items measuring entrepeneurial motivation*

Independence/autonomy
1   Make my own decisions
2   Maintain my personal freedom
3   Self-employment
4   Be my own boss
5   Personal security

Intrinsic reward
1   Personal growth
2   Gain public recognition
3   Prove I can succeed

Extrinsic reward
1   Sales and profits
2   Achieve a comfortable living
3   Increase personal income
4   Achieve business growth

Security
1   Build a business that can be passed on (or sold)
2   Be closer to my family
3   Provide security for my family
4   Build up wealth for retirement

Source: adapted from Robichaud et al. (2001)

Growth opportunities

Entrepreneurial success

Although examples of entrepreneurial success make fascinating reading, it is necessary to recognise that the vast majority of people launching or running a small firm will never have that 'big idea' which will make them fabulously wealthy. In fact the reverse is more probable. Many small businesses cease trading within 18 months of their launch and even those which continue to operate, usually only provide their owners with a relatively small income.

Over the years, researchers have attempted to identify a magic formula which can explain entrepreneurial success. Despite all their endeavours, nobody has yet been able to identify a business model which might guarantee that every entrepreneur can become extremely wealthy. To date, all that has been achieved is the identification of certain guidelines to minimise the risk of failure and improve the chances for an adequate level of profit to be generated. In relation to these guidelines, having undertaken small business research, mentored owner/managers, developed small business training schemes and launched new businesses, there are two rules which are this author's personal favourites. These are to seek to operate in a market (1) that is growing and (2) where customers exhibit a diversity of needs.

Growing markets are attractive because incremental revenue is generated from new customers entering the market. Furthermore, as the market is growing, the intensity of competition remains relatively low. This scenario can be contrasted with mature or declining markets, where the only source of additional sales is to steal customers from the competition. This means the combined costs of attracting new customers while concurrently protecting market share from competition will be extremely high, with a consequent reduction in company profitability.

Changing need opportunities

Where customers exhibit a changing need this provides opportunities for a firm to offer products and services which are radically different from those available from competition. Additionally, because many large firms prefer to operate in markets where high absolute profit can be generated, smaller firms can often find security by occupying sectors of the market which companies from the less proactive large firm sector do not yet perceive as offering significant new opportunities.

One such example of large firms ignoring emerging customer trends is provided by the tendency of virtually all large consumer branded goods companies to continue to focus their marketing efforts on the 18–49 year age group (Chaston 2009). The reason for this preference is rooted in the past when this customer group, often known as the 'baby boomers', represented the greatest source of absolute spending power in virtually every developed nation economy. The phrase 'baby boomers' was originally coined in America to describe people born between 1946 and 1964. The problem facing many large firms in Western nations is that population ageing is leading to a decline in the size of the 18–49 customer target group. Few consumer goods companies, however, appear to believe sales growth in their domestic markets can be generated by marketing more products to other age groups (Anon. 2006a).

This myopic attitude among large branded goods companies is likely to create new opportunities for the more entrepreneurial organisations in Western nation markets to exploit this increasingly important alternative customer segment. In the USA, for example, retirees comprise 30 per cent of the adult population, yet control 70 per cent of the net worth of US households. American retirees spend over $1 trillion a year on goods and services. A similar scenario is to be found in the UK where the highest median income within the entire UK population are individuals in the 60–64 age group with people aged 50+ accounting for 60 per cent of Britain's savings and 80 per cent of all personal assets.

The other reason for firms to focus on older consumers in developed nation economies is that individuals in the 18–49 age group will be most adversely affected by the recession which commenced in 2008. This is because the lax attitude of the financial institutions over the last ten years has resulted in younger people accumulating a huge level of personal debt, the scale of which has been exacerbated in many cases due to the collapse in house prices, leaving people in a negative equity position. Although nobody is able to predict either the depth or duration of the 2008 recession, what is clear is that the debt problems facing younger people will mean that this group's level of discretionary spending will remain depressed for the foreseeable future. The level of discretionary spending within this group will also be reduced because they will be forced to pay higher taxes in the future in order to pay off the huge public sector debts their Governments have created in an attempt to stimulate their respective economies.

CASE STUDY

The Saga saga

Case aims: To demonstrate (a) how an entrepreneur identifies an emerging market opportunity well ahead of potential large firm competitors, (b) the importance of sustaining entrepreneurial growth by responding to changing customer needs and (c) the use of collaboration to support growth through market diversification.

An excellent example of one of the first entrepreneurs to exploit the opportunities offered by the provision of services to older people is provided by Sydney de Haan, the founder of the UK firm Saga Ltd. Having recognised that large firms in the tourism industry were concentrating on the provision of holidays to families, he exploited this situation by entering the market offering holidays specifically designed to meet the needs of retired people. The first product was low-cost coach trips to the seaside. From the outset, de Haan was strongly committed to the concept of creating a competitive advantage through building close relationships with customers. He recognised this approach creates stronger customer loyalty, which inevitably leads to customers exhibiting a higher level of repeat purchasing. One aspect of Saga's relationship building is to monitor customer needs and where dissatisfaction or change in demand was identified, to immediately seek ways to further upgrade product and service provision. For example, within a few years after launch, Saga recognised that an increasing number of retirees, instead of visiting a UK seaside resort or taking a coach tour around England, had begun to desire more exotic holidays. Hence the firm moved into offering a range of overseas travel packages and subsequently, also entered the cruise ship market.

Growth orientated entrepreneurs often adopt the philosophy that once the core business has been established, ways should be found to sustain the revenue trends through product diversification. Some entrepreneurs know that once a large, loyal customer base has been created, organisations from the large firm sector may be interested in expanding market coverage. In return for the privilege of being granted access to an entrepreneurial firm's customers, they can be willing to enter into a commercial alliance. This is the concept which Saga has so effectively exploited. Since the early 1980s, the company has diversified into areas such as insurance, investments and web-based retailing. In those cases where Saga lacked the financial resources and expertise to supply a service, they formed a partnership with an existing major provider (e.g. offering Saga brand savings accounts operated in partnership with a Building Society).

Niche marketing

As well as often being slow in recognising the emergence of a new market segment, major corporations rarely have the flexibility or capability to service smaller market segments which initially only contain a limited group of customers who exhibit specialised needs. In many cases these specialist needs emerge as customers gain experience of the standard products offered by the mass marketing companies and begin, often due to the emergence of a lifestyle shift, to desire access to better, higher quality products. This scenario is why small firms can often avoid confrontations with large firms by adopting the philosophy of 'niche marketing' (Weinrauch et al. 1991). The potential drawback with this approach, however, is that should customer needs be easy to satisfy, the niche will rapidly become filled with other small firms all offering the same 'me too' propositions. Examples of this scenario are provided by independent grocery stores and small gift shops. Entrepreneurial firms are very aware of this risk and to avoid becoming involved in 'me too competition', seek to identify markets where the customers exhibit a unique product or service need which initially few competitors are able to satisfy.

CASE STUDY

Starbucks

Case aims: To demonstrate how entrepreneurs can compete with larger companies by (a) identifying a consumer niche ignored by large firms and (b) over time expand the niche into a major new market segment.

Since the emergence of a consumer-based economy in the USA, one of the sectors where there has been an intensive war for brand share is coffee. The primary players were Maxwell House owned by General Foods and Nestlé, followed later by Procter & Gamble's launch of Folgers coffee. Although these major companies occasionally attempted to build brand share through the introduction of improved products, their fundamental marketing assumption was that the main factor influencing consumers' purchase decision is price and there was little interest among consumers in being offered a superior quality product. In the early 1980s, Howard Schultz was a coffee buyer for the Starbucks Coffee Company which sold fresh, whole beans in five speciality stores in Seattle, Washington. On a trip to Italy he noticed the huge number of cafés selling a diverse range of coffee drinks such as latte and espresso. He proposed that the company let him open a café to exploit this potential niche in the US coffee market. The owners refused, so he resigned, raised $1.7 million and opened his first outlets in downtown Seattle. The focus of the operation was on quality as the basis for offering better tasting coffee. Schultz subsequently acquired the Starbucks company and renamed his outlets as Starbucks. Having validated that American consumers were exhibiting a preference for product quality over low price, Schultz expanded from a niche business to a mainstream operation by opening new outlets across the USA and subsequently expanding overseas (Slywotzky 1996).

SUMMARY LEARNING POINTS

- In the industrialised world, small firms are providing an increasingly important source of employment and making a significant contribution to GDP.
- Although small firms can provide an important source of job creation, this process only occurs in the more growth orientated smaller firms.

(Cont'd)

- There is some variation within and between nations about the definition of what constitutes a small firm, although most of these definitions tend to be based upon the number of employees.
- Entrepreneurs are individuals who exhibit an innovative orientation based upon identifying unconventional ways of developing new products and business processes.
- Entrepreneurs exhibit common traits such as being proactive, innovative and being prepared to take calculated risks.
- Entrepreneurs usually succeed by focusing on markets which exhibit high growth or by identification of changing market needs ahead of competition.

ASSIGNMENTS

1   Use available statistics to review the level of employment within a country's SME sector. (In some countries these data are available on Government Websites, e.g. www.dti. gov.uk for Britain, www.sbaonline.sba.gov for the USA.)
2   Select a major, large firm manufacturing sector and analyse probable performance trends for firms based in your country in relation to the potential impact of overseas competition.
3   What are the potential implications of population ageing on a country's economy?

DISCUSSION TOPICS

1   Do you have the necessary personal traits to be a successful entrepreneur?
2   Over the next five years after graduation, would you prefer to work in the large firm sector, the SME sector or the public sector?
3   What do you feel are the causes of variations in the growth rates of small firms?

Additional information sources

Job creation

Dennis, W.L. (1994), Small business job creation: the findings and their critics, *Business Economics*, Vol. 38, No. 2, pp. 123–138.

Small firm growth

Morrison, A., Breen, J. and Shameen, A. (2003), Small business growth: intention, ability and opportunity, *Journal of Small Business Management*, Vol. 41, No. 1, pp. 31–43.

Defining the entrepreneur

Cunningham, J.B. and Lischeron, P. (1991), Defining entrepreneurship, *Journal of Small Business Management*, Vol. 29, No. 2, pp. 42–51.

Entrepreneurial attributes

Corman, J., Perles, B. and Yancini, P. (1988), Motivational factors influencing high-technology entrepreneurship, *Journal of Small Business Management*, Vol. 26, No. 1, pp. 36–44.

D'Intinio, R.S., Goldsby, M.G. and Houghton, J.D. (2007), Self-leadership: a process for entrepreneurial success, *Journal of Leadership & Organisational Studies*, Vol. 13, No. 2, pp. 105–221.

Motivation

Taomina, R.J. and Lao, S.K. (2007), Measuring entrepreneurial motivation: personality and environmental influences, *International Journal of Entrepreneurial Behaviour & Research*, Vol. 13, No. 4, pp. 200–214.

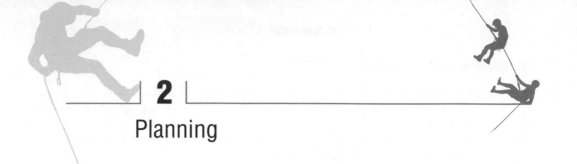

2
Planning

Chapter objectives

The aims of this chapter are to assist the reader to:

- become aware of the importance of business planning
- comprehend the components which constitute the business planning process
- assess the benefits to entrepreneurs of using business plans
- be aware of contradictory research evidence about the benefits of business planning among small firms
- comprehend variations in planning behaviour among entrepreneurs.

Business planning

The planning philosophy

Since humans moved from the role of hunter-gatherer towards producer-trader there have been people who have used business plans to manage their operations. The philosophy behind such activity is to understand the current situation, fix future goals and to determine what actions are required to achieve these goals. As the Industrial Revolution led to the creation of larger, more diversified businesses, managing such operations has become more complicated. One individual who has strongly influenced the acceptance of a structured approach to business planning was Alfred Sloan. This individual, as the CEO of General Motors before the Second World War, demonstrated the benefits of using the concept to manage a large, complex, multi-divisional corporation.

Virtually every major text on management theory provides extensive coverage of the processes and techniques associated with the development of strategic business plans. The roots of this approach are grounded in the principles of Frederick Taylor's theory of scientific management and the classicist school of management thinking (Ansoff 1965). Subsequently a number of justifications for the benefits of adopting a strategic planning orientation have been tabled by academics. A very common perspective is that planning is a process which ensures the policies of different groups within the organisation are co-ordinated and directed towards the achievement of a common set of goals. Planning is also seen as providing a mechanism through which to systematically assess a firm's thinking about its long-term future (Chaffee 1985). Not surprisingly, with strategic planning being given a dominant role in management theories concerning large organisations, as researchers became interested in the SME sector, a frequently articulated view was that strategic planning was also critical in optimising the performance of smaller firms.

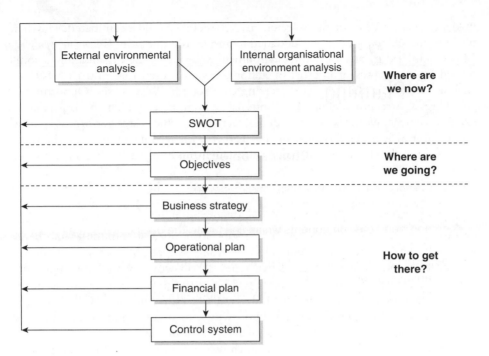

Figure 2.1   *Standard business planning model*

The planning process

The planning model of the type evolved by Sloan and subsequently refined and further developed by other organisations over time is shown in Figure 2.1. This model has been validated by numerous academic researchers and is accepted as the standard template which is found in numerous management texts (e.g. Johnson and Scholes 1999).

The conventional view of planning is that all of the elements described in Figure 2.1 should be analysed in order to make optimal decisions. Furthermore, as illustrated in Figure 2.1, planning is a logical and sequential process. In the development of a plan, adhering to specific rules about the length and structure of the document is not a vital issue. What is critical, however, in the case of entrepreneurs is that these individuals do not delegate the task. They need to provide leadership and be involved at every stage of the process (O'Reagan and Ghobadian 2002). Entrepreneurs should not get fixated on a highly innovative new idea such that when warning signs emerge during the analysis, these are ignored. Should acquired data indicate major problems with a new business concept, then unless a solution can be identified, the idea should be dropped. A new project should then be initiated which can offer an alternative way of generating business growth.

The recommended entry point into the planning process described in Figure 2.1 is an initial review of the market proposition of interest to the entrepreneur. Any review should include an assessment of existing business activities (Quinn 1980). Should the evaluation of current operations indicate these still offer further opportunities for significant revenue growth, this is a much lower risk option than expansion into a new market sector. Assuming the preliminary review indicates that a new opportunity has the potential to become a source of future growth, then a more in-depth examination of the selected market sector should be initiated. This first phase in the planning process is designed to answer the question 'Where are we now?' This is achieved by analysing the environment external to the organisation accompanied by an analysis of internal operations. Data are used to construct a SWOT analysis, this being the acronym referring to Strengths, Weaknesses, Opportunities and Threats. Strengths define those internal operations at which the organisation excels, whereas Weaknesses are internal activities which are performed poorly. Opportunities identify the areas of the market which could provide the basis for business growth. Threats are market trends which might place the organisation in a vulnerable position.

The second phase in the planning process is to define the future objectives for the business by answering the question 'Where are we going?' Most business texts will propose organisations should have a number of objectives ranging from sales and profit targets through softer issues such as supporting local communities and being seen to be environmentally responsible. The reality is that unless an organisation is financially viable, fulfilling these latter types of objectives would be impossible. Hence the primary focus in most plans will be in the definition of numeric financial objectives such as sales, profits and Return on Investment (ROI). For these objectives to be an appropriate basis upon which to build future plans, they must meet the criteria of being realist, achievable and measurable.

The final phase of the plan is the area which will consume most of the management's time with the aim of answering the question 'How to get there?' As shown in Figure 2.1, the first component of this third phase is to determine a business strategy. This is a generic statement describing the primary focus of the organisation's market activities. For Frank Land, the inventor and founder of Polaroid Corporation, for example, his first initial business strategy was that of confronting the photography market global leader Kodak, by developing and launching the world's first instant camera.

The operational components of the plan describe how the various business functions within the organisation will contribute to the delivery of the aims and strategy. These business functions will usually involve areas such as marketing, production, procurement and human resource management. These operational proposals provide the basis for being able to define the costs of implementing the business plan. A financial plan can then be generated by linking these costs to the sales targets that have been specified as the firm's future objectives. The final component of the plan is to define the control system that will be used to monitor actual business performance in relation to forecasted performance once the plan has been implemented.

CASE STUDY

Planning and commitment

Case aims: To demonstrate that having a plan is rarely sufficient, the entrepreneur will often have to draw upon prior experience and exhibit commitment in order to overcome the obstacles that can emerge while seeking to implement the plan.

James Dyson, having graduated from the Royal College of Art in London in 1970, first worked as a designer in the world of theatre (Sheshandi and Henry 2006). While at college he had worked on the design of a new type of boat for Rotork Ltd, whose Company Chairman was a close personal friend. The final product, named the Sea Truck, could carry a considerable load and be easily moved in and out of the water. After a period of zero sales, Dyson created a more commercially viable design which led to sales of over 250 Sea Trucks around the world. From this project he learned the lessons of (a) recognising when a design is wrong and immediately making changes, (b) never start an inadequately funded project and (c) 'one size does not fit all' (i.e. it is usually better to customise a product to meet the specific needs of one or more group of customers).

In 1974, Dyson resigned from Rotork to work on his new idea, the 'Ball Barrow'. This was a wheel barrow where the traditional front wheel is replaced with a large ball. Development took five years and having sold some 45,000 units, the company sales manager went to the USA, the ostensive reason being to develop a new market opportunity for the firm. Upon arrival, he joined an American company who then started manufacturing the Ball Barrow themselves. Against Dyson's wishes, his Board entered into a lengthy and costly legal battle about breach of patents and copyright. By now Dyson's interest had shifted to developing a vacuum cleaner that did not lose sucking power as the machine's dust bag becomes full. His fellow directors were not impressed with the idea, so Dyson resigned and launched a new company, the Air Power Vacuum Cleaner Company, to develop his 'bagless' cleaner. The new machine exploited the concept of using centrifugal force in which an outer cone removes large debris and dust while an inner cyclone uses gravitational force to push smaller particles out of the air. By 1982 and 5,000 prototypes later, Dyson had developed the final product but lacked the funds to manufacture the new cleaner. He spent two years travelling across Europe and America trying to sell the design to various major firms. Frequently the potential partner company tried to steal the design. To protect his ownership rights, Dyson was forced to become involved in a number of law suits. One of these was the US corporation, Amay Inc.

Then in 1985, a Japanese company, Apex, agreed to manufacture the product under the name G-force for the Japanese market and to pay Dyson a royalty based upon a percentage of sales. Having received a cash settlement from Amay Inc. which covered most of his outstanding debts, Dyson sought to raise £750,000 to cover the costs of the machine tools needed to start manufacturing his own vacuum cleaner in the UK. Most venture capital firms seemed unimpressed with the fact that he had spent years and several millions of pounds developing the product. He eventually raised £600,000 and this, plus another £750,000 from selling his rights to G-force to the Japanese company meant he could fund a move into manufacturing. He registered a new company, Dyson Appliances, hired an Italian firm to develop the tools and mouldings and in 1993 contracted with Philips Plastics in Wales to assemble the product.

Within a short time there were problems with Philips who demanded a price increase which even applied retrospectively to products which had already been assembled. Having gone to court and won the case, Dyson moved the equipment out of Philips and started his own assembly operation. By 1995, the Dyson DC01

(Cont'd)

was the best selling upright cleaner in the UK. Then came the cylindrical version, the DC02. By 1996, annual company sales had reached £85 million and the Dyson machines were outselling the UK's previous market leaders, Hoover and Electrolux. Subsequently the company has expanded overseas and is now operating in over 15 countries across the world such as France, Germany, Japan and the USA.

When one compares Dyson's unconventional management approach to the other, conventional, large consumer electrical goods companies there are some clear differences. Dyson tends to enter markets offering a superior quality product at a significantly higher price than competition. His philosophy is that consumers appreciate good design and hence products should be aesthetically pleasing. He places less reliance upon promotional activity such as heavy weight television advertising campaigns. Instead he believes in using 'word of mouth' recommendations by satisfied customers, effective PR and some newspaper advertising. Within the company, his view is that creativity should be the driving force and to support this view, he invests over 15 per cent of sales revenue into R&D (compared with competitors' 3–5 per cent of sales). All key activities such as design, engineering, development, marketing, patenting are kept 'in-house'. Offices are open plan to ensure people interact. Engineers and designers work together, not separately. Everybody is granted the right to be creative and 'dialogue, not memos' is the preferred communications medium. People dress casually and there is no canteen because catering is based on an informal café style. Dyson has articulated the following philosophy in relation to design:

- Ideas do not appear at a drawing board, so make models, create prototypes because these will generate additional ideas.
- New technology is only new if it can be patented and thereby protected.
- Believe in yourself, keep testing and re-testing until you, not other people, are completely satisfied.
- Continue to re-think, re-design and improve.
- Challenging convention requires immense stamina.
- Ideas should be managed from start to finish by the originator.

Planning and the entrepreneur

Benefits of planning

Management texts, when covering the issue of business success and failure, usually recommend that it is critical for managers to adopt a structured approach to performance planning (Mintzberg 1990). It is very common that academics, having been convinced that research has validated the benefits of planning in large firms, believe that the same concepts and practices are applicable in small firms (Norbert 1990). The perspective about the importance of business planning is reflected in the importance given to business planning in most University courses on small business or entrepreneurship. This viewpoint can be illustrated by one group of academics writing about entrepreneurship education in which they proposed that 'entrepreneurship should be defined as a profit-orientated activity which applies principles of strategic management and planning in the development of a business and the promotion of its growth' (Sexton and Upton 1987 p. 37). Hence it is perhaps not surprising to also find that many texts on small business management (e.g. Fry 1992) stress the importance of developing a detailed plan to both identify opportunities and to define how various elements of the organisation will contribute to achieving the firm's specified performance goals. This bias is a little worrying because some years ago, certain leading management theorists recognised that even in the large firm sector, entrepreneurs are apparently able to successfully run their company without reliance on the use of formal plans (Mintzberg and Waters 1982).

The accepted view of the importance of business planning is also reflected in the philosophy underlying many of the training programmes which are offered to SME sector firms. In the UK, for example, within training schemes funded by the Government for individuals interested in starting a new small business, it is usually the case that over 50 per cent of course content is concerned with constructing a business plan. Outside of the world of education and training, business planning is also considered important in organisations providing guidance, such as Government funded business support agencies or accountants providing professional financial services to the small firms sector. To a certain degree this latter perspective is understandable. Both accountants and bankers, for example, find there is a significant advantage when assessing the viability of a business idea to have their clients provide a formal, written business plan. The document is also extremely useful to these professionals as a control device when reviewing their clients' actual business performance.

Venture capitalists from as far apart as London (England), Silicon Valley (California, USA) and Auckland (New Zealand) will confirm their common experience that the more charismatic and enthusiastic is the entrepreneur, the less likely this individual(s) is prepared to provide any detailed information about their new business proposition when first beginning a search for investment funding (Chaston 2000a). In these cases, the usual next step in the funding negotiation process is to provide the entrepreneur with guidance and support in developing a detailed business plan. The other common experience of these venture capitalists is that although they will continue to use these plans to monitor the subsequent performance of their investment, they find their entrepreneurial partners can rarely be convinced of the benefit of using business plans to assist in the day-to-day management of their businesses.

Published evidence does appear to support the view that under certain conditions, even small organisations can gain benefit from creating a strategic business plan to guide their operations (Ibrahim et al. 2004). One of these conditions is that of business or market stability. It appears that when an industrial sector enters maturity, a dominant technology prevails and market growth is minimal, even small firms can benefit from using detailed business plans to guide future operations (Robinson and Pearce 1984). Another appropriate condition for detailed planning is when a firm needs to make a large capital investment to achieve specified revenue goals. In such a situation the firm will probably benefit from undertaking a detailed evaluation of the financial implications associated with making a significant expenditure on new capital assets (e.g. a new biotech company needing to invest in a state-of-the-art laboratory). The reason for the conclusion is that given the irreversibility of the major investment in a new fixed asset, neither management nor external stakeholders should approve any large scale project unless the proposal is underpinned by a detailed plan (Berry 1998).

McCarthy and Leavy (1998) and McCarthy (2003) posit that when reaching conclusions about the use of business plans by small firms one does need to take into account the personality of the owner/manager. These two studies reveal that the *charismatic entrepreneur* tends to be driven by the strength of their own convictions, they exude massive self-confidence in their ideas and are passionately certain their venture will succeed. Such individuals rarely perceive the need to develop a detailed business plan and cannot understand why potential investors, without being provided with a plan, will question the probability of commercial success. In contrast the *pragmatic entrepreneur* tends to adopt a more conservative attitude when assessing opportunities and is not prepared to commit their own or others' resources unless there is clear evidence that success is reasonably certain. This latter type of entrepreneur tends to believe business planning can be an effective process through which to identify appropriate future actions.

In trying to persuade entrepreneurs of the advantage of having well documented business plans, one might mention possible benefits such as (Chaston 2000a):

- it forces an assessment of the external environment
- it forces an assessment of the organisation's internal competences
- it quantifies the expected performance goals for the new venture
- it identifies the scale of required resources and the degree to which these will have to be met through the attraction of external funds
- it creates a 'road map' which can be used to monitor actual performance versus plan upon launch of the venture.

Although such arguments will be accepted without question by a graduate from any business school, it will often be almost impossible to convince inventors, creative artists, entrepreneurial owner/managers and scientists or technologists working in laboratories of the merits of diverting themselves away from working on their 'big idea' to spend time writing a business plan. A source of evidence supporting their attitudes on the very limited benefits of business planning amongst entrepreneurs is provided in the materials documenting the development and commercialisation of many of the world's most famous inventions. Thomas Edison, for example, appears to have had minimal interest in the need for planning while developing the electric light bulb. Frank Whittle, when working on his jet engine in the 1930s in the UK, made no real attempt to quantify the commercial implications of his radical new approach to aircraft propulsion. Similarly it seems that Steve Jobs was not really bothered about the need to develop detailed proposals for the future market opportunities for Personal Computers whilst working on the first Apple Computer in his garage at his home in California.

Nevertheless, the experience of many individuals who work as advisers to companies is there are definite merits of developing a business plan in relation to specific situations facing the organisation (Robinson 1979), including those such as:

1　An inventor is at the stage in the life cycle of their enterprise where further progress is blocked unless the individual is able to attract significant external borrowings and/or equity capital.
2　An existing small firm has grown rapidly, new managerial staff have been recruited (or employees promoted to managerial positions) and the entrepreneurial owner/manager wishes to increasingly delegate downwards, the firm's 'future visioning' activities.
3　An owner/manager is engaged in succession planning and wishes to ensure their nominated replacement is capable of sustaining the firm's entrepreneurial behaviour.

CASE STUDY

Does planning help?

Case aim: To demonstrate that (a) a founder entrepreneur may be able to operate without a plan even as their business becomes very large, (b) a plan is usually a prerequisite to attempting to raise external capital and (c) problems may emerge concerning the lack of a plan as new senior managers take over the running of the business.

In 1917, Mrs Ida Steinberg opened a small fruit and vegetable store in Montreal, Canada (Mintzberg and Waters 1982). Her second eldest son Sam worked in the store after school and at the age of 13 became a full-time employee. The first evidence of Sam's entrepreneurial aptitude occurred in 1919. The shop's landlord asked him to post a 'for rent' sign on the shop next door. Instead Sam decided to rent the site so that his family's shop could expand. By the time Sam died in 1978, from these small beginnings, he had built a business empire generating over $1 billion in annual sales from a portfolio of 191 supermarkets, 32 department stores, 33 catalogue stores, 119 restaurants, 15 pharmacies, 25 shopping centres, a flour mill, a sugar refinery and a food manufacturing operation.

Between 1919 and 1929, Steinberg only opened two stores. Until 1933, the basis of the store expansion programme was to open another store when a new member of the family needed a job as a shop manager. Then in 1933, a new store ran at a massive loss. Over the weekend, Sam changed the name of the outlet to Wholesale Groceteria, slashed prices, removed all forms of customer service and created Canada's first self-service retail outlet. The action was highly effective. As a consequence he introduced the philosophy of discount pricing and self-service into all other existing stores and all new stores which were subsequently opened. Also in the 1930s Sam, instead of renting stores as he had always done in the past, began to create the new stores using mortgage financing. He also started buying land which he thought would be good for retail development some time in the future. In 1946 with the war over, Sam returned to opening new stores and buying more sites with future retail potential. The company moved into food manufacturing and acquired a huge warehouse to develop a more effective store distribution system.

During the early 1950s, Sam boasted that the family had never needed outside investors. In response to questions about his future plans, his standard answer was 'who knows?' Then in late 1952, Sam announced a $15 million, five-year expansion programme. The problem was the firm did not have sufficient internal financial reserves to support the scheme. In seeking a new source of funds, Sam rejected the idea of the family having to give up their shares in the business. Eventually he found a financial institution that would support a general debenture issue for $5 million and allow the company to retain 100 per cent control of the business. In order to be able to issue the debentures, for the first time in his life Sam was required to develop a detailed business plan. Raising the loan meant the financial community had a strong interest in monitoring the company's performance. The financial community also applied pressure to persuade Sam to create a more formalised hierarchical management structure and to recruit new, experienced senior executives from outside of the family. Further external pressure was placed on the firm to base all future operations on

(Cont'd)

clearly defined, formalised plans when in 1955, the company made its first ever public share issue. None of these shares had voting power, so the family retained 100 per cent authority over any key decisions with Sam being able to formally vote all the family shares at any Board meeting.

The period of 1950 to 1960 saw the company continue to open new stores and expand into Ontario. During the 1960s, Sam stood back while his professional executive team implemented a major diversification programme moving into depart-ment (later re-badged discount) stores, restaurants, flour milling and sugar refining. These activities were accompanied by a massive centralisation of authority and withdrawal of the delegated authority which stores had enjoyed in the past.

By 1968 due to both economic conditions and the move towards becoming a much more formal, ponderously slow organisation, sales began to plateau. In almost an exact duplication of Sam's 1933 response to poor trading conditions, a new scheme Miracle Pricing was rapidly introduced into the company's super-markets. This programme involved permanent across-the-board price reductions, stocking mainly only very basic grocery items, cutting back on in-store staffing levels and reducing the advertising budget by 50 per cent. The only difference between this move and the 1930s scheme was that the project champion was not Sam, but the head of the Quebec store operations. This time, however, the new organisational structure meant significant time was lost whilst attempting to convince other senior executives of the viability of the idea.

By the early 1970s, Sam was beginning to feel his age. No potential succes-sors had emerged from within the Steinberg family. In the face of pressure from the financial community new Board level executives were brought into the opera-tion. Unfortunately, the 1970s in Canada were a period of high inflation and labour unrest. To survive the company needed to exhibit a more entrepreneurial orientation in order to be able to develop fast, flexible reactions to new threats as they emerged in an increasingly difficult retail environment. The new senior executives had come from large corporations and were committed to an organi-sational philosophy based on detailed formal planning accompanied by complex control systems to monitor business performance. The outcome was Steinberg's faced a period of labour unrest and when the need to make staff redundant arose as sales continued to decline, this led to a series of strikes. By the time of Sam's death in 1978, the company was in deep financial trouble. The situation was exacerbated by feuding inside the Steinberg family over issues such as who should be in control of the business, whether to accept recommendations being made by the company's professional managers and if all or some of the business should be sold. By the mid-1980s, the company finances had deteriorated to the point where the only solution was to accept a takeover offer from another corpo-ration. Sadly even this company failed to turn the business around and in 1992 Steinberg's went bankrupt.

Conflicting evidence

A review of the research studies which have been undertaken to validate the hypothesis that strategic planning is critically important for small firms will reveal somewhat contradictory conclusions. Some studies such as Lyles et al. (1993) are able to convinc-ingly demonstrate a positive, strong correlation between having a plan and improved business performance. Other researchers, however, when attempting to validate the relationship between planning and performance have been unable to reach such a definite conclusion (Berman et al. 1997).

When seeking to understand the possible causes for these inconclusive findings, it is necessary to recognise a number of factors can complicate the generation and interpretation of research results concerning studies of business planning in the small firms sector (Chaston 2002). For example, in one project where the researcher concluded that owner/managers consider business planning as extremely important, the sample frame was drawn from individuals who had previously all participated in a University course on small business planning. Another concern about sample selection is the common practice of using a sample frame from across industrial sectors and/or to generate data from firms ranging in size from micro-business through to medium size operations. In these instances, the researchers then often fail to provide any statistical analysis about whether planning practices might vary across either different sectors or different size firms.

Even where researchers have attempted to control the potential influence of multiple sectors or firm size, one may still encounter somewhat questionable decisions about research tool design. One research group, for example, having decided to classify respondents in relation to the level of planning sophistication, did not include intuitive planning in their typology. This decision was made because industry experts advised them that intuitive planning was 'not a characteristic of the individuals who might own and manage firms' (Sexton and Van Auben 1985, p.10). Another potential research problem is using data on a very specific scenario as the basis for justifying generalisations about the entire SME sector. Two different researchers, for example, having respectively concluded that business planning assists small retailers and owners of dry cleaning businesses, used their results to justify the view that business planning will assist the performance of small firms in any sector of industry.

CASE STUDY

Plan, what plan?

Case aims: To illustrate that extremely successful business ideas can be developed and launched apparently without the founders being too concerned about the need for a formal business plan.

In 2003, Tom Anderson – a musician and member of various bands – had the idea of creating a Website where unknown Indie bands could for free, add videos, biographical materials and/or sound tracks of their performances so that these could be accessed by their fans. He and his partner in the venture, Chris Dewolfe, created MySpace.com (Kelleher 2005). Initially to persuade bands to use the site, the two entrepreneurs spent their nights visiting Los Angeles live music venues to promote the idea that the new world of music was all about using social networks to expand bands' fan bases and to be seen by people living outside of California. Only two years later, the site had built up a membership of 14 million members, with 65,000 new users joining daily. By this time MySpace was generating more than $20 million in advertising revenue from firms such as Nike and Sony who realised the site was an extremely cost effective medium

(Cont'd)

(Cont'd)

through which to reach the 16–34 age group who constituted 65 per cent of the user base. One of the reasons why demand for advertising space was so high was that in 2004, Procter & Gamble reaped massive rewards in terms of increased sales for their deodorant for young women, Secret Sparkle, by the innovative approach of sponsoring the singer Hilary Duff's MySpace pages. Recognising the huge revenue potential which the site offered, only two years from launch the two founders sold the business to Rupert Murdoch's News Corporation for $580 million.

Planning in practice

Despite the extensive support which planning as a key business process has received over the years in the academic literature, a question still exists about the degree to which the development of a business plan can have a positive influence over the performance of small firms (Shrader et al. 1989). Other researchers, however, when attempting to validate the relationship between planning and performance have been unable to reach such a definite conclusion. The latter perspective is supported by observations of the actual behaviour of owner/managers. These have revealed that many successful small firms do not appear to bother with developing a formal, annual business plan (Carson 1985). Researchers such as Allison et al. (2000) and Kets de Vries (1977) have concluded that few entrepreneurs engage in formalised, long term planning or follow formal, logical models of business process. Instead there is a tendency to act on the basis of instinct, intuition and impulse.

In view of the contradictory evidence concerning the benefits of formalised planning in small firms and some of the potential problems that may be caused by research methodology or data analysis, it is really impossible to reach a solid and certain conclusion either way on this issue. Possibly the safer option is to accept a contingency approach; namely for certain firms in certain industries managed by certain individuals facing certain circumstances, the use of a strategic plan will contribute towards improving business performance. It also appears reasonable to conclude that depending upon their preferred management style, individuals engaged in managing a successful entrepreneurial small business in a complex and changing environment may find that the business planning process is an advantageous method through which to reach key business decisions.

Beaver (2007) has presented a very thoughtful review about the issues associated with the debate about the use of strategic planning in small firms and the advantages this may confer. In presenting his conclusions he made the following observation that:

> It is easy to state the obvious – that thinking and managing strategically is an essential pre-requisite of business success and superior performance for all firms, whatever their size, sector or complexion. To do so is to court naïveté and ignore the role and meaning of strategy and its effect on enterprise prosperity. This is not to deny the value and importance of corporate strategy and business planning but rather to appreciate the complexity of the subject matter and its relationship with organisational achievement in the face of possible difficulties in the operating environment. (Beaver 2007, p. 19)

Entrepreneurial planning behaviour

In providing guidance on strategic planning to SME sector managers, it is important to recognise that many entrepreneurs prefer action over reflective thinking. Their desire is to minimise the time spent planning and instead, immediately move into active trading. Some entrepreneurs also exhibit a business philosophy based upon intuitive decision–making, linked to a preference for learning by experience. Hence given that published research studies have not categorically proven business planning is a beneficial activity, then if some entrepreneurs are adamant about starting to trade without having previously constructed a formal strategic plan, it is probably fruitless trying to persuade them otherwise.

Despite entrepreneurs' preference for action, when working with these individuals, academics and small business advisers do have a responsibility to bring to their attention that there are circumstances when business planning is possibly the wisest option. For example, if there are numerous unanswered questions about the market to be entered or existing market conditions appear to be undergoing major change, then the planning process can generate new knowledge that supports a more informed decision about the viability of the business proposition under consideration. The existence of a plan is also beneficial where there is a need to communicate with others outside the firm (e.g. a bank or venture capitalist when seeking external funding), to generate input of the company directors or management team and to brief employees on their specific roles in relation to achieving the firm's performance goals.

Many small business support service advisers and sector professionals will confirm that even where the entrepreneur can be persuaded to undertake some form of business planning, the process utilised will frequently not mirror that shown in Figure 2.1. Instead, as summarised by Anderson and Atkins (2001), entrepreneurs exhibit a wide range of different approaches depending on market circumstances, the current financial position of the business and the managerial style of the owner/manager. Two examples of the variation in behaviour which they identify are:

1   *Butterfly planning* which is a deliberate attempt to experiment with various situations and scenarios to gain a wider understanding of situations.
2   *Lottery planning* which involves experimenting with various situations or scenarios by a process of random selection.

A common trait which these authors propose exists among entrepreneurs are the differences in the entry point into the planning process and the degree to which the components in the conventional sequential process are actually analysed as the basis for selecting preferred future actions. As shown in Figure 2.2, one way to communicate this situation is to present the planning process as being similar to a spider's web. At the centre is the major issue of most concern to the entrepreneur; namely the future performance objectives for their business. In deciding whether these objectives are both feasible and realistic, different entrepreneurs will opt for reviewing few, some or all of the key topics summarised in Figure 2.2. Furthermore, one can also expect significant variation in the order with which entrepreneurs will review these topics.

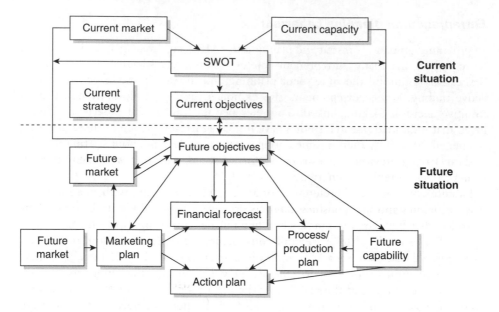

Figure 2.2   *Possible components in an entrepreneur's approach to planning*

CASE STUDY

Planning by trading

Case aims: To demonstrate that because the scale success of a new entrepreneurial idea may be highly dependent upon non-forecastable, non-controllable external events, then the ability to develop an accurate, structured, formal plan in the early years of a new business may not be a feasible proposition.

Chad Hurley and Steve Chen cut their respective teeth in the on-line world as two of the first twenty people ever to be hired by the hugely successful electronic Internet payment system company, PayPal (Wasserman 2006). Their backgrounds could hardly be more different. Hurley had a degree in fine arts, whereas Chen's was in advanced computing. In January 2005 they wanted to share some videos they recorded over the holiday season on their mobile phones with some other friends. At this juncture they became extremely frustrated by the difficulty which then existed sending video materials over the Internet. In an approach highly reminiscent of Steve Jobs, the founder of Apple, the two worked together in Hurley's garage. By May 2005, the beta version YouTube.com was in operation. Initially the site only had 30 video clips, and most of these were of Chen's cat.

The new company was not making a huge impact in terms of site visitor numbers but it was attracting the attention of people in the media industry and more importantly, rapidly became the video transfer and download system favoured by teenagers using MySpace. It was not until December 2005, however, that the site finally caught the world's attention when somebody posted a copy of a video of a section of an NBC programme. The presence of this clip on the site spread mainly by word of mouth, generated millions of new visitors, virtually all of them teenagers. Heavy blizzards trapped many Americans at home at the beginning of 2006 and this is thought to be the reason that early in that year, monthly visitor levels reached over 4 million. People started posting their home videos, then the idea took off of teenagers doing something crazy (e.g. four Chinese students singing rap songs) and within a short time YouTube was where many young people turned for entertainment.

A further stimulus to site visitor levels was generated when well known members of the entertainment industry also started posting video clips on the site. The site does not offer a suitable framework for traditional on-line advertising, but some of the more perceptive people in the world of advertising realised that products could be promoted by either sponsoring video clips or shooting videos which included usage of the product. One of the first to recognise this opportunity was the sportswear company Nike which posted a short video featuring the Brazilian football star, Ronaldinho. This clip, publicised by word of mouth among YouTube users has been viewed over 20 million times. By late in 2006, YouTube fans were uploading 65,000 videos a day and the site had built a global audience of over 100 million users. Most of these users, mainly young people, were individuals most difficult to reach via conventional media channels.

Not surprisingly the level of audience size represented a huge opportunity for the on-line advertising industry. The outcome was that another global Internet success, Google™, which had been started only a few years earlier by two other on-line entrepreneurs, Larry Page and Sergey Brin, purchased YouTube for $1.65bn (Anon. 2006b).

SUMMARY LEARNING POINTS

- Business planning is considered as a critically important process in the successful management of organisations.
- The business plan involves the three-stage process of determining 'Where are we now?', 'Where are we going?' and 'How to get there?'.
- The conventional view is that the use of business planning is extremely important in ensuring successful performance within the SME sector.
- Many entrepreneurs either do not develop a business plan or alternatively, adopt a more informal approach to determining appropriate future actions for optimising the performance of their enterprise.

ASSIGNMENTS

1 What external Government support services exist in your country to assist small firms to develop business plans and/or to develop the business planning skills of owner/managers?
2 What differences would you expect to encounter in the management of the business planning process in large versus small firms?
3 How might the number of employees influence the need and nature of the business planning process in a small firm?

DISCUSSION TOPICS

1   Can an entrepreneur be successful if instead of developing a formal business plan, the individual uses intuition to reach decisions about managing the future?

2   What are the possible obstacles that can confront the owner/manager undertaking business planning at (a) business start up and (b) during the early years of trading?

3   Select and visit the Websites of two major banks and review the small business support services offered by these two organisations. Prepare an analysis comparing the services offered as the basis for a discussion about why you would prefer one or other of the banks if you were starting a small business.

Additional information sources

The planning philosophy

Chanin, M.N. and Shapiro, H.J. (1985), Dialectical inquiry in strategic planning: extending the boundaries, *The Academy of Management Review*, Vol. 10, No. 4, pp. 663–676.

Benefits of planning

Berman, J.A., Gordon, D.D. and Sussman, G. (1997), A study to determine the benefits small business firms derive from sophisticated planning versus less sophisticated types of planning, *The Journal of Business and Economics*, Vol. 3, No. 3, pp. 1–12.

Planning in practice

Miller, D. (1987), Strategy making and structure: analysis and implications for performance, *Academy of Management Journal*, Vol. 30, No. 1, pp. 7–33.

Entrepreneurial planning behaviour

McCarthy, B. (2003), The impact of the entrepreneur's personality on the strategy formation and planning process in SMEs, *Irish Journal of Management*, Vol. 24, No. 1, pp. 154–171.

Russell, R.D. and Russell, C.J. (1992), An examination of the organisational norms, organisational structure and environmental uncertainty on entrepreneurial strategy, *Journal of Management*, Vol. 18, No. 4, pp. 639–657.

3

Opportunity Research

Chapter objectives

The aims of this chapter are to assist the reader to:

- become aware of the benefits of using market information to assist decision-making
- comprehend the components which constitute the market research process
- be able to assess the various sources of secondary information
- comprehend alternative primary information generation methodologies
- understand the concepts of identifying different customer needs through market segmentation
- become aware of the role of intuition in the opportunity discovery process utilised by entrepreneurs.

Why, how and what

Benefit

Small firms are not renowned for spending time undertaking extensive research studies before launching a new business proposition. Many entrepreneurs decide no additional information is required because they have an intuitive faith in the validity of their ideas. Others hold the opinion that research is an expense they cannot afford or they lack the skills to implement the activity (Barnes et al. 1982). The outcome is a significant proportion of small start-ups make the classic mistake of rushing into a new venture without any assessment of the available facts. Only after things go wrong do they perceive there would have been significant benefits in acquiring additional information before expending funds on a new proposition or buying an existing business. Of those individuals who survive to 'trade another day', this learning experience may persuade them that time spent on research can be a wise investment in considering any future ventures (Chaston 2002).

Process model

The conventional recommendation concerning market research is the use of a sequential process model of the type shown in Figure 3.1. This process model was developed and validated by large consumer goods companies such as Nestlé and Procter & Gamble operating in mature markets where the potential customer is easily identifiable, has extensive experience of the product and is able to provide data on why one product is preferred over another. One aspect of the model which will appeal to the

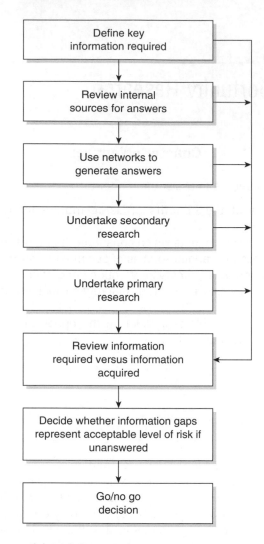

Figure 3.1   *The sequential market research process*

resource constrained small firm is that early phases of the process involve minimal expenditure. Should the small firm be fortunate enough to acquire all the required information early into the research process, this will mean the more expensive activities, such as undertaking a survey, can be avoided.

Academics and market research companies, in making recommendations about the use of standard research methodologies by small firms undertaking market research, typically recommend extremely extensive studies involving the collection of vast amounts of information across a huge diversity of variables (e.g. Boughton 1983). The drawback for the small firm is the immense amount of time and effort required to then analyse the acquired data (d'Amico 1978). Furthermore, most small firms prefer to implement their new ideas in the shortest possible time. Nevertheless, in terms of balancing the risk of immediately entering the market versus undertaking some research before reaching an entry decision, then at a minimum the owner/manager would be advised to at least acquire key information about:

- the size of the market
- who is the customer
- the benefit(s) sought by customers
- how and when customers acquire market information
- the nature of competition which exists within the market.

Networks

Standard market research texts recommend that any business exhausts all sources of existing, documented information (or 'secondary data') before expending efforts to generate new data (or 'primary information') by implementing actions such as initiating a survey. Fortunately many entrepreneurs exhibit the fascinating habit of ignoring the well intentioned advice of academics. Instead they tend to adopt real world approaches which they have discovered are more effective. Such is the case in relation to data acquisition through networking.

Networks are constituted of individuals who have common interests and seek to assist each other through being part of a group within which members freely exchange information (Carson et al. 2004). The commonest networks are informal, involving contact between small firms located in the same geographic location. Most entrepreneurs are aware that the fastest way to acquire zero-cost market information is to contact other network members. Research on the characteristics of successful entrepreneurs reveals a tendency to be very active in building and seeking ways of expanding their business and personal networks (Littunen 2000). The effectiveness of networks for resolving market research issues are influenced by factors such as the structure of the network (i.e. size, formality, diversity and stability), strength of the linkages which exist between members and the marketing management skills which exist within the network (Burke and Jarratt 2004).

Export networks

Possibly one of the riskiest SME strategies is entry into a new overseas market. The conventional advice is that the firms should undertake extensive market research prior to initiating an export-based growth strategy. This again is an area where the conventional advice seems to be ignored by entrepreneurs. As demonstrated by Mort and Weerawardena (2006), small firms place reliance upon networking to gain both an understanding of international opportunities and assistance in the specification of an appropriate market entry strategy.

These two researchers undertook a study of small Australian firms operating in business-to-business (B2B) high-technology markets where at least 25 per cent of respondents' revenues already come from exporting. Their conclusion was that there were two capabilities influencing successful exploitation of international networks. One was the fundamental networking capability of the founder who, usually through prior business experience or links with the scientific community, has already formed key links with individuals and organisations located in key overseas markets. These links are used to acquire necessary data on issues such as local market need, nature of competition and identification of the most effective path through which to initiate market entry. The second capability, which emerges once the firm has entered a new market, is further evolution of existing networks which provides more in–depth information on a more accurate assessment of market potential, customer reactions and identification of possible counter attacks being planned by larger, incumbent competitors.

Social capital

Social capital is the term applied to the set of social resources which are embedded in the relationships which individuals create within both their social and business lives. The assumption in the small firm literature tends to be that all owner/managers invest time in the creation of increased social capital through participation in business networks. One of the few studies, however, which has sought to validate this assumption was that undertaken by Liao and Welsch (2005). These researchers concluded that the average owner/manager exhibits no greater level of social ties than members of the general public. More importantly, however, they found that a significant differentiating factor between the average owner/manager and the entrepreneur is that the latter has definitely sought to enhance their abilities and business capabilities by strengthening their personal level of social capital. Furthermore, it emerged in their study that the level of social capital is much higher among high technology entrepreneurs than entrepreneurs involved in low technology sectors.

These researchers posit that the higher social capital achievements of high technology entrepreneurs reflects both their working environment, which is characterised by the sharing of information to solve complex problems, and their recognition that participation in networks can greatly enhance their prospects that their high technology idea can be converted into a commercially viable business proposition. This latter perspective is supportive of the idea that a key benefit for the entrepreneur is the new knowledge which the network can provide in relation to enhancing the speed and direction of innovation (Fukugawa 2006). Fukugawa found that in the case of very innovative firms, having defined a possible future business plan, this is then followed by a proactive search to seek new network opportunities and contacts. Furthermore, as revealed by Mort and Weerawardena's (2006) study, as an entrepreneur becomes successful and the scale of the business increases, the individual will gradually reduce contact with those networks which were important at the time of business start-up. This is because these older contacts no longer appear able to be of further assistance to the firm.

Secondary data

Electronic sources

Over the last ten years, the lives of firms in the SME sector seeking market information has been revolutionised by the advent of the Internet (Weiber and Kollman 1998). Through utilisation of search engines operated by organisations such as Google™ and Yahoo!, anybody can now access invaluable, rich sources of data on a global scale. In relation to socio–demographic data, the most prolific sources are Government departments and agencies. The breadth of data from Government sources, however, does vary by country. One of the best examples of a well constructed informational Website in terms of both quality of data and ease of use is that provided by the US Census Bureau (www.census.gov). This site provides not just a breakdown of income by age group, but also additional information on expenditure by age group across a wide range of product categories such as food, housing, healthcare, utilities and consumer durables.

When small firms start to utilise the Internet for market research, their tendency is to focus upon seeking information about their competition and customers (Wood 2001). Wood also found that as experience is gained in recognising the benefits of on-line research, small firms then begin to expand their search into new areas such as economic trends, on-line bulletins published by trade associations or reports issued by local economic development services and the business press. Perceived benefits of the Internet as a research tool among small firms include ease of access, value for money, quantity of information available and up-to-date data.

Before leaving cyber world in the search for additional information, small firms can also benefit from searching through two other, relatively new, sources of data (Henry 2007). These are chat rooms and blogs. Chat rooms are created by individuals or organisations as electronic platforms through which interested parties can exchange information and views. The term blog is a derivative of the phrase 'web log' which was proposed by Jorn Barger to describe sites that permitted links to other, related sites. Similar to chat rooms, there are a limited number of blog sites concerned with purely commercial, technological or political issues. In most developed nations these are sites created by influential bloggers whose opinions about products and services which they have purchased may adversely impact the offending supplier's market image. Small firms should sample sites containing criticisms of larger companies because these can often provide invaluable insights about the scale of customer dissatisfaction. This information may then permit identification of a new product or service opportunity that could be exploited by the entrepreneur.

CASE STUDY

Blog mining

Case aims: To illustrate how on-line marketing can exploit blogs to acquire and distribute market information.

Greg Selkoe launched Karmaloop (www.karmaloop.com) in 1999 as a sideline to his day job as an urban planner with the Boston Redevelopment Authority (Seybold 2006). The aim of the new business was to help young adults to locate 'cool clothes' which are just not available in mainstream retail outlets. Early into the venture, Greg persuaded four clothing brands to give him clothing to sell in consignment in exchange for promoting their brands. Launched from the basement of his parents' house, in the early years the business relied upon word of mouth recommendations and viral marketing to build visitor levels to the company's Website. Having validated the business model, Greg raised $2 million from investors to move the business to a downtown warehouse. By 2006 the company had 20 employees, 750,000 customers in 40 countries, a Website and a Boston shop. Now any clothing firm wanting to become a trendsetter among streetwise young people is desperate to be featured by Karmaloop.

Early in the life of the firm, Greg recognised the critical influence that customer opinions can exert on identifying the latest trend in youth culture. To exploit this variable, he created a blog area on the company Website where customers can submit postings in a variety of categories such as music, fashion, art and culture. Karmaloop staff vet submissions to ensure the site remains perceived as only providing high quality information. By analysing submitted materials, the company is

(Cont'd)

able to rapidly identify newly emerging trends in fashion, music and youth culture. Many customers wanted greater recognition of their contributions in terms of influencing the lifestyle trends of young people. Hence in 2004, the company permitted individuals to apply to become members of the Karmaloop Street Team. These individuals are located in various countries around the world and are permitted to create their own Website banners, put advertisements into their MySpace site and operate customised blog pages.

Terrestrial sources

Over the last thirty years, various Governments' recognition of the important role small firms play in both wealth and job creation has led to a significant increase in the level of public sector resources to support the creation of SME sector advisory services. Some services are operated by Government departments. Others are commercial or not-for-profit organisations that are partially or totally funded by national or regional Government bodies. Research studies concerning the quality and effectiveness of the data provided by these advisory services typically reveal that the quality of the information is highly variable (Jocumsen 2004).

Trade associations can also be a useful source of secondary information (Jurek 1997). These organisations range in size from those with an international or national footprint through to some constituted of a small number of firms trading within a single town. These organisations exist to assist their members' commercial endeavours, but the nature and scope of the support available can vary significantly. Many markets are also covered by sector specific, trade magazines. To retain the interest of their readers, these magazines will contain articles covering a diversity of topics such as market trends, changing supply sources, new technology and pending Government legislation.

Included in any secondary information study should be identification of competitors and an analysis of their trading activities (Smith 1999). Once competitors have been identified, acquiring basic data about their operations is extremely simple because this will be contained in the materials they make available to the market such as brochures and price lists. If the competitor is a limited company, then financial data on sales, operating expense and profits are readily available by accessing a commercial, on-line database at a local library. Obtaining financial information on sole traders or partnerships is not usually feasible because most Governments do not require these organisations to file annual accounts that are then placed into the public domain.

Primary data generation

Alternative methodologies

In those cases where data acquired from secondary sources still leaves key questions unanswered, the small firm will be faced with the necessity of undertaking primary research. The various techniques associated with primary research include experimentation, observation, interviews and surveys. Selection of the most appropriate approach will be influenced by the nature of the data being sought and also the degree to which the entrepreneur feels sufficient skills exist within the firm to undertake the research (Chaston 2002).

Experimentation is intuitively appealing because it appears simple and logical. This is not the case, however, because experiments can be adversely impacted by extraneous variables over which one has no control. Hence the advice to most small firms is, in most cases, to avoid experimentation as a way to acquire data. This situation can be contrasted with observation. This also is a simple process and one that is often underutilised by market researchers. Most entrepreneurs already possess observation skills because they often exploit the activity during the identification of new opportunities. Hence to apply the same capability to market research, the only required change in behaviour is to replace their more typical random approach to data acquisition through observation with a more structured approach of defining what information is to be acquired before commencing the research activity.

Should a small firm need to acquire new data, usually the best approach is to use interviews, focus groups or surveys (Smith 1990). The focus group approach works best with a group size of not more than eight to ten people. During an interview, the direction of the discussions can be altered depending on the information being provided by the respondent. Furthermore, where the respondent exhibits a detailed understanding of an issue, supplementary questions can be used to probe for more data. Interviews can be conducted on a face-to-face basis or by telephone.

Surveys

Where the small firm decides data are required from a large number of people, it will usually be necessary to undertake a survey. The following are key issues which need to be considered when planning this activity (Evans and Mathus 2005):

1 How to identify the names and contact details of the individuals who will participate in the survey.
2 How many people to survey. In many statistical analysis techniques the number of respondents is defined by the level of variation within the population from which the sample is to be drawn. Although the next statements are no doubt statistical heresy, as far as the typical small business is concerned, deciding the samples size can usually be based upon the following simple guidelines:

    (a) When the total population is small (e.g. in an industrial market such as seeking the views of buyers employed by major retailers), then try to obtain response from at least 30–40 per cent of the population.
    (b) When the population is quite large (e.g. most consumer markets), then try to generate answers from at least 150–200 individuals.
3 Which medium to use for delivery of the survey. Where gaining access to respondents is difficult, an intercept method such as stopping people in the street or visiting them at home should be used. Should the names and postal addresses of respondents be available then the survey can be mailed. Alternatively if one has access to respondents' telephone numbers, then a telephone-based survey may be a viable option. The other method which is gaining in popularity is on-line surveys (Michaelidou and Dibb 2006). Their appeal is their low cost and respondents being able to self-schedule their participation time. Reports about the effectiveness of this approach when used by small firms remain, however, somewhat mixed.

4   The other issue is the design of the survey tool. There are numerous books on this
    subject ranging from simple 'how to' texts through to weighty academic publications.
    It is not clear how useful such sources are in assisting small firms to acquire survey
    design skills (Huang and Sukant 1990). However, whichever method is used, at a
    minimum the tool should be assessed prior to implementation by reviewing the issues
    covered in Table 3.1.

Table 3.1   *Survey design assessment*

1   Is the survey written in a language respondents can understand?
2   Is the answer being generated by any question actually relevant to the study or can some
    questions be omitted?
3   Does the structure of the survey logically progress the respondent through the questions being
    asked?
4   Can the survey be completed in a timespan acceptable to respondents?
5   Will respondents feel secure in terms of (a) answering the questions posed and (b) their expecta-
    tions over privacy and confidentiality being respected?
6   Does the survey ask questions about the respondent sufficient to classify them into appropriate,
    specific, socio-demographic, subgroups (e.g. income, age, gender, education, location, marital
    status, accommodation, etc)?
7   Is returning the completed survey a zero-cost proposition for the respondents (e.g. by the provision
    of a stamped, addressed, return envelope)?
8   Is there any incentive being offered for participation in the research (e.g. mailing a gift voucher
    along with the survey form)?

Qualitative research

For many years the conventional view of market research held by academics and
marketing practitioners was that only quantitative data was of any real benefit to
organisations (Hill and Scott 2004). The basis of this view is that only empirical data
permit forecasts or marketing decisions to be made with any degree of accuracy.
More recently, however, there is growing acceptance that qualitative research can be
as valuable as any quantitative study (Carson and Coviello 1996). The reasons for this
change of opinion are that (1) qualitative research will reveal 'soft data' such as
motivation or beliefs that can rarely be identified in purely quantitative studies and
(2) various analysis techniques have been developed whereby qualitative data can be
analysed to generate quantitative data. The purpose and differences between the two
techniques are summarised in Table 3.2.

This growing acceptance of qualitative data has influenced the approach now
being adopted by professional market research firms when assisting smaller
firms. Goodman (1999), in reviewing the role of professional market researchers,
has identified the need for service providers to recognise the limited availability
of secondary data in many of the markets where SMEs operate and the financial constraints facing smaller firms which prevents utilisation of large scale
quantitative studies as used by large firms. In illustrating the effectiveness of
qualitative studies, Goodman provides examples of how in-depth interviews
among knowledgeable sources such as intermediaries and key customers can
generate a richness of data sufficient for the small firm client to make a more
informed marketing decision.

Table 3.2   *A comparison of qualitative and quantitative research*

Qualitative research	Quantitative research
Why respondents do?	How many respondents do?
Explaining and understanding	Describing and measuring
Interpretative/impressionistic	Precise/definitive/scientific
Taps consumer creativity, dynamic, flexible providing depth/richness of understanding	Standardised, repeatable
Intensive, limited data sets	Detailed subgroup sampling or comparisons possible
Quota sampling of individuals/groups covering a range of opinions	Structured probabilistic sampling to represent a segment of the market
Topic guide, open ended questions	Pre-coded questions using structured questionnaire
Interpretation	Numerical analysis/statistics
Provides ideas, insights, hypotheses	Provides conclusions

Source: adapted from Chaston (2002)

CASE STUDY

Understanding customer need

Case aims: To demonstrate how market research can permit identification and understanding of market need and thereby enhance the probability of entrepreneurial success.

Mary Obana and Mike Lannon are both committed to leading healthy lives and exercising regularly. Having entered middle age, they noticed it was becoming increasingly hard to lose weight. They decided that others no doubt faced the same problem, and so an opportunity probably existed to offer a new solution to the American health and fitness market (Seybold 2006). However, without the benefit of having been able to identify a solution based upon intuitive reasoning, in 2003 the couple embarked on an extensive market research study. They observed people in health clubs and gymnasiums and then interviewed them at the end of their exercise sessions. Having interviewed approximately 600 middle aged individuals, they identified a common concern of people wanting to remain fit and thereby enjoy a better quality of life than their parents. Most people were very interested in using strength training to maintain muscle tone and lose weight but felt the existing fitness equipment was not easy to use. The couple concluded there was an opportunity for a new product, but that the probable cost of the new fitness machine would mean it would have to be marketed to health clubs, not consumers.

Secondary data and interviews with health club owners revealed that customer retention is critical to success and that expenditure per client increases if they are provided with access to personal trainers who can create and then guide individuals through a customised, eight to twelve week, training programme. Based upon this knowledge it was decided that the new machine must exploit digital and sports engineering technology which could guide the user through their exercise session and then use the data from the user's

(Cont'd)

workout to automatically generate an updated, personalised training regime. To translate their entrepreneurial idea for a new strength training product into reality, the couple hired a sports equipment designer, the owner of a fitness consultancy, a design firm which specialises in designing consumer electronic products and a software development company.

In late 2004, prototypes of the new product, the Koko Smartrainer, were tested in a YMCA gymnasium in Springfield, Massachusetts. Users were extremely enthusiastic about the product even though they often had to face the software exhibiting 'bugs' and the machines exhibiting mechanical problems. It took almost two years to identify and resolve all of the machine's problems and hence the initial launch did not occur until early 2006. Initial market response from local gymnasiums and health clubs located in leading national hotel chains all indicate that the Smartrainer is a very successful new entry in the health and fitness market.

Variety of life

Emergence of market segmentation

Large mass marketing firms first began to recognise the potential of offering a range of products to meet the needs of different market segments in the 1950s. Their attention was drawn to this opportunity because as consumers become wealthier, in most product categories they begin to exhibit a desire for a greater variety of goods. Once this trend emerges in a market sector, a mass marketing firm may decide to cease offering a standard product. Instead the revised marketing philosophy can be to offer a range of products each targeted at meeting consumer needs within a different market segment.

Segmentation is only feasible if the criteria of measurability, accessibility and viability can be met (Kotler 2006). Measurability requires that a segment's parameters can be determined using variables such as customer need, the number of customers and their location. Accessibility is concerned with being able to contact the customer in order to deliver the product and associated promotional messages. Viability is the issue of whether the revenue from the segment can exceed operating costs, thereby generating an adequate level of profit. The degree to which small firms use market segmentation to grow sales revenue seems to vary by both country and industrial sector. To a certain extent most small firms, because of their bias towards serving a specific market niche, have always used some form of segmentation philosophy. A study of SME firms in the USA identified that the three most popular approaches to identifying segments are geography, demographic and product benefits sought (Petersen 1991).

CASE STUDY

Intuitive segmentation

Case aims: To illustrate how an entrepreneur can identify a new, unsatisfied market segment by drawing upon their own product needs and purchasing experiences. Although most academic texts would advise undertaking market research to identify segments, there are a number of entrepreneurial firms whose founder started the business by having an intuitive understanding that there existed a market segment which had yet to be effectively exploited. Validating the existence of the customers who constitute the segment opportunity is usually due to the fact that customers share the same motivations and product needs as the company founder. An example of identifying an unsatisfied segment is provided by the UK firm Bravissimo which markets fashionable lingerie and swimwear for large-breasted women (Guthrie 2003). When the founder Sarah Tremellan was pregnant, her breasts became a G cup size. Her own shopping experience made her decide that many women must be very dissatisfied with large retail stores. This is because these outlets tend to only stock cup sizes A to C and even where larger sizes are stocked, the styling tends to be very unfashionable.

Deciding to back her intuition about an unsatisfied market segment, in 1995 she launched a mail order business. Success caused her to decide to open a specialist retail outlet because she felt women would appreciate shop staff trained in the skills of being able to help women seeking guidance over the purchase of suitable products. Within eight years of starting up her operation was employing 140 people in four shops, the warehouse and head office. In 2003, annual sales were £15 million. Despite large retailers beginning to stock similar products, she has been able to sustain a premium price for the product range by stocking a much larger range of goods in her stores, carrying an even larger range in the warehouse, promising next-day delivery and having more staff in-store to deliver outstanding customer service.

Simple segmentation

The evolution of simple segmentation has been dependent on the ease with which customer data can be acquired (Shaw and Cresswell 2002). The gender of an individual is easy to determine. It is, however, a somewhat crude measure. To gain any benefit from this knowledge would usually require a second variable to be added such as age or income. Age has been a basic segmentation variable for many years. This is because although obtaining data on any individual's precise age can be difficult, observation does permit a reasonably accurate subdivision of customers into groups such as children, teenagers, young people, middle aged people and old people. Different age groups tend to exhibit variation in their requirements for products and services. Discretionary income is another popular single segmentation variable because this can be easily correlated with certain types of purchase behaviour.

Support for the concept that the stage in a person's life can provide a more accurate basis for segmentation by small firms has been provided by various studies comparing the purchase behaviour of different consumer groups. Widgery et al. (1997), for example, researched retired versus working women of similar ages. Although both groups sought to optimise value, working women were most interested in issues such as manufacturer rebates, loan interest rates and monthly repayment plans. This can be contrasted with retirees who were more concerned about warranties, dealer reputation for integrity and developing a trust in the salesperson.

Problems have emerged over the accuracy of single variable approaches and has led to the conclusion that the greater the variety of information acquired about customers, the more accurate are the definitions of differences between market segments. This view has led most market researchers to favour composite data sets. One popular composite approach is to use age, marital status and family size as the basis of classifying people into segments based upon their position on the family life cycle curve (McCrohan and Finklemen 1981).

CASE STUDY

Similar segment characteristics

Case aims: To illustrate the entrepreneurial approach of entering a market satisfying customers with a segment profile similar to that of the business founder.

Another approach to segmentation is for the entrepreneur to use intuitive market analysis which involves focusing on customers with similar demographic or family life cycle behaviour. One such example is provided by a UK company, The White Company, which markets a range of stylish home accessories and clothing (www.thewhitecompany.com). The original idea for the company came to Christian Rucker in 1993 when, on the basis of her own frustrating shopping experience, she decided fashion orientated young women were unable to locate well designed, white home accessories when setting up their first home. Her solution was to create a small mail order business and then relied mainly on Public Relations to get her company mentioned in newspapers and fashion magazines. Over time the product range has expanded and virtually all of the product lines are made exclusively for The White Company. The nature of the product range has evolved as a reflection of Christian's own changing lifestyle. She has moved into furniture and subsequently into clothing. In 2001 the company opened its first store in Chelsea. There are now 14 stores located across the UK. In 2006, combined annual sales from on-line, catalogue and the retail outlets were £56 million.

CASE STUDY

Self-identified segments

Case aims: Illustrating the opportunity offered by customers indicating a need that reveals the existence of an unfilled segment as yet unnoticed by competition.

Occasionally an entrepreneur who intuitively perceives an emerging segment opportunity ahead of competition may ultimately become so successful as to become a significant new market force exceeding the financial performance of many existing large companies in the same industrial market sector (Rafferty 2004). An example of this scenario is provided by the UK specialist recruitment company Ambition. In 1996 the founder Penny Streeter opened a one-person recruitment agency in Croydon, South London. At that time the large national recruitment agencies focused their efforts on the supply of secretarial and clerical staff. Some months after launching her small, single office recruitment agency, Penny was contacted by a local nursing home late one afternoon after most other agencies had closed. The home was desperately looking for nursing staff to cover the night shift. Intuitively perceiving that round-the-clock market coverage in the provision of healthcare workers was an unfilled segment, Penny focused her efforts upon recruiting more healthcare staff onto her books. While other agencies ignored the segment, Ambition just continued to grow by opening new offices elsewhere in the UK and by entering other, related market sectors such as social workers, teachers and doctors. Six years later Ambition has become a major national player in the UK recruitment agency business. Annual sales are £60 million, the company has opened 19 branch offices and has over 13,500 professional staff on the books.

Geodemographic segmentation

Socio-economic data measure such factors as age, income, occupation and social class. The latter measure is especially useful because it can be used as a surrogate to identify variations in consumer lifestyles and purchasing patterns. Researchers have noted, however, that within any social class there can be significant differences between the purchase behaviour of individuals. Concern about the possible errors which may develop using socio-demographic information has led to the development of geodemographic data as a more accurate way of classifying consumer groups (Kaynak and Harcar 2005).

A leading innovator in geodemographics has been the UK market research company, CACI Ltd (www.caci.co.uk). This firm used statistical analysis of population census data, a classification of residential neighbourhoods, Government expenditure surveys and data on consumer behaviour generated by proprietary research to create the ACORN classification system. Their latest version of ACORN classifies the UK population into five primary groups. Each group is further subdivided into groups from A through to U, thereby yielding a total of 21 subgroups within each primary group. Each subgroup is then further subdivided in relation to neighbourhoods exhibiting specific, common characteristics. Geodemographics of the type developed by CACI are now utilised in most nations in the Western world.

CASE STUDY

Cannondale Corporation

Case aims: To demonstrate the utilisation of geodemographic segmentation.

ACORN's main competitor in the USA is PRIZM (Lee 1990). The company acronym comes from the technology behind the product; namely Potential Rating for Zip Markets. The company's founder was a computer scientist Jonathon Robbins who became interested in the ability of computers to match Postal Zip codes with US Government census data and results from consumer surveys. One successful user of the PRIZM system is a specialist state-of-the-art bicycle manufacturer, Cannondale Corporation, based in Georgetown, Connecticut. The company sells through a network of mainly independent retail

(Cont'd)

stores. There is no sales force; all the selling activities are undertaken by an in-house tele-marketing sales team. By using the PRIZM system to classify 15,000 names and addresses the company was able to determine the nature of their primary customer segment and to use this knowledge to determine the geographic location of such customers. The primary customer profile is dedicated bikers with high disposable incomes. By comparing total population of this segment in a geographic area versus actual sales for that area, the tele-sales team is able to determine market potential and to set realistic sales targets for each of the retailers stocking the Cannondale product range.

Other segmentation techniques

In the 1970s, in an attempt to use personality measurements in market segmentation, advertising agencies in the USA and Europe began to pioneer the idea of using consumer lifestyles to identify different customer groups (Marshall and Greenbergronald 1983). The concept underlying lifestyle classification is to group consumers on the basis of certain activities (e.g. leisure, work, shopping), interaction with other people (e.g. perception as a teenager, adult, parent) and opinions (e.g. politics, social issues). To develop a lifestyle classification system requires large scale surveys to obtain respondents' degrees of agreement with questions concerning activities, interaction and opinions. Statistical tools are then used to classify respondents into specific groups based on their responses.

Segmentation approaches using product usage, benefits or lifestyles to classify markets all have their supporters and their detractors (Wright 1996). Whoever is correct, it should be recognised that developing any of these segmentation concepts will require significant expenditure on primary data research. This will be followed by extensive application of relatively sophisticated analytical tools to identify the characteristics of different consumer segments (Chye et al. 2003). Most small firms are unable to afford such large scale research projects and also often lack the skills to use the required statistical tools. These approaches are likely to remain primarily the preserve of large firms. Hence with rare exceptions, these more advanced techniques are unlikely to be considered by entrepreneurs as being applicable to generating data to assist their decision–making (Kale 2004).

CASE STUDY

Lack of data problems

Case aims: To illustrate an alternative approach to opportunity identification by the entrepreneur where market research or identification of a potential segment prove to be non-viable propositions.

The UK academic, John Mullins (2007 p. 8), has researched the success and failure of numerous entrepreneurs. In his opinion, 'surveys and focus groups are simply not designed to resolve the kinds of uncertainty that the new product or new venture entails'. This is because in many cases there is uncertainty about who is the customer, what they need and whether the new technology can deliver. His perspective is that entrepreneurs are usually so convinced that their idea has merit, their mindset is on proving their idea will work. Mullins' proposed solution to this attitude is that the entrepreneur should focus on discovering the unknown, unknowns (or 'unk-unks'). To achieve this objective the most practical approach is to implement in-depth, lengthy one-to-one interviews with people who have a detailed understanding of market trends and needs.

Unlike conventional interviewing where the researcher uses a series of structured questions to guide the respondent in a long interview, the researcher asks a few open-ended questions and then lets the interview go in the direction which most appeals to the respondents. One example Mullins provides is that of Kenn Jorgenson and Cassian Drew who as avid rock climbers had the idea of installing indoor climbing walls in health and fitness clubs. Initial feedback from fitness club operators indicated the multi-purpose nature of fitness club rooms meant there would be space to install a climbing wall. They then discovered their unk-unk; namely, clubs operate on the simple target metric of achieving an operating cost per participant per fitness class in the region of $1.50/person/class and the maximum acceptable cost is $1.88. Unfortunately the costs of installing and operating their climbing wall were greatly in excess of this figure and hence the two entrepreneurs were forced to drop their business idea.

Another example is provided by Silverglide Surgical Technologies based in Boulder, USA. The company acquired the rights to a proprietary non-stick technology which had the potential to be used in wound cauterisation. The proposed benefit was their new surgical probe would not stick to tissues whilst being used to cauterise blood vessels. Initial sales were poor. Then the company discovered the unk-unk. In this case it was surgeons not using the new probe in a way which was compatible with their way of operating. Fortunately some early users articulated the view that what they really needed were reusable forceps with the non-stick capability. This caused Silverglide to introduce electro-surgical non-stick forceps which have rapidly gained market acceptance.

Opportunity discovery

New to the world

Conventional market research techniques are based on the fundamental assumption that both the potential customer and the entrepreneur have sufficient understanding of a new product or service that they are able to assess the scale of the potential market opportunity using standard data generation techniques (Golder and Telus 1997). A problem will possibly arise, however, during the development of a 'new to the world' proposition. This is because the nature of the market opportunity may not be understood by either, or alternatively both, the customer or the entrepreneur.

Although most potential customers also may lack an understanding of future opportunity, in high technology industries there are often lead customers who, because of their extensive understanding of an industrial sector, are able to collaborate with the

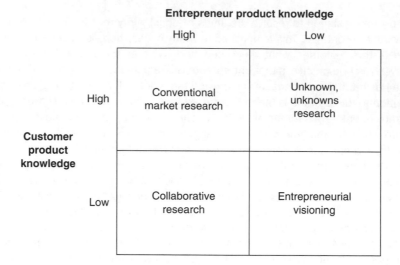

Figure 3.2   *Alternative strategic options*

entrepreneur in evolving a potentially successful, commercially appealing product proposition (Von Hippel 1986). The use of a highly knowledgeable source to provide input about product viability is known as lead customer research. For example, in the semiconductor industry Von Hippel found cases where the entrepreneur would have probably failed if it were not for lead customers who were prepared to fulfil the role of directing the evolution of a commercially viable new product.

Intuition

Where neither the entrepreneur nor the customer has sufficient product knowledge about the market, the product development decision of the entrepreneur will have to be based upon their intuition. In a large scale study undertaken by Carland et al. (1997), the researchers used a scale to assess whether individuals are logical, fact orientated problem solvers, or preferred to rely mainly on their own intuition. The results showed there is a much higher probability that entrepreneurs will be intuitive problem solvers, whereas managers will tend to rely on the acquisition and analysis of facts in reaching a decision. This study also suggested that compared to managers, entrepreneurs have a much higher preference than managers in the reliance on intuitive innovation in the generation of solutions. However, both the entrepreneurs and the managers had similar scores in relation to the issue of being tolerant of risks.

Intuition is not a concept which appeals to some academics because they feel more comfortable with the concept that success is achieved by understanding and responding to customer needs. The conventional thinking on how entrepreneurs develop 'new to the world' propositions is that they are successful because they acquire market knowledge about customers' unrecognised future or latent needs ahead of competition (Slater and Narver 1995).

The concept of opportunity discovery originated with the 'Austrian School' of economics. Their theory originally assumed managerial identification of opportunities evolved out of a careful accumulation of relevant information. In the specific context of the entrepreneur, however, observation reveals the individual does not search out information on which to base a decision (Sanz-Velasco 2006). Instead the entrepreneur seems to just recognise an opportunity when it is encountered. This perspective provides the basis for the theory that entrepreneurs differ from managers in that the former are able to discover or create opportunities, whereas managers in their identification of opportunities typically utilise some form of causative model involving an empirical assessment of factors such as market conditions and the nature of competition.

In reviewing the entrepreneurial process of opportunity discovery the individual engaged in the process must have the ability to recognise that the idea has some form of commercial value. Shane (2000) has also noted that when a number of entrepreneurs with different educational or industrial experience are exposed to a situation leading to opportunity discovery, there will often be wide variance in the ideas which they produce. The explanation for this outcome is that the nature of opportunity discovery is significantly influenced by the entrepreneur's existing knowledge and expertise. The consequence of this situation is that entrepreneurs will be influenced by their prior experiences when determining which market opportunities offer the best prospects for the successful exploitation of a newly discovered opportunity.

In order to validate the concept of how prior experience influences entrepreneurial behaviour, Shane researched the activities of eight entrepreneurs in the period following them being granted licences to develop a process known as three-dimensional printing. This is a manufacturing technology developed and patented by MIT in the USA. As part of the licensing procedure, MIT provided all eight individuals with the same briefings and full access to the same research data. Despite this commonality of new knowledge provided, in all eight cases the new products which were developed all involved very different approaches to exploiting the new technology. When these entrepreneurs were later shown the products developed by the others, all of them felt they would never have been able to identify any application other than their own.

SUMMARY LEARNING POINTS

- Identification and assessment of new opportunities can be greatly assisted by undertaking market research.
- The standard approach to market research is to minimise costs and maximise benefits. This is achieved by undertaking a sequential process of firstly identifying existing (or secondary information) before undertaking the more expensive process of primary research to generate new data.
- Small firms rely heavily on personal and business networks as a key source of low-cost information.
- Small firms' access to secondary data sources have been greatly enhanced by the advent of the Internet and on-line search engines.
- There exist a number of alternative quantitative primary research methodologies of which surveys are probably the most popular.
- Small firms can often avoid confrontations with large firms and also identify new opportunities by focusing on the customer needs within specific market segments.
- As well as market research, many entrepreneurs rely heavily on intuition as a mechanism through which to identify new opportunities.

ASSIGNMENTS

1   In what ways has the Internet expanded the ability of small firms to undertake more extensive market research?
2   Compare and contrast the different techniques which exist for generating new data through primary market research.
3   Compare and contrast the different approaches to market segmentation that might be used by a small firm.

DISCUSSION TOPICS

1   Do you feel that small firms tend to be averse to undertaking market research to assist in developing their understanding of markets? If so, why?
2   What are the potential benefits and risks associated with using qualitative market research data?
3   What are the problems confronting the entrepreneur who is seeking to determine the scale of opportunity offered by a new-to-the-world business idea?

Additional information sources

Research benefits

Greenbank, P. (2000), Micro-business start-ups, challenging normative decision-making, *Marketing Intelligence & Planning*, Vol. 18, No. 4, pp. 206–215.

Networks

Curran, J., Jarvis, R., Blackburn, R.A. and Black, S. (1993), Networks and small firms: constructs, methodological strategies and some findings, *International Small Business Journal*, Vol. 11, No.2, pp. 13–25.

Research Techniques

Goofman, R.V., (1999), The pursuit of value through qualitative market research, *Qualitative Marker Research*, Vol. 1, No. 2, pp. 111–122.

Primary data generation

Lazer, J. and Preece, J. (1999), Designing and implementing Web-based surveys, *The Journal of Computer Information Systems*, Vol. 39, No. 4, pp. 63–68.

Segmentation

Marcus, C. (1998), A practical yet meaningful approach to customer segmentation, *The Journal of Consumer Marketing*, Vol. 15, No. 5, pp. 494–503.
Markely, R., Ott, J. and du Tioit, G. (2007), Winning new customers using loyalty-based segmentation, *Strategy & Leadership*, Vol. 35, No. 3, pp. 32–46.

Intuition

Isaak, T.S. (1981), Intuition needed in managing the small business, *Journal of Small Business Management*, Vol. 19, No. 2, pp. 74–82.
Levangie, J.E. (2003), Musings of a social entrepreneur, *New England Journal of Entrepreneurship*, Vol. 6, No. 2, pp. 65–77.

4

Growth, Chasms and Money

Chapter objectives

The aims of this chapter are to assist the reader to:

- be aware of the concept of the life cycle curve in small business
- assess the high failure rates among small firms
- be aware of how cash flow management can influence small firm success
- review conflicting evidence about SME support service effectiveness
- understand how management roles change as firms grow
- examine sources of external funding utilised by small firms.

Business growth

Life cycle curve

Some of the earliest academic research on small firms focused upon the nature of growth and the factors influencing business performance over time (Greiner 1972). There was widespread acceptance of the idea that small firms exhibit a standard organisational life cycle and various models were proposed to describe the stages which firms passed through from start-up to maturity (Dodge and Robbins 1992). The popularity of the life cycle model among academics has declined in recent years. This is because a number of research studies failed to validate the existence of the stages of growth posited by the earlier writers in real life scenarios (Hill et al. 2002). Another criticism about life cycle theory presented by Beverland and Lockshin (2001) is the model does not acknowledge the fact that the sequencing of actual business events may be different from the standard activities usually defined for the various phases of the growth curve. These researchers also feel another drawback is the model ignores the activities associated with the very important phase prior to start-up, which can take an extensive period of time to complete and may require a significant financial investment.

The probable situation in 'real life' is there are stages of growth in the life cycle of the small firm but very often actual behaviour will not fit the precise geometric curves which academics have posited. Nevertheless, the theories proposed by supporters of the life cycle model (Parks 1977) do provide an extremely useful conceptual framework through which to assess the nature of the business problems facing the entrepreneur over time. By identifying the different challenges which may face the small firm, Kroeger (1974) has proposed this permits conclusions to be reached about which managerial issues should be given priority at any specific point along the life cycle curve.

CASE STUDY

A flawed succession

Case aims: To demonstrate that replacing an entrepreneurial leader with a highly experienced executive from a large, mass marketing company may be inappropriate in terms of sustaining ongoing business success.

Possibly the most difficult leadership role is being hired to replace a visionary entrepreneur. Such was the scenario facing Roberto Goizueta, the ex-CEO of Coca-Cola who was brought in by the board of Apple Computers to replace Steve Jobs, the company founder (Anon. 2002). Steve Jobs was renowned for his highly entrepreneurial and visionary approach to management which the board felt was becoming a major obstacle in achieving market leadership within the PC sector of the computer industry. Hence Jobs was fired in 1985 because the board, major shareholders and certain financial institutions held the view that Apple's expansion required a more disciplined, conventional leader who could implement a more structured, carefully planned expansion of the company to create a global brand.

Goizueta's style, which he brought with him from Coca-Cola, was judged as appropriate for achieving and retaining brand leadership for a major consumer brand. His actions involved a shift towards a more centralised, formalised approach to management. This was apparently accompanied by a massive curtailing of the freedom of the employees to control their own activities, exhibit creativity and to be innovative. Unfortunately, what probably was not required at Apple to retain a strong market position was the introduction of a consumer goods marketing philosophy of spending massive sums on advertising to increase market awareness in the hopes this would lead to a significant increase in market share.

Survival in the computer industry typically requires an ability to develop the technological capability to manufacture large volumes of product at a cost lower than competition or to use innovation to continually launch new generations of product offering performance superiority. Soon after Steve Jobs' departure, sales of Apple computers went into decline. It must have been highly satisfying for Steve Jobs, therefore, when he was re-hired in 1997 to rebuild the innovative, creative high technology business which he had originally founded. His charisma and vision soon rejuvenated a very demoralised workforce whose faith in their returning saviour was almost immediately rewarded by the launch of the massively successful iPod™ music player.

Crossing chasms

As illustrated in Figure 4.1, the life cycle concept suggests that at specific points on the life cycle curve, the small firm faces a new chasm which has to be crossed before the next stage of growth can commence. Crossing each chasm will usually require the entrepreneur to acquire new management skills as well as being prepared to revise the priorities being allocated to specific managerial tasks inside the organisation.

At the pre–business, start-up, stage the focus of the entrepreneur will be on validating whether a viable business opportunity exists. Activities may include assessing market potential, determining the feasibility of a new technology or persuading an external funding source to lend money to the proposed business. The time between deciding

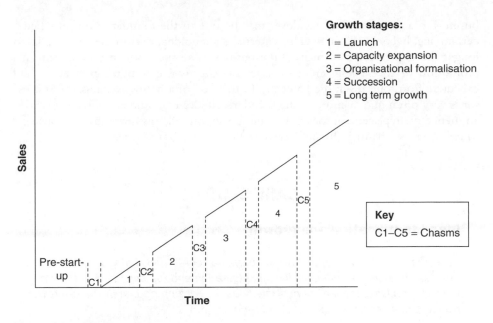

Figure 4.1   *Growth and chasms*

to enter the industry and launching the business can range anywhere from a few months to several years (Beverland and Lockshin 2001). It is to be expected that during this phase, some entrepreneurs will decide against progressing the proposition. The most usual reason is an inability to attract financial backing or being unable to develop a commercially viable version of a new technology which is being developed. A failure to achieve a key aim such as the technology not proving viable will mean the business will not manage to get across Chasm 1 (Dunn and Cheatham 1993).

The next phase of the business is start-up, where the primary focus is on identifying customers and generating initial sales (Luger and Koo 2005). Should the entrepreneur only be able to persuade a few customers to buy the product, then Chasm 2 will not be crossed. During the subsequent capacity expansion stage, the entrepreneur's attention will usually need to be focused on finding ways of satisfying rising demand for the product. For some this may involve moving premises or opening a factory. In a high-technology service sector such as a dotcom start-up, capacity expansion will probably involve investing in new servers and associated data processing systems in order to handle the rapidly rising number of customers visiting the company's Website. Failure to match the demand with a capacity to supply will typically mean the business is unable to cross Chasm 3.

In the early years of a new business, entrepreneurs have a tendency to want to remain in control of everything, from key decisions about strategy through to ensuring every product shipment is leaving on time from the warehouse. Eventually the workload will become too much for one person and there emerges the need to create a more formalised organisational structure. Typically this involves hiring or promoting staff to become responsible for functional activities such as marketing, production management and finance. A failure to implement these changes will mean the business will not cross Chasm 4 (Anon. 1984).

Should the founder remain the owner or major shareholder for many years, eventually the time will arrive where they need to consider handing over the business to a successor. This handover may be due to the founder having reached a certain age, becomes ill or because external shareholders decide the founder is no longer the right person to manage the business. The successor may be an internal promotion of an existing senior manager or can involve bringing in a new chief executive from outside of the company. In the case of a family business, the successor is very often one or more of the founder's children. Should an individual who is an ineffective replacement for the founder be appointed, this may cause the business to fail to cross Chasm 5 (Ip and Jacobs 2006).

CASE STUDY

Idea identification and growth

Case aims: To demonstrate (a) how personal goals and life experience of a business founder will influence idea identification and (b) can continue to determine the ongoing management strategy as an entrepreneurial business grows from a small operation into a global brand.

Anita Roddick, the founder of the globally successful retail chain Body Shop, was one of four children of Italian immigrants who spent her childhood working in her parent's café in Littlehampton, UK (Oates 1988). While employed by the United Nations she visited various countries and was fascinated to discover how local people in countries such as Sri Lanka used vegetables and fruits as skin care products. Upon returning to the UK she married and with her husband, opened a restaurant. He then developed a wander lust and went off on a horse-back ride from South America to New York that would take him two years. Anita did not feel she could manage the restaurant on her own, so she decided to open a shop. Anita's eco-orientation caused her to believe that women wanted products made from natural, organic ingredients and that none of the products whilst being developed by suppliers, should be tested on animals. She opened the first Body Shop store with a bank loan of £4,000.

In the early years, although committed to her idea of eco-friendly cosmetics and skin care products, her primary business aim was survival in what was at that time, a very undercapitalised business. Gordon Roddick's horse died, so he returned to assist in managing the administrative side of the business. Having proved there was a growing demand from eco-orientated women, the Roddicks persuaded a friend to invest in their business expansion plans. Even with this injection of capital, the company lacked the financial resources to rely on opening new shops as the way to grow the business. So the decision was made to offer people the opportunity to buy a Body Shop franchise. This proved an exceptionally effective mechanism through which to build the business not just in the UK but in numerous other countries around the world.

In developing a global business, Anita placed emphasis on ensuring the Body Shop remained loyal to her personal values of seeking to assist less advantaged people. To fulfil this aim she travelled tirelessly finding new sources of product in developing nations. Where necessary, Body Shop provided financial assistance to local people in these countries to support the expanded production of ingredients and the manufacture of skin care products. Eventually the need for further capital to support business growth led the Roddicks to float the business on the UK stock market in 1984. The injection of additional cash sustained the further expansion of the business and by 1988, Body Shop had 1,200 stores spread across the world, of which 90 per cent were franchise operations.

However, by going public, Anita Roddick was exposed to pressure from major shareholders such as pension funds to make what in their eyes was a more conservative, properly run, professionally managed business (Davidson 1996). These investors attempted to apply pressure for a change in business philosophy, especially during periods when sales were affected by economic downturns in key markets such as America and the UK. Anita's reaction was to remain unaffected by such demands. She continued to travel the world seeking new ways of helping people in developing nations and assisting in the creation of community support programmes for the unemployed. These activities and her decision to become a corporate member of environmental protest organisations such as Greenpeace and Friends of the Earth made the financial community extremely nervous.

By the mid-1990s, it was apparent that Anita Roddick was increasingly frustrated by the constraints and criticisms of major investors which had the potential to frustrate her desire to ensure the core values upon which the Body Shop business philosophy had been built, remained unchanged. Although she remained involved in developing new product ideas and overseas production sources her level of participation in the day-to-day management of the business significantly declined. Instead she committed more of her time to social issues, such as promoting ideas concerned with the new ways of educating and developing the next generation of young managers in the UK. Then in 2006, the last business surprise she sprang on the world was to sell Body Shop to the French cosmetics firm L'Oreal for £100 million. Her supporters in the environmental movement accused her of selling out to a large multi-national which was involved in animal testing and was not perceived as being environmentally responsible. Anita Roddick defended her actions, pointing out that she negotiated a deal in which L'Oreal has undertaken to become more environmentally aware and to cease participation in testing new products on animals. Only time, however, will tell whether these promises prove to be correct.

Success and failure

Business failure

The high number of new start–up firms that cease trading within 18–24 months of their launch has understandably attracted the interest of academics, banks and small business support agencies in terms of understanding the factors influencing success and failure (Gaskill et al. 1993). It is necessary, however, to be aware there is an apparent myth and also an unrecognised problem in relation to research on this subject. The myth concerns frequent mention in the popular and business press of 80–90 per cent of small firms failing in their first year. The origins of this myth remain unsubstantiated (Cochran 1981), but regretfully it is frequently mentioned in small business start–up training programmes. Presumably the statistic is stated to justify the benefits to the participants of attending the training scheme. In reality, however, the main impact upon being told this failure rate is often to severely reduce people's confidence in their personal ability to succeed in small business.

The unrecognised research problem is the assumption that business failure is the reason why any small firm has ceased trading. As noted by Cochran – one of the researchers who have attempted to analyse available data – many small firms identified in the available statistics as having ceased trading, and hence considered as apparently failed businesses, where in fact successful operations. In reality there are a variety of reasons, other than business failure, which can cause the founder to close the business. From his study of US small firms, Cochran concluded, for example, that the most frequently quoted reasons why successful businesses are closed are the founder has decided to re-enter employment, retire or sell the business.

To gain further understanding of the issues associated with failure versus closure, Headd (2003) undertook a statistical analysis of the US Census Bureau's data set that has been generated by large scale surveys of American small firms. The data set showed that 66 per cent of new small firms survive for two years, 50 per cent for four years and 40 per cent for six years or longer. In terms of predicting the probable long term survival of a small business, his analysis indicated this was highest for businesses where the founder had access to at least $50,000 in capital, a college degree and started the firm because they wanted to create a new, very successful business. Success rates also generally increased with age, the number of founders involved in the start-up and previous experience of owning at least one small business. The highest rates for business closure were among small firms established by a relatively young person with little or no capital, engaged in running a trading entity which required a high level of labour intensive input (e.g. window cleaning, gardening etc.). Headd points out that these latter types of businesses are easy to close or to sell. Hence his conclusion is that in many cases, the closure of a small business is not related to failure, but merely reflects the founder deciding against remaining in self-employment or has been successful in finding more rewarding, permanent employment.

Cash flow

In the vast majority of the research papers published on small firms in the early years after initial launch, the primary cause given for business failure is the owner/manager ran out of cash (Lane and Schary 1991). Explanations of why this occurred include (1) an inadequate level of market demand for the product, (2) higher than expected operating costs, (3) not recognising the level of cash needed until sales revenue exceed costs, (4) a major customer not paying an invoice and (5) an inability to persuade an external source, usually a bank, to lend money to the business at the outset or being prepared to increase the size of the overdraft when trading problems are subsequently encountered.

Demonstrating how a cash crisis can occur can be achieved by examining the simple example of a single person who decides to make aromatic candles and sells these as gift products to friends, relatives and local gift shops. The numbered elements which constitute the trading process are shown in Figure 4.2.

At start-up, the owner will need to part with cash to buy raw materials to make candles for sale (1, 2). During this period the business will be incurring costs (3), receiving

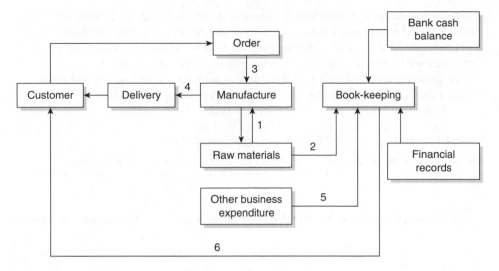

Figure 4.2   *Business processes for the start-up candle business*

no revenue and hence be running at a loss. Upon receipt of an order (4), the owner delivers the product, issues an invoice (5) and eventually is paid (6). The business cycle now becomes that of obtaining more orders, buying in and paying for raw materials, shipping new orders and being paid (1–6). The cash will be held in the company's account at the bank. The financial records that describe the business activity are the Profit & Loss (P&L) statement and the Balance Sheet. The elements which constitute a P&L statement are revenue inflows from sales (plus any other sources such as interest on bank deposits) from which, by deducting cost of goods and operating expenses, net profit is calculated. Typical items in a P&L statement are illustrated in Table 4.1.

Most organisations own items purchased for operating the business (e.g. computers). These are collectively known as 'fixed assets'. The other type of assets are those known as 'current assets'. These are items that are either cash (e.g. bank deposits) or can rapidly be converted into cash (e.g. debts owed by customers). Liabilities define what the firm owes to others. Liabilities can be payable within 12 months, in which case they are known as 'short term liabilities' (e.g. the telephone bill). Other liabilities which are not due for payment for at least a year are known as 'long term liabilities' (e.g. a mortgage taken out to fund the purchase of the firm's office building). The elements which constitute the balance sheet are shown in Table 4.1.

Once any new business starts trading, hopefully sales revenue will soon at least be equal to costs. This point is known as 'break even'. It is not unusual for new businesses to have to survive for 18–24 months before break even is achieved. In terms of possible cash crises that might force closure of the candle business, these could include:

1 Paying for the raw materials to make the first candles and then discovering nobody wants to buy the product.
2 Having delivered the candles, customers do not pay their bills.
3 Sales remain too small, running at a level below costs and hence the break even is never achieved.

4   The business approaches the bank for a temporary overdraft and because cash inflows are running behind cash outflows, the bank refuses to lend the firm any money.

5   Sales growing very rapidly causing the owner to invest in purchasing new stock and expanding capacity only to discover cash outflows to support the expansion are greater than the rate with which new customers are settling their invoices. This situation is known as 'over trading'.

Table 4.1   *Components of a P&L statement and Balance Sheet*

Components of a P&L statement	Components of a Balance Sheet
Sales	*Fixed Assets*
Other revenue	Land & buildings
Total Revenue	Plant & equipment
Cost of Goods Sold	Vehicles
Gross Profit	*Total Fixed Assets*
(= Revenue – Cost of Goods)	*Current Assets*
Operating Expenses	Cash
Salaries	Debtors
Rent	Finished goods
Utilities	Work in progress
Postage & telephone	*Total Current Assets*
Travel	*Current Liabilities*
Motor expense	Creditors
Advertising	Bank overdraft
Professional fees	Loan repayments due
Misc. expense	Tax
Total Expense	*Total Current Liabilities*
Net Profit	*Net Current Assets*
(= Gross Profit – Operating Expense)	(= Current Asssets – Current Liabilities)
	Long Term Liabilities
	Long term loans
	Shares issued
	Retained profits

Other failure factors

In terms of explaining how a cash crisis may arise, there is a tendency of many researchers to focus on operational and tactical business processes to explain the underlying reasons for business failure (Watson et al. 1998). As a consequence the usual conclusion is to explain failure in terms of the poor management skills of the owner/manager, usually by highlighting their deficiencies in managing the financial aspects of the business or understanding the real nature of market demand. In commenting upon this situation Beaver and Jennings (2003 p. 115) have expressed the view that these findings are 'simplistic, immature and dangerous'. Their concern is that such research findings are often used to justify the majority of funding for small support schemes being directed towards providing small business training programmes covering topics such as business planning and financial management. As a consequence, potential and existing owner/managers are not provided with a broader understanding of such issues as: (1) the impact of external environmental factors on business performance (e.g. an economic downturn, changes in Government legislation), (2) the motivation, ability to handle stress, problem solving and interpersonal skills of the owner/manager and (3) the critical

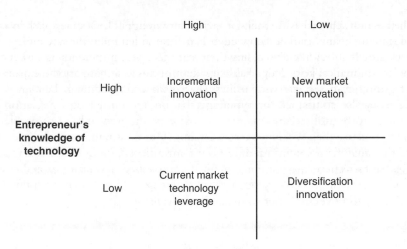

Figure 4.3 *Technology/market options*

Source: modified from Saemundsson and Dahlstrand (2005), How business opportunities constrain young technology-based firms from growing into medium-sized firms, *Small Business Economics,* Vol. 24, No. 2. With kind permission of Springer Science and Business Media.

role the creation of effective personal and business networks can play in assisting the owner/manager to develop and implement their business ideas.

High technology start-ups

An example of the nature of the interaction which can occur between internal capabilities and the external environment is provided by Saemundsson and Dahlstrand's (2005) study of the constraints to growth facing technology-based start-up firms. These researchers proposed that key influencers of performance in technology-based firms are the founder(s)' understanding of the market and the technology upon which the business venture is based. By combining these two variables, they proposed that, as illustrated in Figure 4.3, the new business faces four different possible scenarios.

The researchers posited that the fastest business growth rate will occur in businesses using incremental innovation in existing markets because these enterprises have already acquired technological and market expertise. They also felt the key constraint facing the start-up enterprise is the ability to persuade the financial institutions and potential investors to provide the high level of funding which is usually necessary in order to successfully launch a new, technology-based product. Should these be valid hypotheses, then the enterprises having the fewest problems raising financing will be those firms intending to use incremental innovation. This is because (1) the enterprise will usually need to borrow less money than for a project based on entirely new technology and (2) funding sources will perceive lending risks to be lower in those cases where the entrepreneur has extensive prior knowledge of the technology or the market sector to be entered.

The researchers examined data from 262 young, technology-based Swedish firms. The results indicated that the fastest growth rates occurred within firms which exploited new opportunities based on the founder(s) utilising technology about which the individual(s) had extensive prior knowledge. Their study also concluded that degree of prior market knowledge had little apparent influence over business growth rates. It should be noted, however, that this finding contradicts earlier studies where lack of market knowledge has been identified as an inhibitor of business success for a technology-based start-up business (Kirpalani and Macintosh 1980).

The study also confirmed the hypothesis that limited knowledge in relation to the technology to be utilised and market sectors to be entered did create problems for the entrepreneur when seeking external funding. This constraint seemed to be greatest where the small firm sought funding from conventional, traditional lending sources such as banks. Where the entrepreneur had approached a venture capital company for funds, a lack of technology or market knowledge did not seem to influence the lender's decision over whether to make funds available.

CASE STUDY

Persistence

Case aims: To illustrate that (a) starting a new business is rarely easy and (b) the importance of the entrepreneur retaining their business vision in the face of repeated obstacles needing to be overcome.

Tom Managhan, the founder of the American Domino Pizza empire, having been raised in orphanages and foster homes, joined the US Marines in the 1950s (Jakubovics 1989). Upon leaving the service in 1959, his first business venture was to put all of his life savings into an oil drilling venture. This turned out to be a swindle and he lost all his money. Then, instead of going to college as he had planned, in 1960 he and his brother purchased DomiNicks, a pizza store in Yspilanti, for $500.

The store was small and the brothers relied more on carry-out sales and home deliveries than on in-store sales as a revenue source. After a few months his brother wanted to leave the business and so Tom gave him the delivery car in exchange for his share in the business. Now reliant upon just his own skills, Tom focused on how to satisfy customers who wanted the speedy delivery of a hot pizza. He developed a stiff, corrugated box and a 'hot box' to maximise the quality of the product in transit. Additionally he introduced the idea of the 30-minute free delivery concept (i.e. if the delivery takes more than 30 minutes, the customer gets the pizza for free).

Sales rapidly grew from $99 to over $750/per week and Tom decided that to build the business he needed to open more stores, especially in better markets such as college towns. He met a chef who offered new expertise and bought a half share in the business for $500. Together they opened two more pizzerias which Tom managed and two restaurants that the chef ran. Unfortunately, while Tom was working over 100 hours a week to build the business, the chef was spending most of his time renovating his house. They decided to dissolve the partnership with Tom keeping the pizzerias and the chef retaining the restaurants. It was at this stage that the Domino's Pizza name was born, primarily to communicate to customers that he and the chef were no longer working together.

A year later in 1965, the chef was declared a bankrupt and Tom was left to cover unpaid back taxes of $75,000. Having worked out an agreement with his creditors, there was then a $150,000 fire which wiped out Domino's commissary and offices. The solution to not having any cash to open more outlets was to follow the McDonald's hamburger model and to launch Domino's Pizza as a franchise operation. Within only 12 months, 12 stores had opened and a further 12 were near to being launched. At this juncture Tom hired an investment broker who was excessively enthusiastic about growing the business. He persuaded Tom to change to a large, expensive accountancy firm and to increase the size of the management team. This expansion rapidly spiralled out of control.

Eventually the banks who had funded the expansion stepped in and took control. They retained Tom as an employee with the promise that he could buy back 49 per cent of the shares if he turned the business around within 24 months. In 1971 the banks decided they wanted out, so they gave Tom back all of the shares, leaving him to run the business and at the same time needing to find other ways of paying off the creditors. Through all of these trials and tribulations, Tom retained the same basic strategy of focusing upon take-out and delivery sales, offering limited sit-down facilities in the outlets, limiting the menu to just pizza and soft drinks and continuing to offer the 30-minute delivery promise. By 1978, there were over 100 stores in operation. By the late 1980s, Domino's had become the second-largest pizza chain in America, operating approximately 5,000 outlets and generating annual sales in excess of $2.8 billion.

Support services

Support service expansion

It was only in the 1980s that Western Governments began to recognise the SME sector as an important component of their respective economies. The primary reason for this shift in attitude was that with large companies closing down or moving their operations offshore, politicians realised that persuading people to start a new small business was an excellent way of reducing unemployment levels (Curran 2000). Adverse employment trends caused Governments to allocate huge sums of money to expand existing support schemes such as business counselling and to underwrite the creation of a diverse range of new forms of small business support. These new schemes included the opening of local support agencies, offering start-up business training, grants and access to subsidised work spaces. Delivery of these new schemes was usually contracted out to the private sector.

Some of the published research paints a very positive picture about such schemes being extremely successful in terms of assisting the participants (Brown 1990). There is also strong evidence that owner/managers can clearly benefit from being provided with access to an effective support service such as one-to-one counselling or mentoring delivered by individuals with extensive small business management experience (Sullivan 2000). However, certain question marks must exist about some of these published findings regarding the actual effectiveness of support provision, because in most cases the study is often concerned with a support scheme for which the researcher or their organisation has received funding to deliver the activity (Storey 2002).

Where attempts have been made to acquire a more balanced view, the evidence of successful outcomes is somewhat less impressive. In terms of whether such schemes are perceived as beneficial by owner/managers, in most countries only a minority of small firms ever seek assistance from public sector support agencies or participate in the free or subsidised training which is available. Lewis et al. (2007), for example, in assessing the impact of 20 years of spending on support schemes in New Zealand, found that the majority of small firms still relied upon the traditional sources of accountants, banks and personal networks to assist them in creating and managing small businesses.

Support effectiveness factors

There are a number of reasons why schemes may not prove to be effective. For example, Muhammad Yunus (1998) – the founder of the Grameen Bank to provide micro-finance for villagers in Bangladesh and winner of the Nobel prize for his work in social enterprise – has criticised the standard solution of seeking to reduce unemployment and poverty by offering people training programmes. In his view many of these schemes fail because there are insufficient opportunities available for the people who have been trained and even more importantly, the training providers have a financial incentive to ensure economic development policies remain focused on training, not investing in social infrastructure. For a training scheme to be beneficial, in his view the programme should be delivered and managed by a local community instead of being placed in the hands of a profit orientated commercial training provider.

Another problem with many schemes is politicians prefer outcomes that are low cost, offer a simple measurement of achievement and participant numbers are extremely high (Chaston 1992). Hence large scale, very short duration, business start-up training programmes are extremely popular with Governments. This is because the programmes are easy to assess by just measuring the number of people attending the training sessions and high participant numbers sound very impressive when used by politicians to claim success for their policies. Unfortunately, in order to fund such mass market schemes, programme content tends to be extremely simplistic and only provide participants with a minimal level of knowledge (Robson and Bennett 1999).

In relation to the issue of why only a very small proportion of existing SMEs take advantage of available support initiatives, politicians and commercial training providers, Governments will usually explain that this reflects lack of commitment towards training within the small firms sector. In reality, however, the available research contradicts the view that owner/managers are anti-training. Most studies reveal that the majority of SMEs do undertake training, but virtually all of this is delivered in-house to meet company specific, skills development needs. The reason small firms do not attend external courses is many owner/managers have discovered public funded schemes have usually been designed by the training providers who have little or no understanding of the real employee development needs of SMEs (Curran and Blackburn 2000).

Another common error in relation to the provision of effective support is the assumption that concepts which have proved effective in large firms will also be of benefit to SMEs (Smith and Collins 2007). For example in the UK, for over ten years the Government has funded Investors In People (IIP). This scheme is designed to promote, assist and evaluate the utilisation of structured human resource management (HRM) policies within small firms. The programme represents a very significant revenue source for the numerous consultants employed to enrol owner/managers and to then ensure their client firms will be awarded the IIP accreditation. However,

Figure 4.4 *Universal and entrepreneurial competence*

Source: modified from Sandler-Smith, Hampson, Chaston and Badger (2003), Managerial behaviour, entrepreneurial style and small firm performance, *Journal of Small Business Management,* Vol. 42, No. 1, pp. 47–68. With kind permission of Wiley-Blackwell.

as demonstrated by Smith and Collins, research question marks exist about whether this programme can be of benefit to smaller firms.

Managing growth

Managerial responsibilities

Once a small firm becomes successful, the usual outcome is that growth leads to the business becoming larger and activities such as decision-making, problem solving and fulfilment of specific management functions can no longer be controlled by the founder. Assuming this individual recognises and accepts there is a need to change the firm's operations, new staff will be appointed from either within or outside of the firm to take on specific management roles such as marketing, finance and personnel management (Jennings and Beaver 1997). At or soon after this point, many small firms move away from a somewhat ill-defined organisational structure to one where specific functions are departmentalised and there is a clearer definition of lines of authority between employees and managers.

In a study to determine whether entrepreneurs exhibit any variance when compared with non-entrepreneurial firms in relation to formalising and undertaking managerial tasks, Sandler-Smith et al. (2003), did find both similarities and differences. As summarised in Figure 4.4, all of the small firms in the study indicated a common need to manage certain aspects of their organisations' activities; namely functional roles involving responding to environmental change and achieving performance goals. The entrepreneurial firms, however, also identified the additional roles associated with working with employees in the effective management of the firm's vision and culture.

To gain an understanding of how small firms respond to the need to manage growth, Kotey and Slade (2005a) undertook a study of the process within Australian SMEs. Their research confirmed earlier studies that as small firms grow, it becomes increasingly difficult for the owner/manager to use informal approaches in areas such as communicating with employees, the allocation of resources and problem solving. The usual solution is for the owner/manager to introduce a more formalised style of management and to increasingly delegate day-to-day tasks to subordinates. This study also confirmed that when a firm is small and remains under the control of the owner/manager, this individual usually perceives there is little need for documentation and standardisation of activities such as recruiting and managing staff. As the company grows, however, in order to ensure there is consistency in the tasks undertaken by subordinates, formal business practices begin to be established. In many cases this formalisation is undertaken by those individuals who have been appointed to specific managerial roles such as finance or marketing. In the case of the hiring of the first ever personnel manager, for example, this appointment would probably be followed by actions such as creating detailed records and job specifications for all employees, adopting a more formalised approach to recruitment, implementing staff appraisals and developing a staff training programme.

At some stage in the life history of a new small business, the founder(s) will have to consider who will be their successor. The need for this decision can be for a number of different reasons. These include retirement, illness, inability to cope with the increasing complexity of the business, boredom, the emergence of a new, more exciting opportunity or pressure from major shareholders who have concerns about the individual's managerial performance (Sambrook 2005). The degree to which this change in leadership proves successful will depend upon how effectively the founder has developed and implemented a succession plan for the business. Unfortunately, it is all too often the case that the leadership transition is an abrupt, totally unplanned event. This may occur because the founder either dies or is taken seriously ill. The other scenario is where major shareholders orchestrate a board room coup and the founder is immediately ousted from the business. Whichever are the events that lead to the founder no longer being the leader, the individual who takes on the role under such circumstances will face the virtually impossible task of being accepted by the workforce as capable of 'filling the founder's shoes'.

CASE STUDY

'Morphing'

Case aims: To illustrate that when entrepreneurial firms respond to competitive pressures in a rapidly changing high technology market, the outcome in terms of the winner and loser is dependent upon the firms' respective business strategies.

Rindova and Kotha (2001) have used the phrase 'managing by morphing' to describe the process whereby entrepreneurial firms when confronted with rapidly changing markets or technologies, respond dynamically by rapidly revising their strategy or redirecting their resources to implement an effective response to a perceived opportunity of threat. To demonstrate the application of their morphing concept, the researchers undertook a comparative analysis of two of the leading US firms who were early entrants into the world of Internet search engines, Yahoo! and Excite.

In 1993/94 a team of students at Stanford University in California set themselves the goal of developing software which used a computer program to search and index Websites. Their technology included some very advanced features such as concept extraction, which involves searching for families of words instead of just single words. The students formed a company called Architext, subsequently renamed Excite. Meanwhile two other Stanford students, Jerry Yang and David Filo, were creating their own list of favourite Websites which they organised into a hierarchical directory of categories. Encouragement from other techies was the stimulus for these two individuals to start visiting and categorising in the region of 1,000 new sites/per day. The sense of humour that is a characteristic of these two individuals led them to describe their site as 'Yet Another Hierarchic Officious Oracle', which was the origin of their very memorable business name, Yahoo!.

The organisational structure of these two operations was very different. At Yahoo! the directory which formed the basis of their search engine was maintained and expanded by a large team of 'surfers' who identified, visited and then classified new Websites. The Californian lifestyle and orientation of the Yahoo! operation business was reflected in the names on the two navigational buttons on the Website; namely 'new' and 'cool'. In contrast, Excite's operation was software driven using a search technology known as 'spiders' to scan the Internet and automatically develop an index listing new Websites as these are identified. The company employed fewer staff and instead ran the operation using row upon row of computer servers linked to very powerful workstations. Initially Excite's computerised search engine generated results faster and in greater quantity than Yahoo!. The latter's search engine, however, was seen by users as providing more relevant information.

By licensing spider technology from third party suppliers, Yahoo! was soon able to match Excite's search speed. In response to this situation, Excite developed an in-house editorial staff to review and categorise new Websites. Both companies rapidly needed external financing to fund their expansion. Excite negotiated funding from a Silicon Valley venture capital firm, Kleiner, Perkins, Claufield and Byer and Yahoo! obtained funding from another Silicon Valley venture capital company, Sequoia. Only two years later, both companies made their stock market debut through IPOs. On 4 April 1996, Excite raised $31 million in new capital. This was then exceeded by Yahoo! who on 12 April raised $85 million. By 1996 new competitors such as Google™ and HotBot were entering the market and the ability to operate fast search engines as the basis for sustaining a competitive advantage began to decline in importance.

Yahoo!'s response was to seek to build awareness for the brand by exploiting the firm's reputation as being the really switched on, coolest company on the World Wide Web. This identity was extremely useful in generating revenue from other Internet firms. For example, Yahoo! was adopted as the default engine by the then leading browser company, Netscape. In 1996 Yahoo! launched a $5 million television advertising campaign. This was the first time a major Internet company had used an off-line, terrestrial medium to build brand share. Excite responded by launching their own $8 million television campaign built around Jimmy Hendrix's classic rock song, 'Are You Experienced?' Despite this higher level of spending, Yahoo! still remained a more highly recognised brand name

(Cont'd)

than Excite. The key reason for Yahoo!'s success was the strategic decision in 1996 to start offering new content such as stock market quotes, maps, news, weather, sports, classified advertising and 'chat rooms'. Content differentiation was achieved by creating specifically labelled sections such as Yahoo! Finance. The company then moved to strengthen regional and international brand identity by creating ten regional sites in the USA and seven sites overseas. To execute these activities Yahoo! exploited their existing relationships with companies such as the Reuters News Service and the Japanese media conglomerate, Softbank. Lacking such well developed market contacts, Excite was forced to rely on reaching agreement with companies such as AOL and MSN-Europe to provide content and to expand the distribution of their search engine's services.

By 1997 the number of surfers employed at Yahoo! had dropped to below 50 per cent as the company evolved to become a more formalised organisation structure in order to effectively implement marketing and brand building activities. Excite's attempts to match Yahoo!'s success had by the end of 1997 caused the company to virtually run out of cash. To overcome this problem, the company fired about 50 per cent of their in-house editorial team. The cost cutting exercises failed to solve the cash problem. To survive the company was forced to accept a takeover offer from @Home, a US provider of high-speed, on-line access services. The acquiring company's plan was to use this and other acquisitions to build a business based upon providing search engine products to other companies in both on-line and off-line markets. Yahoo! in the meantime continued to evolve and began to generate ever increasing revenue growth from again 'morphing' their strategy into concentrating on selling on-line advertising space. From then on, the firm's main rival has remained the even more successful, but perceived as somewhat more conservative firm, Google™.

Funding growth

Sources of funds

As illustrated in Figure 4.5, the start point for virtually every owner/manager is to fund their new business from their own resources or to borrow money from family or friends (Justis 1982). Should there be a need to inject additional cash during the early months of trading, this is often achieved by using additional informal sources such as the owner/manager's personal credit cards or being granted credit by suppliers. At the point where these sources are unable to continue to provide the funds needed to support ongoing trading or permit the implementation of a growth plan, most small firms then turn to their banks for an overdraft or a business loan. For individuals with either a poor or no credit history such as first generation immigrants into a country, persuading banks to lend them money can be extremely difficult. In some cases these individuals may be able to raise money from relatives or other members of their community. Very often, however, this may not be feasible and in these cases the only solution is to

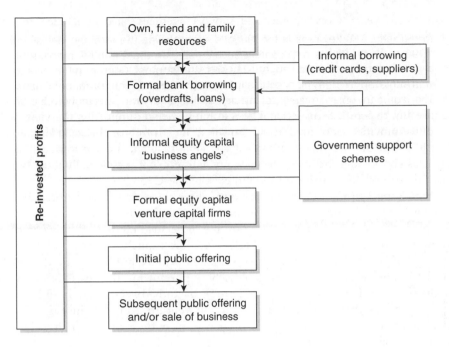

Figure 4.5   *The money raising progression*

accept that the size of the business will remain constrained by a lack of funds for the foreseeable future (Hussain et al. 2006).

The majority of small firms have no plans to expand beyond being a business able to support the lifestyle and income needs of the founder(s). Hence these organisations usually have few requirements to seek any other sources of external finance (Boocock 1990). Firms which wish to grow, especially those engaged in high technology product development requiring massive spending on Research and Development (R&D) or the acquisition of expensive production equipment, will usually need to identify additional borrowing sources. Taking on more loans is usually not an option because this would create an unmanageably high interest repayment burden for the organisation. Hence the more usual source of additional monies is either from applying for Government grants or bringing new shareholders into the business.

Organisations seeking funds in the region of £50,000–£200,000 are usually perceived as being too small to be of interest to venture capital companies. Hence raising these smaller amounts of money will often involve working with informal investors, known as 'business angels'. These are wealthy private citizens, who having often previously run their own company, are willing to make a small investment in new firms in return for a 10–20 per cent equity stake (Mason and Harrison 2000). In many cases the motivation behind being a business angel is not the financial return, but the excitement and mental stimulation of helping another entrepreneur. Sudek's (2007) study of business angels in California found that critical factors influencing an angel's decision to invest in a new venture include trustworthiness of the entrepreneur, quality of the management team, enthusiasm of the lead entrepreneur, and exit opportunities for the angel.

In recent years, Governments and support agencies have concluded that the unwillingness of venture capitalists to invest small sums of money has resulted in the emergence of an 'equity gap' in some countries. In an attempt to overcome this problem, Governments have sought to bridge this gap by establishing regional investment funds dispersed by specialist support agencies and in some cases, have also offered major income or capital gains tax breaks to private citizens who are willing to invest in the small firms sector. The research evidence supporting the view of the need to provide such funding is, however, far from conclusive. Harding and Cowling's (2006) study, for example, indicated that the perceptions of support agencies concerning the scale of the equity gap problem was actually much greater than the size of the actual gap found to exist in the UK.

Once a small firm has reached the point where the scale of the cash requirement is of interest to a venture capitalist, the founder(s) will then become involved in developing a business plan and presentation for use in persuading one of these companies to invest in the business. The critical role of venture capitalists in assisting the development of the US dotcom industry has been widely publicised by the media. To determine whether this role was equally important in other parts of the world, Audretsch and Lehmann (2004) undertook a study of German business. Their conclusion was that without the existence of venture capitalists investing in new, small, innovative firms, then the scale of success for entrepreneurial high technology businesses will be greatly reduced.

In those cases where venture capitalists are attracted by the proposition, they will usually expect to be offered a significant share of equity in the region of 20–50 per cent of the business in return for investing in the proposition. The ultimate aim of venture capitalists is to recover their investment within a reasonably short period (e.g. three to four years) by selling their shares at a high price when the new business goes public through the mechanism of an initial public offering (IPO). Venture capitalists are sometimes criticised both in the media and by entrepreneurs because of their desired target of wishing to make a 40–50 per cent return on their investment. Such a high return is necessary, however, because only a minority of the firms in which they invest ever prove to be commercially successful and hence can be 'taken public'.

To gain further understanding of why some firms fail despite the support of venture capitalists, Zacharakis et al. (1999) undertook a study of unsuccessful small US companies which had growth plans requiring an injection of venture capital. The study sought the views of both the founder(s) and the venture capitalist about their perceptions about the cause of the business failure. Both parties concluded that the commonest reasons for failure were: (1) the firm's management team lacked the necessary skills to grow the business, (2) the firm's management team had implemented the wrong business strategy and (3) upon implementation of the business plan, the need for external funding proved to be significantly higher than originally estimated. Other reasons given by the venture capitalists to explain failure included external events such as an economic downturn, market conditions being more difficult than originally expected or the emergence of unexpectedly strong reaction by competitors. This can be contrasted with the founder(s) who tended to place greater blame on themselves and their own management team for not having the skills to develop and implement a marketing plan appropriate for the trading conditions which were encountered.

SUMMARY LEARNING POINTS

- The concept of the business life cycle divides the development of the small business into the four phases of start-up, capacity expansion, professionalisation and succession, each of which create different managerial priorities for the small business.
- The conventional view of the high failure rates in small business typically ignore that included in these data are owner/managers who cease trading for reasons such as returning to employment, sale of the business or retirement.
- The commonest cause of business failure is cash flow management but there are a diversity of reasons that can lead to the business encountering a cash flow crisis.
- High technology start-ups face the additional risk of developing and/or gaining market acceptance for their new product or service.
- Recognition of the importance of the SME sector has led to a significant expansion of Government small business support services in Western nations but questions exist over the actual effectiveness of many of these schemes.
- As the small business grows this leads to the owner/manager needing to develop additional management skills and eventually to accept the need to appoint others to become responsible for certain aspects of managing the business.
- At start-up the primary sources of funds are the owner/managers themselves, relatives or friends. Where these sources are inadequate, bank borrowing is likely to occur.
- Very successful high growth entrepreneurial firms will eventually need to access equity capital through channels such as business angels, venture capitalists and the stock market.

ASSIGNMENTS

1 How could an owner/manager avoid the problem of lacking relevant skills when seeking to cross each chasm on the business life cycle curve?
2 What are possible causes of Government small business support schemes failing to provide effective assistance to the SME sector?
3 How can small firms avoid or reduce the possibility of a cash flow crisis during a significant economic downturn?

DISCUSSION TOPICS

1 What are the advantages and disadvantages of starting a new small business in a high technology industry?
2 How could Governments develop or revise small business support schemes in order to make them more relevant to the actual needs of the SME sector?
3 What are the potential problems associated with borrowing start up funds from (a) friends or relatives and (b) banks?

Additional information sources

Cash flow

Gaskill, L.R., Van Auken, H.E. and Manning, R.A. (1993), A factor analytic study of the perceived causes of small business failure, *Journal of Small Business Management*, Vol. 31, No. 4, pp. 18–32.

Support scheme effectiveness

Land, N. (1975), Too much emphasis on management assistance, *Journal of Small Business Management*, Vol. 13, No. 3, pp. 1–12.

Managerial responsibilities

Graeme, M. and Staines, H. (1994), Managerial competences in small firms, *The Journal of Management Development*, Vol. 13, No. 7, pp. 23–35.

Sources of funds

Colombo, M.G. and Grilli, L. (2007), Funding gaps: access to bank loans by high-tech start-ups, *Small Business Economics*, Vol. 29, No. 1/2, pp. 25–47.

5

Market Assessment

Chapter objectives

The aims of this chapter are to assist the reader to:

- be aware of the factors influencing potential sales that can be achieved
- understand the problems with assessing market potential for new products
- be aware that even industry experts can make market forecast errors
- comprehend how variables external to the core market can have a significant impact on business performance
- examine the influence of variables such as economics, politics, legislation, finance, technology, socio-demographics and culture on market size.

Market potential

Potential sales

An important dynamic in determining potential revenue is the current and expected future size of a market. Large markets offer greater opportunity because they usually generate much higher total sales. Additional appeal exists in those cases where a large market is expected to continue to grow over time. Conversely any markets in late maturity or decline are typically a threat because potential future revenue will eventually fall (Lam and Postle 2006).

When assessing revenue potential it is necessary to recognise that markets exist at two levels. The inner or 'actual' market is made up of customers who are actively purchasing the products or services. The outer or 'potential' market contains both customers who are active purchasers and those who are prospective buyers, but have yet to enter the core market to make an actual purchase. Most owner/managers, when undertaking an evaluation of a new market, tend to focus their attentions on current, actual market size. This is because these data define how many customers are actively engaged in purchasing goods and services. In terms of determining future opportunities and threats, small firms should also focus on changes in the size of the potential market which might lead to an increase or decrease in the size of the actual market over time. Such changes can occur because the number of customers actively purchasing goods may alter over time, as can the average total purchase expenditure per customer. These variations in purchase activity are the outcome of influences such as an alteration in the economic conditions or the product need preferences of purchasers (Jun and Peterson 1991). In terms of determining whether any variation might occur, one approach is to examine demand in relation to the following three types of purchase behaviour:

1 *Economic preference*: need which is based on whether customers feel they can afford the potential purchase.
2 *Benefit preference*: need which reflects the degree to which the customer perceives whether a product or service offers greater purchase satisfaction than alternative expenditure on some other product or service.
3 *Practicality preference*: need which is an indication of the degree to which the customers decide whether the proposed purchase is a practical proposition at a specific point in time.

CASE STUDY

Assessing the opportunity

Case aims: To demonstrate that in some cases an entrepreneurial idea will be even more successful than the most optimistic expectations of the individual introducing the new product into the market.

Being able to quantify the potential sales for a new idea in development is relatively easy where the entrepreneur has identified an opportunity to exploit a perceived changing need in an existing market. For almost 40 years, with annual global sales of $2 billion, Mattel Corporation's Barbie doll has dominated the children's toy market. Hence only an extremely optimistic entrepreneur considering entry into this market would assume the potential sales revenue will exceed $1 billion (Warner 2006). The Barbie doll has always been presented as an Anglo-Saxon blond who can be dressed in different outfits, including a whole range of career outfits such as those worn by astronauts, doctors and lawyers. For many parents Barbie presented an image which they perceived as acceptable in terms of their aspirations for their child's future on becoming adults.

In 2000, a designer Carter Bryant showed Isaac Larian, the owner of a small business – MGA Entertainment Inc. based in Los Angeles – a very different idea for a doll. Larian felt the doll looked weird and ugly, but his daughter Jasmin was fascinated by the toy's almond eyes and full, pouty lips. Larian's entrepreneurial flair caused him to realise that in the twenty-first century, young girls were becoming less interested in their future image as adults and instead wanted a doll which closely resembled themselves or the teenage girls which they emulated. MGA developed a range of multi-ethnic dolls, much curvier and shorter than Barbie. The other critically important distinguishing factor was the dolls, launched under the generic brand name of Bratz, came dressed in knock off products (i.e. highly discounted branded goods) such as hip hugging jeans, tight tank tops and platform shoes.

The initial market reaction from retailers, who retained the same view of the world as Mattel, was that this new product was so unconventional it would never appeal to children. Their perspective appeared to be validated by the sales in 2001 of only $100,000. Twelve months later the annual sales for the Bratz dolls had reached $1 billion and the brand replaced Barbie as the top selling doll in the USA. This achievement convincingly proved to the world that Larian had a better understanding of the changing product needs of young girls than other, more conventionally minded individuals within the toy industry. Revenue continued to grow, in 2003 equalling the previous historic sales volume achieved by Barbie and by 2004 reached the amazing figure of $3 billion.

Market size

It is important for the entrepreneur to determine whether the personal circumstances of potential customers might change over time. Such an event will influence the actual market size as customers either depart or enter the market. Determining the nature of current customer need and whether this may change in the future will also influence decisions in relation to the relative importance of elements within the marketing mix such as the product benefit claim, pricing, promotional message and distribution (Whitlark et al. 1993). Although forecasting market size for many firms may merely involve the simple task of extrapolating current customer data, such is rarely the case when entrepreneurs are engaged in seeking to enter a totally new or emerging market. In these latter markets, even large firms encounter problems developing accurate forecasts (Bemmaor and Lee 2002). This is because the number of potential customers cannot be accurately defined as there is a lack of understanding about customers' possible desire to purchase. Hence the firm may be forced to rely on industry experts to develop predictions for the future. But in some cases these individuals may make an extremely erroneous forecast.

CASE STUDY

Forecast error

Case aims: To illustrate how industry experts can make quite significant errors when attempting to forecast how a new technology will influence market size and opportunity over time.

An illustration of the possible scale of forecasting error by an industry expert can be achieved by undertaking a hindsight evaluation of predictions. This is done by comparing actual outcomes with forecasts made some years earlier. For example, at the end of the 1980s, Young (1988), an American Professor in Technology, published an article about leading technology trends and how these would impact various industrial sectors by the year 2000. In his view the most important application of any emerging new technology would be in the exploitation of superconductivity which would revolutionise approaches to propulsion systems. He predicted that by the year 2000 there would be widespread use of magnetic levitated trains, superconducting-driven ships, unmanned satellite launching systems and electromagnetic-driven space vehicles. Hindsight reveals that the technology has not advanced as rapidly as expected and with the exception of a few small magnetic levitated train systems, this forecast was completely inaccurate.

Young did correctly identify that computers would continue to be a dominant area of commercial growth based on further exploitation of new technologies. He also forecast that the then current 80:20 ratio of hardware/software sales would be reversed to become 20:80. Clearly these two predictions have proved accurate. In terms of forecasting the future market size for software products, however, he predicted that world sales would be in the region of $800 billion by the year 2000. It appears that to calculate this figure he applied costings and development frameworks based on the software industry's prevailing 1980s focus on developing bespoke customised products for supercomputers,

(Cont'd)

mainframe and mini-computers. Currently the actual global market for software is estimated to be in the region of only $300 billion. The probable reason for this huge variance between forecast and actual outcome was that Young was not in a position to modify his forecast to accommodate the subsequent combined impact in the 1990s of such factors as (1) the massive upgrade in the processing power of microchips, especially in relation to their use in PCs, (2) the advent of the Internet, (3) the adoption of open language systems such as Linux and (4) outsourcing of software development to countries such as India.

CASE STUDY

Market, what market?

Case aims: To demonstrate that where there is no way of determining customer reaction, in some cases the only way to determine market potential is from launching the business.

Assessing market opportunity for a completely new technology is often virtually impossible. This was the case in the early days of the Internet when entrepreneurs began to perceive the opportunities which might exist for using the technology to create on-line, social networking services. An early example of this scenario is provided by Steve and Julie Pankhurst's idea in 1999 to use the Internet to help old friends in the UK get back in touch with each other (Murphy 2006). Their new business Friends Reunited (www.friendsreunited.co.uk) started life in the back bedroom of their small house in Barnet, North London. Within a few weeks of going live, the founders received an e-mail telling them how one of their early members had used the site to meet up with an old school friend.

Initially the site survived by word-of-mouth recommendations with people telling their friends how the site was a great way of tracking down friends from their school days. The site was officially launched in July 2000 and by December had 3,000 registered members. At that point the Pankhursts had no idea of the business' eventual size. Then the site was featured on a national radio show, nominated as the 'Website of the Day'. That night their single server collapsed several times as thousands of radio listeners tried to log on. By February 2001, membership had reached 19,000 and the founders realised the ongoing operation was becoming a full-time job.

Originally the Pankhurst's business model was to generate revenue from companies advertising on the site but this was not generating sufficient revenue. In order to survive, a membership charge was introduced. This was not a deterrent to potential customers and by the end of 2001, membership had exceeded 4 million.

At the beginning of 2003, the Pankhursts hired three individuals as the basis for establishing a new senior management team. This team focused on both continuing to expand the operation and to introduce a higher level of professionalism into the back office operations. New features were added to assist people's social networking activities such as on-line dating, job hunting or locating people with similar hobby or sporting interests. As is often the case where the large company elephants have slept through a time of market change, their response when they recognise the scale of the missed opportunity is to acquire the entrepreneurial upstart. This is what occurred with Friends Reunited. Britain's largest television company, ITV, realised that the Internet represented a totally new medium through which to sell advertising space. Hence in 2006, Steve and Julie sold their shares at a very handsome profit to ITV, for whom the purchase meant they now had access to the vast audience of what was, at that time, the UK's eighth most visited Website; namely 12 million registered members and on average, attracting 5,000 new members every day.

Expert fallibility

Further evidence concerning the fallibility of experts as forecasters is provided by a study undertaken by Galbraith et al. (2006). These researchers examined 69 high technology development projects funded by the Center for Commerlization of Advanced Technologies (CCAT) in the USA. Their analysis examined the documentation submitted to support each firm's grant application and then over time, tracked the outcome of each project. This approach permitted an assessment of the scale of actual success achieved relative to that forecasted by the firm and the three to five experts employed to assess the viability of the technology claims made in each of the original funding applications. Statistical analysis revealed that in virtually every case, the expert reviewers exhibited extremely poor levels of competence in terms of accurately predicting project outcomes. In contrast, an equation developed by the researchers based on generic variables such as the age of the firm, number of employees, education level of the development team, diversification skills, previous funding received and the stage of technology development provided an extremely accurate prediction of whether the new project would be successful.

On the basis of numerous examples of the failure of organisations to correctly identify the impact of change, it seems reasonable to posit that a number of interacting variables need to be taken into account when assessing technology in relation to the scale of potential opportunity. The core determining variable will always be that of the degree to which there is market need for the product or service outcome created by the new technology (Von Hippel 1986). This level of need is controlled by both the existing needs of customers and as yet, unidentified potential customer needs. In some cases, the outcome of the new technology is a substitute for a current product. Hence existing customer need will be the key influencer of demand in this scenario and market forecasting will be relatively risk free. An example of this is provided by the situation facing Japanese firms when first seeking to determine potential sales for offering the digital camera as an advance on the traditional, film-based, camera technology. Forecasting becomes significantly more difficult, however, where potential customers have little understanding of how a technology offers completely new benefit propositions. For example, it was difficult to assess the potential consumer demand for the PC at the stage when Steve Jobs was working on the first Apple computer in his garage in California.

CASE STUDY

Videodisc meets VCR

Case aims: To illustrate that (a) commitment to one product concept may reduce the ability to perceive the potential for an alternative proposition and (b) even large firms, when relying on industry experts, can reach totally incorrect conclusions about market potential.

In many cases industry experts are individuals that have been heavily involved in the development of technology and as a consequence tend to have an excessively optimistic view about market demand. Under these circumstances it is extremely probable that a highly optimistic customer uptake forecast will be produced. The experts' views are then used to make commercial decisions about future profitability and these will also be dramatically inaccurate. An illustration of this scenario is provided by Klopfenstein's (1989) analysis of the development of two competing consumer electronics products, the videodisc player (VDP) and the videocassette recorder (VCR).

VDP uses the technology of a stylus riding in the grooves of the videodisc to translate variations in electrical capacitance into video and audio signals that can be displayed on a standard television set. Laser optical disc technology, which uses a laser beam rather than a stylus to play back sound and video images, was developed jointly by MCA and NV Philips in the early 1970s. The benefit proposition offered to consumers was VDP provided a much higher quality visual and auditory experience than that delivered by a television signal. Both firms planned to launch their products accompanied by a major library of videodiscs that could be purchased for use with their machines. The companies' management teams and some experts within the entertainment and consumer electronics industry predicted a huge potential market demand for the new technology.

Parallel to the development of the VDP, various electronics companies were working on how to translate existing industrial market videotape recording technology into a system that could be used as a product to be offered to consumers. Initially the cost of producing a consumer VCR machine meant that the product would be somewhat more expensive than the VDP. Also the picture and sound quality of the latter was clearly superior. These facts were contributory influencers which caused many in the US consumer electronics industry to forecast that the VDP would significantly outsell the VCR. Unfortunately, these forecasts ignored two key factors. Firstly, the Japanese recognised that the VCR would only achieve high market penetration if priced at a level similar to an expensive television. Hence while the US manufacturers priced their first VCRs at over a £1,000 to generate an adequate level of profit, companies such as Sony entered the market offering VCRs at below-cost prices in the range of £500–600. This aggressive pricing strategy assumed, quite correctly, that as production volumes increased and new technological advances were incorporated into the VCR, production costs would fall dramatically.

The other key factor influencing market demand was that while VDPs only offered a small number of pre-recorded titles that could be played on the systems, as well as being able to play pre-recorded tapes, the VCR also allowed consumers the additional key benefit of being able to record and play back television programmes. By the early 1980s, while annual VCR unit sales in the USA were in their millions, VDP unit sales were much lower. This outcome eventually caused most of the manufacturers of VDPs to withdraw from the market.

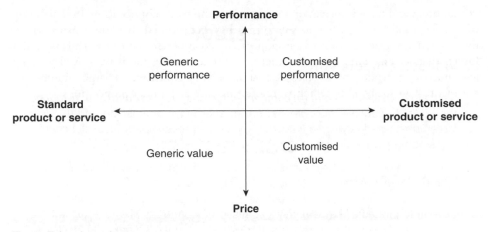

Figure 5.1   *A product space map*

Source: modified from Chaston (2000), *Entrepreneurial Marketing*, Macmillan Business, Basingstoke. Reproduced with permission of Palgrave Macmillan.

Competition

Competitive mapping

The other potential external influence which may result in revenue change over time is the current or future activities of competitors (Gaskill et al. 1993). In most cases, competitors will be considered as a threat because they can be expected to steal customers from the small business. Occasionally, however, competitors' inability to meet customer needs can result in dissatisfaction being the cause of a newly emerging trend within a market which in turn can create a new opportunity for another firm.

One approach to determining how to avoid costly competitive battles is to map the nature of the propositions being offered by other firms. An effective approach to mapping is to assume firms offer products which are constituted of the two dimensions, product and customisation. As illustrated in Figure 5.1, it is suggested that product performance can range from high to low, with the latter being offered at a lower price. In the case of product or service choice, it is proposed that this can extend from offering a standard product or service to all customers through to each customer being offered a proposition customised to meet their specific, often unique needs (Quader 2007). Combining these two dimensions generates four different product propositions that can be offered to the market.

Large firms, by exploiting internal capabilities such as production capacity and extensive logistics capability, are usually the organisations most likely to offer value as the important attribute of their product or service proposition. To avoid potentially expensive confrontations with large firms, new entrepreneurs should usually focus on using superior product performance as the path through which to build market share.

By analysing the market behaviour of other firms, the entrepreneur can map the strategic positions occupied by competition. Where the mapping process reveals a large number of other firms clustered in a single sector, competition will tend to be intense and ability to achieve an adequate level of profitability will be limited. Hence the small firm seeking to understand how to avoid a competitive threat would be well advised to select another area of the market in which to operate. Steiner and Solem (1988) demonstrated the benefits of avoiding market sectors containing numerous competitors and the advantages of competing on the basis of innovation. In their study of small manufacturing firms in Wisconsin they determined that those firms which focused on using innovation to develop improved processes and products enjoyed a higher than average rate of sales. Furthermore the less successful firms, as well as being less innovative, tended to operate in market sectors containing a larger number of competitors virtually all of which were offering similar product propositions.

CASE STUDY

The browser war

Case aims: To illustrate that even a successful entrepreneurial firm can be defeated by an incumbent larger organisation should the latter have the resources and commitment to defeat the new entrant.

Although the accepted mythology is that elephants are frightened by mice, in the real world the exact opposite prevails. This is because although large firms may adopt a slow or cautious response to change, when they do eventually decide to act, their financial resources, process capacity and control over market systems can usually guarantee the complete destruction of any smaller competitors. Such was the outcome in the 1990s during the Internet browser wars between Netscape and Microsoft (Windrum 2001).

The first commercial browser, Mosaic, was developed by the National Center for Supercomputing Applications (NCSA) in 1993. The research institute licensed the browser to established firms such as Fujitsu and IBM with the intention of using revenues generated to fund their ongoing research activities. Then in 1994, Jim Clark and Marc Andreesen launched Netscape Navigator. This product was able to load graphic images ten times faster than Mosaic, easier to use and offered text formatting options that simplified the production of Web pages. To differentiate the product from Mosaic, Netscape added proprietary extensions to the HTML code which meant that Netscape's browser could not be accessed by people using Mosaic. The other aspect of the Netscape launch was that the company provided a Client Application Programming Interface that commercial Website development companies could use to create products that complemented the browser. Unlike Mosaic, the Netscape product did not come with an Internet dial-up access or e-mail system because Netscape believed most users already had these facilities and did not want the complication of having to create a new dial-up connection. To achieve rapid market penetration Netscape used the Internet to supply their software as a downloadable product. Furthermore potential customers were able to download the browser for a free 90 day trial. By 1995 Netscape was market leader, the company was loved by Wall Street and the founders had become, on paper at least, multi-millionaires.

Initially Microsoft had paid little interest in the Internet and their first browser, Internet Explorer was basically a licensed version of Mosaic. Then in late 1995, the 'elephant spoke', when Bill Gates proclaimed Microsoft's intention of becoming the leading player in this rapidly expanding sector of the computer industry. Internet Explorer 3.0 was a significant improvement over the firm's earlier products. The new software, similar to Netscape, had proprietary HTML code so that it could not be viewed by Netscape users. The weight of the elephant's foot was demonstrated by Microsoft's strategy of integrating the browser at no cost into the company's Windows 95 operating system which was being installed in virtually every PC being manufactured in the world. The company then added the browser free-of-charge to all of the Microsoft Windows applications software. This essentially meant consumers buying new Microsoft products were also being given the browser for free. To ensure an even faster demise of the Netscape product, Microsoft set up deals with the major Internet Service Providers (ISPs) – AOL, MCI and CompuServe – to offer Internet Explorer as the standard default browser available on their Websites. Microsoft also invested funds to create their own ISP, Microsoft Network. Netscape never really had a chance. Eventually the company was sold to another US corporation at a share price which was a fraction of the price quoted on Wall Street back in the halcyon days of the mid-1990s.

Wider forces

Macro-environmental factors

Most small firms take a relatively short term perspective about future customer demand. They tend only to be interested in possible changes that might influence the size of the market over the next 12 months. However, entrepreneurs hoping to achieve sustained business growth or establish a business dynasty can benefit from determining whether opportunities or threats exist which might impact potential market size over the longer term (Becherer et al. 2006). Fortunately governments, trade bodies and the academic community regularly undertake and then publish research about the influences of wider forces on market structure, product usage and factors influencing customer purchase decisions. Hence these reports can provide an invaluable source of information that can be used to examine trends in market size. An example of such data in relation to the American food service industry is provided by Eun-Jung (2002). His report provided an analysis of total food consumption, sales by industry segments and the influence on economics and socio-demographic variables on the expenditure patterns of US consumers. Another example is Lea and Worsley's (2006) study of the organic food market in Australia. On the basis of a large scale survey, these researchers were able to determine in consumer markets how personal values and socio-demographic profiles influence purchase patterns for organic foods.

As illustrated in Figure 5.2, there are a number of variables which can influence the potential market, which in turn will ultimately determine growth or shrinkage in the size of the actual market.

Economics

Prevailing economic conditions will strongly influence consumer spending. During a period of economic growth, employment prospects improve, average earnings rise, consumers become more confident and spending levels increase. This effect feeds

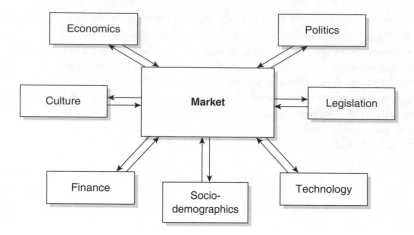

Figure 5.2   *Factors impacting market size*

back into industrial markets which also exhibit higher demand for goods and services. The situation can be contrasted with a recession during which unemployment grows, earnings fall and the decline in consumer confidence results in a downturn in spending. Upturns and downturns in the economies of industrial nations occur on a somewhat cyclical basis. Hence astute managers in any size of firm can adjust their future business plans to reflect their perceptions of potential changes in consumer spending.

In the current 2008/09 recession, the scale and depth of the downturn has yet to be understood (Anon. 2008a). What is apparent, however, is that the recession will be of a global nature as evidenced by the decision of the G8 nations to meet in Washington in November 2008 to examine possible coordinated approaches within their respective countries. The aim of the meeting is to attempt to identify actions that will minimise the impact of the downturn on their own economies and also to sustain a reasonable level of consumer spending. The magnitude of concern about this current recession is starkly illustrated by the fact that for the first time in history, the Chinese Government has taken actions aimed at achieving compatibility with responses being initiated by the other G8 members. On 9 November 2008 an economic stimulation package of approximately $600 billion was announced which in fiscal terms is four times larger than announced by the US Government earlier that year.

Data on the direct impact of economic conditions on the SME sector is that during an economic decline, the number of new small business start-ups increases as unemployed people seek an alternative income source (Yusuf and Schindehutte 2000). The majority of these new firms, however, tend to be survivalist ventures and there is little evidence that the onset of a recession has any impact on the creation rates for new, innovative, growth orientated enterprises. Nevertheless, if the entrepreneur is establishing a new venture dependent on strong consumer spending, then attention should probably be given to the medium term economic prospects of the market which is intended to be entered.

In relation to the sustained health of major economies around the world, consumer spending is more likely to rise if a country's economy is based on increasing economic output due to strong increases in average wages or the performance of the country's firms in export markets. Currently this scenario is clearly apparent in the case of the two new tiger nations, China and India. In contrast, since the mid-1990s consumer spending in the Western world has been driven by rising house prices and low interest rates. This trend has made consumers more willing to use their 'plastic friend' to fund a consumptionist lifestyle and to take out mortgages to buy houses. Unfortunately the mortgage lenders, especially in the USA, responded to this demand by approving more and more riskier loans. Certain banks then combined these 'sub prime' loans into complex credit instruments for sale in the world's financial markets. All appeared wonderful until a slow down in the US economy and rising interest rates began to be reflected in falling house prices. At this juncture in 2007, the world's financial institutions began to recognise the true value of debt instruments based around sub prime loans. This was followed by major banks being forced to acknowledge massive write offs which in turn triggered a fall in share prices and the emergence of a financial liquidity crisis (Anon. 2007). By early 2008 economists have been forced to recognise that the after shocks of these events will very probably dampen consumer spending in many Western nations for several years.

Politics

The prevailing political philosophy of the party currently in power will impact the lives of people as Governments seek to implement the manifesto on which they were elected to office. Two areas which tend to be emphasised in most political manifestos are the provision of public sector services and management of the economy. Since the Second World War, major parties in democratic nations have received a favourable response from electorates over the provision of free or subsidised access to services such as education or healthcare. Over time, the cost of these services, and the number of public sector employees engaged in their delivery, has risen dramatically. With most Western nation economies exhibiting limited growth in GNP over recent years, funding of public sector services has usually required ongoing increases in both personal and corporate taxation.

Although Governments have understood the financial implications of population ageing in relation to the funding of healthcare provision and pensions, the negative impact on any manifesto of admitting the need to increase personal taxation means it is only in the last few years that politicians have finally been forced to admit to the real scale of this fiscal problem (Hau and Jiang 2005). Whether the solution is to increase personal taxation to fund public sector services or make the general public more responsible for self-funding their needs in old age, either way the medium term perspective is that in many countries disposable consumer spending will shrink in the face of declining average per capita incomes.

There has only been limited research on the specific impact of different business tax regimes on high-growth small firms. The prevailing view is that lower rate tax regimes offer a more positive business climate because they stimulate higher investment in innovation and new technology. In the UK, research by Poutziouris et al. (2000) has shown that in the SME sector internal tax administration costs per employee are significantly higher than in the large firm sector. Of even greater concern, however, is the conclusion that small high technology firms pay proportionately higher taxes (when defined in relation to total assets) than low technology firms. This occurs because high growth enterprises are usually more profitable and hence will face higher tax bills. Small firms also are usually unable to utilise the complex financial instruments used by large firms to exploit the benefits available from tax allowances on interest charges and depreciation. The adverse outcome for tax legislation has recently been demonstrated by the impact on small firms of the UK Government's decision to significantly alter the tax regime on capital gains. This is probably going to act as a major disincentive to growth in small, entrepreneurial organisations (Anon. 2008b).

A similar conclusion over how high levels of taxation and the inability to accumulate the wealth necessary to invest in implementing growth strategies has reduced the number of high growth, entrepreneurial firms has been reached in Sweden (Davidsson and Henrekson 2002). This study examined data over the period 1980–2000. In 2001 the Swedish Government reduced corporate tax by 50 per cent and introduced a uniform 30 per cent flat capital gains tax. Additionally, the highest marginal personal income tax rate was lowered from 90 per cent to 56 per cent and actions had been facilitated to transfer delivery of certain public sector services to private sector providers. The impact of these changes was reflected in a massive upswing of initial public offerings (IPOs) among new Swedish small firms, especially in the IT sector.

Legislation

One approach Governments adopt to define rules of behaviour in business is to introduce new legislation which can be enforced by legal sanctions. New laws are usually invoked when politicians cannot obtain the voluntary co-operation of the general public or commercial organisations (Garnett and Wall 2006). Governments often telegraph their future plans for new legislation through mechanisms such as publishing discussion papers, permitting periods of consultation with interested parties and 'leaks' to the media. Under such circumstances, an entrepreneurial firm usually has a reasonable length of time during which to determine whether legislation represents an opportunity or a threat to a market sector.

A significant proportion of Government legislation is aimed at ensuring firms are not putting their customers and employees at risk and to protect minorities in society from discrimination. An unfortunate outcome of these laws is that they are perceived as burdensome red tape because firms have to create expensive administrative systems in order to ensure compliance with every regulation (Atkinson and Curtis 2004). Similar to taxation, system expenditure as a percentage of sales is often much greater for small businesses than for their counterparts in the large firm sector. An even more worrying aspect of such legislation is that it can reduce the ability of entrepreneurial firms to respond flexibly and rapidly to changing market circumstances. Davidsson and Henrekson (2002), for example, proposed the lower number of entrepreneurial firms in Europe versus the USA strongly correlates with the inflexibility of EU employment legislation. This is because European employment laws can reduce labour mobility and dissuade owner/managers from implementing a growth plan if this requires a significant expansion in the size of the workforce.

CASE STUDY

One winner, one loser

Case aims: To demonstrate that changing legislation can represent either an opportunity or a threat to the entrepreneur.

For a number of years, the activities of the UK Inland Revenue were a clear indication that the Government would eventually seek to gain greater control over taxing the incomes of freelance professionals in sectors such as IT and engineering. Then in 2000 the Government introduced the IR35 tax laws which greatly complicated the lives of self-employed contractors, the large companies who employ these individuals and recruitment agencies. The entrepreneurial response of Paul Bishop was to develop and launch Actinium which creates and then administers a limited company on behalf of a contractor, thereby reducing tax and national insurance liabilities. Revenue is generated from a commission on the invoices Actinium issues on behalf of the contractor. The company also generates fees from providing legal documentation, tax advice and employment-law compliance to contractors, large firms and recruitment agencies. Over a three-year period, annual sales have risen by 282 per cent per annum and in 2005 reached £40.7 million which resulted in the company being identified as the fastest growing private company in the UK (*The Sunday Times* 2006).

The entrepreneurial firms on the Internet which have enjoyed the highest growth rate in recent years have been the on-line gambling companies. Some of the leading firms originally started as private entities which, on subsequently going public, made their respective founders overnight millionaires. Over 50 per cent of the industry's income came from gamblers living in the USA. From the outset there was always the risk the American Government would on the grounds of public morality, act to legislate against the industry (Weinberg and Pruitt 2006). This risk was clearly stated in the prospectuses of firms which went public, but everybody seemed to believe the American Government would never be able to enforce a law banning this type of gambling. Then, seemingly out of nowhere, the Unlawful Internet Gambling Enforcement Act (UIGEA) appeared on the floor of the US Senate and within record time had been ratified to come into effect on 13 October 2006. The law did not criminalise on-line gambling but instead prohibits banks and credit card companies from processing transactions related to placing bets on the Internet by people living in America. The publicly traded on-line gambling companies were forced to close their US operations resulting in a dramatic crash in both their revenue and their share prices. In the first half of 2006, for example, PartyGaming PLC, the industry's biggest operator, was generating 76 percent of total revenue from the US market. The passage of the UIGEA wiped 72 per cent off the traded share price in London.

Finance

Financial conditions will always be a focal point of concern for virtually every small firm because cash flow tends to be volatile and the ability of entrepreneurs to implement a business start–up or subsequently a growth plan, can often be constrained by limited access to external funds. Traditionally these external sources have often been friends or relatives and where these prove inadequate, taking on a bank loan (Ou and Haynes 2006). Banks will usually require security. In most cases this will involve the owner/manager putting their only significant asset, the family home, at risk. Although the large banks heavily advertise the availability of services specifically designed to meet the needs of the small firm, these financial institutions often claim that this is not a profitable sector within their product portfolios (Mason and Harrison 1996). Furthermore, the strength of the banks' desire to lend to small firms varies over time. During the economic downturn at the beginning of the 1990s, small firms in the UK, for example, found their banks much more reluctant to fund loan requests from both new or existing small business customers. As the economy improved in the mid-1990s, the banks re-acquired an interest in the SME sector and embarked on aggressive promotional campaigns to attract new customers (Sternberg and Wennekers 2005). The outcome of the sub prime crisis in 2007 and the subsequent liquidity crisis within the banking system totally reversed the financial institutions' desire to lend to small firms. This was demonstrated early in 2008 when there was growing evidence that some major banks in the Western world had become less willing to make loans to new small business customers and concurrently reduced the size of approved overdrafts to existing customers (Browning and Silver 2008).

Once an entrepreneurial small firm has entered the market and is beginning to grow, the need for additional funds will usually increase dramatically. Even if the banks are willing to offer additional loan facilities, the owner/manager would face a very major increase in the scale of interest charges that would have to be covered. One way of reducing this burden is to consider acquiring additional funds by issuing equity. There now exist a number of private and public sector venture capital firms who specialise in raising equity funding for small firms (Fisher 1988). These organisations came to prominence in the USA due to their activities in funding a massive number of new dotcom start-ups in the mid-1990s. Their aim was to identify a new opportunity in the booming Internet industry and to grow the enterprise to the size when the company could be taken public through selling shares via an IPO. For a brief period dotcom entrepreneurs were becoming overnight paper millionaires. Unfortunately the euphoria surrounding investing in new Internet companies seemed to result in myopia in the financial services industry with the share prices during the IPO in no way reflecting the real earnings potential of these new enterprises. Eventually the world came to recognise this fact which led to the bursting of the dotcom bubble in the late 1990s.

After the dotcom market crash, the number of venture capital firms was somewhat reduced. Those which remained have since adopted a more conservative view about the earnings potential of the new enterprises in which they consider making an investment. The majority of these organisations are usually only interested in deals requiring at least a £1 million equity injection (Harding and Cowling 2006). Although this scale of investment may be of interest to high growth entrepreneurial firms during a second or third cycle of equity funding, most small firms seeking equity only wish to obtain an injection of capital in the region of £50,000–£250,000. Access to this smaller scale of funding is usually through the informal venture capital market by linking up with a 'business angel'. These are individuals, typically experienced business people, who are looking to invest small sums of money in what they perceive as growth orientated small firms. In many cases, the primary attraction for the business angel is not the financial return, but instead the satisfaction of being involved in assisting and guiding a new entrepreneur to achieve market success (Sudek 2007).

Technology

New technology can have a dramatic effect on the fortunes of both large and small firms. This is reflected by business history being littered with examples of firms, and in some cases entire industrial sectors, failing to comprehend how the advent of a new technology would dramatically alter the industrial landscape. In most cases, the introduction of the new technology has been led by a small band of technologically orientated entrepreneurs who comprehend the potential impact of a new technology (Vermeulen 2005). These 'first movers' subsequently enjoy significant financial reward for their initiative. In contrast the sleeping elephants in the large firm sector often continue to operate as if nothing has changed and eventually may be forced into terminal decline.

A popular explanation of why entrepreneurial firms frequently exploit new technology ahead of the large firm elephants, is the former are more innovative, flexible, proactive and 'fleet of foot'. More recently, however, Christensen et al. (2002) have posited that another common reason is market leaders often face huge pressure from their customers and competition to continually improve the performance of their current products through the application of increasingly sophisticated applications of existing technologies. Thus, for example, while the German camera industry was valiantly responding to market pressures to invest in further improving their products' optical and mechanical systems, the Japanese industry was left unchallenged to experiment with the development of the first generation of digital cameras.

CASE STUDY

A new medical frontier

Case aims: To illustrate how a completely new technological solution to well understood problems may provide entrepreneurs with the basis for a significant new business opportunity.

As the large pharmaceutical firms face increasing difficulties developing new 'wonder drugs', their attention in recent years has switched to the field of biotechnology such as recombinant DNA, gene therapy and stem cell research in their search for new sources of future commercial opportunity. Consequently development in another area of biomedical development, neurotechnology, has remained primarily the preserve of smaller, entrepreneurial firms (Cavuto 2002). Scientists have known since the eighteenth century that nerve tissue responds to electrical stimulation, but it was not until the second half of the twentieth century that advances in medical research began to generate a more adequate understanding of the nervous system, particularly in relation to the human brain. Neuroscientists have been greatly aided in their search for deeper understanding of the human physiology by advances in IT in relation to human–machine interfaces and the development of biomaterials that can be implanted or attached to the body.

(Cont'd)

This technological convergence has permitted neurotechnology to begin to successfully treat certain medical disorders. An early area of success has been in the field of functional electrical stimulation (FES) to treat certain types of spine injury. This approach permits the artificial stimulation of nerves and muscles to partially restore mobility in paralysed areas of the body. Possibly one of the most significant successes to date has been the use of neurotechnology to develop auditory prothesis systems for the treatment of deafness. The medical solution in this instance is based on cochlear implants that activate the auditory nerve using electrical stimulation. The devices operate by separating incoming sound into different frequency ranges, with each frequency range feeding into a stimulating electrode.

The prospects for an expanding neurotechnology industry based on entrepreneurial innovation by small firms and spin-offs from University research centres appear to be excellent. Various potential areas for the application of this science to offer new forms of medical treatment have already been identified. These include rehabilitation of stroke victims, control of incontinence, obesity, certain psychiatric disorders such as schizophrenia, neurological disorders such as Parkinson's disease and chronic pain management. Compared with conventional forms of medical treatment, at the moment the global market for neurotechnological solutions remains extremely small. Nevertheless average revenue growth over the last few years has been in excess of 40 per cent per annum. To a large degree this low share of the total healthcare market is because entrepreneurial firms do face a number of market obstacles. The two largest barriers are that medical insurance companies are slow to accept neurotechnical treatments as being covered by their healthcare policies and the length of time it takes to gain Government approval for new medical products in relation to the issues of safety and efficacy.

Socio-demographics

These are the variables which describe the structure of a population in terms of income, age, employment, education, household size and geographic location. Most industrialised nations undertake a regular census of their inhabitants and make these data freely available to any interested parties. By examining how data change over time, the small firm can identify emerging shifts in socio-demographic profiles (Chaston 2009). It is now extremely easy to acquire on-line data from Government agencies on, for example, the forecasted trend in the different types and numbers of people living in a specific location. This information can be used to determine whether the trend represents an opportunity or a threat in terms of influencing future potential market size. There are also a number of Websites where the entrepreneur can gain further understanding of the impact of socio-demographic change. The advent of computerised databases has also greatly increased the entrepreneur's ability to undertake further analysis of socio-economic trends in relation to variables such as behaviour, age, income and lifestyle.

Culture

This is a key factor in determining the prevailing attitudes and behaviours of a population. Identifying the early signs of a culture shift is not easy because typically it only involves a small subgroup within a population. Once recognised, these early signs can provide a significant, new opportunity. An example of an emerging culture shift is people's changing attitudes towards the impact of tourism on local communities and the need to protect the environment in exotic locations (Goodwin and Francis 2003).

CASE STUDY

Culture and entrepreneurship

Case aims: To illustrate how cultural differences between nations may result in a different approach to identifying and implementing entrepreneurial ideas.

An issue which emerged during the 1980s as Japan successfully entered world markets offering consumer goods such as televisions, VCRs and cars superior to those available from Western producers, was whether the Pacific Rim nations exhibit a different approach to innovation during the development of new or improved products? The conclusion reached in relation to creativity and entrepreneurship, is Pacific Rim nations tend to focus on an adaptor (or 'do things better') approach whereas Western nations tend to exhibit an innovative (or 'disruptive') orientation (Herbirg and Jacobs 1996). The reason for this difference is believed to be in part based on prevailing societal values. Western creativity and entrepreneurship is centred on individual freedom. This is supportive of the approach that discovery of new ideas is the best form of innovation and reflects a social values system based on admiring competition and personal success. In contrast, Japanese innovation is usually more concerned with application and the refinement of existing ideas.

In Japanese companies a desire for innovation is accompanied by a need to foster teamwork, conformity and a sense of harmony. This behaviour is a reflection of a strong preference for co-operation and conformity within Japanese society as a whole. Problems are viewed as complex, incoherent and vague. Responding to this perspective demands incremental, diffuse, open ended solutions (Hickman and Raia 2002). In Western nations, many major advances in science and technology have involved intuitive leaps of imagination from a position grounded in scientific reality. This can be contrasted with adaptor behaviour in Japan which has resulted in the country's base of scientific knowledge and approaches to research being less developed than in the Western world. An entrepreneurial orientation to developing radical solutions requires curiosity, adventurousness and risk taking. Westerners are comfortable with such traits, but the Japanese prefer the comfort of working with proven ideas and tend to avoid involvement in newly emerging, unproven technologies. Further constraints to innovative behaviour are that the group takes precedence over the individual. Hence Japanese society does not look with favour on brilliant, outspoken mavericks.

SUMMARY LEARNING POINTS

- Ultimately the scale of success for an entrepreneurial proposition will depend on the final level of market demand for the product or service.
- Accurate estimates of potential sales and market size are significantly more difficult for new-to-the-world propositions.

(Cont'd)

- Even where there is extensive understanding of a new technology, sector experts may be unable to accurately forecast ultimate market size for a new product.
- Market size can also be influenced by macro-environmental factors which are totally beyond the control of the entrepreneur.
- Variables which can influence market size include economics, politics, legislation, finance, technology, socio-demographics and culture.

ASSIGNMENTS

1   How and why have the business strategies of the low-cost airlines such as EasyJet and Ryanair caused the total European market for the number of airline passengers to increase in size over recent years?
2   Review the political manifestos of the two largest political parties in your country to compare and contrast how their differing philosophies might impact on the performance of SME sector firms.
3   Develop a competitive map for the car industry and then review how hybrid, electric and other lower emission/lower hydrocarbon vehicles might be positioned on this map.

DISCUSSION TOPICS

1   What is the validity of the view that excessive legislation can be detrimental to ensuring a country has a vibrant, growing SME sector?
2   What socio-demographic changes are likely to occur within your country over the next decade and how might these affect the future size of consumer goods markets?
3   How can bank lending practices influence (1) the level of demand in consumer goods markets and (2) the ability of entrepreneurial firms to develop and launch new products?

Additional information sources

Competitive mapping

Fahey, L. (2003), Competitor scenarios, *Strategy & Leadership*, Vol. 31, No. 1, pp. 32–45.

Macro-environment

Erdener, K. and Orsay, K. (1993), Successful marketing for survival: the airline industry, *Management Decision*, Vol. 31, No. 5, pp. 32–44.

Economics

Barker, K. (2005), Economic stability and the business climate, *Bank of England Quarterly Bulletin*, Vol. 45, No. 4, pp. 489–497.

Finance

Lund, M. and Wright, J. (1999), The financing of small firms in the United Kingdom, *Bank of England Quarterly Bulletin*, Vol. 39, No. 2, pp. 195–212.

Technology

Oke, A., Burke, G. and Myers, A. (2007), Innovation types and performance in growing UK SMEs, *International Journal of Operations & Production Management*, Vol. 27, No. 7, pp. 735–748.

Socio-demographics

Peterson, M. (2007), Effects of income, assets and age on the vacationing behaviour of US consumers, *Journal of Vacation Marketing*, Vol. 13, No. 1, pp. 29–44.

Culture

Harcar, T., Spillan, J.E. and Kuchemiroglu, O. (2005), A multinational study of family decision-making, *Multinational Business Review*, Vol. 13, No. 2, pp. 3–22.

6

Internal Capability

Chapter objectives

The aims of this chapter are to assist the reader to:

- be aware of factors influencing loss of market leadership
- understand the critical importance of effective leadership
- examine the concept of the 'resource based view' of the firm
- review how a small firm's approach to managing strategic issues can influence performance
- review how internal capabilities across the areas of innovation, productivity, human resources, quality and information management can influence performance.

Growing and capability

Market leadership

The history of business is littered with examples of companies which were born, achieved market domination and then went into decline. Sometimes the final outcome has been that of the firm disappearing completely (e.g. the US airlines Pan Am and TWA). In other cases, the business survived, but only by evolving into a somewhat different trading entity and in many cases, becoming a significantly smaller operation. For example in the 1950s, the UK motorcycle company Triumph was a global brand. Then due to various internal operational problems, the company failed to respond to the emergence of the Japanese in the world market. Eventually what arose from the ashes of a once huge operation was a small company which specialises in the manufacture of a limited range of up-market motorbikes. These are primarily sold to people who retain a nostalgic attachment for what was once a world famous brand name.

Some marketing texts tend to suggest that most major corporate downturns are the result of a radically new, innovative product entering the market. However, in their analysis of pioneers who became market leaders and subsequently went into decline, Tellis and Golder (1996) concluded that a more frequent reason for the loss of leadership was a failure to continue to emphasise the importance of continued improvements in existing products as a fundamental aspect of company culture. To explain the reason underlying this behaviour trait, Fraser (2004) has posited that in many cases this problem occurs because senior management place excessive focus on maximising sales to sustain a high market share, accompanied by de-emphasis of allocating resources to support ongoing investment in developing new and improved products. A tragic example of this scenario is provided by the two originators of the global car industry, Ford and General Motors (GM). Over the last ten years, these two companies have permitted competitors such as Toyota and Honda to catch up and eventually overtake them in world markets.

Resource-based view of the firm

When one examines case materials about large firms behaving as sleeping elephants and losing market share to smaller competitors, what often emerges is customer needs have not undergone any real fundamental change. Instead, the incumbent leading firm has not remained alert to the need to continually seek ways of upgrading internal capabilities to sustain product performance leadership and the organisational processes necessary to retain superiority in areas such as productivity or quality. This failure to invest in remaining ahead of the competition thereby provides other firms with the opportunity to exploit their superior internal capabilities to deliver greater customer satisfaction (Bate and Johnston 2005).

The managerial philosophy concerning market success based on exploiting superior internal capability is known as the 'resource-based view of the firm' (RBV) (Hamal and Prahalad 1996). Exploiting the philosophy offers two strategic options. Firstly, a company may develop the capability to develop and launch improved existing products (e.g. Toyota's excellence in product development leading to the launch of Prius, their electric hybrid vehicle) or enter new market sectors (e.g. Honda's excellence in engineering capability to support their entry into the marine outboard engine market). Alternatively, a firm may be able to initiate price-based competition by passing onto the customer savings achieved through the exploitation of superior operational technologies and processes. This latter approach is exemplified by the way major supermarket chains in the USA lost market share to Wal-Mart who exploited superior capabilities in the areas of procurement and logistics as the basis for offering much lower prices to the American consumer.

In comparison with reports on the large firm sector, Rangone (1999) notes the application of RBV theory to explain superior performance of small firms has received somewhat less attention in the literature. Instead academics have tended to propose other reasons to explain small firm success. These include concepts such as effectiveness in responding to competition, adoption of a strong marketing orientation or utilising a niche-based business strategy. In seeking to gain wider acceptance of the application of RBV to the SME sector, Sanchez and Sanchez (2006) have posited that a small firm's internal resources and capabilities constitute a much more stable point of reference in terms of providing a primary source of benefits and crucial determinants in terms of formulating an effective organisational strategy capable of sustaining business growth. These researchers supported their viewpoint by demonstrating the critical influence of internal capability in terms of influencing the performance of Spanish SMEs. A similar conclusion was reached by Hadjimanolis (2000). In this latter case, however, the researcher expressed the view that one of the most critical internal resources in the case of the smaller firm is the entrepreneurial capability of the owner/manager.

The critical capability

Leadership

The influence of individuals such as Jack Welch at General Electric, Lord King at British Airways, Lou Gernstner at IBM and Stuart Rose at Marks & Spencer in the large firm sector is strong evidence to support the view that possibly the most critical internal capability in any successful organisation is the presence of an effective leader

(Savage and Sales 2008). In today's highly competitive world, any business leader in the large firm sector who fails to satisfy shareholder demands for sustained year-on-year growth in profits is usually removed from office very rapidly. This situation can be contrasted with the small firm sector (Fernald et al. 2005). Owner/managers are less likely to face pressure from external stakeholders to continually improve the firm's financial performance. In fact most owner/managers have no interest in growing their firm. One reason for this is many small firms are operated as lifestyle businesses. The owner/manager merely requires the business to generate sufficient income to support their desire to pursue their leisure interests. Another reason is that some owner/managers are not prepared to undertake the increased level of administrative tasks required by Government legislation or face visits from Government inspectors that will occur once the firm begins to employ more than just one or two people.

One of the earliest quantitative studies on vital areas of organisational competence within small firms was undertaken by Stoner (1987). His research concluded that the most critical small firm capability is the knowledge/experience/skills of the owner/manager. His study revealed that only a very limited number of a diverse group of small businesses located in Illinois, USA understood that to succeed, the owner/manager needs to create a 'distinctive competence' for the business. He posited that distinctive competence is critical in providing the basis for a competitive advantage that can provide the foundations upon which to base business growth. Stoner concluded that in the case of small service businesses, the most common distinctive competence selected by the owner/manager was ensuring the firm is differentiated from competition through the delivery of superior service quality. A similar theme has emerged in many subsequent small firm studies in both Europe and the USA in terms of identifying the critical importance of owner/managers having the leadership skills to grow the operation into a larger, highly successful business. O'Reagan et al. (2005), for example, concluded from a study of 194 small manufacturing firms that strong leadership led to much better market performance than organisations where the owner/manager exhibited an uncertain or weak leadership style.

CASE STUDY

The Midas Touch

Case aims: To illustrate that success can cause some entrepreneurs to believe they are infallible at identifying and exploiting new opportunities.

There is the risk that extremely self-confident entrepreneurs having been lionised by the media after one extremely successful product introduction may possibly begin to believe they have the 'Midas Touch'. This attitude may blind the entrepreneur to their own fallibilities. Hence these individuals continue to launch what they believe will be hugely profitable enterprises which actually turn out to be a series of failures. Such is the case of Sir Clive Sinclair, knighted for his services to British industry, who in the late 1970s launched the highly successful consumer product, the Sinclair PC. On the basis of this success, Sir Clive predicted huge opportunities for the pocket television, wristwatch radios and electric cars. In terms of his ability to perceive future trends, he was no doubt totally accurate. His problem, however, was his lack of skills in the design, development and manufacture of viable products using the technology then currently available. Many of his subsequent ventures in these areas of new consumer products were commercial failures. Perhaps the most notorious example was the launch of his electric car, the C5. This did not go very fast, could only carry one person and after only a few miles, came to a stop because the batteries needed re-charging.

Leadership style

The leadership skills of the owner/manager are especially important in an entrepreneurial firm (Apospori et al. 2005). This is because the owner/manager will usually be the originator of the unique idea which will provide the basis for major business growth. As well as being responsible for leading the innovation process, this individual will have the added burden of being responsible for managing day-to-day operations until these responsibilities can be delegated to new senior managers when they are eventually hired. This perspective is supported by research undertaken by Sariona and Martinez (2007). In their study of 100 small firms, they concluded that an entrepreneurial, participative leadership style had an important influence on the entrepreneurial spirit of the organisation. This spirit was absent from those firms where the owner/manager exhibited an autocratic, task-orientated management style.

Ojasalo (2004) has proposed that how entrepreneurs are portrayed by the media has a very strong influence over the general public's perception of the image, personality and behaviour of these individuals. The mass media has always been interested in documenting the business and social activities of well-known entrepreneurs. In the late nineteenth century and for much of the twentieth century, for example, the popular socialist broadsheet newspapers usually characterised individuals who built large business empires as having succeeded by creating monopolies or cartels, exploiting their employees or forcing them to work in unsafe situations. By the late twentieth century, however, as small business has become recognised as an increasingly important component of Western economies, the media seem to have adopted a more balanced view in presenting information about successful entrepreneurs.

In contrast with the media image of entrepreneurs, research studies aimed at developing a specification of the leadership qualities which can be attributed as being common to the majority of successful entrepreneurs have, however, been unable to validate the idea of all entrepreneurs exhibiting similar behavioural traits (Stanworth and Gray 1991). Their research suggests that the only firm conclusion that can be reached is a tendency of owner/managers, especially in matriarchal family firms, to resist delegating key tasks and limiting the degree of autonomy which they are willing to grant the employees (e.g. McKenna 1996). Other studies, however, have identified small firms where delegated authority is granted to the staff and the owner/manager actively promotes the philosophy of people collaborating with each other as members of a team (Kickul and Gundry 2002; Littunen 2000). Hence the safest conclusion is probably that there is no one single leadership style which can be attributed to ensuring achievement of entrepreneurial success.

CASE STUDY

Visiting the dark side

Case aims: To examine the scenario that not all entrepreneurs are unselfish individuals committed to the common good of the organisation.

Beaver and Jennings (2005) have proposed that in most cases the fundamental cause of small business failure is the managerial incompetence of the business owner. As part of their examination of managerial incompetence in small firms, these authors present a number of disguised cases where leadership was not just inadequate but exhibited evidence of morally indefensible behaviour. In one family firm, for example, the three sons who inherited the business from their father drained the profits from the operation to fund excessively opulent lifestyles and expenditure. Any expenditure on company assets tended to demonstrate an appreciation of the latest trends in interior design, not asset functionality. Then one of the sons was discovered to be having an affair with the wife of the managing director of a key customer. The immediate loss of this key customer added a further strain on the cash flow and within weeks the company went into receivership.

Richardson et al. (1994) had earlier expressed a similar view about the highly dubious behaviour and questionable decisions made by entrepreneurs whose business subsequently failed. The authors suggest that some entrepreneurs are insatiably driven to be more successful than anybody else in the same industry. Such individuals will exhibit extreme arrogance about their early success and remain certain that new, even greater achievements lie ahead. When expenditure on attempting to generate these greater achievements creates not success but major financial problems, the entrepreneur may actually continue to borrow money. An inability to repay such borrowing then emerges, often accompanied by evidence of some very questionable financial activities inside the business (e.g. withdrawing funds from the company pension scheme) which eventually leads to bankruptcy. Such was the outcome in the case of the UK media mogul Robert Maxwell who died in a boating accident in 1991. After his death it soon emerged his business empire was struggling to service a total loan burden of £1.8 billion. The subsequent outcome was the profit-making flagship business, Mirror Group Newspapers, being sold off by the administrators appointed to salvage what they could from the collapse of the Maxwell empire.

Strategic capabilities

Defining strategy

Many of the articles published about the influence of internal capabilities on small firm performance tend to be based on anecdotal evidence concerning observations of a very limited number of firms. The risks associated with using such findings are the data may not be of sufficient validity to provide the basis for generalisations that are applicable to other SME scenarios. To overcome this potential risk, Plymouth Business School, in collaboration with a UK Government small support agency, used a number of published studies to evolve the qualitative small firm capability model

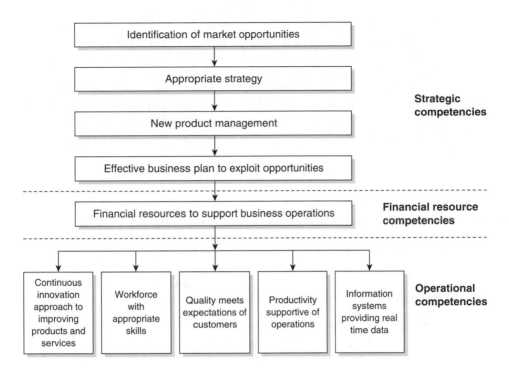

Figure 6.1 *A qualitative model of organisational competencies to support and deliver an entrepreneurial strategy*

shown in Figure 6.1 (Chaston and Mangles 1997). The model provided the basis for a large scale quantitative study of small firms in both the manufacturing and services sectors. Discriminant function analysis was applied to the survey data which permitted the creation of a quantitative model describing how variations in capability can be expected to influence business growth rates. This model demonstrated that in addition to the entrepreneur's leadership skills, other important internal small firm capabilities that influence business growth are those which are either of a strategic or operational nature.

The entry point of the model is the organisations's critical capability to identify emerging opportunities and to evolve an effective strategic response. Day and Schoemaker (2005) have suggested that exploitation of this competence often requires an ability to identify weak signals in the external environment. In commenting on weak signal identification, MacKay and McKiernan (2004) posit that conventional business planning tools are somewhat ineffective. Furthermore, they feel that individuals who exhibit this skill seem to exhibit an unusually highly developed intuitive ability to identify such signals and evolve entrepreneurial responses well ahead of their competitors.

New products

Exploiting a newly identified opportunity involves developing a concept to service the new opportunity in a way which will be superior to any existing offerings in the market. The model shown in Figure 6.1 indicates the need for some form of planning activity to assist the entrepreneur to assess the validity of the proposed strategy and to define the actions required to successfully exploit identified opportunities. This conclusion is supported by other research studies. For example, in a study of small Texas manufacturers, Khan and Manopichetwattan (1989) found that non-innovative respondent firms exhibited a limited understanding of strategy, had poor planning skills and lacked the ability to implement an integrated response to changing environments.

These researchers concluded that it is not unusual for small firms to discover that their existing products are not satisfying customer demand. Under such circumstances, success can only occur if the business has the capability to develop and launch one or more new products. Similar findings are presented by Martin and Staines (1994). They also concluded that growth orientated small firms tend to be led by individuals who exhibit high levels of managerial competence in the areas of innovation, providing visionary direction and facilitating the effective performance of other staff within their organisations.

Financial resources

There is a common adage used by bankers that 'actual plans take twice as long to implement and actual costs will be twice as high'. Parks' (1977) research supports this perspective. He found a very common scenario among small firms is that new products frequently encounter cost overruns, generate less than forecasted sales revenue and take much longer than expected to progress through to market launch. Given this situation there is a critical need for small firms to have sufficient financial resources to be able to survive any problems which may emerge during the development of a new product (Hogarty 1993). Hence entrepreneurial firms must ensure that they have the financial resources needed to successfully implement a strategy which is heavily reliant on the development of new products. These funds can be from sources including retained profits, cash inflows from trading, external borrowing or raising equity.

One study which validates the importance of the effective management of financial resources is provided by research undertaken of Canadian small firms by Chaganti and Chaganti (1983). These researchers surveyed 1,200 small manufacturing companies located in Saskatchewan, seeking the views of senior managers about the degree to which specific internal organisational variables influence their companies' performance. Application of discriminant function analysis indicated that optimal management of financial resources was one of the most important factors in terms of influencing profitability. Those firms which reported a high level of financial asset management competence were also those which enjoyed the highest level of profits as measured in terms of achieved Return on Investment. These conclusions are confirmed by the experience of venture capitalists who tend to find that successful entrepreneurial small firms typically have created strong, healthy balance sheets (Hellman and Puri 2000).

The issue of financial competence is extremely important during periods when the banks, who are the primary source of external funds for small firms, adopt a highly conservative lending orientation. In the UK, for example, the emergence of the 2008 liquidity crisis in the financial sector was followed by reports in the media of banks refusing to approve new loans, redefining the terms of recently approved loan applications and reducing the ceiling on the level of approved overdrafts granted to their small firm clients (Thomas 2008). When faced with criticism from both the UK Government and trade bodies such as the Federation of Small Business, the banks' response was that no constraints had been placed on lending to those customers whose business case demonstrates potential growth. Clearly very few small firms will remain unaffected by a recession. Hence the probability of new loans or overdraft ceilings being offered will remain low until bank profitability has returned to pre-2008 levels (Aldrick 2008).

Organisational capabilities

Innovation

The degree to which product performance has actually been enhanced by major brands announcing the launch of a 'new, improved product' can range from marginal (e.g. Parazone bleach being sold in a 'new, spill proof bottle) to significant (e.g. Nike's launch of a new design of football boot to coincide with the 2006 World Cup). The scale of change and the frequency with which improved products are launched into the market by large companies varies between industries (Biggadike 1979; Levitt 1965). In mature, low technology consumer goods markets such as soaps or detergents, product change may be quite minimal and improved products only appear every two to three years. This can be contrasted with growing, high technology markets such as telecommunications and electronics (Montoya-Weiss and Calantone 1994). In these latter markets, any delay in product launch will have a dramatic impact on revenue. This is because consumers tend not to wait for the postponed market introduction, but instead switch to another supplier. An example of this scenario is provided by Sony's failure to launch their latest generation PlayStation product in time for the key 2006 Christmas season.

Published information about the product improvement capabilities of SME firms is somewhat less informative. Based mainly on anecdotal evidence, it appears that in small firms in mature, low technology sectors, product improvement introductions are relatively infrequent. This can be contrasted with high technology sectors such as software, where small firms also need to introduce product upgrades on a regular basis (Thom 1990).

CASE STUDY

Networked innovation

Case aims: To demonstrate that in low technology sectors, successful innovation by small firms may require interaction between organisations.

The founder and managing director of the Australian company, Harvest Industries, believes that small firm success in the food industry can only come from using innovation and creativity to differentiate the company from competition. Implementation of this strategy is based on marketing unique products with the current focus being the launch of the seedless watermelon, mango, pineapple and avocado (Hyland and Beckett 2005). The company's core competencies are marketing and distribution. To acquire new products the firm has, therefore, needed to establish a strong network of growers, suppliers and contractors as

(Cont'd)

the basis for creating a highly effective supply chain operation. The company has created a network of suppliers who are under contract to grow unique food crops that Harvest has the sole right to produce in Australia. To support innovation these suppliers participate in regular meetings with Harvest at which all parties exchange knowledge on both product and process technologies. To widen the knowledge base Harvest has also created other networks involving packaging consultants, food scientists and market researchers.

Chaganti and Chaganti (1983) determined that the highest level of profitability in small manufacturing firms is among those organisations which offer a broad range of products, use innovation to frequently update their product line and are prepared to respond positively to market demands for product customisation. They noted, however, that innovation has an equally important role in being used to implement improved process changes inside the organisation. The usual focus of this activity will be to achieve one or more of the three key aims of reducing costs, improving quality and saving time. Although the entrepreneur will probably act as project leader, ultimately success is critically dependent upon involvement of the entire workforce.

An important area where internal process innovation can impact performance is the activities associated with the generation of a firm's product or service outputs. Laforet and Tann (2006) concluded that in relation to sustaining business growth in small UK manufacturing companies, there was much greater reliance on process rather than new product innovation within these organisations. Innovation activities they identified included the utilisation of new computer-based technologies and the automation of production lines. The conclusion about the dominant role of process innovation in this one sector, however, should not be considered to be a generalisation that can necessarily be applied to other sectors of industry. For example, in the case of the US timber industry, Wagner and Hansen (2005) posited that process innovation was more important among large firms whereas product innovation was a more certain path for achieving business growth among smaller companies. Similarly Wolff and Pett's (2006) study of factors contributing to business growth for small firms operating in international markets also concluded that product innovation was much more important than process innovation.

CASE STUDY

Collaborative innovation

Case aims: To illustrate how collaboration can assist in implementing an effective innovation strategy.

Boers Industries, located in Sydney, Australia, is a small engineering firm committed to sustaining growth through innovation. Started more than 20 years ago, the company has specialised in designing special purpose machine tools for clients across a diverse range of manufacturing industries. In the face of increasing international competition the founder of the business, Carlos Boers, opted to specialise in working collaboratively with clients to undertake more difficult projects. This permitted entry into toolmaking for the aerospace industry and the manufacture of automated machine tools.

Boers' usual approach to product and process innovation is to initiate change through a series of small, sequential steps. Where rapid change is required, however, the firm is willing to act more radically, being prepared to terminate current practices and adopt a totally new approach. With the aim of broadening the range of available market opportunities, in the mid-1990s the company entered into a collaborative network with other toolmaking companies. This allowed a pooling of resources that increased production capacity, thereby assisting network members' to take on larger contracts and pursue new export market opportunities.

Productivity

The primary role of any firm is to convert inputs into a product or service that can be sold for a profit. Survival can only be achieved when the product or service can be sold at a price that exceeds total operating costs. The difference between price and costs can be described in terms of the profit generated. This profit describes the 'added value' achieved by the workforce. Productivity is a measurement of added value. The importance of productivity is reflected in the fact that many Governments consider firms' productivity data to be a key indicator of the competitive capabilities of their economies (Mayhew and Neely 2006).

One way of determining the effectiveness of a small business is to compare productivity in relation to that achieved by other firms (Lawton 1999). To permit comparisons between firms, productivity is usually expressed in terms of added value per employee. This figure is calculated by dividing annual profit by the number of employees. Although small firms are considered to be more responsive, flexible and able to react more rapidly to new opportunities, in most countries SMEs are less productive than their counterparts in their large firm sector (Taymaz 2005). This reflects the influence of factors such as large firms being able to exploit economies of scale, having the buying power to procure inputs at much lower costs and an ability to afford to hire highly trained staff.

In most small firms, labour costs are often the highest single area of expenditure. For small firms seeking to achieve higher productivity, there are a number of capability enhancement options available which can save time or reduce direct costs. Gunasekaran et al. (2000) have proposed that in many cases, small firms can make very cost effective productivity gains by focusing on improving workflows. Typically this will involve simple actions such as improving procurement practices, identifying and removing bottlenecks on the production line, introducing a more structured approach to switching between items being manufactured and investing in upgrading workforce skills. The researchers also reviewed the alternative solution of replacing employees with machines. They concluded that this approach should only be considered where the combined costs of purchase and operation of the new machines are greatly exceeded by the costs of continuing to use employees to undertake the task. Aris et al.

(2000) reached a somewhat different conclusion about investing in advanced manufacturing technology. In their view this can be an extremely effective strategy through which to improve productivity in smaller firms. These authors did note, however, that obstacles such as lack of awareness of the latest technology, an inability to select the best solution or inadequate workforce skills can lead to the return on such investments being much lower than had been anticipated at the time of making the decision to invest in new equipment.

CASE STUDY

New technology

Case aims: To illustrate how new technology by a small firm can enhance both productivity and product quality.

New technology can both improve productivity and concurrently permit the entrepreneurial small firm to operate in sectors where the customer is seeking a high quality, customised product. An example of this approach is provided by an American manufacturer of steel saw blades, the Peerless Saw Company based in Groveport, Ohio. The company was facing potential bankruptcy in the face of foreign competition offering equivalent quality saw blades at much lower prices. Although one solution was to replace the firm's obsolete machinery with modern, higher output, punch presses, the president recognised this only offered a temporary solution. He decided to invest in the possibility of cutting saw blades with a laser and contracted with Battelle Laboratories to develop menu-driven software to permit utilisation of laser cutters. Once the new system was operating effectively, it permitted the firm to respond more rapidly to customer orders. When customers found the firm had reduced the time of the order-to-delivery cycle, they began to order smaller batches more frequently. Peerless was also now in a much stronger position to respond to orders involving product customisation. As customers became aware of this capability, they began to experiment with saw blade designs that could improve their own production processes. The outcome is that Peerless has not only improved productivity, it is now virtually the only occupant of a niche manufacturing high margin, customised products.

Human resources

Large firms frequently claim their employees are the company's most valuable asset, especially in the service sector. In many of these markets there are minimal differences between the services offered by suppliers, so consequently exploiting the skills of employees is often the only way to ensure that customers receive a service experience superior to that available from a competitor (Fuchs et al. 2000). An example of this approach to differentiation is provided by Singapore Airlines where the capability of their staff has permitted the airline to regularly be rated as one of the world's best international carriers.

Unlike in the large firm sector, although owner/managers are usually aware of the importance of optimising the performance of their employees, in most cases formalising the people management function through the appointment of a personnel manager does not happen until employee numbers have risen significantly (Barrett and Mayson 2007). There are a number of reasons for this. Firstly, in very small firms, owner/managers often believe they are qualified to handle all aspects of the activities associated with the hiring, managing and firing of employees. Secondly, many owner/managers perceive the only important aspect of the personnel function is to ensure the firm is fulfilling Government employment legislation in areas such as health and safety, recruitment, equal opportunity and dismissal procedures. In the eyes of many owner/managers to hire an additional individual to undertake these tasks represents a major increase in non-recoverable overhead costs. To avoid such expenditure they tend to undertake the task themselves or, as employee numbers begin to rise, delegate the role to an existing employee such as an office manager (Kotey and Slade 2005b).

This tendency to adopt somewhat myopic attitudes towards the personnel function may result in a small firm missing the opportunity to exploit the competitive advantages arising from the creation of a working environment that provides high levels of job satisfaction. In more successful small firms, there is a strong commitment to the adoption of appropriate people management practices. These can include structured recruitment systems, ensuring job satisfaction, determining how to enhance employee motivation, assessment of employee skills, creation of training schemes and regular employee appraisals (Raymond et al. 1988). Where such systems exist most owner/managers perceive the benefit of appointing a full-time personnel manager or training an existing member of staff who can then be promoted into this role.

Small firm success is often based on an ability to build stronger relationships with customers than their large firm counterparts. For a small firm seeking to dominate a market niche or enter a new market sector, an issue which should be examined is whether the nature of their existing workforce is appropriate for building relationships with key customers (Rowden 2002). Anecdotal evidence suggests that in many service sector firms, consumers prefer interacting with older people because of their acquired knowledge and also because they tend to exhibit greater respect for customers than younger staff. Hence, according to Hilpern (2004) small firms are more likely to be successful building market share if the workforce contains some appropriately skilled, older employees.

This is illustrated by an Oregon firm, Poorman-Douglas Corporation. In their view, it is the older, not the younger, employees who exhibit the highest level of productivity. This company specialises in high speed cheque, invoice and other mailing services and through its legal division, legal noticing and claims processing. About 10 per cent of the permanent workforce is aged over 65 and many of them have been with the company for all of their working lives. There are times when the volume of work exceeds workforce capacity thereby necessitating recruitment of more employees on a short term contract. The firm has found that older people are the best source of hard working, highly flexible, temporary staff.

CASE STUDY

Not just people problems

Case aims: To illustrate that in many cases business problems can be a mixture of both human resource and other managerial issues.

Tri-Seal of New York is a plastics extrusion company founded by Joe Dukess, who raised the seed money for the venture by playing cards on a troop ship when

(Cont'd)

returning home from Europe (Retkwa 1989). The company name comes from Dukess' invention of a patented triple layer sealing process plastic liner which fits into the bottle top of products ranging from household chemicals, detergents, cosmetics and beverages. This individual's entrepreneurial leadership created a highly successful business which in 1978 was acquired by Atlantic Research Corporation. After the acquisition, Dukess left and without his technical and entrepreneurial expertise, the business went into rapid decline.

Within three years of Dukess' departue the business was running at a loss. The new owners recognised the need to hire a new CEO. Harvey Fickelstein – an industrial engineer with no prior experience as a CEO – applied and to his surprise, was offered the job. By 1983, the company was again profitable. In 1985 Fickelstein organised a Leveraged Management Buyout (LBO) in order to purchase 70 per cent of the company equity. The plan was to consolidate operations across four different sites by moving into a single, new factory in July 1984 while the business was still owned by Atlantic Research. In fact they did not move into the new premises until May 1985, when the building was still incomplete and they had incurred numerous cost overruns.

Fickelstein's plan had been to maximise output by running the factory seven days a week with the staff working a concentrated 12 hour, three-day week, being paid for 40 hours, and then being off for three days. While these plans were being developed, about one-third of the staff decided they would not work on Sundays. No Sunday working would mean some staff working a 48-hour week which is unacceptable under Federal law. Production declined massively and the only solution was to introduce new engineering processes into the manufacturing operation. However, the Vice President of Manufacturing was not up to the job of managing this change and Fickelstein was forced to fire him.

With the company facing a financial crisis, no US banks would consider lending the company any more money. The founder Dukess was still receiving royalties for his Tri-Seal patents. He introduced the firm to a Danish bank that wanted to enter the US small business lending market. The bank provided the necessary additional funds to run the business. By the end of 1988 annual sales had exceeded $10 million with the company achieving a 70 per cent share of the US plastic bottle liner market. Fickelstein recognised that as the primary supplier of cap liners for plastic containers for companies such as Unilever and Procter & Gamble, this would guarantee the ongoing financial survival of the business. Nevertheless, in order to support further sales growth he decided there was a need to duplicate the founder's entrepreneurial spirit and to strengthen the business through new product innovation. The company's first success was the development a new fold-over, re-sealable pull tab which was immediately adopted by firms such as Minute Maid and Coca-Cola.

Quality

During the 1970s, many Western manufacturers, fighting to sustain profitability in the face of both inflation and the refusal of trades unions to permit revisions in working practices, allowed the topic of quality to disappear from their organisational radar screens. Countries such as Japan were quick to realise the vulnerability that this situation created and moved into world markets offering higher quality, reliable products at reasonable prices. It was only after inflation started to decline and unions began to adopt a more co-operative attitude that European and American firms began to introduce Japanese inspired concepts such as Total Quality Management (TQM) to re-inject quality into their operating philosophy (Anderson and Sohal 1999).

During the 1990s, Government support agencies in countries such as the UK decided that because of the success of structured quality evaluation schemes in the large firm sector (e.g. ISO 9000), small firms should also seek quality management accreditation. The outcome was small firms were advised to invest in formalised internal systems which greatly increased operating costs. These costs could not be recovered through sales because customers refused to accept price increases (McElwee and Warren 2000). As is often the case, however, most entrepreneurs rejected this advice. Instead they continued to utilise the philosophy of exceeding customer expectations over quality, but only if this could be achieved at a cost which permits the generation of an adequate level of profit.

A key reason for the SME sector to rely on quality as the basis for competitive advantage, especially when expanding internationally, is the ever present threat of larger firms offering goods at lower prices (Kaynak et al. 1987). This is primarily due to the larger companies enjoying cost advantages associated with being able to bulk buy or to exploit economies of scale. Sanjay and Golhar's (1996) research indicated that perceptive entrepreneurs realise that the small size and the more flexible nature of their workforce means that they can be more responsive to those customers who are seeking higher quality products and services. Upton et al. (2001) have posited that to achieve this goal, the small firm does require strong internal capabilities in areas such as measuring customer perceptions, identifying causes of customer dissatisfaction, diagnosing the cause of quality failures and implementing appropriate changes in organisational processes.

CASE STUDY

Global quality

Case aims: To illustrate the benefits of quality in seeking to build a successful small firm.

Although Portec Flowmaster of Canan, Colorado (www.prtec.com) has only 125 employees, the company has achieved global superiority in the design and manufacture of power-turn conveyors (Anon. 2006c). The company's first customer for airport baggage handling was American Airlines. Since then, Portec's materials handling expertise has permitted diversification into other industrial sectors including retailing, food processing, fertiliser plants, cement plants, slat plants and parcel handling. A key competence which has greatly influenced the company's global success is a total commitment to quality across the entire organisation. New staff are required to undergo extensive training leading to task certification for operations, quality and safety. All staff then participate in regular monthly quality training which has virtually eliminated scrap, rework, and most importantly, warranty claims from customers. All employees are empowered to take personal ownership for the quality of their work and all have the authority to stop production flows if they perceive a quality problem emerging.

Information

Data stored in a person's mind is known as tacit information. Providing others with access to such knowledge usually requires a one-to-one interaction between individuals. This contrasts with explicit information which is stored in a form accessible to others (e.g. in a written report or computer file). The complex nature of large firm operations has long caused their managers to recognise the critical importance of ensuring information is in an explicit form so that it can be accessed by others. Small firms, however, tend to adopt a somewhat more cavalier approach to the management of information. Much is stored in a tacit form, which means employees may be forced to reach decisions without having an adequate understanding of a situation (Chaston 2004).

Mukherji (2002) posits that the advent of low-cost computer systems in the SME sector has made a significant impact on the creation of explicit sources of knowledge in areas such as financial information and customer records. Nevertheless, many owner/managers still perceive most data as only needing to be collected for purely administrative or statutory purposes (e.g. filing year end tax returns). They tend not to exploit stored information as the basis for building competitive advantage. The more enlightened entrepreneurs, however, are beginning to accept that explicit information offers a vast range of new opportunities for employees to undertake tasks that permit the organisation to outperform competition.

Beal (2000), for example, determined that small manufacturing firms which scanned the environment to assess the nature of competitor behaviour were more able to identify effective responses to new market threats. Kotzab et al. (2006) concluded that information management was critical to firms in business-to-business markets when seeking to optimise their performance within the supply chain of which they are a part. Tanabe and Watanabe (2005) reached similar conclusions about the critical importance of managing information as the basis for optimising the performance of small service firms.

CASE STUDY

The on-line goldmine

Case aims: To illustrate how a firm rediscovered new market opportunities and a return to a more entrepreneurial orientation following entry into on-line retailing.

Getzs is a Michigan-based retailer founded in 1898 and specialises in the supply of outdoor clothing (Chen et al. 2003). Retail sales had been flat for some years. In an attempt to generate business growth, in 1997 the company, which until then had been a somewhat traditional retailer following prevailing industry conventions, took the entrepreneurial decision to move on-line. Their aim was that the move would create a national footprint for the company.

Although the Website was successful in attracting new customers, the unexpected and much greater benefit was the wealth of additional information that was generated from their on-line activities. These new data were immediately recognised as having profound implications on Getzs' future marketing strategy, product mix, storefront usability, and inventory control. In studying the server log data, Getzs discovered four very important things about its customers and current marketing strategies. First, none of the on-line orders were from customers living within 70 miles of the Getzs store. Second a large percentage of visitors come to Getzs.com for Carhartt-brand clothing. Hence 'Carhartt' and other variations of the spelling were the most commonly used keywords that directed visitors from search engines to Getzs.com. Third, Getzs found banner advertising's effectiveness to be poor in relation to cost. In addition, traditional advertising channels, newspapers and television, failed to generate increased Website hits. Fourth, search engine advertisements and placements showed signs of definite promise in terms of driving traffic to the on-line store.

A customer source research study revealed that almost 60 per cent of Getzs' customers came from America Online (AOL). In light of this fact, it became clear this is where the company needed to concentrate their on-line advertising dollars.

An analysis of customers' purchase behaviour at the on-line store indicated that a large portion of Getzs' customers did not bother to get more detailed information about products before placing orders. A closer look at these customers' profiles revealed that they were repeat customers who re-ordered the same products on a regular basis. It was also apparent that 80 per cent of Getzs' on-line customers only ordered from 20 per cent of the products that Getzs carried. This gave the management crucial insights on how to attract customers with promotions and how to meet their needs more efficiently. This knowledge also permitted more accurate product forecasts, thereby reducing procurement lead times and minimising the number of back orders, and costs associated with procurement.

SUMMARY LEARNING POINTS

- Sustaining competitive advantage can be critically influenced by the internal capabilities of the firm.
- The theory of exploiting internal capabilities to achieve competitive advantage is known as the 'resource-based view' of the firm.
- Areas of critical capability in relation to the performance of small firms exist at both the strategic and organisational level.
- Key small firm strategic capabilities involve being able to identify the most appropriate market position and the effective utilisation of new products to sustain performance.
- Key small firm organisational capabilities include innovation, productivity, human resources, quality and information.

ASSIGNMENTS

1   Review why an entrepreneurial firm is more likely to succeed, at least during the early years after business start-up, by implementing a niche-based marketing strategy.
2   Compare and contrast the ways of enhancing productivity in small manufacturing firms versus small service businesses.
3   What role can a personnel manager play in enhancing the performance of a small firm?

DISCUSSION TOPICS

1   How can access to adequate financial resources influence the performance of the small firm?
2   Why is excellence in quality management possibly more critical in a small service firm versus a small manufacturing company?
3   How can advances in IT be of assistance to small firms seeking to exploit information for enhancing business performance?

Additional information sources

Resource-based view (RBV)

Pascale, R.T. (1984), Perspectives on strategy: the real story behind Honda's success, *California Management Review*, Vol. 26, No. 3, pp. 47–73.

Defining strategy

McDoougal, P., Robinson, R.B. and Richard, B. (1990), Competitive strategies for entry, *Strategic Management Journal*, Vol. 11, No. 6, pp. 447–468.

New products

Panigrahi, B., Ede, F.O. and Calcich, S. (2003), A comparison of test marketing practices of large and small consumer goods manufacturing firms, *Management Research News*, Vol. 26, No. 6, pp. 1–20.

Human resources

Vinten, G., Lane, D.A. and Haves, S. (1997), People management in small and medium sized enterprises, *Management Research News*, Vol. 20, No. 11, pp. 1–66.

7

Strategy and Culture

Chapter objectives

The aims of this chapter are to assist the reader to:

- understand the strategic concept of mass marketing
- examine the benefits of strategies based on a merger of marketing and RBV
- review the evolution of small business theory
- comprehend the benefits of using a niche-based marketing strategy
- understand the importance of sustained innovation
- examine the concept of company culture
- review alternative company cultures and team orientated small businesses.

Conventional wisdom

Mass marketing

Most new management theories are based on research about successful real world practices, leading academics to identify an operational philosophy that has proved beneficial to a number of organisations. In the case of marketing management, early theoretical foundations were based on studies of major consumer goods companies such as Procter & Gamble and Unilever in the decades immediately following the Second World War. The success of these firms was attributed to their adoption of a mass marketing philosophy that involved identification of a large consumer market need that could be satisfied by offering a standard product (Kotler 2004). Large market size has the potential to support very high sales volume. The resultant economies of scale created by high sales in turn generate large profits that can be re-invested in significant levels of promotional expenditure.

The low technology manufacturing processes required to produce consumer goods such as detergents, soaps, coffee and frozen food means it is virtually impossible to create products which are technically very different from those offered by competitors. Under these circumstances, market leadership is often determined by variables such as spending on advertising at a level greater than competition which, when linked to widespread distribution in outlets such as supermarkets, permits firms to dominate markets (Tedlow and Jones 1993). The behaviour of the large branded goods companies has led to the accepted theoretical wisdom that mass marketing is the most effective route to dominating markets. The concept is still widely practised by major multinational companies (Beard and Easingwood 1992). The philosophy is especially relevant where few or no opportunities are perceived to exist to permit the launch of radically different product propositions or to introduce a fundamental change in process technology that can completely alter industry cost structures.

Mass marketing companies usually have to confront markets for their products moving into the maturity phase. At this juncture the only source of significant new incremental revenue is to persuade consumers to switch brands (Linvol and Razzouk 2006). The need to stimulate brand switching behaviour in consumer goods markets has been an important influence in the evolution of the concept of evolving a Unique Selling Proposition (USP). As there are minimal variations in the performance characteristics of many branded goods, the identified USP will have to be based on some form of perceived difference. This difference is usually established through the medium of advertising. For example, in the UK lager industry, Foster's advertising platform is based on the platform of a product drunk by Australians. This can be contrasted with Carlsberg Export's promotional message of being 'so good, Danes hate to see it leave'.

Theory merger

The risk associated with being completely focused on outperforming existing competitors in a mature market is the major companies may fail to recognise early signs of a fundamental shift in customer needs. This myopia can provide an opportunity for an entrepreneurial firm to enter the sector as a market challenger. Observations of the successful entry of market challengers led to a theory being proposed by some academics as an alternative to mass marketing. This proposed that given most major companies are marketing orientated and understand how to implement a mass marketing strategy in order to defeat other brands, to become a market leader a challenger organisation should adopt a resource-based view (RBV), based on the exploitation of a unique, superior, internal core competence(s) (Hamal and Prahalad 1996).

In the mid-1990s, some academics, such as Chandler and Hanks (1994), began to question whether the success of market challengers such as Apple Computers or Microsoft were compatible with the purist view of RBV that success is totally attributable to having developed superior internal competences. The view which authors such as Levitas and Ndofor (2006) articulated was that only after having acquired a detailed understanding of market conditions, could a successful challenger evolve the core competences which permitted them to offer a superior product. This alternative perspective has led to the acceptance of a more balanced view in which both market orientation and internal capability are both seen as critically important in the selection and implementation of a successful strategy.

CASE STUDY

Challenging sector conventions

Case aims: To demonstrate that by combining an understanding of markets with expertise in developing new internal competences, an entrepreneur can successfully challenge the market dominance of well entrenched large firm competitors.

Samuel Moore Walton personifies the entrepreneur whose understanding of consumers combined with his ability to identify new forms of internal competence permitted him to successfully challenge the conventional strategies being utilised by large, well entrenched, incumbents. As a consequence his company, Wal-Mart, has become one of the largest retail operations in the world (Bell 1999). The 1960s saw American consumers, who were traditionally very brand loyal, beginning to exhibit price resistance. This trend was exploited by the emergence of large discount chains such as K-Mart, typically situated near or in large cities.

In the 1960s Sam Walton and his brother John were managing a regional chain of Ben Franklin stores. Sam's experience was that large retailers tended to hold the incorrect view that small town America contained minimal sales potential. Having failed to persuade the owners of Ben Franklin to exploit this opportunity, in 1962 he opened his first Wal-Mart store in Rogers, Arkansas offering a broad range of products at discount prices in a no-frills setting. While other retailers accepted the conventional view that success is founded upon economies of scale in procurement, large city locations, promotional spending and effective merchandising of goods in large, modern outlets, Walton realised that the more important influencer of profitability was logistics and communications. His initial strategy was to situate a regional cluster of stores within 24 hours travel distance of the Wal-Mart warehouse. The warehouse was the centre which did all the purchasing and managed distribution.

Another convention breaker was the introduction of cross docking as the focal element in the warehouse operation (Dess and Picken 1999). This process involves goods continuously arriving at the warehouse remaining on the loading dock to be selected, repacked and dispatched to stores thereby reducing inventory and out-of-stocks. This new concept in logistics when linked to the location of stores in smaller towns permitted the company to offer brand name goods at discount prices in places where there was little competition from other major chains.

Having proved the validity of the new approach to retailing, the company expanded rapidly. By 1977 it owned 190 stores and by 1985 this figure had risen to over 800. A key aspect in the expansion was seeking new ways of enhancing logistics processes. There was emphasis on using electronic technology to link suppliers, distribution centres and stores to ensure real time monitoring of product movement through the retail supply chain. By owning 2,000 trucks and building 19 distribution centres, the company was able to ensure rapid and responsive transportation of products. To monitor truck movements the company even invested in creating the world's first ever non-commercial satellite tracking system.

Sam Walton did not make the mistake of many other retailers of assuming once proven, the company's retail model should remain unchanged. In 1983, he launched SAM's Clubs, a chain of deep discount warehouse outlets. This was followed in 1987 by Supercentres which were even bigger than any existing Wal-Mart store.

Sam Walton died in 1992 and soon after his death the company decided to expand overseas, initially entering markets such as Canada, Mexico, Germany and the UK, then more recently into China and India. To date international achievements have not been as successful as some industry experts had predicted. Additionally in recent years the company has faced image problems in the USA over issues in relation to the treatment of their workforce and the emergence of other retailers attempting to duplicate the Wal-Mart strategy. Hence there is a question mark of whether without the entrepreneur Sam Walton, Wal-Mart will be able to enjoy the same scale of success which the firm enjoyed for the 30 years following Sam's opening of his first store in Rogers, Arkansas.

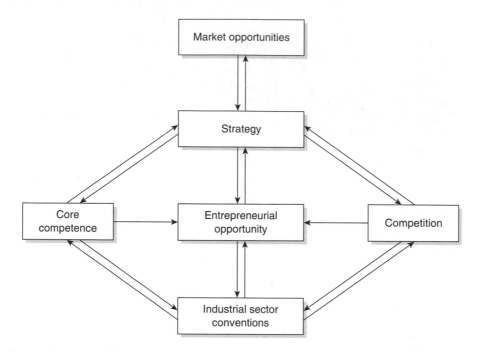

Figure 7.1　*Determinants of strategy*

Small business theory

Two dominant sources of small firm management theory are (1) those based on transferring large firm theory into the SME sector and (2) identifying sector specific management practices that have been developed by entrepreneurs seeking to cope with the unique factors known to influence small firm performance (Sanders 2007). In relation to the first of these, some management theorists tend to dogmatically present one single perspective. For example, for some this might be that small firm success stems from being market orientated, whilst others may posit the view that the superior performance is completely dependent on exploiting a core competence.

Fortunately, entrepreneurs tend to adopt a more broad-minded attitude when listening to the advice being proffered by management gurus (Anderson and Atkins 2001). Hence most entrepreneurs would be more comfortable with a concept of the type illustrated in Figure 7.1 which proposes there are a number of variables to be considered in the strategy selection process.

Most successful entrepreneurs are very aware that a head-on confrontation with a sector's existing large firm market leaders by offering only a marginally better product or service is an extremely dangerous strategic concept. There is a good reason for this perspective. As noted by Weinsten (1994) a key capability of large firms is their ability to access additional resources such as finance or to exploit their domination of distribution channels in order to respond to competition. Thus should a large firm decide that a smaller entrepreneurial firm is becoming a significant threat then they can be expected to respond with actions such as increased promotional spending, heavy price cuts and blocking the smaller firm's attempt to achieve widespread market distribution. Consequently most entrepreneurs aspiring to create a new, large

Product

		Same	New
Process	Same	Market domination by established major firms	Challenging leading firms by launching the next generation of products
	New	Challenging the established firms by introducing a new superior process	Making the entire industrial sector obsolete by introducing fundamental convention changes

Figure 7.2   *Alternative strategic options*

commercial entity will opt for a strategy which is based on challenging the validity of the accepted rules (or 'conventions') currently being utilised within an industrial sector (Chaston 2000a). As summarised in Figure 7.2, this challenge can involve the introduction of a new process technology, the launch of a new, next generation product or a combined strategy involving both product and process change.

CASE STUDY

Avoiding a market confrontation

Case aims: To demonstrate how an alternative strategic positioning can be utilised by an entrepreneurial firm to avoid directly challenging large firms that have the resources and market dominance to defeat the smaller organisation.

The risk facing the entrepreneur is that their new product attracts the attention of a larger firm which perceives the activity as a very significant, potential threat. An example of an entrepreneur who was very aware of this risk was Jeff Hawkins who launched his Palm Pilot electronic organiser product into the hand-held computer market in 1996 (Yoffie and Kwak 2001). Hawkins perceived Microsoft as the greatest potential threat. Hence he adopted a very low key approach when initially launching his product. For example, the parent company US Robotics wanted to debut the new product at the Las Vegas Electronics Show. Instead Hawkins opted to quietly direct marketing efforts to individuals who worked in the computer industry, earning more than $100,000 a year. This generated 50,000 customers who were so impressed they told others about the Palm Pilot. By Christmas, the product was one of the fastest selling new consumer electronic devices in the world.

(Cont'd)

Some entrepreneurs in the American computer industry do have a tendency to be very vocal about their success. For example, Jim Clark, the co-founder of the web browser Netscape, called Microsoft the 'Death Star,' depicting Netscape as part of a rebel alliance ready to liberate the galaxy. Hawkins took a very different approach. He positioned the company on the periphery of the personal computer industry. Actions included not calling the product a computer or personal digital assistant. Instead the Palm was positioned as companion not a replacement for a user's PC. By adopting this position, Microsoft totally ignored the growing market success being enjoyed by the Palm Pilot. Hawkins also recognised that market leaders succeed by defining the criteria by which customers assess the relative offerings available in the market. Instead of following the usual industry philosophy of maximising the number of clever activities that could be undertaken by the device, he focused on offering a product which was simple, elegant, easy to use and did those things deemed critically important by customers such as organising the calendar and address book extremely rapidly. In addition he insisted on the software meeting the operating criteria of working 99.999 per cent of the time. This meant unlike most PCs of the time, the Palm Pilot rarely ever crashed. To achieve this goal the company kept all hardware and software development in-house.

By the end of 1996, Palm Pilot had achieved a 51 per cent market share of the personal organiser market. This prompted Microsoft, who had previously already launched two hand-held products that failed, to offer a third generation pocket-size operating system to major computer manufacturers such as Compaq and Hewlett-Packard. To defeat this move, Hawkins launched the next generation Palm Pilot. This launch was followed by another significant product upgrade and the incorporation of new design features which reduced manufacturing costs. Probably the next most significant achievement was the launch of Palm VII which delivered an integrated wireless-connectivity at a time when no other company could offer such a product benefit. To maximise market penetration of the Palm Pilot operating system Hawkins persuaded software developers to create new applications for integrating the Palm Pilot with users' PCs. To achieve this goal he took the totally unknown step in the industry at that time of publishing the source code for the product and making available a software-development kit. In 1997 3Com acquired US Robotics. The new owners were concerned about Hawkins' strategy of driving down the price to increase market penetration and making source code available to other people in the computer industry. Their view was that such actions were completely unnecessary because by this time the Palm Pilot had achieved a greater than 65 per cent market share. They did not understand that as demonstrated by Microsoft, long term survival in the software industry is dependent on achieving a virtual monopoly position. In 1998, Microsoft launched their new Palm PC. The new device offered a number of new features such as a voice memo recorder, an LED light that flashed to remind users of their appointments and a larger screen. Hawkins came under intense pressure to match these features by adding them to the Palm Pilot. He held the view that simplicity, elegance and price were still the key factors in the market. His recommended response to the Microsoft threat was to move into new markets by linking the Palm Pilot to other products such as MP3 players and digital cameras.

Senior management rejected this view. Hence in 1998, Hawkins left the company to create a new business, Handspring Corporation. In 1999, this new business launched the hand-held device Visor which is totally compatible with the Palm Pilot but offered an expansion slot which could be used to link the device to an MP3 player, a digital camera or a mobile phone. Within only a few months Visor became the fastest selling hand-held device in the market, with approximately 40 per cent of sales coming from people who previously would have purchased a Palm Pilot.

Small firm wisdom

Successful strategies

There is a tendency for some small firm researchers to use a very small number of qualitative case studies as the basis for justifying why a specific management strategy is successful in the SME sector. One of the earliest studies which attempted to overcome this questionable methodological approach to evolving new management theories was undertaken by Cavanagh and Clifford (1983). These individuals adopted the view that validation of theories should involve a quantitative assessment of a very large number of small firms. Hence they undertook a large scale survey of high growth SME sector firms across the USA. From this study they were able to identify a number of commonly occurring variables in relation to how owner/managers evolved their business strategies.

In their study, the majority of the firms opted for the strategy of using innovation as the basis for developing new products that permit achievement of business growth. Importantly this focus on innovation is not just apparent in the early years after business start-up, but is retained as a long term aspect of strategic orientation. This latter fact is illustrated by over 25 per cent of respondents reporting that a significant proportion of their current sales came from products that were not being offered five years earlier. Over time, however, many firms also indicated that they have needed to re-focus innovation by shifting emphasis from new products to developing new business processes.

Niche strategies

Cavanagh and Clifford's (1983) study also confirmed the view that small firm success is often dependent on the strategy of occupying a specialist market niche as a mechanism for avoiding confrontations with large firms. In most cases the entrepreneurial firm will continue to operate a 'focused' strategy aimed at serving the needs of a subset of customers with specialist needs within a market sector. Only rarely were the small firms so successful that they were able to expand into other areas of the market and take market share from large companies. Another aspect of the study was confirmation of the standard guidance to be found in the academic literature that small firms should avoid competing on price and instead rely on a 'differentiation' strategy. This latter philosophy is based on making available products or services which deliver superior performance. When determining the foundation on which to construct a strategy, the high growth firms in the sample reported heavy reliance on exploiting a key competence such as knowledge of technology, research expertise or marketing skills.

Aurand et al. (2004) are supportive of this strategic philosophy but also note that exploiting these competencies is an extremely effective system for the entrepreneurial firm to be involved in differentiation through product customisation. In those cases where the entrepreneurial firm determines their original niche can no longer sustain further growth, their usual response is to develop their core skills as the basis for permitting entry into new niches or finding new approaches to innovation.

CASE STUDY

The need to respond to change

Case aims: To illustrate that even a niche-based strategy can fail due to changing market conditions, declining commitment to innovation or poor financial management decisions.

A characteristic of the retail sector is the emergence of a new firm which will exploit an emerging new market niche by utilising an innovative, entrepreneurial approach to the merchandising (Hollander 1996). Over time, however, the successful firm often begins to exhibit non-entrepreneurial behaviour or is replaced by a new market entry offering a more attractive consumer benefit more suited to prevailing market conditions. This behaviour pattern, described as the 'wheel of retailing' by the American academic Professor Malcolm McNair, has been challenged by other researchers on the grounds of excessive simplicity (Brown 1987). Nevertheless, the concept still provides a useful framework for examining market change in the retail industry.

A well known example of the wheel of retailing cycle is provided by the American retailer, Levitz Furniture Corporation (Carnnes 1997). In the 1960s the company adopted a more entrepreneurial orientation and established a niche position based on opening warehouse outlets offering families immediate delivery of inexpensive furniture at competitive prices. By the early 1980s the problems associated with sustaining rapid growth of the firm apparently caused management to forget the need to retain an entrepreneurial orientation. Consequently Levitz failed to identify and implement a proactive response to changing consumer trends such as rising incomes causing the American middle classes to begin to seek more contemporary designs. Further problems were created by the huge debt which was created by a leveraged buyout in the 1980s and by the late 1990s the company's poor financial position resulted in the largest unsecured creditor, Northwest Bank of Minnesota, forcing the organisation to file for protection from creditors under Chapter 11 of the US Bankruptcy Code.

The 1990s provided a stimulus for new entrepreneurs to enter the market opening stores which focused on serving a specific, specialist market segment (Greco 1997). One example was Zany Brainy, a multimedia educational toy store which was the brainchild of David Schlessinger. The company strategy was to exploit parents' growing interest in the education of their children. Each outlet offered a selection of 25,000 items in around 12,000 square feet of retailing space. Sections of the store were subdivided by activity types such as 'discovery' or 'creativity' and further subdivided by age and product group. Staff were trained to interact with parents and children in an enthusiastic and supportive way by acting as learning advisers. Growth was rapid and the company eventually opened 187 outlets with annual sales exceeding $400 million. Unfortunately expansion was not accompanied by a sustained commitment to innovation, operational control or in-store customer service. Additionally competition emerged in the form of a similar 'super-nicher' Noodle Kidoodle and the dominant toy retailer Toys R Us adding educational items to their product line. The company was also somewhat slow to recognise the implications of on-line retailing and rather belatedly spent $10 million on a joint venture which failed. Eventually, in the face of declining sales, excessive operating costs and excess inventory problems, in 2001 the company was forced to make a Chapter 11 bankruptcy filing (Bannon 2002).

Sustained innovation

Most small firms recognise there is a major risk with using a price–based strategy because new market entrants or the response of larger firms will often render this approach impossible after a short time (Chaganti et al. 2002). Hence even in market sectors where the customer is known to be price orientated, by focusing on offering superior value the entrepreneurial firms are able to continue to command a premium price for their output. In many cases this superior value is achieved by being strongly customer orientated and using the knowledge generated by close relationships to develop ways of augmenting their basic product proposition with additional services. These incremental services include activities such as keeping inventories near or at customer locations, offering free technical support services and providing training to their customers' employees.

CASE STUDY

Sustained innovation

Case aims: To illustrate the benefits of sustained innovation as a strategy capable of ensuring ongoing business growth for an entrepreneurial company.

Whilst head of the chemistry department at Trinity College in Hartford, Connecticut, Vernon Krieble discovered that anaerobic resins, unlike conventional sealants or adhesives which have to be mixed and heated in order to become a permanent plastic, can quickly harden and form a durable bond between assembled surfaces when kept away from air (Wantuck 1982). In 1953 he founded the American Sealants Company, later to be renamed Loctite and in 1955, at the age of 70, implemented the first test market for the Loctite adhesive. During the following year he raised $100,000 to fund the market launch of the business. A year later he persuaded his son Robert Krieble, to join the fledgling operation. Within four years sales had reached $1 million.

(Cont'd)

The company culture was orientated towards working in partnership with customers to solve difficult bonding problems, whilst inside the operation emphasis was given to assisting employees to acquire additional job skills. An initial area of product development was in the creation of specialist applicator systems to solve specific manufacturing problems being encountered by customers. For example, when General Motors needed to find a better approach to the assembly of hubs on the rear axles of cars on their production line, Loctite designed and developed a totally new type of adhesive applicator. The company's in-depth understanding of product chemistry was exploited to permit entry into new market sectors and eventually supported entry in consumer markets.

The first consumer product was a plastic material to fill small dents in car bodies. From this small base, a whole range of household adhesive products were then introduced. The most successful of these was Super Glue. Unlike many other smaller US firms, which tend to avoid expansion outside of North America, early in the life of Loctite opportunities were sought to generate export sales. Market entry was usually through the medium of a distributor. However, once sales volume had achieved a certain level, the company usually sought to establish a wholly owned subsidiary.

Entry into the German market brought the firm into contact with the Henkel Corporation, which in the mid-1980s became a passive investor by acquiring a 35 per cent interest in Loctite. The Henkel Corporation is a diversified conglomerate which in the early 1990s commenced an aggressive programme of growth through acquisition. In 1996 Henkel mounted a successful hostile bid to take over Loctite (Adams 1997). Although Henkel has been supportive of Loctite continuing to be active in new product development, no member of the Krieble family remains as a member of the senior management team. The organisation has gradually morphed into becoming a conventionally managed subsidiary within a multi-national corporation.

Company culture

Single culture theory

A characteristic of icebergs is that only one-eighth appears above the water with the other seven-eighths remaining unseen beneath the waves. This is analogous to the process of strategic management. Selecting and then announcing a new company strategy has a high level of visibility within an organisation. The activity which often remains opaque, and therefore often misunderstood by the workforce, is the effective implementation of the strategy that has been chosen (Sull 2007). Although a number of factors have been identified which can influence successful strategy implementation, one of the most important is company culture.

Culture is constituted of the prevailing values, beliefs and attitudes which determine the overall behaviour of the firm's employees. Some writers have a tendency to evangelise the idea that there is but one model of culture which should be adopted by all organisations (Blackburn and Benson 1993). Authors promoting this theory tend to select certain well publicised cases to justify their views. For example, some American writers with absolute faith in the superiority of a culture based on employee empowerment, will typically cite two firms, Marriott Hotels and the department store chain, Nordstrom, as examples which validate the impact on performance of organisational empowerment (Reichfeld and Sasser 1990; Schlesinger and Haskett 1991).

CASE STUDY

Lotus Corporation

Case aims: To illustrate how a change in leadership in an entrepreneurial firm can be accompanied by a culture shift which may not be beneficial to business performance.

In many cases the culture of an entrepreneurial organisation reflects the leadership style of the founder. When this individual retires or is removed from the organisation, the arrival of a new CEO may be accompanied by a culture shift. An example of this is provided by the US company, Lotus Corporation. This initially entrepreneurial company launched the world's first leading spreadsheet software product, Lotus 1–2–3. The founder Mitch Kapor was famous for his preference for informality. He established an organisation where active collaboration between employees permitted rapid identification and development of new software products. As the company grew, similar to the Apple scenario, external stakeholders became concerned about the apparent chaotic approach to business which they perceived existed inside Lotus. An ex-McKinsey consultant, Mike Manzi, was appointed to run the company. He was a great believer in major decisions being the preserve of his office and preferred rigid organisational structures accompanied by extensive control systems. His impact on the business was dramatic. Many of the key software developers soon departed the business. The firm was then unable to sustain the pace of innovation required to counter the increasing threat of new office software products being launched by Microsoft. Eventually after some years of declining performance, the highly weakened business was taken over by IBM.

Alternative cultures

Some academics believe there is probably no single culture which is applicable to every organisation. This viewpoint is supported by the extensive research undertaken in the USA by Dr William Schneider (1985). He concluded that to optimise performance, management should concentrate on ensuring the same culture prevails across the entire organisation. He further recommends that, depending on both the attitudes and beliefs of both the leadership and the workforce, firms should attempt to embed one of the four following culture types into the organisation:

1   A control culture orientated towards predictability and order. Leadership is authoritative and conservative.
2   A collaborative culture favouring close internal and external relationships. Leadership is supportive of high employee participation and cohesive teams.
3   A competence culture which pursues innovation and employee capability excellence. Leadership is visionary and promotes the idea of individuals setting themselves high personal standards of performance.
4   A cultivation culture favouring life enrichment for individuals both within and outside the organisation. Leadership is charismatic and inspirational.

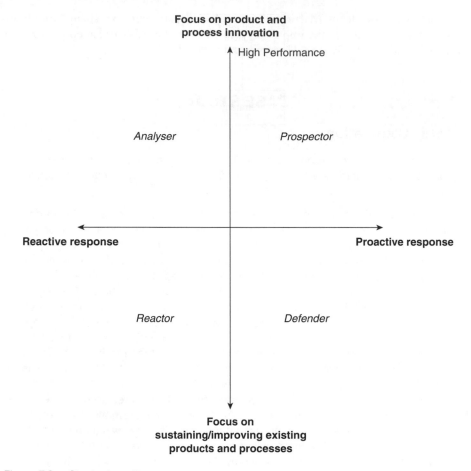

Figure 7.3   *Strategic options*

With the aim of gaining further understanding of the relationship which may exist between strategy and culture in the SME sector, O'Reagan and Ghodadian (2006) undertook an empirical study of small UK manufacturing firms. In relation to identifying different strategies being used by respondent companies, the researchers used the Miles and Snow (1978) typology of prospectors, defenders, analysers and reactors. As illustrated in Figure 7.3, prospectors are first-to-market companies that succeed by being proactive leaders in the development of new products and technologies. Defenders attempt to locate and maintain a secure niche in a relatively stable industrial sector, sustaining the sale of high quality, relatively unchanging products or services. Analysers exhibit both a prospecting and defending capability, but base their decisions on careful, detailed analysis of available information. Reactors tend to shift strategic priorities in response to what they perceive to be the latest market threat confronting their organisation.

O'Reagan and Ghodadian concluded that to a large extent entrepreneurial firms in their sample could be classified as prospectors. Within this group, the dominant company culture was that of being orientated towards creativity, close working relationships with key customers, a high degree of inter-departmental co-operation plus permitting employees a significant degree of freedom in decision-making and task completion.

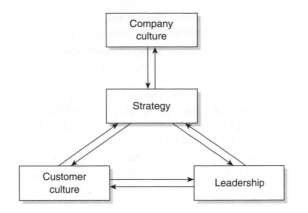

Figure 7.4 *Strategy influencing variables*

In seeking to ensure culture is supportive of strategy, firms must recognise that culture will need to be compatible with the values of both the customers and the communities from which employees are recruited. As summarised in Figure 7.4, it is important to ensure strategy is supported not just by culture, but also by an effective leadership style. O'Reagan and Ghodadian's study also examined leadership style. They concluded that within most entrepreneurial small firms in their sample, the leadership style was orientated towards being transformational, welcoming change, a strong emphasis on delegation of authority, promoting employee flexibility and minimisation of rules and regulations. This contrasts with defenders where the leadership favour an autocratic centralised control and a hierarchical, functional organisational structure.

The importance of the influence of leadership style on company culture in relation to sustaining entrepreneurial behaviour has also been identified by Golan (2006). His study focused on process innovation in small US manufacturing firms which achieve business growth through exploiting their ability to undertake customised engineering projects. He concluded that success could be greatly impaired in those cases where the organisation operated a rigid management structure in which all key decisions about process change had to be authorised by senior managers before new actions could be implemented on the shopfloor.

CASE STUDY

Polaroid Corporation

Case aim: To demonstrate that the dominant influence of a founding entrepreneur can cause successors to not recognise that changing market environments or technologies require the introduction of an alternative business strategy.

Edwin Land was an entrepreneur who had a total commitment to the idea that science is the best instrument through which to develop products that can satisfy deep human needs (Tripsas and Gavetti 2000). He also felt such needs could rarely be understood through market research. In 1948 his company Polaroid

(Cont'd)

Corporation launched the world's first instant camera. To sustain the company's growth from small firm to global player Land funded ongoing research to improve picture quality, decrease the photograph development time and to introduce colour.

Originally manufacturing had been outsourced, but in the 1960s Land bought both camera and film manufacturing in-house. To avoid direct competition with traditional cameras sold through specialist outlets, Polaroid focused on gaining distribution in mass market retailers such as K-Mart. There was a strong corporate belief in the 'razor blade' business model. This involved selling cameras at low prices and making a high profit on the sale of film. Land's philosophy remained that success comes from innovation based on long-term, large scale research. In 1972, after 8 years of research and half a billion dollars of expenditure, this philosophy led to the launch of the SX-70, a camera which ejected the picture which then developed as the customer watched.

By the mid-1970s, Land decided to delegate some of his role and appointed Bill McCune as CEO. This individual was a colleague who shared Land's vision over the importance of research. In 1985, the new CEO committed substantial funds to undertake R&D on digital imaging technologies with the aim of combining digital imaging and instant photography. The goal was to develop an instant digital camera and printer product (called 'Printer In The Field' or PIF). Senior management mistakenly believed that digital imaging could be made to fit their beloved razor blade business model. Scientists with understanding of digital imaging recognised that it was not possible to duplicate the razor model because digital imaging is a profoundly different market. Additionally fundamental to success was the requirement to invest in overcoming the firm's basic weaknesses in the areas of low cost electronics, manufacturing and rapid product development. Senior management were highly resistant to any recommendations about addressing these problems and were concerned that the products under development did not fit the razor blade model. They also felt consumers would also want instant prints, not the ability to take a digital photograph and store the picture on a computer for printing at a later date.

Despite having created a viable prototype in 1992, Polaroid did not launch their first digital camera until 1996. By this time there were over 40 other firms in the market selling digital cameras. The other problem was the retail price of $1000 required the product be marketed through specialist retailers, whereas the Polaroid marketing and sales team only had prior experience of gaining distribution in mass market, price-based retailers. The product failed to gain market share. In 1996, Polaroid brought in an outsider, Gary DiCammillo, as the new CEO. His management background was consumer marketing so he immediately applied this philosophy to the Polaroid operation. Research expenditure was drastically cut and funds diverted into up-weighted spending on advertising. The historic commitment to large scale invention through research was replaced with a philosophy of only funding the development of improved versions of existing products. The dominant players in the world of digital cameras were consumer electronics giants such as Sony, Toshiba, Hitachi and Canon. Polaroid was unable to compete against these firms. The final nail in the Polaroid business model occurred because as consumers became familiar with digital cameras, their interest in instant cameras virtually disappeared. On 12 October 2001, Polaroid Corporation filed for bankruptcy.

Team-orientated culture

Owner/managers have a reputation for wishing to retain control over any and all activities which may have a significant impact on the future performance of their firm. This is totally understandable given that should the business fail, unlike employees, the individual risks the loss of the family home. Nevertheless, it is critically important in relation to the successful management of growth, that entrepreneurs recognise they cannot do everything or be in two places at once.

There are case materials and small scale qualitative studies which indicate that the growth rate of entrepreneurial firms will usually be higher when there is an orientation towards delegation and using a team-based approach to innovation management (McNamara and Watson 2005). One of the few studies based on a large scale empirical validation of this perspective was that undertaken by Littunen and Tohmo (2003). They surveyed over 200 small firms in Finland to determine which factors most influence company growth over the first seven years after establishment. A common characteristic among the high growth entrepreneurial firms within their sample was the emphasis that the company founders placed on using entrepreneurial teams within their organisations. The identified benefits of this approach were the positive impact on areas such as creating competitive advantage, new product development and organisational productivity. This occurred because compared with relying on a single entrepreneur, an entrepreneurial team has the advantage of being able to draw on the combined knowledge, skills and personalities of a diverse group of individuals.

CASE STUDY

Team-orientated entrepreneurship

Case aims: To illustrate the benefits of a team orientation to achieving superior business performance.

Possibly one of the most difficult consumer service propositions in the USA is attempting to create a successful, independent ice-cream store operation. Owners face competition from both national brands such as Baskin Robbins and new independent outlets entering the market on the basis of price. Amy Millar's entrepreneurial solution for her seven outlet ice-cream operation in Texas was to position her company as a place of fun and entertainment (Case 1996). This is achieved by employees acting more as performers than shop assistants, wearing strange outfits and persuading customers to participate in the activities such as singing songs, dancing or telling a joke. The concept is successful because all the staff share the common perspective that their role is to entertain, not just scoop ice-cream. To communicate this philosophy to potential employees, instead of providing an application form, people are given a plain white bag and the instruction to do anything with it and bring it back in a week. The success of the concept in terms of placing emphasis on creativity when hiring new staff is demonstrated by the company going from zero to over $2 million in sales in less than ten years.

(Cont'd)

The importance of ensuring the founder's philosophy is shared and supported by all employees is also illustrated by Black Diamond Equipment. The company is based in Salt Lake City, Utah, and competes in the highly competitive, narrow niche of selling trendy rock climbing equipment. The company's approach is to be perceived as more committed and more passionate about their products than their competitors. A key aspect of achieving this goal is to only hire employees who are already rock climbing enthusiasts. Customers thereby share common experiences with the company staff, and even more importantly, the staff's deep involvement in the sport makes them an extremely fruitful source of new product ideas.

SUMMARY LEARNING POINTS

- Major branded goods companies have based their success on the implementation of mass marketing strategies.
- Small business theory has evolved from both drawing on management practices used by large firms and by sector specific concepts evolved from within the sector.
- Effective business strategies tend to be based on merger of marketing and RBV theory.
- Most small firms find that adopting a niche-based strategy is the most effective market position.
- Company culture is a reflection of the prevailing attitudes, values and beliefs which exist within an organisation.
- Strategy implementation is influenced by the culture which prevails within an organisation.
- Leadership style will have a significant influence on company culture.
- A team-orientated culture seems in many cases to be the most appropriate environment for sustaining innovation within small firms.

ASSIGNMENTS

1 Select a well known major national or international brand. Undertake research to identify the various marketing practices which the brand utilises to sustain a selected market positioning.

2 Select a well known international B2B company such as Boeing, British Aerospace, Du Pont or Rio Tinto Zinc. Through research identify which internal capabilities appear most critical to the company in terms of successful business performance within their specific market sector.

3 Select a service sector such as tourism or retailing which contains both large and small firms. Compare and contrast their marketing activities to identify differences between mass and niche marketing strategies and business practices.

DISCUSSION TOPICS

1 What do you feel are the variables which provide an assessment of organisational culture and what research techniques would you use to measure these different variables?
2 Discuss the view that mass marketing is bad for society because the strategy promotes excessive consumerism and materialism within society.
3 Based on your personal experience of working in a team environment, what are the possible factors that can impede the effectiveness of a team? How can these factors create obstacles for a team seeking to contribute to creating a more innovative organisation and how might such obstacles be overcome?

Additional information sources

Mass marketing

Kotler, P. and Singh, R. (1981), Marketing warfare in the 1980s, *Journal of Business Strategy*, Vol. 1, No. 3, pp. 30–42.

Niche strategies

DeCarlo, J.F. and Lyons, P.R. (1980), Toward a contingency theory of entrepreneurship, *Journal of Small Business Management*, Vol. 18, No. 3, pp. 37–46.
Parrish, E.D., Cassill, N.L. and Oxenham, W. (2006), Niche market strategy for a mature marketplace, *Marketing Intelligence & Planning*, Vol. 24, No. 7, pp. 694–703.

Single culture

Loewe, P. and Dominiquini, J. (2006) Overcoming the barriers to effective innovation, *Strategy & Leadership*, Vol. 34, No. 1, pp. 24–32.

Team-orientated culture

Benko, C. and McFarlan, W. (2004), Managing a growth culture: how CEOs can initiate and monitor a successful growth-project culture, *Strategy & Leadership*, Vol. 32, No. 1, pp. 34–42.

8

Entrepreneurial Innovation

Chapter objectives

The aims of this chapter are to assist the reader to:

- be aware that significant innovation may be caused by a market disruption
- accept that process innovation can be as effective as seeking to develop a new product
- comprehend the role of the leader in visioning and guiding the development team
- be aware that successful innovation depends on a development team maximising the number of new ideas generated
- accept that the stage gate model may not be appropriate when seeking to develop a highly entrepreneurial new product or process
- comprehend that entrepreneurs adopt a more flexible approach to innovation, only utilising components of the stage gate model they perceive as relevant
- understand that the limited resources of small firms mean that participation in a network will often enhance innovation activities.

Innovation pathways

Disruptive innovation

Christensen (1997) has used the phrase 'sustained innovation' to describe the orientation of most large corporations focusing their R&D efforts towards introducing incremental improvements in existing products or organisational processes. The potential problem with this managerial philosophy is that the future performance of these firms is highly vulnerable to a new player entering the market offering a significantly different product or the introduction of a new, more effective, organisational process (e.g. Dell's use of direct marketing of computers to US consumers while major firms continued to use a sales force or distribute their products through retail outlets).

The conventional theory of large firm failure is of an event that occurs because an incumbent market leader fails to recognise the scale of the threat posed by a new firm entering their market and their speed of response is inadequate (Paap and Katz 2004). The alternative view posited by Christensen (1997) is that market leaders' desire to respond to changing market circumstances is often constrained by existing customers' insistence on key suppliers concentrating on further improvements to existing products. As a result many large firms tend to focus on product or process innovation which can sustain the company's current market position in terms of staying ahead of other large organisations operating within the same market sector (Demuth 2008). Thus for example, although IBM recognised the potential of minicomputers to provide smaller organisations with access to more affordable computer technology, the firm's existing large company clients articulated a desire for IBM to continue to develop the next generation of mainframe computers capable of offering even greater, more powerful, data processing capability. This behaviour permitted an MIT-trained entrepreneur, Ken Olsen, operating from an old textile mill in Massachusetts to launch the Digital Equipment Corporation (DEC). The new firm's success was based on the strategy of making computers affordable to smaller organisations by supplying them with the first generation of minicomputers.

Christensen's theory suggests that an entrepreneurial small firm seeking to achieve significant growth should develop a very different product or organisational processes which permit offering a benefit not yet satisfied by the incumbent, large firm market leader. This approach to new product or process development is known as 'disruptive innovation'. The terminology applies to those situations where the new proposition is significantly different from the prevailing business conventions being followed by large firms. The outcome is either the creation of a very different customer usage pattern or the offering of a radically different benefit proposition.

CASE STUDY

Technology disruption

Case aims: To illustrate that disruption can be achieved even in relatively new markets and areas of technology.

At the outset, the three founders of the Swiss company Logitech – Daniel Borel, Pierluigi Zappacosta and Giacomo Marini – operated on the basis of the somewhat indistinct aim of wishing to transfer computer technology from Silicon Valley to Europe (Jolly and Bechler 1992). Their initial product was a word processing system for desktop publishing. This project was terminated when the sponsor, a large Swiss company, cut the funding. Logitech's near term cash flow was protected because the firm's reputation as an entrepreneurial innovator had led to the award of a development contract to design a graphics workstation for the Ricoh Corporation.

As the founders gained experience of how to survive in the rapidly changing computer industry their interest began to focus on identifying an opportunity to exploit technology as the basis for developing a product which avoided being in confrontation with major computer manufacturers, component suppliers or software companies. Observing the development work on computer interface devices in progress at the Ecole Polytechnique Fédéral de Lausanne (EPFL), Logitech became convinced that the mouse would play a critical role in making computers easier to use. This was at the time when the mouse was only being used by a small number of computer engineers and scientists around the world.

In 1982, Logitech acquired the rights to a hybrid optical-mechnical mouse which had been developed by Professor Nicoud of EPFL and was being manufactured by a small Swiss firm. Logitech developed an improved version and transferred the production to a larger Swiss manufacturer. Unable to have sufficient control over product quality, in 1983 Logitech acquired the rights to

(Cont'd)

a new generation of mouse design and established their own small manufacturing operation with an annual output capacity of 25,000 units. At this point, sales of personal computers began to grow at an unprecedented rate and it became clear that the potential for computer control devices was huge. Other firms such as Mouse Systems Corporation, Mouse House and Microsoft had already entered the US market but were focusing their primary efforts behind establishing strong retail brands.

Logitech's solution was to focus on their reputation for innovative design and high product quality as the basis for developing a sales base supplying major Original Equipment Manufacturers (OEMs). Logitech's first customer was Hewlett-Packard who wanted to source a high quality mouse built to their specification. The strategy of other mouse companies was to subcontract manufacturing to low-cost, off-shore suppliers. Logitech took the view that quality and product development demanded ownership of the manufacturing operation and to locate the operation near to customers in order to permit maximum speed of response and provide easy access for inspecting output. Hence they opened a new, large manufacturing facility in California.

At that time the two prestigious OEMs, Apple and IBM, were buying their mice from Alps, a large Japanese firm that also supplied Microsoft. Logitech knew it could supply a technically better product but also needed to fulfil the requirement of being able to produce high volumes at low cost. Their solution was to take advantage of the Taiwanese Government's offer of heavily subsidised space in an industrial park in Hinschu. The new facility was soon outproducing the US plant and as the scale of manufacturing increased, the firm successfully negotiated supply contracts with both Apple and IBM.

Whilst building their B2B operations, Logitech also sought to enter the huge US retail market. Their first attempt, the technically advanced C7, generated little interest from either consumers or major retailers. In order to bypass the traditional channel members, Logitech entered the mail order business and placed advertisements and coupons in specialist computer magazines offering a $99 mouse at the time when the leading brand was selling for $179. Almost straightaway the company became the largest mail order mouse supplier in the USA. This success caused retailers to want to stock the brand.

Entry into the European OEM market was simplified because of the firm's relationships and reputation with large US multi-nationals. With Apple operating a manufacturing base in Ireland and other firms such as IBM and Compaq located in Scotland, 18 months after opening their Taiwanese facility, the company built a new manufacturing operation in Ireland. By the end of the 1980s, the company had developed a full range of products covering the upper-end, middle and lower-end of the market.

Logitech's continued success in countering intense, price-based competition from Pacific Rim producers was to offer technically superior, customised products. During the evolution from being a small entrepreneurial firm based in Switzerland to a global, multi-location market leader, the founders focused on the need to sustain an entrepreneurial culture. The company culture is founded on delegating managerial autonomy to each company site whilst promoting the exchange of ideas and knowledge between all employees around the world. Logitech recognised the potential trap of becoming a 'single product' company and in the late 1980s began to diversify into other areas of technology associated with managing the user–computer interface. The first move was to launch a hand-held optical scanner. This has been followed by acquiring majority interests in other firms. This provided access to new technologies such as pen-based computing and computer gaming equipment. The strategy of sustaining high quality output at low cost whilst being located near to OEMs has not, however, been neglected. For this reason the company has now opened a new manufacturing facility in Shanghai, China.

Process innovation

There is a tendency for entrepreneurs to assume that disruptive innovation should always be based on a new product. This ignores the fact that consideration should be given to whether opportunities exist to use organisational process innovation as a pathway through which to achieve the desired significant improvement in financial performance (Gilbert 2003). Consequently, at the outset of an innovation project, the small firm should firstly determine whether the product or internal processes are to be the focus of entrepreneurial action. This can be achieved by undertaking an analysis of the growth options described by Figure 8.1, to determine which approach offers the greatest opportunity and potential for success. Operational innovation activities that might be considered include the product/service production system, promotion, distribution or logistics. The appeal of process innovation is that typically it will involve a smaller level of expenditure to successfully attract customers. It has the added advantage of often being a lower risk proposition than developing a new product.

Research by Aris et al. (2000) has confirmed the preference of small firm entrepreneurs to focus on product innovation. These researchers also concluded, however, that especially in those industrial sectors where the generic product design has been available for some years, then a small firm seeking to achieve significant future profit

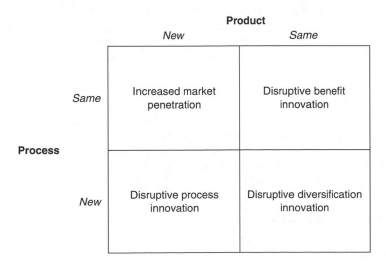

Figure 8.1   *Growth pathway matrix*

growth through innovation is more likely to enjoy this from concentrating on the development of a new, more productive, operational process.

CASE STUDY

Process disruption

Case aims: To demonstrate that even in an industry which has for many years utilised the same process technology, process disruption can still offer an entrepreneurial opportunity.

In the 1950s and 1960s, the US steel industry was dominated by eight major American companies who operated large, integrated plants using economies of scale as the basis of achieving a competitive advantage (Slywotzky 1996). In the mid-1960s, however, the Japanese steel industry entered world markets offering lower priced steel produced from more modern, vertically integrated steel plants. At the same time, US manufacturers in sectors such as the car and drinks industries were switching to aluminium and plastics as lower cost raw materials. The reaction of the US steel industry was not to re-examine their future process technology or be concerned about responding to substitutes for steel. Instead the industry focused on persuading the US Government to create tariff barriers to stop steel imports.

One entrepreneur who recognised the need to introduce an alternative process technology into the US steel industry was Ken Iverson at Nucor. He focused on the use of small production units, or mini-mills, located near to customers which used scrap steel instead of iron ore as their raw material. By 1985, Nucor's success was reflected in the company's stock market value of $1 billion, almost equal to the market value of one of America's largest steel companies, Bethlehem Steel. Iverson was an entrepreneur who realised that standing still in a price sensitive, commodity orientated industry is not a viable option.

In the early 1980s, the price of the mini-mills' raw material, scrap steel, was rising dramatically and also expansion by competitors was causing mini-mill capacity to begin to approach total market demand. Iverson's response was to avoid price competition by moving up-market, offering a higher grade product at a higher price. Nucor built a thin-strip, continuous casting plant in Indiana to produce flat-rolled steel for use in manufacturing sectors such as domestic appliances and the car industry. To reduce reliance on scrap, the company built an iron carbide plant in Trinidad which processed low-cost iron produced in Brazil. The iron carbide which provided an alternative to scrap was shipped to Nucor's US mini-mills on barges which were routed through the port of New Orleans. Other American mini-mills could not compete with Nucor's new business model. Furthermore, not even Japanese steel producers could match the low cost of production for flat-rolled steel which had been achieved within Nucor's re-designed operation.

Entrepreneurial leadership

Leadership style

Ensuring a successful outcome from entrepreneurial innovation is possibly one of the more difficult managerial tasks facing any organisation. In the case of small firms, the task is complicated by a requirement to organise the process such that it is compatible with the owner/manager's leadership style (Chaganti et al. 2002). Research reports on the behaviour of owner/managers, especially in matriarchal family firms, tends to characterise these individuals as being highly autocratic, directing staff to undertake specific tasks with minimal interaction with other employees (Hunt and Handler 1999). This style of leadership is often accompanied by an unwillingness to seek the opinion of employees before reaching any key decisions, and can be extremely destructive, especially in the case of new product development projects requiring inputs from a significant proportion of the firm's workforce.

Although a number of researchers have identified examples where new product success was accompanied by one specific leadership style, as noted by Becherer and Maurer (1999), researchers have not yet categorically decided whether an autocratic or integrated management style is more likely to result in the most successful new product outcomes. In an attempt to gain further understanding about this issue Mosey (2005) undertook a case-based analysis of SME UK manufacturing firms known to be seeking to develop new-to-market products. He concluded that the most critical issue was that either the owner/manager or a nominated senior manager was seen to be leading and participating across four key areas during the creation of a successful new product; namely, opportunity identification, acquisition of market knowledge, defining strategy and managing the development process. Nevertheless, even this study was unable to determine the degree to which project outcomes are influenced by the project leader exhibiting a participative leadership style. The case materials did suggest, however, that a cross-functional team approach is preferred when attempting to create a new-to-market proposition involving a relatively complex product or process technology.

Team leadership

Harper (1991) has proposed that whichever management style is being exhibited by an entrepreneur, this individual needs to put equal emphasis on both improving current operations and developing future solutions. By adopting a proactive, long-term view, rather than waiting until an actual business downturn occurs, the firm will have enough time in which to develop new products or processes.

Based on both earlier research and media articles about successful entrepreneurs, Sweirz and Lydon (2002) concluded that entrepreneurial leaders cannot just restrict their activities to directing or implementing disruptive innovation programmes inside the organisation. They must also orchestrate all aspects of their firm's operations. To validate this view and also to acquire data about the actual activities undertaken by entrepreneurial small firms' owner/managers, the researchers undertook an in-depth study of 27 CEOs of small firms in the American biotech, software, hardware and Internet industries. They concluded that the role of the successful entrepreneurial CEO includes 'visioning', defining and creating appropriate operational competences, being the primary company fund raiser, leading the development of a customer relationship orientated organisation and guiding the creation of an effective human resources management system. This latter role is seen as critical so that the company can respond to the need to expand organisational capacity as sales increase. This capacity building activity will have the specified aims of ensuring the workforce is of an optimal size, appropriate new employees are recruited when needed, existing employees continue to acquire new skills and all members of the organisation are well rewarded and highly motivated.

CASE STUDY

Sustaining the vision

Case aims: To illustrate the importance of sustaining a long-term vision based upon innovation to achieve ongoing business success.

Reilly Industries, an Indianapolis-based manufacturer of speciality organic chemicals was founded in 1896 by Peter C. Reilly, a 27 year old, self-educated technologist whose entrepreneurial vision was that science is the main source of new commercial opportunities (Gywne 1996). In the early years, the founder was the operation's sole R&D capability even though he had no formal techni-cal qualifications or education. The company's initial area of focus was on discovering and developing new applications for coal tar. In the 1900s Reilly received a patent of a still for producing coal tar. The device dramatically increased the yield of tar during the distillation process. This improvement permitted more effective exploitation of the emerging market for wood preser-vation, such as railroad ties, marine pilings and telephone poles. In the 1920s, Reilly entered the market for bituminous road paving made of coal tar rather than petroleum asphalt.

Prior to the Second World War the manufacture of aluminum created a demand for anodes made of carbon obtained from coal tar. Reilly Industries satisfied much of that demand, and in the process made the tar side of its business much more sophisticated. As early as 1918 Reilly's commitment to research was reflected by hiring Ira Derby, a Ph.D. chemist from the University of Minnesota, as the company's research director. Reilly recruited scientists with the zeal of a college sports coach. In 1936, Derby was succeeded as research director by Frank Cislak. These two individuals helped the company move into the organic chemical industry by focusing upon the production of pyridines, the demand for which rose dramatically following the discovery of sulfa drugs. Added demand for pyridines occurred due to DuPont's invention of water-repellent canvas and the discovery of the benefits of using vitamin B3 to combat pellagra.

In 1952, when P.C. Reilly died intestate, the company had to sell off part of the business to settle the estate taxes. Nevertheless, Reilly Industries, run by the founder's son, Peter C. Reilly, Jr, continued to support a high level of R&D expen-diture. This investment paid off when the manufacturers of herbicide recognised that manufacturing the key ingredient pyridine, was best contracted out to a specialist supplier such as Reilly Industries.

Now under the direction of the founder's grandson Thomas Reilly, Jr, the company understands the need to develop a more structured, focused approach to R&D. This focused approach emphasises both research orientation based around customer needs and selecting research priorities on the basis of which opportunities seem to offer growing market demand. The key element underly-ing this philosophy is to continually identify where new core research compe-tences may be required in the future and to act to fill any identified skills gaps. The company' s overall business strategy still remains that of developing commercially viable manufacturing technologies for new molecules where it is perceived there will be rising future market demand.

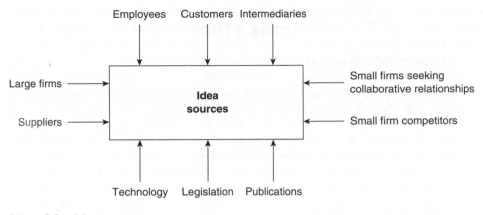

Figure 8.2   *Idea sources*

Idea generation

Generation obstacles

The success of a new product development programme is often dependent on maximising the quantity and quality of new ideas that are generated at the beginning of the project. As summarised in Figure 8.2, case materials from both the large and small firm sectors suggest new ideas can come from a variety of different sources. Hence where the small firm perceives the benefit of following a conventional managerial approach, it is important that as many as possible of these sources are examined during the idea generation phase.

Vermeulen et al.'s (2005) research identified the following issues which can act as potential obstacles that can inhibit idea generation in small firms:

1   Many organisations use 'lightweight' teams for idea generation, thereby not exploiting the best of the expertise which may exist within the company.
2   There is a tendency not to involve key customers in development activities.
3   Companies, having faced problems over incremental development of existing product, avoid examining radically new ideas.
4   Firms suffer from a lack of resources for new product development.
5   Those individuals assigned the task of idea generation have limited experience in the process.
6   Senior managers typically fail to provide incentives that could stimulate employees to become involved in the generation of new product ideas.

To gain further understanding of the obstacles confronting idea generation and to determine how these might be overcome, Petersen (1988) surveyed 483 owner/managers in the USA to determine the source of their firm's most profitable ideas. Respondents indicated that the most important source were their own inspiration and spontaneous thoughts. This finding led the researcher to conclude that in many small firms, new product ideas are inspirational thoughts by the entrepreneurial owner/manager without recourse to implementing the formalised, structured processes commonly encountered within the large firm sector. His conclusion was that this excessive reliance on personal judgement was the primary reason why some entrepreneurial firms failed to exploit the expertise of other sources such as employees, key customers and other external sources when seeking to maximise the number of potential ideas which could provide the basis for a successful new product. The other risk associated with entrepreneurs' self-reliance on their ideas is ideas may not be carefully screened for viability. As a result new product development may commence even though the firm's employees perceive fundamental flaws exist that will mean the idea will fail.

In theory the advent of computer-based customer records and access to the Internet has greatly increased both the speed and breadth of data access that can assist in the identification of new ideas. Exploitation of electronic data is enhanced by requiring employees to record their findings in a common database. Even though over recent years, one might expect the advent of the Internet to have altered the approach to idea generation within small firms, Petersen's (2006) most recent study reveals that many owner/managers still continue to rely on inspiration and spontaneous thought.

Idea relevance

Blumentritt (2004) identified that another barrier to idea generation is that small firms in mature, non-growth industries tend to adopt the philosophy that innovation is either not relevant or productive in their industry sector. He proposes that owner/managers should revise their perspective on this matter and seek to promote greater innovative thinking among the workforce. In his view the owner/manager should initially focus their actions on those employees who exhibit curiosity, talent and motivation. Keiningham et al. (2006) expressed another concern; namely another potential barrier to success is the overoptimistic views of some entrepreneurs who suffer from observing the world through 'rose tinted spectacles'. Such a behavioural trait runs the risk of ideas being progressed which even from the outset have little chance of ever being translated into a successful new product.

During the idea generation process it is important not just to focus on positive information. This is because negative data, such as customer complaints or an e-mail from an angry supplier, can sometimes lead to the identification of a new idea. For example, the Coleman Corporation, a US pioneer of camping equipment such as lanterns and stoves, launched a smoke detector with a big 'broom button' alarm tester. The idea came from newspaper articles about some older people who were frustrated with kitchen fumes repeatedly triggering their smoke alarms, and were removing the batteries from their existing alarms as a way of achieving peace and serenity. This added feature of 'broom buster' is specifically aimed at older people who cannot climb onto a stool or ladder to turn off an alarm that has been accidentally triggered by burning the toast.

Idea bias

When exploiting any source, the small firm must recognise that the information provided may be biased (Greve 2007). This can occur when a source lacking in commercial integrity has a vested interest in gaining acceptance for their suggestions. For example, a supplier wishing to sustain future sales may propose a design idea to ensure their company's components will remain an integral part of any new product. Intermediaries such as large retailers often place their own commercial aims ahead of those of their suppliers. Typically they favour new product ideas capable of maximising their profit per unit of retail space. When relying on consumers as a source of ideas, it is necessary to accept that most consumers tend to extrapolate from their existing beliefs and experiences when expressing an opinion that might lead to the identification of a new product concept. This situation is effectively illustrated by Henry Ford's statement that should he have listened to his customers, he would have focused on developing a faster horse. Hence the small firm must find ways of 'thinking outside the box'. This will occur where the owner/manager or a trusted employee is a very capable entrepreneur. In other cases where the small firm determines there is a requirement for a more creative or far-sighted input, sources that might be exploited can be those such as advances in a technology, futuristic magazine articles, trade body reports or output from researchers in the University sector.

New product development process management

The stage gate model

The linear (or 'stage gate') new product management model is to be found in virtually every marketing text ever published. It is presented as a sequential process constituted of the seven components of idea generation, idea screening, concept development, business planning, prototype development, test marketing and launch (Cooper et al. 1997). Originally evolved to assist large firms minimise the risk of new product failure, the model is an excellent example of the 'moving from one box to the next' managerial philosophy often presented as the 'holy grail' by Business Schools around the globe. Supporters of the model strongly adhere to the view that managers should execute every component within the model prior to market launch. Furthermore, the manager is urged to stick to the rule of totally completing all the activities associated with the tasks specified for each box before progressing to the next stage in the model.

Even in the large firm sector, questions have been raised about the universal validity of the stage gate model. Millier and Palmer (2001) note, for example, that the utilisation of the model assumes certain critical assumptions. These are that the product can be characterised as having features or benefits which potential customers can understand and that the market for such a product is identifiable. In those cases where these assumptions prove invalid Millier and Palmer posit that alternative new product process systems will be required. As summarised in Figure 8.3, there are three scenarios where, due to lack of understanding by either customers or developer, it would be inadvisable to apply the conventional linear new product process model. The three scenarios of avoiding working in isolation of the market are during (1) concept definition (2) prototype development and (3) market launch.

In all scenarios where at least one party has a low understanding about the proposition under consideration, successful new product development will require collaboration between the developing company and key customers. This is because collaboration will be necessary in order for the developer to acquire sufficient understanding of the new proposition such that a product specification with strong market appeal can be created. Even where the developer has an understanding of the proposition, customers will need to be involved at the beginning of the development process in order that they can acquire sufficient understanding such that upon launch they comprehend how they can benefit from purchasing the new product.

Developer understanding of the new proposition

Customer understanding of the new proposition	High	Conventional linear new product development process	Collaborative development programme with developing company and key customers working in close partnership
	Low	Collaborative development programme led by developing company	Collaborative development programme led by key customers
		High	Low

Figure 8.3   *Customer/developer interaction matrix*

Source: modified from Milllier and Palmer (2001), Turning innovation into profit, *Strategic Change*, Vol. 10, No. 2, pp. 87–98. With kind permission of Wiley-Blackwell.

Alternative process approach

Various researchers have used survey data or case studies to assess whether the linear model is in widescale use among small firms. Typically they discover it is not (e.g. De Toni and Nassimbeni 2003; Vinson et al. 1975). The conclusion often then reached is that new product failure rates in the SME sector would be greatly reduced if owner/ managers learnt from their large firm counterparts and adopted a structured, stage gate management model. Not surprisingly these studies have led to the creation of some Government small business support programmes aimed at persuading the SME sector that adoption of this managerial technique could improve new product success rates. The usual outcome from being exposed to such thinking is that of reinforcing many owner/managers' existing opinion that few support programmes offer new knowledge which is of any real benefit to their firm. This attitude prevails because entrepreneurs tend to respond intuitively when assessing the validity of theories that have originated from the large firm sector or are evangelised by a management guru.

Undertaking qualitative, informal research with small firms will reveal that although small firm entrepreneurs usually reject strict adherence to a stage gate approach, they often do perceive that there are some clear advantages to using one or more of the components contained within the model. But as is shown in Figure 8.4, actual utilisation tends to be based on a less formalised approach with the small firm exhibiting a menu-based orientation involving varying the order of action sequencing or totally ignoring certain component activities within the model.

There are several reasons to explain this difference in the use of the process model by large versus small firms. In some cases it is a reflection of managerial culture. For example, the entrepreneur who is prepared to jump immediately from idea generation to prototyping may reflect the impatient enthusiasm of an owner/manager to immediately prove the technical viability of a new idea. Another common scenario is that the cash flow may mandate there can be no delay in bringing the new product

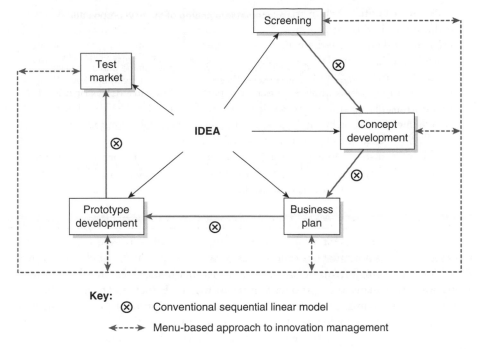

Key:

⊗   Conventional sequential linear model

◄---►   Menu-based approach to innovation management

Figure 8.4   *Innovation management model*

to market. There are also some individuals who, based on previous success, hold the view that their proven entrepreneurial skills totally justifies their decision to move from idea identification to market launch without validation of project viability. Whichever is the reason for selecting how to use the process model, the critical issue is that the small firm comprehends the purpose of every component in the model. This understanding can then lead to acceptance of the advisability of implementing one or more stages of the model as a path by which product success rates may be increased and product failures avoided.

Process effectiveness

Whether or not the small firm accepts the validity of using the stage gate model for managing new product development, research by individuals such as Owens (2007) has revealed that project success can be undermined due to certain failures in effective project management. Respondent firms indicated that in their organisations these factors have led either to project failure or the project breaching agreed time schedules or financial budgets:

1   Lack of overall strategic thinking and purpose to guide the development process.
2   Failure of senior management to exhibit strong commitment to new product development because of a tendency to be more involved in resolving crises that arise in day-to-day business operations.
3   A failure to ensure that adequate financial and staff resources are assigned to the project.

4 Lack of scientific, technical or engineering skills to overcome unexpected technological problems.
5 Inadequate skills within the manufacturing operation to convert a prototype into a viable product suitable for manufacturing or an inability to produce the new product to meet cost or quality specifications.
6 Poor communications between different departments causing delays or miscommunications that lead to incorrect decisions being reached.
7 A tendency to use a hierarchical structure accompanied by limited interaction between the different departments involved in the project.
8 A failure to involve potential customers in the development process at a sufficiently early stage such that lessons learnt from their feedback can be incorporated into the final product specification.

Another key factor that can strongly influence the successful implementation of a new product development project is the company's ability to acquire appropriate information from potential customers to assist with the product launch. The conventional view that small firms do not engage in formal market research has led to the assumption that many new product failures in the SME sector can be attributed to inadequate data acquisition and analysis during the development process. Sultan and Barzack (1999) have challenged this view on the grounds that (1) the evidence of small firms not valuing market research tends to be of a limited, anecdotal nature and (2) where formal academic research studies have been undertaken, the results typically indicate that most small firms do draw upon market sources to assist their product development activities.

In their study, Sultan and Barzack found that the nature of the market interaction process rarely involved the classic, positivist approach to market research of undertaking customer surveys. Instead they found small firms relied on a more informal, qualitative approach where data about markets and views of customers are generated through one-to-one meetings between a key customer and the company. Additionally, the firms often arrange focus groups constituted of intermediaries or potential end users.

In most cases the small firms involved in the study reported that they undertook all or most of their market research activities without the involvement of a professional market research agency. The primary reason given for this behaviour was these firms' prior experience of market research firms wanting to undertake expensive, lengthy quantitative data generation exercises. What the small firm actually wanted was a very rapid, qualitative evaluation of a specific issue. Some small firms also felt that in those cases where there was a need for additional market or customer data on complex technological issues, they were better qualified than any market research agency to acquire such information. Sultan and Barzack also identified cases where the benefits of the market research that had been undertaken were reduced or nullified by the way the firm utilised the acquired data. In some cases they found that where the new information conflicted with the existing opinions of key executives within the company, there was a tendency to dismiss the acquired data as being erroneous. The other problem which the research identified was the tendency of executives responsible for acquiring data to not always share new knowledge on a timely basis with others within the organisation involved in the new product development programme.

CASE STUDY

Developing new spectacles

Case aims: To illustrate some of the variables which can influence the effectiveness of the new product development process in small firms.

Due to location inside the EU and sector labour costs, the Italian spectacle (or eyeglass) industry is in no position to compete on the basis of low price. Ongoing success is critically dependent on positioning their products as fashion goods. This means there is strong pressure to continually update and introduce new designs with at least 30 per cent of product lines being replaced every year. This situation makes the sector an extremely interesting candidate for research on SME sector new product management (De Toni and Nassimbeni 2003).

The start point in creating a new spectacle product is the generation of a new design. This new design provides the template from which to construct a prototype to evaluate both the aesthetics of the design and the viability of manufacturing the new product. A common problem which can emerge is poor interaction between designers, the marketing team and the manufacturing group. As a result, delays occur in decision-making. In some cases a lack of a close collaborative working relationship can result in the new product evolving into a completely non-viable proposition. A further complication in some firms appeared to be an orientation towards emphasising the importance of product functionality in terms of the role of improving users' vision. As a result the issue of the aesthetics aimed at maximising consumer appeal of the new design sometimes became forgotten or neglected in the battle to ensure new product development schedules were not disrupted.

To be able to manufacture the new design, raw materials, components and sometimes even new machine tools will need to be acquired. A problem which can emerge is poor collaboration between the company and suppliers. Delays occur while appropriate components are sourced or designs modified to reflect the need to utilise an alternative, lower cost input. Some of these problems could be mitigated by the use of computers to link together members of the spectacle supply chain. At the time of the study, there was an unwillingness of the firms to start utilising IT to improve inter-organisational communications.

The last phase of the new product development process is the effective management of the market launch. In the spectacle industry there is a significant time lag between a product being shown to the market, distributors making a stocking decision and goods finally being delivered. Another error which can occur in the industry is for a company not to initiate communications with the market until product manufacturing is about to commence. This will inevitably lengthen the time taken to successfully establish the new product in the market. The solution is to maintain closer links with distributors and involve them in the new product development project much earlier.

Innovation networks

A common problem among small firms is the scenario of resources constraints acting to limit business performance. Successful new product development is critically dependent on access to adequate resources in key areas such as market information, knowledge of new technologies, employee R&D skills, finance and access to specialist equipment. One way to overcome this problem is to collaborate with other organisations in the development of new products. A relatively common approach to become involved in a collaborative approach to innovation is to join a business network (Rogers 2004).

Research undertaken by Piore and Sabel (1984) was one of the catalysts for creating widespread interest in the potential for small firm innovation being able to benefit from the formation of business networks. Their study focused on certain industrial districts in Northern Italy to provide evidence about the benefits of networks for sustaining economic growth. The widespread acceptance of their views concerning the superiority of small firm networks in 'post-Fordist economies' (i.e. Western economies no longer dominated by large corporations exploiting mass production and mass marketing) caused the concept of network formation to be accepted by some Governments as a dominant economic regeneration model. For example, in Denmark, the Danish Technology Institute led a small business scheme promoting network formation which for a period utilised virtually the entire Danish Government's small business support budget (Chaston 1996).

Although other researchers have demonstrated the benefits of using small firm networks to assist innovation to achieve economic regeneration in industrial districts, subsequent studies have concluded that the interpretation of available data by Piore and Sabel may not have been totally accurate. Lazerson and Lorenzoni (1999), for example, raised doubts about the validity of the concept and conclusions which had been drawn. They undertook a longitudinal analysis of economic events in certain industrial districts in Italy. The researchers noted that the concept of a post-Fordist industrial model was not necessarily relevant. This is because many of the small firm artisan networks in Italy have existed since well before the twentieth-century move to exploit mass production. Furthermore, they noted that the destiny of small firms within business networks are under the complete control of the very large firms who are their customers. Unfortunately, some of these large firms, by continuing to operate a non-innovative, myopic strategy and apparently ignoring changes in world markets, have instead acted as an obstacle in terms of innovation being a primary business philosophy within some industrial regions.

The adverse influence of local large firms is described by Lazerson and Lorenzoni as 'over embeddedness'. This trait reflects an excessively inward looking orientation. These researchers believe the only reason growth through innovation has occurred is because of the arrival of 'external pollinators'. These latter sources have in many cases been intermediaries from overseas markets such as major upmarket US retailers. These firms are keen to purchase Italian fashion goods, but firstly have to persuade network members that their current products are not those being sought by customers in other countries.

As other researchers have concluded that not all small firms wish to participate in business networks, a more balanced view has begun to emerge about how these organisational structures can play a role in assisting entrepreneurial achievement in the SME sector (Kingsley and Malecki 2004). For example, evidence exists concerning the different ways in which small firms utilise networks to assist their new product development activities and will be influenced by the nature of their relationship with other network members (Elfring and Hulsink 2003). These are usually described in terms of 'weak' and 'strong' ties. Weak ties tend to be informal and the level of inter-firm interaction tends to vary over time. This type of tie is typically used when the small firm is seeking to access new or novel information. Such knowledge often exists in a tacit form in organisations such as research laboratories or Universities. The small firm will be required to extend their contacts beyond other network members in order to undertake a broader search to acquire information on 'leading edge' knowledge or technologies. Weak ties are also used by small firms in the resolution of a highly complex problem with which other regular network members have no experience.

Strong ties are usually associated with frequent interchange of information between network members with whom the small firm has established a relationship based upon mutual trust and commitment. The nature of the relationship is critical because innovation often involves the exchange of confidential or commercially sensitive data. This type of information is something which small firms would not be inclined to share with organisations about which the owner/manager has minimal prior experience. Hence the majority of collaborative new product development activities are associated with drawing on strong ties with existing network members to progress the project from idea identification through to market launch.

The actual structure of innovation networks will vary between industrial sectors and by country. In some cases the network will be a horizontal format with collaboration between firms at the same level within the supply chain. An example of this structure are small Nordic firms manufacturing equipment for fish farming who collaborate in both developing new products and in the joint exploitation of overseas markets. Other networks are of a vertical nature where suppliers, intermediaries or end users are seen as having a critical role in the provision of knowledge or resources. Mohannak's (2007) examination of small Australian firm networks in a bio-technology cluster, for example, revealed that these operations relied heavily on strong links with Universities, public sector research laboratories, large pharmaceutical firms and specialist medical staff working in hospitals. This latter group were perceived as a critical source of information. They provided information that led to new idea generation within the small firms and also guidance over product performance or specification during the prototype development phase. This researcher also concluded that a common view of small high technology firms using networks to achieve innovation may not always be a valid assumption. An illustration of this perspective was provided by a study of small Melbourne firms in the Australian IT industry. Although these firms faced severe challenges in the development of new products or services, most of these firms considered in-house R&D and other knowledge sources within the firm to be the crucial components for successful innovation. Very few firms used collaborative links with other firms in the supply chain as a source of assistance or providing access to scarce resources.

SUMMARY LEARNING POINTS

- Significant innovation may be caused by market disruption.
- Process innovation can be an effective way of developing a new product.
- The company leadership needs to be both visionary and guide the activities of the development team.
- Successful innovation depends on maximising the number of new ideas generated.
- The stage gate model may not be an appropriate process for managing entrepreneurial concepts.

(Cont'd)

- Entrepreneurs exhibit a more flexible approach to innovation process management.
- Participation in a business network will often enhance the ability of a small firm to be highly innovative.

ASSIGNMENTS

1 Using the Internet as a source of biographical data, demonstrate the degree to which you believe Steve Jobs is an effective developer of disruptive innovations.
2 Using the Internet as a source of biographical data, compare and contrast the innovation leadership skills of Henry Ford and Bill Gates.
3 How and why can business networks be utilised to assist the innovation process?

DISCUSSION TOPICS

1 Assume you are a member of a college/University team which has been asked to exploit innovation to generate higher future revenue for the organisation. Generate some ideas of products or services which might have potential.
2 Consider an organisation of which you have some familiarity such as a college/University or business in which you have worked. Identify how process innovation could assist in areas such as reducing operating costs, enhancing service quality and delivering teaching programmes.
3 Identify a possible new product idea that a college/University might adopt and determine the advantages/disadvantages of using the new product stage gate model to manage the development process.

Additional information sources

Disruptive innovation

Christensen, C.M., Johnson, M.W. and Ridgby, D.K. (2002), Foundations for growth: how to identify and build disruptive new businesses, *Sloan Management Review*, Vol. 43, No. 3, pp. 22–31.

Process innovation

Weiss, P. (2003), Adoption of product and process innovations in differentiated markets: the impact of competition, *Review of Industrial Organization*, Vol. 23, No. 3/4, pp. 301–312.

Entrepreneurial leadership

Kuratko, D. (2007), Entrepreneurial leadership in the 21st Century, *Journal of Leadership & Organizational Studies*, Vol. 13, No. 4, pp. 1–12.

Idea generation

Stasch, S.F., Lonsdale, R.T. and Lavenka, N.M. (1992), Developing a framework for sources of new-product ideas, *The Journal of Consumer Marketing*, Vol. 9, No. 2, pp. 5–16.

New product development process management

Cooper, R.G. (1994), New products: the factors that drive success, *International Marketing Review*, Vol. 11, No. 1, pp. 60–77.

Innovation networks

Harris, L., Coles, A. and Dickenson, K. (2000), Building innovation networks: issues of strategy and expertise, *Technology Analysis & Strategic Management*, Vol. 12, No. 2, pp. 229–242.

9

Entrepreneurial Promotion

Chapter objectives

The aims of this chapter are to assist the reader to:

- recognise that small entrepreneurial firms may lack adequate financial resources to support large scale promotional activity
- understand the entrepreneur as a personality can often provide the basis for an effective promotional platform
- comprehend that effective planning is critical in enhancing promotional cost–benefit relationships
- recognise that entrepreneurs should usually focus on promoting benefit superiority
- accept that benefit messages will need to change to reflect different customer purchase motivations
- understand a wide variety of different promotional channels options exist
- recognise the Internet is a very effective new channel through which to build customer awareness.

Promotional process

Promotional affordability

No matter what the size of the firm, the aim of promotion is to build awareness among potential or existing customers through the provision of appropriate information. In contrast with the large multi-national, branded goods companies, however, many smaller entrepreneurial firms face the obstacle of being constrained by very limited financial resources (Snell and Agnes 1994). The level of promotional spending in small firms can also be influenced by the owner/managers who may believe that the appeal for their new, innovative product is so strong that there is little need to spend significant funds on building awareness among potential customers.

Optimising the cost–benefit outcomes for any promotional campaign requires a detailed understanding of buyer behaviour (Araghna et al. 1991). Large organisations can draw on their accumulated market experience, market research studies or the skills of their advertising agency to assist in the acquisition and exploitation of data about how customers use information when making a purchase decision. One obstacle facing some small firms is their somewhat uninformed perception of what they consider is the very poor cost–benefit relationship associated with the cost of employing a market research agency and the fees charged by advertising agencies (Madden and Caballero 1987). It is also the case that the more successful advertising agencies prefer to avoid working with SME sector organisations. This is because they find that owner/managers tend not to appreciate how agency input can greatly improve the effectiveness of a promotional campaign (Dart 1980). With many entrepreneurs concluding that promotional campaigns are an expense they just cannot afford this can mean missing out on the more rapid growth in sales that might accrue from funding an adequate scale of promotional activity.

Personality promotion

In the case of well-known entrepreneurs, these individuals may be able to achieve increased market awareness without expending significant funds on promotional activity. This is because they are able to get free media exposure from being extremely newsworthy with journalists always keen to feature them in broadcasts or articles. For example, Sir Richard Branson's enthusiasm for activities such as cavorting around the sky in hot air balloons has been an invaluable source of media exposure for building awareness for his global Virgin brand. Sometimes the entrepreneur that has established a reputation as an entertainer will actually be paid to be the star of their own television show, thereby gaining additional promotional exposure for zero cost. Two recent examples of this phenomenon are provided by the television series *The Apprentice*, featuring Donald Trump in the USA and Sir Alan Sugar in the UK.

CASE STUDY

Taking the mousetrap to the customer

Case aims: To demonstrate how a change in promotional channel communication assisted the creation of what eventually became a highly successful, international entrepreneurial business.

An intentional misquotation of the American philosopher Ralph Waldo Emerson, in the marketing adage designed to communicate the important role of promotion is that 'one can invent the greatest mousetrap, but do not expect the world to beat a path to your door'. An entrepreneur who discovered the truth behind this guidance is Earl Tupper, the inventor of Tupperware (Brennan 2007). This individual was born in 1907 in New Hampshire and although he received only a minimal level of formal education, he was a serial inventor who achieved little success in selling any of his ideas to large companies. After his landscaping business collapsed during the Great Depression, he joined the plastics division of the chemical manufacturing giant, Du Pont. Although the early plastics were brittle and had an unpleasant odour, Tupper had the foresight to see the material as having huge potential. He discovered a lighter, more flexible plastic which could be shaped into small containers.

In 1947 he patented Tupperware's unique selling proposition, the sealing lid which forced out air and kept food fresher for longer. The product was not an instant success. Stockists were unwilling to spend time explaining the product's benefits to consumers and housewives did not understand how to use the special lid. Tupper was saved by Brownie Wise, a single mother from Detroit. She realised that to communicate the product's unique features, one had to communicate

(Cont'd)

directly with housewives. So she built up a network of women, paid on commission, who organised gatherings of friends at which to demonstrate the product. The idea of the 'Tupperware Party' was born and by 1951, the company had ceased marketing the product through retailers and relied entirely on promoting the brand using the direct selling approach.

Tupper could never have implemented this action because like many inventors, he was a shy recluse who only understood how to produce the containers. In contrast, Wise was an outgoing, flamboyant individual who drove a pink Cadillac, dyed her hair canary pink and was the first woman to be featured on the cover of *Business Week*. Unfortunately her behaviour was resented by Tupper whose rather puritanical attitude to life caused him to disapprove of her well publicised activities. Hence in 1958 he fired Wise on the grounds that she had betrayed the company ethos by endangering its reputation. By this time Tupperware was a successful, well established brand and Wise's departure had no adverse impact on company sales.

CASE STUDY

The founders are the promotion

Case aims: To illustrate how the activities and values of business founders can provide the basis for a firm's promotional strategy and consumer communication.

An example of entrepreneurs who achieve significant market awareness utilising very limited promotional expenditure are Ben Cohen and Jerry Greenfield, the founders of the highly successful ice-cream brand, Ben & Jerry's (Hanna 1995; Rigby 1998). In the 1970s, these two former hippies spent $5 on an ice-cream manufacturing correspondence course from Pennsylvania State University. They borrowed $12,000 to purchase and renovate an abandoned petrol station in Burlington, Vermont, in which to make ice-cream using old-fashioned rock-salt freezers. Their ice-creams were differentiated from other companies because the Ben & Jerry's formulations used only natural ingredients, featured chunks of fruit or chocolate and were marketed under memorable names such as 'Chunky Monkey' and 'Cherry Garcia'.

From day one in the new business, the two founders articulated very strong views about issues such as equality within their workforce, creating informal, relaxed working environments, the importance of strong business ethics and a commitment towards protection of the environment. Customers were attracted to the company by both their experience of buying products from a laid back, caring workforce and by the wide press coverage that Ben and Jerry achieved for both their opinions and their entrepreneurial activities. On the company's first anniversary they announced they would be giving away free ice-cream to all their loyal customers.

When a decision was needed about opening a West Coast manufacturing operation, the company opted to remain in Vermont and pay above market prices to help the state's declining dairy farming sector. At the point where sales hit $10 million, the company founded the Ben & Jerry's Foundation through which the company gave away 7.5 per cent of pre-tax profits to charity. The firm's unusual activities – when compared with other, more conventional US food companies – generated widespread media coverage. This, along with strong word-of-mouth recommendations from loyal customers, helped to sustain sales growth on a very limited promotional budget.

Another example of generating high awareness is provided in 1983 when the company decided to expand into Boston to determine their ability to survive in an urban market. At the beginning of their market launch, they plastered the city with posters announcing 'Two Crazy Vermont Hippies Invade Boston With Their Ice Cream'. When Häagen-Dazs, which then held a monopoly in the premium quality ice-cream market threatened distributors with the loss of their business if they also carried Ben & Jerry's, the two entrepreneurs took out a classified advertisement asking readers to 'help two Vermont hippies fight the Pillsbury Corporation'.

By 1984 when the company went public, it was operating 150 retail outlets across the country and also supplying the brand to major supermarket chains. The company shares were initially only offered to Vermont residences in order to encourage ownership among small, like-minded shareholders. The subsequent public listing on NASDAQ created a business valued at $110 million. This event was soon followed by having to fight a predatory takeover bid from Pillsbury. Ben & Jerry's response to this unwelcome approach was to implement various activities based around pillorying Pillsbury's iconic brand identifier, the Pillsbury Doughboy.

Having succeeded in the USA, the later company expanded into other large overseas consumer markets such as the UK and also into developing nation economies in Eastern Europe. During the 1990s, the two owners increasingly focused their personal efforts on the company's social work with communities both in the USA and overseas. These activities continued to create media coverage that further assisted in building stronger brand awareness and customer loyalty in both existing and newly entered overseas markets. After 23 years in the business, the two founders eventually decided it was time to step down and in 2000 the business was sold to Unilever for $326 million.

Promotional management

The planning process

Few entrepreneurs can ever aspire to also becoming media stars. Nevertheless, virtually every small firm does have the potential to create higher customer awareness by drawing on understanding of customer buying behaviour to implement low-cost, effectively targeted, promotional campaigns. The combined sources of experience gained through trading, membership of business networks and secondary data can all be exploited to generate information about customer buying behaviour (Bunn 1993). This knowledge will provide the basis from which to optimise the effectiveness of even a low budget, promotional campaign. Achieving this goal can be assisted by following the management process illustrated in Figure 9.1. The only significant difference between the process model shown in Figure 9.1 and

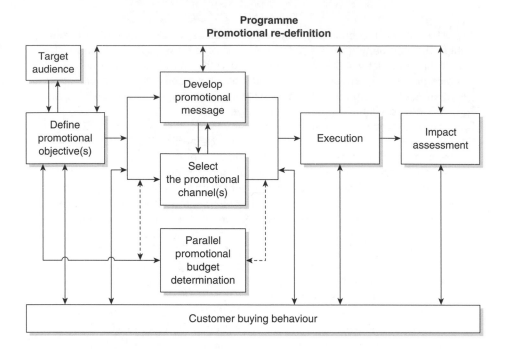

Figure 9.1   *The promotional planning process*

the large firm models presented in standard marketing texts, is the latter tend to recommend determination of the promotional budget prior to the development of the promotional message or the selection of a promotional channel. In contrast, most small firm entrepreneurs prefer to determine the promotional budget by adopting a more reiterative approach based on reassessing the scale of promotional expenditure on the basis of the new understanding which emerges during the message and channel selection process (Stewart and Gallen 1998).

All firms, no matter their size, must decide the target audience to whom the promotion will be directed (Stewart and Gallen 1998). Usually the choice of target will be between that group who are the largest new potential users or alternatively, current, existing users. The promotional objective is concerned with the specification of the communication task to be undertaken (Jones 1994). In those cases where the aim is to build new demand, the primary target audience will be new customers and the promotional task will be concerned with educating the target audience about the product benefit being offered. Where the promotion is aimed at existing customers, the task will be usually that of further persuasion which will focus on communicating product benefit or product value.

Crossing the chasm

A well established concept in new product marketing is the diffusion of innovation curve which proposes that customers can be divided into five groups known as innovators, early adopters, the early majority, the late majority and laggards. The

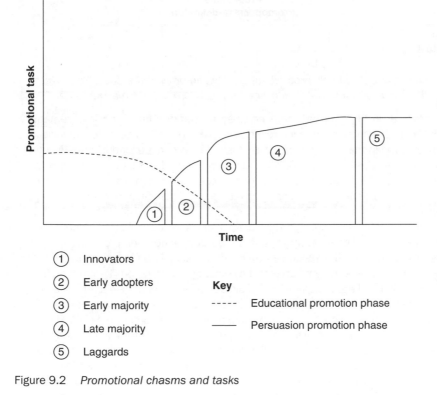

Figure 9.2   *Promotional chasms and tasks*

1. Innovators
2. Early adopters
3. Early majority
4. Late majority
5. Laggards

Key

- - - - -   Educational promotion phase
———   Persuasion promotion phase

time taken for a potential customer to purchase a product will depend on which group an individual is a member of. The first purchasers will be members of the innovator group. Having reviewed the launch of numerous high technology products, Geoffrey Moore (1991) proposed that the needs of each of these five groups are somewhat different. Innovators purchase the product because they wish to own the latest technology and are prepared to accept performance problems with the new product. Early adopters need to be persuaded that the product will work and thereby offer a new way to fulfilling their vision of how to exploit technology. The early and late majority will postpone purchase until they are persuaded the product offers a functional benefit not provided by existing products. Laggards are price sensitive and hence wait until the product is virtually obsolete before entering the market.

Moore used case materials from a number of product launches to demonstrate that these different needs will require the promotional message to be changed as the company seeks to 'cross the chasm' which exists between each of the five customer types. As illustrated in Figure 9.2, the implications of linking Moore's chasm theory with the requirement about overall promotional purpose of education followed by persuasion, are that the entrepreneur will need to revise the promotional message in recognition of the motivation to purchase within the customer group to whom the main focus of the promotional campaign is being directed.

CASE STUDY

Building a brand

Case aims: To illustrate how product superiority can provide the basis from which to build a successful international brand through word-of-mouth advertising.

The computer industry is fortunate because it operates in a high involvement environment in which customers respond rapidly to news about technological advances. Even in this situation, however, customers are influenced by prior experience and awareness of available brands within the market. This situation can create a huge obstacle for an entrepreneurial firm whose brand name is not known and where success is dependent on changing market attitudes. Such was the scenario facing the founder of the Taiwanese Acer company, Stan Shih (Barun 1989), because in the 1970s American firms were perceived as technological leaders and Taiwan had a reputation for supplying lower cost, prior generation products.

First established in 1976, Acer was launched with only $25,000 of equity. These funds and relatively low revenue meant the company was in no position to fund the scale of promotional expenditure which would be needed to change negative market attitudes towards Taiwanese electronic goods. The company survived by producing a diverse range of products for other Original Equipment Manufacturers (OEM) firms in sectors such as telecommunications, computers and computer games. From the outset, Shih's objective was to establish the Acer brand as a leading supplier of innovative, high quality products. In 1981, the company launched a learning kit called MicroProfessor which helped engineers and students learn about microtechnology. The firm was then one of earliest to enter the emerging home computer market offering an 8-bit and then a 16-bit PC. This was followed by the launch of the Acer 20 MHz 386 computer and in 1988 the Acer 1110/25 which was recognised as one of the world's fastest PCs. At the same time, the company was achieving added brand name recognition through being the first non-Japanese supplier of an English/Japanese bilingual software system and contributing to Microsoft's development of the first Chinese MS-DOS operating system.

Further recognition of the company's technological superiority came from being acknowledged as the leading designer of application specific integrated circuits (ASIC) chips. The consequence of these activities was that Acer was able to exploit 'word-of-mouth' advertising by IT experts in the computer industry which meant that the company's distributors had to expend much less promotional effort when seeking to attract new business-to-business (B2B) customers to the product range. In the late 1980s, further unprompted additional new customer interest was generated by Acer cracking the secrets of the IBM PS/2–30 model and launching a compatible system. Then in 1989, Acer launched their 80486 product which at that time was the fastest PC in the world. Despite the company continuing to only fund a relatively low level of promotional activity when compared with brands such as IBM, in 1990 Acer annual sales exceeded $1 billion.

Communication

No matter which promotional channel is selected, as shown in Figure 9.3, there are certain standard components influencing the communication process (Kotler 1997).

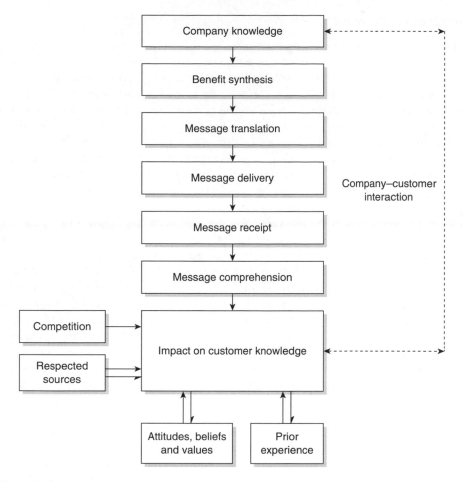

Figure 9.3 *The communication process*

The volume of information that can be delivered may be constrained by delivery time (e.g. the 30 second television commercial), available space (e.g. the size of a print advertisement) and the time the customer is prepared to allocate to receiving the information. This constraint usually necessitates the company distilling the knowledge into a briefer communication that will provide the basis for the promotional claim (see Figure 9.3).

As companies and customers rarely share a common language, the product claim will have to be translated into a form understood by the target audience. Once the promotional message has been received, the customer will process the information to comprehend what has been communicated. This new information will add to the customer's existing level of knowledge about the product. The impact of the promotional message will be influenced by a number of factors. These vary between product categories. Persons with a satisfactory prior experience of a product will have a more positive reaction to the benefit claim being communicated (Percy and Rossiter 1992). Customer response to a promotion will also be influenced by their existing attitudes, beliefs and values in relation to the depth of their interest (or 'involvement') in the product or service.

Product involvement

Houston et al. (1987) have suggested there are three types of involvement. Product involvement is the influence of the customer's prior purchase and consumption experience on their current individual needs and values. Situational involvement describes the individual's concern for their behaviour at each stage in the buying process. Response involvement refers to the persuasiveness of information which is provided to the customer. Munch and Hunt (1984 p. 32) posit response involvement is the most critical variable in terms of determining the effectiveness of a promotional message. They propose that 'involvement is the level of perceived personal importance and/or interest evoked by a stimulus (or stimuli) within a specific situation'. From this definition it can be concluded that in cases of low involvement goods (e.g. the decision to purchase a commodity such as potatoes) the customer will rapidly progress through the problem solving model of the type shown in Figure 9.3.

Some academics believe that in assessing potential response to promotional messages, it is necessary to recognise the influence of customer personality. Wilson (1973 p. 22) defines personality as a 'general disposition to behave' and contrasts this with attitude which he describes as 'opinions on something in the world outside'. He further posits that personality is a continuum. At one extreme customers seek consistency in their lives through the purchase of items which are familiar, comforting and reassuring. At the other extreme, there are customers who continually seek to be exposed to new and different experiences. Foxall and Goldsmith (1994) have concluded that this latter group are more likely to respond to entrepreneurial (i.e. unconventional) products and promotions because they are flexible thinkers, can tolerate a higher level of ambiguity, have high self-esteem and a positive attitude towards seeking out new sources of sensation.

Where the customer has a high level of involvement, but requires a high volume of information to acquire an adequate understanding of the product benefit, promotional budgetary constraints will usually require that the message be targeted at a relatively narrow target audience. In those cases where the customer is highly involved in the product and only needs a minimal volume of additional information, the promotional message should be directed at closing the sale. Low information needs occur when the customer feels sufficient knowledge has been acquired through product usage or input from respected sources. The attraction of this type of high involvement product is that even small firms with very limited promotional budgets can expect to enjoy promotional success.

Most low involvement products normally require a high level of promotional expenditure to achieve higher customer awareness. Products exhibiting this requirement are less appealing because usually a large promotional budget will be necessary to achieve an adequate level of product awareness (Pascale and Smart 1998). This is the typical scenario facing mass market, branded goods. Customers have a low information need, but numerous companies are all seeking to gain market share. It is the most expensive promotional environment in which to operate. Most entrepreneurial small firms would be advised to avoid this scenario because they lack the scale of financial resources required to execute a successful campaign. Furthermore should the small firm's promotional message begin to have an impact in the market, there is a high probability that the large firm incumbent elephants will finally awaken to the new threat and respond by dramatically increasing their level of promotional spending.

Communication channels

Firms selecting an appropriate promotional channel are able to choose from a number of options, such as the following:

- *Personal selling* which permits representatives of an organisation to enter into a dialogue with potential customers.
- *Advertising* which involves paying a fee for time or space to a third party such as a radio station or a local newspaper.
- *Word-of-mouth (or referral) advertising* whereby satisfied customers recommend the product or service supplier to others.
- *Direct marketing* which focuses on individual customers by using techniques such as direct mail or the telephone.
- *Public relations* which involves persuading the media to feature the firm in articles and broadcasts.

Face-to-face dialogue is the most effective form of communication. Given access to an unlimited promotional budget, most organisations would opt to rely on personal selling as their only channel through which to deliver customer information. In a world where cost–benefit outcomes determine decisions, the use of salespeople will be restricted to those situations where there are few customers and each makes high unit value purchases. Hence both large and small firms tend to restrict personal selling to B2B markets.

Any organisation considering the use of advertising to deliver a promotional message has a variety of media from which to choose. These include channels such as television, radio, newspapers, magazines and directories. Selection of the most appropriate media is influenced by factors such as required market coverage, the absolute cost of the advertising space and the channel through which the majority of customers within a market sector acquire information. Research on advertising selection decisions indicates that most smaller entrepreneurial firms tend to use newspapers and business directories. These are perceived as both more affordable and appropriate than other mass market media such as television or radio (Van Aucken et al. 1992).

Yellow Pages is possibly the most popular directory vehicle among small firms. This is because *Yellow Pages* is the medium most frequently used by consumers seeking to identify a local supplier. How long this situation will last is questioned by some industry observers. The advent of the Internet and the ease with which people can undertake on-line searches is reducing the proportion of the population who use paper-based directories to locate products and services (Klassen 2006). The response to this scenario is that *Yellow Pages* has moved on-line through the creation of the Yell.com Website. Nevertheless, in recognition of the fact that the majority of potential customers prefer to use Google™ or Yahoo!, Yell.com has also become a major advertiser on these two search engine sites.

Once an entrepreneurial firm has established a loyal customer base, word-of-mouth referral by existing, satisfied customers can often become the most effective method through which to attract new business (Money et al. 1998). Once this outcome is achieved this may then permit a decrease in advertising expenditure. Another factor which has assisted both large and small firms to enhance the cost–benefit effectiveness of their promotional activities has been the declining costs of postal services and increasing levels of telephone ownership in most developed countries (Jones and

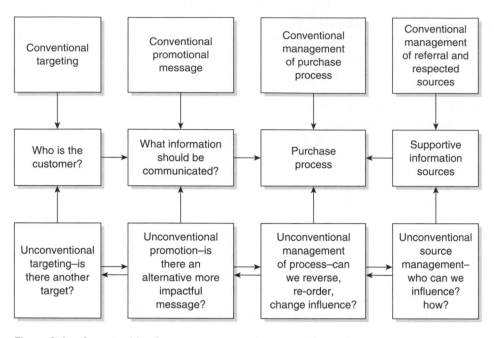

Figure 9.4   *Opportunities for an entrepreneurial approach to promotion*

Source: Chaston (2000), *Entrepreneurial Marketing*, Macmillan Business, Basingstoke. Reproduced with permission of Palgrave Macmillan.

Chudry 2001). These trends have made direct marketing an extremely cost effective proposition. In many consumer markets, spending on direct marketing now exceeds that of television advertising. The medium is also extremely popular in B2B markets because of the low costs of being able to rapidly distribute customer-specific communications across an entire market sector.

Public relations can be an effective low-cost promotional vehicle where the small firm is the source of a newsworthy story of interest to the media (Moss et al. 2003). Sometimes owner/managers may self-manage contact with the media. Additionally there is always the chance that a local media story may subsequently be taken up by the national media. In most cases, however, where the small firm is depending on public relations to ensure a consistent, regular appearance in the media, this will usually require the services of a public relations agency. Furthermore, a public relations agency will usually become a mandatory expenditure in those cases where the small business needs to deflect the potentially damaging influence caused by media interest in organisational problems (e.g. guests at a hotel taken to hospital due to an outbreak of food poisoning).

In planning a promotion, most organisations opt for following the current conventions which prevail in their industrial sector. There are, however, two potential problems with this philosophy (Chaston 2000a). Firstly, should competitors act aggressively and increase their level of promotional expenditure, then the firm could be forced into also increasing their own promotional activity in order to avoid losing market share. Secondly, smaller firms rarely have the scale of financial resources to counter the threat posed by competitors' increased promotional activity. Given these potential drawbacks of following prevailing conventions, a very feasible alternative is for the small firm to adopt a more entrepreneurial attitude in relation to promotional activities. As summarised in Figure 9.4 the four available options are (1) target a different customer group, (2) communicate an unconventional promotional message,

(3) identify a new way of managing the purchase process or (4) find an unconventional approach to stimulating referrals.

CASE STUDY

Unconventional promotion

Case aims: To illustrate how promotional effectiveness can be enhanced by adopting an entrepreneurial approach to customer communication.

Different customer – Nettimarket.com

In 1998, with initial share capital of $4,100, Aki and Eija Teranto decided to create an Internet grocery store in Finland (Jelassi and Enders 2005). They decided to name their on-line outlet Nettimarket. Aki realised that he would have to compete with existing retailers who were moving on-line, so to achieve price parity and generate an adequate profit, his business model was to link up with an existing grocery products wholesaler which eliminated warehousing and procurement costs. After a few months' trading, Nettimarket was failing to attract Finnish consumers and Aki recognised that to expand there was a need to promote the company to a completely different target audience.

In Finland, changes in the availability of welfare funding has led to more elderly and disabled people living at home or with relatives. The size of this market has been expanded because hospitals are releasing patients much more rapidly after surgery. Aki decided that this situation offered a new opportunity by targeting promotional activity towards home-helpers. To minimise the costs of the promotional campaign Aki worked with the city council's welfare officer responsible for managing the home-helpers employed by the council. The appeal of an on-line service to these individuals is that they can now avoid having to spend 45–60 minutes shopping for each client. Although Nettimarket had to invest resources in training home-helpers in placing on-line orders, this target audience has generated the revenue to make the company profitable.

Different message – The Body Shop

By the time the British entrepreneur Dame Anita Roddick decided to open her first retail outlet selling health and beauty products she had already developed strong personal convictions about issues such as industrial pollution and the need to protect the environment (Anon. 1996). From her earlier travels in the Far East she had already become convinced of the benefits of using natural ingredients and her social conscience prompted her wherever possible to source products from economically deprived areas of the world. Her other very strong conviction was that it was completely wrong of the beauty care industry to use animals as the way to test product safety. Hence when Anita opened her new business, called The Body Shop, instead of communicating the standard promotional message about how her products could fulfil the beauty and skin care needs of women, she focused on communicating that her products were natural, organic and none of her suppliers used animals in any product safety tests. This unconventional product promise was immediately appealing to women and The Body Shop rapidly expanded.

(Cont'd)

Different process – Dell

When IBM moved to open product architecture, this permitted others in the computer industry to produce low priced, IBM 'clones'. One of these new firms, located in Austin, Texas, was founded in 1984 by an outstanding entrepreneur, Michael S. Dell. He concluded that the prevailing industry practice of selling home computers through local distributors was fundamentally flawed. Their sales staff lacked the technical knowledge to effectively service their customers' needs and these outlets were keeping prices high by adding a very high mark-up. His solution was to sell Dell computers direct to the consumer using direct marketing techniques such as telephone selling and mail order catalogues. By removing the intermediary from the purchase process, Dell was able to offer products at a highly competitive price. The direct link with the final user allowed Dell to gain a detailed understanding of customer needs and to develop the proposition of offering people a 'customised' PC.

The competitive advantage created by the Dell business model was sufficient to permit the company to become a global player. Additionally, because the company had already acquired the competencies and technologies associated with direct marketing, this gave the firm a massive lead over competitors when the advent of the Internet permitted the on-line marketing of electronics products.

Different referral – The Arctic Monkeys

Ever since the advent of commercial radio in the 1920s, a critically important referral source about new music stars, bands and groups has been the radio DJs (Anon. 2006d). These individuals' 'word-of-mouth' (WOM) advertising could make or break new musicians fighting to sell their first record. Recognising the massive task associated with achieving mention of their group by leading DJs in the UK, caused the Sheffield band The Arctic Monkeys to adopt a very different referral approach. As with many new groups, they had toured the country and at gigs handed out CD singles to build a loyal base of fans. Having recognised the power of the Internet, they started putting their tracks on-line so that people could download, listen and discuss their music. On-line loyal fans exploited the free, mass communication benefits of the Internet to introduce others to The Arctic Monkeys.

This approach of utilising the Internet to generate product interest by referral is usually known as 'viral marketing'. To exploit the benefits of viral marketing The Arctic Monkeys let it be known they were working on their first album and excited fans were debating their hopes and expectations for months in e-mails and blogs long before the album was released. The result was that when this album, *Whatever People Say I Am, That's What I'm Not*, arrived in the record stores, 360,000 copies were sold in the first week, outselling the combined unit sales of all other albums then in the UK Top 20.

On-line promotion

By the early 1990s, the world had come to accept that ongoing advances in the computer and telecommunications industries were likely to have a major impact across both consumer and industrial markets well into the next century. However, with the exception of a small number of visionary technology futurists, most academics and industry experts had no comprehension of the scale of impact the launch of the World Wide Web would have on revolutionising virtually every aspect of the marketing process (Chaston 2000b). Supporters of the technology tended to perceive the Internet as a communications tool that could provide the basis for a totally new promotional concept. The primary reason for this assumption was that early entrants into cyber world were small firms creating promotional Websites. At that time, the cost of back office technology to permit selling products on-line was prohibitive. The exceptions were organisations such as Dell Computers and Cisco, the leading producer of switches and routers, who already had extensive experience of direct marketing IT-based management systems. This permitted them to rapidly exploit their existing electronic information exchange capability to create on-line purchasing systems.

Initially the World Wide Web was hailed as the technology which would democratise the promotional process. This perspective was based on the fact that even small firms could afford to create an on-line presence and then rely on potential customers locating their Web page through the use of search engines. This claim soon proved invalid, however, because most potential customers were not prepared to extend their search beyond the first ten addresses generated in a search. Additionally, the promise of a more democratic world began to disappear as search engines started to offer the facility of charging a fee to guarantee the appearance of a firm at the top of any on-line search.

In the early years of the Internet, the primary users were buyers in certain industrial markets and the more technology orientated consumer. Awareness of the technology as a new mass market channel was first awakened by the entrepreneur Jeff Bezos when he launched his on-line book store, Amazon.com. The underlying strategic philosophy behind Amazon, however, was less about utilising the Internet as a promotional channel. The primary focus was to offer consumers the opportunity to purchase books electronically. Observing the rapid rate of market penetration for this new retail brand, some academics and industry observers were quick to forecast the demise of many traditional terrestrial businesses. These experts were also highly critical of large consumer goods companies and retailers who they felt had entirely misunderstood the strategic potential of the on-line world. Undoubtedly some large firms were blind to the potential offered by the Internet. In most organisations, however, there was an understanding that the real opportunities would not emerge until the Internet achieved greater market penetration, the technology evolved to the point where faster downloads were possible and the quality of transmission of visual materials had significantly improved. Additionally experienced mass marketing companies such as Procter & Gamble sensibly avoided the new medium until techniques had been developed which could measure the overall level of site visitors, how many consumers were 'clicking through' to a specific site and the number of pages being viewed by each visitor.

Major companies interested in the Internet were also aware that until significants advances had been achieved in software development, it was very expensive to develop the back office systems needed to effectively support on-line purchasing. The more enlightened firms knew they did not have to be first movers in this market because purely on-line operations such as Amazon faced the hugely expensive problem of needing to use traditional promotional methods to build market awareness of their on-line existence. Once software costs began to fall, then major retailers implemented on-line selling to complement their terrestrial outlets (Constantinides 2004). The commercial validity of this strategic philosophy, which became known as 'clicks and mortar' operations, was demonstrated by the success of firms such as Tesco and Wal-Mart. Barnes & Noble, the largest terrestrial book retailer in America, exploited awareness of the company brand name such that within 18 months of their on-line market launch, this company was generating a profit from this new operation. In contrast Jeff Bezos would have to continue to struggle for many years before Amazon became a financially viable business proposition (Mellahi and Johnson 2000).

Other electronic media such as radio and television took many years to become established as effective promotional channels through which to reach a large number of customers. This is in contrast with the speed with which the Internet has rapidly changed the way organisations now communicate with customers. The technology offers the appealing benefits of permitting interactivity, global access, precise targeting, flexibility and message enhancement through the exploitation of multi-media interfaces. Having created a Web presence, any organisation can also amplify their promotional activity by the introduction of on-line advertising campaigns using techniques such as banners and site sponsorship. Interested viewers can then 'click through' to an advertiser's destination site where audio and video permit communication of detailed information about a product or service.

Major consumer brands have recognised that the Internet offers two types of communication opportunity (Cosgrove 2001). Firstly, in the case of established brands, terrestrial promotional activity can be complemented by creating informational sites offering new knowledge and assistance in relation to the context in which the product is utilised. For example, the disposable nappy brand Huggies provides parents with guidance and assistance over issues associated with caring for their babies. Secondly, the Internet offers a way of reaching the teenager and young adult market sectors, both of whom are becoming increasingly difficult to reach through traditional media such as television and magazines. In the USA, for example, the brewer Anheuser-Busch, executed a promotional campaign aimed at young people by sponsoring Golden Tee Golf which is a coin-operated, on-line golf game which is accessible at bars and taverns across the country and is accessed by over 100,000 players every month.

Sales promotions have also successfully migrated to the Web. Numerous companies now use the technology to distribute money off coupons, free samples and to support contests and sweep stakes. One unfortunate side effect of the technology, however, has been the emergence of technology to identify people's contact information and to use this knowledge to distribute millions of unwanted e-mails. Known as 'spams', despite the ongoing activities of major software suppliers to add systems which block these messages, many users continue to find their e-mail account is stuffed full of these unwanted communications.

The acceptance of the World Wide Web has now reached the point where in countries such as the USA expenditure on Internet promotions exceeds that of television advertising. As a result, similar to the scenario that has long existed in other media, the stage has now been reached where the interaction between supply and demand means the cost of purchasing on-line advertising space makes the activity prohibitively expensive for many SME sector organisations. Nevertheless, for even the smallest of firms, especially in service sectors such as hotels and restaurants, operation of a Website has become a mandatory expense without which sales revenue can be severely reduced (Takacs and Freiden, 1998).

CASE STUDY

An entrepreneurial disaster – Boo.com

Case aims: To illustrate that on-line operations is exactly the same as terrestrial marketing in that success is dependent on having a business idea which is based on attracting a high level of consumer demand in order to recover operating costs.

In 1998 Ernst Malmsten and Kasja Leander became one of the world's first dot.com millionaires after selling their bookstore, Bokus.com, to a large Swedish media company (Stockport et al. 2001). Leander was keen to create the first trend setting, global, on-line company selling the latest fashions. She, Malmsten and Patrik Henderson, the financier who managed the sale of Bokus.com, established their new offices in Carnaby Street, London and began to seek financial backers for their new venture Boo.com.

The New York financial sector was desperate to become investors in new on-line ventures. JP Morgan took a 5 per cent stake for $12 million and in less than 12 months, the founders of Boo.com raised almost $130 million. None of these investors apparently attempted to assess the financial implications associated with this level of borrowing. Even the simplest of calculations, assuming a net profit of 10 per cent on sales, would have immediately revealed that to just break even, Boo.com would need to generate annual sales in the region of $1 billion/annum.

Execution of the Boo.com strategy required (a) software capable of managing a global operation and (b) investment in a huge promotional campaign to achieve broadscale consumer awareness of the company brand name. Malmsten and Leander decided to embark on the most notoriously dangerous aspect of IT development; namely integrating state of the art software from various suppliers as the basis for building their electronic trading system. Lacking appropriate in-house staff, they hired the Swedish company Ericsson to manage the integration. This was despite the fact that Ericsson had no previous experience in this area of computing.

Development work commenced in May 1998 with the aim of launching Boo.com within 12 months. Ericsson made slow progress on systems integration and Malmsten decided the company would take over the project. New staff were hired in the UK, USA, Germany and Sweden. To ensure the creation of global brand awareness for the brand, Leander commenced spending her $42 million marketing budget. Billboard and magazine advertising space was booked and in early 1999, television advertising commenced on MTV in America and ESPN in Europe.

With the company still struggling to complete systems integration, the on-line launch was postponed to June 1999. It was not until July, however, that the company was in a position to test their launch platform. The test failed and the whole computer system crashed. JP Morgan was becoming increasingly concerned at the rate the company was burning through funds. Another round of financing was urgently required and Goldman Sachs was persuaded to take a stake in Boo.com. Their participation decision was made at the peak of the dot.com investment hysteria. Ongoing technical problems resulted in the new launch date of October 1999 also being missed. With an extensive television

(Cont'd)

advertising campaign scheduled to commence within weeks on 2 November 1999 Leander appeared on CNN to announce the launch of Boo. com.

Operating problems emerged immediately. The site had been designed for access by people owning high speed computers and the latest Web browsers. Most consumers lacked PCs incorporating such features. Less than 25 per cent of people who tried were able to gain access to the site. Boo.com sought another injection of capital. This time JP Morgan insisted on much more stringent lending terms, including the demand that Boo.com cut staff by 25 per cent. At the beginning of January 2000, Boo.com's burn rate on expenditure was over $1 million/week and sales were still very poor. Everyday on-line prices were no lower than in terrestrial shops, but in order to reduce a massive inventory, discounts of 40 per cent had to be announced. With expenditure still in excess of sales revenue, JP Morgan resigned as Boo.com's advisor. Other investors were only willing to provide more capital if the company raised an additional $25 million from other sources. Unable to fulfil this requirement on 17 May 2000, the company went into liquidation.

SUMMARY LEARNING POINTS

- Small entrepreneurial firms may lack adequate financial resources to support large scale promotional activity
- The entrepreneur as a personality can be an effective promotional platform
- Effective planning is critical in achieving optimal promotional cost–benefit relationships
- Entrepreneurs should focus on promoting benefit superiority
- Benefit messages will need to change to reflect different purchase motivations
- There is a need to evaluate the different promotional channel options that exist
- The Internet is very effective for building customer awareness.

ASSIGNMENTS

1 Using a magazine which you read regularly, select two different advertisements for two different types of product. Based upon the content of these two advertisements, compare and contrast how the two companies are seeking to communicate their promotional message.

2 Prepare a report examining the advantages and disadvantages associated with the various terrestrial promotional channels available to advertisers.

3 Select two Websites run by different consumer goods companies. Based on the content of these two Websites, compare and contrast how the two companies are seeking to communicate their promotional message, and also present your views on which of the two Websites is the most effective.

DISCUSSION TOPICS

1 Obtain a recent copy of a college prospectus. Discuss what you perceive to be the strengths and weaknesses of this promotional vehicle in relation to the target audience(s) to whom you feel the prospectus is aimed.

2 Obtain a copy of a newspaper containing advertisements for managerial posts in the private and public sector. Select an advertisement from an organisation in each of the two sectors. Compare and contrast the promotional approach utilised by the two advertisers. Discuss which of the two is the more effective as a recruitment communication.

3 Visit two different college Websites. Discuss what you perceive to be the strengths and weaknesses of the two Websites in relation to the target audience(s) to whom you feel these on-line communications are aimed.

Additional information sources

Promotional process

Ghingold, M. (1988), Bridging theory and practice in the allocation of sales management resources, *The Journal of Business & Industrial Marketing*, Vol. 3, No. 2, pp. 17–27.

Kelly, K.J. and Hoel, R.F. (1991), The impact of size, color, and copy quantity on *Yellow Pages* advertising effectiveness, *Journal of Small Business Management*, Vol. 29, No. 4, pp. 64–72.

Priluck, R. and Till, B.D. (2004), The role of contingency awareness, involvement, and need for cognition in attitude formation, *Academy of Marketing Science Journal*, Vol. 32, No. 3, pp. 329–345.

Rao, A. and Lilien, G. (1972), A system of promotional models, *Management Science*, Vol. 19, No. 2, pp. 152–161.

On-line promotion

Bharadwaj, P.N. and Soni, R.G. (2007), E-commerce usage and perception of e-commerce issues among small firms: results and implications from an empirical study, *Journal of Small Business Management*, Vol. 45, No. 4, pp. 501–522.

Faber, R.J., Lee, M. and Nan, X. (2004), Advertising and the consumer information environment online, *The American Behavioral Scientist*, Vol. 48, No. 4, pp. 447–467.

Levenburg, N.M., Schwarz, T.V. and Motwani, J. (2005), Understanding adoption of Internet technologies among SMEs, *Journal of Small Business Strategy*, Vol. 16, No. 1, pp. 51–70.

10

Pricing and Distribution

Chapter objectives

The aims of this chapter are to assist the reader to:

- recognise the common error of both entrepreneurs and conventional small firms is to use 'cost plus pricing'
- comprehend that successful pricing of an entrepreneurial product or service is determined by the nature of customer expectations
- understand there is a need to assess the cost implications associated with supplying goods when determining an optimal price
- accept that pricing decisions also have to recognise the influence of macro-environmental factors
- recognise an alternative to a price reduction is to offer a sales promotion
- understand new products face the hurdle of identifying intermediaries willing to link the supplier with the end user
- recognise that selection of distribution channels will be influenced by those pathways which can offer consumer satisfaction
- comprehend a new distribution concept can offer the basis of launching a new entrepreneurial business proposition
- understand the Internet is now dominated by large terrestrial brands
- recognise the Internet has led to the emergence of consumer led on-line communities.

Demand pricing

Pricing error

Price is possibly the most critical variable in the marketing process. On the basis of a number of studies of pricing by small firms Pitt et al. (1997) expressed concern that a common error is a preference for 'cost plus pricing' using the formula: price = cost per unit + desired profit per unit. Their criticism of this approach is that although the formula is intuitively appealing, it will be purely fortuitous if the resultant price is acceptable to customers. This is because, in virtually every situation, customers, not firms, determine price.

Reports in the literature about the high predominance of small firms using cost plus pricing has led to the conclusion by many academics that virtually all owner/managers adopt a very simplistic approach to pricing by merely evaluating costs when determining price. Some researchers, however, either by adopting a qualitative approach in seeking to understand pricing practices (e.g. Curran et al. 1995) or by utilising more carefully crafted survey questions that permit a more in-depth analysis of the data obtained (e.g. Friel 1999) have concluded that price-setting by owner/managers is not the simplistic, mechanistic process that has frequently been described in the literature. By undertaking a more rigorous, in-depth research approach these latter types of study reveal that the more entrepreneurial small firms clearly perceive pricing as a critically important aspect of the marketing mix. Owner/managers are willing to revise prices in relation to both prevailing economic circumstances and also in recognition that different customer segments exhibit different levels of sensitivity to product or service pricing. Hence it can be concluded that these more entrepreneurial firms understand the risks associated with cost plus pricing and recognise the significant benefits that accrue from adopting a more flexible, demand orientated pricing philosophy.

Demand pricing

Demand orientated pricing is an approach that is based on the premise that prices are determined by customer expectations (Cannon and Morgan 1990). Gaining an understanding of customer price expectations can be achieved by acquiring data from potential and existing customers or sometimes, by observing the pricing behaviour of successful competitors. Assuming a small firm is able to measure internal operating costs and prevailing market prices, then by restating the 'cost plus' formula in the form of profit = price – costs, the entrepreneur can calculate the achievable profit per unit of sale associated with setting the price equal to customer expectations. Should the resultant profit figure be unacceptable, the option is to examine whether opportunities exist to either increase price or reduce operating costs.

In reviewing the price response options available in an increasingly turbulent world, Pitt et al. (1997) have concluded that in many cases the more innovative orientation found within entrepreneurial firms will usually cause these organisations to identify specialist market niches that can be occupied where, through product or service modification, it is feasible to charge a premium price. If this type of repositioning is not possible, however, and no opportunities exist to reduce operating costs, then the only other realistic alternative is to identify a completely new market opportunity where competitor pricing behaviour is not a barrier to achieving an adequate level of profitability. A similar conclusion over entrepreneurial pricing behaviour was reached in Cunningham and Hornby's (1993) case-based examination of UK small firm behaviour. These researchers found that virtually all of the firms in their study adopted a highly flexible attitude to pricing decisions in relation to market circumstances and also the financial importance of the customer being served. The firms avoided situations which involved attracting business through aggressive pricing. Instead they used product quality and service provision personalisation as the basis for differentiating their operations from competition.

Cost factors

Further information on the implications of altering price or operating costs is provided in the conceptual diagrams, Figures 10.1 and 10.2. These indicate that as a firm moves from a low to a high product performance specification, costs will rise. Customers are normally willing to pay a price for superior specification products. With most products or services, however, there is a minimum and maximum

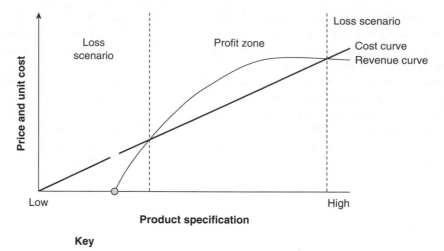

Key

○ Minimum specification acceptable to customers

Figure 10.1   *Price and cost relationships*

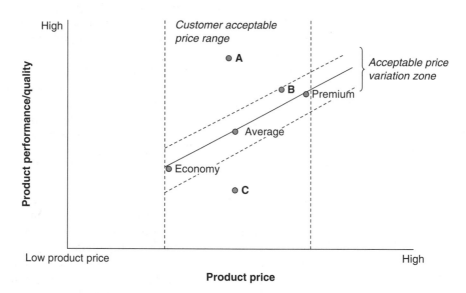

Figure 10.2   *Value price relationships*

specification below and above which customers will not purchase. This means there is only a restricted product specification range within which costs and customer expectations will permit the generation of a profit.

Although customer expectations should dominate the pricing decision firms must also remain alert to how certain key variables can impact operating costs. As illustrated in Figure 10.3, when implementing a price change based on rising operating costs it will be necessary to determine whether a price increase is feasible. Change can only be contemplated where customers will accept the revised price (Moorthy 2005). Premises and equipment are usually considered as an overhead, a proportion of which is allocated to each unit of goods or services produced. Product customisation increases production costs. New technologies usually lead to

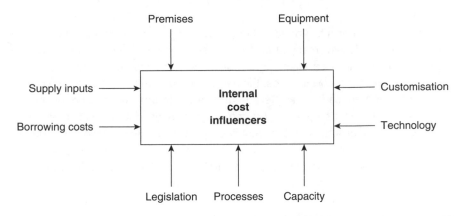

Figure 10.3   *Cost influencers*

a reduction in operating costs. Falling production capacity utilisation will increase operating costs, whereas a rising level of production will reduce unit costs. A firm's total product processing costs can be influenced by other factors such as machine downtime or inefficient use of production equipment.

CASE STUDY

The inconvenience factor

Case aims: To illustrate how consumers are willing to forgo convenience in order to obtain goods at a lower price.

In determining price expectations, it is important to recognise that price expectation can be influenced by the degree of purchase inconvenience the customer is willing to accept. An illustration of the influence of requiring lower prices in return for undergoing greater inconvenience is provided by the purchasing behaviour of older people for prescription medicines in the USA (Brink 2003). The total annual drugs bill in the USA is $160 billion and people over 65 have over five times as many prescriptions filled as individuals still in work. Unlike Europe, where the welfare system often permits prescription drugs to be made available free of change or at a subsidised price, Americans even when in receipt of Medicaid or covered by a private health insurance scheme, still have to find a significant proportion of the drug costs themselves. An added burden is the fact that Americans face the world's highest prices for prescription drugs.

The entrepreneurial solution which has emerged in Canada and Mexico is pharmacists who have opened outlets near to the border to service the needs of Americans who are willing to travel some distance to save money on medicines. In theory it is illegal for private citizens to import prescription drugs into the USA. However, as long as people cross the border with prescriptions and return with not more than a three-month supply of medicines for personal use, the customs and other federal officials leave them alone. The State of Maine, for example, is

(Cont'd)

bounded on the north by Canada where on average drug prices are 60 per cent lower. Not surprisingly, many of Maine's elderly population are willing to suffer the inconvenience of participating in organised bus trips across the border to gain access to these lower prices. Similar behaviour can be found in the southern states of America such as Nevada and Texas. In this instance people head south to cities such as Tijuana in Mexico where savings of up to 70 per cent are available. For individuals who cannot face or are unable to travel to another country, however, Internet entrepreneurs have now intervened to provide a solution. This has resulted in a growing number of on-line pharmacies based in Canada who are more than willing to supply the American market.

Category influencers

Customer expectations

When setting and reviewing prices, as shown in Figure 10.4, firms have to be aware there are a number of category level variables that can cause customers' price expectations to change over time (Theodosiou and Katsikeas 2001). The existence of such variables demands that entrepreneurial small firms must remain extremely alert to any evidence that behaviour shifts are occurring among their target customers. One such factor is the level of personal income. Consumers approaching retirement and whose children have left home, for example, tend to feel financially secure. This causes them to purchase higher quality goods than they may have done in the past. The trait explains why many older couples make purchases such as a luxury car or a world cruise when approaching or commencing their retirement.

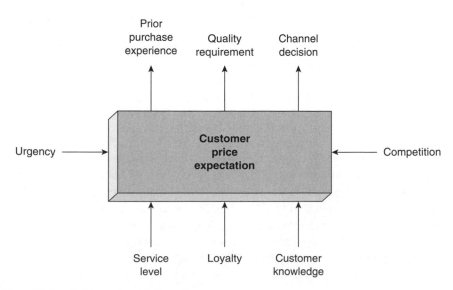

Figure 10.4   *Category level influencers*

In the case of consumer electronic goods, customers' prior purchase experience usually causes them to expect average prices to decline over time (Lal and Rao 1997). This expectation is amplified when prices have been consistently falling for a number of years. The outcome is that when a new technology first appears in the market (e.g. plasma screen televisions), the majority of consumers will postpone their purchase until they perceive prices are beginning to fall. The impact of this behaviour trait on Western nation electronics manufacturers unable to match the rapidly declining prices from nations such as Korea, is that survival has only been possible by relocating or outsourcing their production to low labour cost Pacific Rim countries.

Customer loyalty

The way price influences customer loyalty is not always easy to predict (Shoemaker 2003). Loyal customers for branded goods are usually willing to pay a higher price when purchasing their favourite brand in some product categories. In other cases, however, consumers expect their loyalty to be rewarded through being offered a repeat purchase discount or receiving higher priority when making a subsequent purchase. The degree to which loyalty is influenced by price appears to vary with age (Mogelonsky 1995). Research on American consumers undertaken by the *Better Homes and Gardens* magazine revealed that although lower prices were the dominant factor in causing people to switch supermarkets, this variable has declining influence as people grow older. Pensioners, for example, are much more loyal to their primary retail outlet and less likely to be influenced by lower prices available elsewhere in their immediate neighbourhood. Instead other variables such as attentive employees, rapid response to requests for assistance, positive reaction to complaints and store cleanliness are all factors which are more important in retaining retiree store loyalty.

Macro-environmental factors

As summarised in Figure 10.5, macro level factors can influence customer price sensitivity. Unlike category level factors, where firms may be able to forecast the impact of change, assessing the potential influence of macro level factors on customer behaviour is more difficult. Macro level influencers can cause entire groups within a population to revise their attitudes about personal wealth and financial security (Bigelow and Chan 1992). An increase in the rate of income tax, for example, will cause consumers to be concerned about future disposable income and increase their level of price sensitivity. They will usually cut back on personal expenditure and actively seek out the lowest available prices. National companies seeking to sustain sales in this situation are often forced to put pressure on their suppliers to reduce prices. These cost savings can then be passed on to consumers in the form of lower price. Small firms lack the power to demand a similar response from their suppliers, but nevertheless, to counteract their larger competitors, they may still be forced to reduce prices. Under these circumstances, the probable outcome for smaller firms is a major erosion in profit margins.

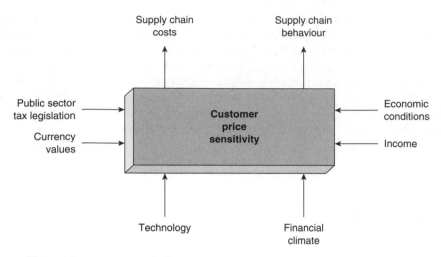

Figure 10.5   *Macro consumer influencers*

CASE STUDY

Pricing innovation

Case aims: To illustrate the implications of innovation in terms of an influence on pricing strategies.

At the end of the Second World War, Akita Morita joined his friend Mr Ibuka in Tokyo to found the Tokyo Telecommunications Laboratory (Anon. 1973). With just seven employees the company focused on producing communications equipment for telephone companies and from there moved into manufacturing tape recorders. In 1952 Mr Ibuka thought that an opportunity existed to develop new products if Western Electric in the USA would grant him a licence to manufacture transistors. At that time everybody thought that because transistors only operated at very high frequencies, the only application for them would be in hearing aids. Through further research, Mr Ibuka developed a new version of the device which could be used to build a transistor radio. Although beaten to the market by a small American company, Regency Corporation, by 1957 Akita Morita's entrepreneurial marketing skills had permitted the company, now re-named Sony Corporation, to become an international market leader in transistor radios.

In recognition of the fact that the small size of the transistor radio was perceived as offering greater value and convenience than the existing, larger valve-based, portable radios, Morita launched the new product at a premium price. The radio was followed by the first transistorised television and even though the screen was much smaller than any other existing TV sets, again the smaller size proposition was seen by Akita Morita as justifying the basis of marketing the product at a premium price. By the time the company launched an even smaller TV, Sony had established a market image of offering innovative, quality electronic goods at a premium price. Consumers' acceptance of Sony's pricing strategy of higher value/higher price was further consolidated by their launch of the first colour television using a single electron gun in place of the much bulkier three guns used in competitors' products.

Price-based competition

Many graduates leave Business Schools around the world imprinted with Michael Porter's theory that the only secure and sustainable strategy is to differentiate the firm from competition by offering a premium priced, superior product. Quantitative validation of the philosophy has been generated by inter- and intra-sectoral organisational performance studies undertaken by the long running Profit in Marketing Strategy (PIMS) project (Besanko et al. 2001). It is not surprising, therefore, to find most entrepreneurs often adopt a differentiation strategy when exploiting a new opportunity. This is because their aim tends to be that of wishing to develop a replacement or new-to-the-world product which is demonstrably superior to alternatives already existing within a market sector. As illustrated by the Sony Corporation case study, the need for highly competitive pricing at the time of market launch is rarely an issue because customers are more interested in acquiring a superior quality product or service proposition.

The alternative to differentiation is a price leadership strategy based on exploiting a cost advantage. Porter (1980) posits this approach should usually be avoided because over the longer term it is non-sustainable. The basis for his viewpoint is that offering a lower price will depend on resource input economies such as lower wages or raw materials costs. In most cases, however, the price leader firm will eventually face rising costs or alternatively the emergence of a new competitor based in another country, where operating costs are even lower (Nagle 1993).

An important exception to the Porterian philosophy that cost leadership is a low scale advantage is where the outcome of an entrepreneurial project is the development of a solution that significantly reduces either product provision or production costs (Venkatram et al. 1994). This will then permit the new or improved product or service to be made available at a price lower than competition. Assuming competitors are unable to duplicate the entrepreneurial firm's new process or product, then the latter organisation will be able to exploit low price as the path for the long term retention of market leadership.

CASE STUDY

Entrepreneurial pricing

Case aims: To illustrate how savings on operational processes can provide the basis for a price-based marketing strategy.

An example of exploiting organisational processes to build market share is provided by the European 'no frills' airlines such as EasyJet and Ryanair. While national carriers such as British Airways or Lufthansa continued to concentrate on competing with other international carriers, the economy airlines developed a new, entrepreneurial process model which focused on making significant savings in operational costs. These savings were achieved through actions such as flying out of less popular airports, only using one model of aircraft, achieving a higher number of flying hours per aircraft per day and requiring passengers to book directly with the company. These savings were then passed on to the market in the form of lower prices and as a result these no frills operations have captured a massive share of the European air travel market.

CASE STUDY

Customer rejection

Case aims: To illustrate how customer self-interest may result in an innovative, lower cost solution encountering market resistance.

In the case of the airline industry, the lower price proposition mainly attracted existing users. There are other cases, however, where having developed a lower price product, this may be rejected by current customers allowing the opportunity to attract a totally new customer group. An example of this scenario occurred in the mid-1970s in the healthcare industry (Gilbert 2003). During the 1960s, heart surgeons in the USA in seeking to treat coronary heart disease developed coronary bypass surgery. This involved rerouting the blood around a blocked heart vessel. The operation required the services of highly trained cardiac surgeons to undertake the task of opening the rib cage and then delicately sewing a bypass graft onto the wall of the heart. To undertake this activity, the patient's heart had to be stopped and a complicated perfusion machine used to replace the heart's pumping function during the operation.

In 1974, a German doctor, Andreas Gruentzig performed the first balloon angioplasty operation which instead of bypassing the blocked artery, used the much less invasive approach of inserting a small balloon catheter to remove the blockage within the blood vessel. Cardiac surgeons ignored this development which they perceived as an inferior solution for their most lucrative customer group, namely patients with advanced heart conditions. In contrast cardiologists who until then were primarily involved in assessing patients' conditions using angiograms rapidly perceived balloon angioplasty as a whole new area of medical opportunity. Until the early 1990s, bypass surgery and angioplasty existed in tandem. Then the last remaining problem with angioplasty, that of a post-operative re-narrowing of the artery, was overcome by the development of a device called a stent. As a result the number of angioplasties undertaken has risen dramatically while cardiac surgeons have faced a significant downturn for the demand of their services to undertake bypass surgery.

Sales promotions

As prices fall, demand for most products will rise. This means firms can use temporary reductions in price as a mechanism through which to stimulate a short term increase in sales. Available incentives can be classified into three types; discounts, sales promotions and sale pricing. Sales promotion is a term given to a range of offers which share the common characteristic of providing a temporary increase in the value of goods. Examples include free product, price pack, coupons, premiums, competitions and sweepstakes. This type of promotion is a dominant feature of branded goods marketing. Although precise data on large firm sales promotion expenditure is unavailable, for most brands approximately 70 per cent of their marketing budget is allocated to supporting sales promotions (Davies 1992).

There are many reasons to explain this scale of expenditure. Probably the most important reason is that because supermarkets recognise the appeal of in-store specials, they demand that leading brands fund these events. Another important influence

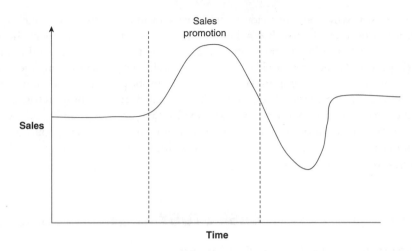

Figure 10.6   *Sales promotion revenue curve*

is that brand managers know sales promotions have an immediate impact on revenue, and so are often used to avert a sales downturn (Srinivasan and Anderson 1998). What seems to be ignored by most manufacturers and major retailers is, as shown in Figure 10.6, sales promotion merely brings sales forward into an earlier period. Unfortunately the increased sales during the promotional period are generated at a reduced price. Sales promotions are less frequently utilised by small entrepreneurial firms. Why this is the case has not been established. Possibly it may reflect an awareness of the sales curve shown in Figure 10.6 which indicates sales promotions will have a minimal impact on total sales volume over the medium term. The other possibility is that many small firms do not distribute their products through one or more dominant national retail chains and hence are less likely to face pressures from intermediaries to offer sales promotions to their customers.

Distribution

Intermediaries

In most consumer goods markets, producer firms have the option of delivering their product or service direct to the customer or using an intermediary to fulfil this responsibility. The role of the intermediary will only be sustainable where these organisations are adding value to the distribution process (Markely and Davis 2007). One dimension of added value is the reduction in unit price by the intermediary exploiting economies of scale to optimise delivery costs (Anderson et al. 1997). Supermarkets achieve this by purchasing truck load quantities, mixing goods from different suppliers and displaying the products in-store. Another role of an intermediary is to add value through actions that can enhance the product benefit. A hairdressing salon, for example, adds value to a shampoo and conditioner by using the product when restyling a client's hair.

In many consumer markets, small firms tend to sell direct to the final customer. With many small service firms such as household maintenance or repair companies this is because they have to visit the consumer's home to fulfil their supply responsibilities.

Another reason why sales are made to the final customer in a market sector is that numerous conventional small businesses are end user outlets such as retail shops or garages. A third reason for direct distribution is consumer goods markets are dominated by large, powerful supermarket chains (Gallagher et al. 2000). These organisations have two primary commercial aims; maximising in-store profit per square foot and sustaining shopper loyalty. Supermarket buyers minimise product costs by purchasing large quantities from lower cost, often overseas, sources. Large retailers rarely perceive any benefit in purchasing more expensive products from small domestic producers unless consumers are demanding major supermarkets exhibit greater social responsibility by sourcing more products locally.

CASE STUDY

Overcoming the distribution hurdle

Case aims: To illustrate how small producers have been assisted in gaining distribution for their goods in developed nation economies.

In recent years a number of Fair Trade Organisations have been created to improve the earnings and cash flow stability of small independent producers based in developing nations (Randall 2005). Many of these ventures are assisted by social entrepreneurs who perceive that one way of utilising their acquired skills is to assist in the creation of charitable trusts responsible for supporting producers to improve their production capability and to export their output to developed nations across the world. One of the biggest hurdles in the marketing process is achieving distribution because major retail chains are rarely interested in stocking goods from a diverse range of small suppliers.

In Canada one relief agency has created the Ten Thousand Villages operation which distributes products through 30 retail stores, half of which are managed as franchise operations. Fair Trade in New Zealand assists producers to form community co-operatives and imports the items into New Zealand for sale through the charity's network of 30 small retail outlets. Tearcraft in the UK is the trading arm of Tearfund UK which assists small producers across the world to market their products in the UK. The distribution process in this case is that volunteers in the UK sell products through in-home events, churches, persuading retailers to carry the product and through a mail order catalogue.

Channel assessment

In assessing which is the optimal distribution system, the small entrepreneurial firm needs to recognise that there are a number of factors that will influence this decision (Figure 10.7). Possibly the most important issue is responding to customer need. Where the customer has a preference (e.g. on-line purchase) this should be met. For example, in the 55+ age group in most Western nations, some individuals prefer on-line versus terrestrial purchasing because the former offers convenience, zero travel distance or because of personal mobility limitations, can only accept delivery to their home. The issues of convenience and mobility are also important reasons why many 55+ individuals exhibit a positive inclination towards purchasing products by mail

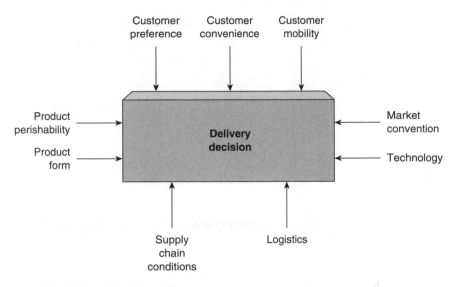

Figure 10.7   *Delivery decision influencers*

order (Jones and Chudry 2001). Products promoted through a catalogue have the added appeal of permitting retirees to reach a decision in their own homes and over a time frame that suits them. As the mail order business is possibly one of the easiest ways of starting a new small business, a preference for this distribution channel among 55+ individuals is good news for both start-up and existing small firms.

For some products, customers have become accustomed to using one delivery channel over the years. Their purchase behaviour will be based on a well established convention (e.g. home purchase of cosmetics from an Avon representative). Conventional behaviour may alter, however, where technological change offers a more attractive distribution proposition (e.g. buying a car on-line instead of from a terrestrial dealer). Occasionally the firm which breaks a long established distribution convention and offers the customer the option of purchasing a product through a completely different channel can exploit this first mover advantage and eventually become a leading national or international brand (e.g. Dell's direct marketing of computers). In relation to this issue Canavan et al. (2007) posit that in most cases where the customer is willing to switch to a new, alternative channel there needs to be a trade off in terms of being prepared to forgo the benefits offered by the conventional channel because there are compensatory benefits available through altering their purchasing behaviour. These researchers found, for example, that consumers who have traditionally bought speciality foods in retail outlets are willing to forgo the social aspects of the terrestrial shopping experience when buying products on-line. This is because a shift to Web-based purchasing is seen as offering the alternative benefits of convenience and being provided with access to a much greater variety of products.

Although the tendency of most owner/managers when considering the launch of a new product of service is to use the same channel of distribution as the competition, this trait can result in an opportunity being missed of exploiting an alternative channel which is a more effective system through which to reach the customer and thereby compete more effectively with especially larger national branded goods operations (Stasch et al. 1999). The possible channel alternatives are summarised in Figure 10.8. This proposes there are four alternative options available if the small

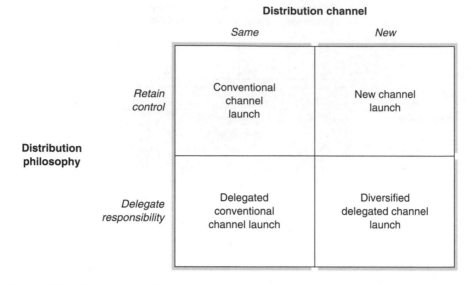

Distribution channel

Figure 10.8   *New product distribution options*

entrepreneurial firm decides to avoid duplicating the conventional distribution strategy utilised by the majority of the competition in the same industrial sector.

Of the four options shown in Figure 10.8, possibly the rarest is the concept of distribution delegation. This involves persuading a supplier to incorporate a product or service into their operation and have them fulfil some or all of the distribution management task. One sector in which this occurs is computer software (Anon. 2004). A software developer may purchase a standard system from a major software company which is then used as a platform to develop a specialist application (e.g. building a customised database management system for doctors' surgeries). The supplier or the developer may perceive this customised software has broader market potential and agreement is reached whereby the specialist system is incorporated in the supplier's software product. This latter organisation becomes responsible for managing future distribution for the newly bundled product proposition.

CASE STUDY

Distribution assistance

Case aims: To illustrate how a downstream customer can take over the distribution and marketing role.

In the case of the company having a customer undertake the distribution function, this approach is of appeal where the company's product enhances another product which is being marketed by the customer (Campbell-Kelly 2001). This route was adopted by the founder of the specialist software company Autodesk, John Walker, in 1982 when the company was constituted of just five employees. The focus of the new business was to develop specialist software for the rapidly growing PC market. One of the company's most successful products was AutoCAD which was a computer aided design (CAD) system for desktop computers. The company initially tried to sell the software direct to engineering companies which already used PCs. What Autodesk soon realised, however, was that a more effective distribution channel was to link with Value Added Resellers (VARs) which specialised in supplying complete CAD systems to their customers. The Autodesk new distribution channel involved the VARs specifying an appropriate hardware specification for the client wanting to create a PC-based CAD facility and would then recommend AutoCAD as the preferred software solution. By 1990 this alternative distribution strategy permitted Autodesk to become a global player with annual sales in the region of $180 million.

Substitution and hybrids

The substitute distribution channel strategy often involves marketing a company's product through both the conventional channel used in an industrial sector and then adding the substitute as an alternative route to market. This approach typically occurs where there is a need for close interaction between the supplier and the final customer (Ojala and Tyrvainen 2006). Hence in some markets, similar to competition, the company may follow the conventional route of selling direct to customers using the organisation's own sales force. There may be other specialist market sectors where there are distributors who have more extensive understanding of the end user and in these cases, sector specific distributors will be used as the substitute channel for reaching this latter group of customers. This concept of utilising more than one channel is known as a 'hybrid distribution strategy' (Webb and Hogan 2002). In their study of hybrid channels, these researchers concluded that hybrid channel conflict is an important determinant of both channel performance and satisfaction. Their results further suggest that the relationship between hybrid channel conflict and channel performance is moderated by the life cycle stage. Data supports the view that the frequency of conflict, but not its intensity, has a negative effect on channel system performance.

The route of moving into a completely new channel completely removed from the conventional market system of which a company is a part is clearly extremely risky. This is because there is the requirement that customers perceive the new channel as a preferable way of purchasing the product or service. If, however, the company is a first mover and end users perceive significant added benefit in using the new channel, then the outcome can be for the entrepreneurial distribution strategy to permit the organisation to become a sector leader (Anderson et al. 1997).

CASE STUDY

First mover advantage

Case aims: To illustrate the benefits of being an entrepreneurial first mover in the creation of a new distribution concept.

Peter Wood is the entrepreneur who founded Direct Line which is now a market leader in the UK insurance industry. At the time he launched the business the

(Cont'd)

conventional way to distribute car insurance was through major insurance firms having their own offices in major cities staffed by their own sales force and by distributing insurance cover through the offices of insurance brokers. Wood's concept was that a more cost effective approach in the car insurance market would be to centralise the entire operation at one location and then use the telephone and mail systems to both sell insurance, administer the document flow and to manage customer claims. The approach permitted a significant reduction in costs and by offering lower premiums than the major firms in the market, Direct Line was immediately embraced by UK car owners. Following the subsequent acquisition of the business by the Royal Bank of Scotland, Wood's alternative distribution strategy netted him somewhere in the region of £65 million.

The on-line world

Founding philosophies

The founding fathers of the PC and software such as the Windows operating platform grew up in California during the era of 'flower power' and hippies. This environment influenced some of the industry's entrepreneurs to exhibit both commercial and social aims. For example, Steve Jobs wanted everybody to have access to computer technology in their everyday lives through the provision of personal computers such as his Apple product. The other dimension of these entrepreneurs' social conscience was a desire that new technology should be available to everybody at a reasonable price. To fulfil this aim, they attempted to create systems that could stop large firms such as IBM establishing sector monopolies.

These highly commendable attitudes are best demonstrated by the creation of the World Wide Web. Developers of this technology were keen to create a system that used open source languages and in a very insightful decision, established a global not-for-profit organisation to manage domain name allocation. The influence of such philosophies did cause some experts to predict that the Internet was a commercially democratic institution because any size firm was provided with a zero cost distribution system for reaching global markets. By moving on-line, small entrepreneurial firms who could not afford conventional terrestrial promotions such as television advertising would in theory be able to attract customers by their Websites being locatable through search engines. Hence the ability to offer an on-line purchasing facility was seen as a distribution system which circumvented the terrestrial channels dominated by large multi-national corporations (Chaston 2000b).

Large firm domination

Events in the mid-1990s appeared to support this perspective of a brave new world. The Internet was dominated by the launch of totally new, small enterprises. Tragically, however, the hopes of business democratisation were defeated by reality. Once the commercial viability of the technology was proven, large firms took actions to ensure their dominance of the new channel. By allocating huge promotional budgets to

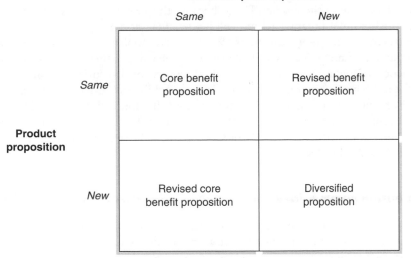

Customer price expectation

Same   *New*

	Same	*New*
Same	Core benefit proposition	Revised benefit proposition
New	Revised core benefit proposition	Diversified proposition

Product proposition

Figure 10.9   *Distribution option assessment*

support their on-line marketing programmes, large firms were able to secure a prime position in on-line searches. Their ability to also fund the purchase of banner advertising on major Websites greatly stimulated click throughs to their own Websites. By the end of the decade, the activities of the large companies meant that achieving a high awareness about a firm's on-line presence demanded massive expenditure on traditional terrestrial media such as television advertising. Budgets on this scale are an unaffordable option for most SME sector firms. It also became apparent that most consumers prefer to trade with firms with whom they are already very familiar. Consequently large 'clicks and mortar' firms have continued to enjoy much higher Website visitor numbers than lesser known, smaller firms. This outcome again validates the business reality that when a market is attractive to large firms, the elephants are usually able to ensure small firm competitors are rarely able to remain a threat over the longer term (Frank 1997).

The possibility that limited opportunities exist to use a Website to significantly increase sales should, however, not deter small entrepreneurial firms from considering the medium when examining new distribution channel options. Web distribution can reduce operating costs and permit the organisation to reach a much larger target audience. As with any distribution decision, however, the small firm should assess the cost–benefit implications of the Internet prior to investing in the medium as either the sole or complementary distribution pathway. The operational characteristics of different channels may permit a small firm to offer alternative versions of the same product. This implies that where a channel strategy is being considered, the product proposition may need to be changed to be compatible with a specific channel. Price expectations of consumers within respective channels need to be assessed. This can generate the alternative options summarised in Figure10.9.

The other issue which the entrepreneurial small firm might consider is whether moving on-line will lead to conflict with existing terrestrial intermediaries. This is because these organisations may perceive the move as an act of disloyalty of a supplier who they have assisted over the years. Tay and Agrawal (2004) developed a model to generate some managerial insights into the issue of conflict between a small firm moving on-line and continuing to rely on using existing terrestrial intermediaries. They concluded that a direct channel alongside a terrestrial reseller channel is not necessarily detrimental to the reseller. This is because the supplier is likely to adjust prices in a hybrid channel situation which will be beneficial to both parties and even more importantly, to end user customers. To assess the applicability of the model the researchers examined real world scenarios concerning issues such as changes in wholesale pricing, paying the reseller a commission for diverting customers towards the direct channel, or conceding the demand fulfilment function entirely to the reseller. Their conclusion was that such actions are mutually beneficial to supply chain members because they more effectively exploit the competitive advantages that exist due to the organisational capabilities which each party exhibits in the optimal distribution of products and services.

Distribution communities

An important aspect of the Internet is that it permits real time or asynchronous interaction between individuals and between customers and suppliers. Young people are the heaviest users of the Internet. For them the medium has become an important aspect of both their social activities (e.g. utilising sites such as Facebook) and also exchanging information about their satisfaction with products and services they have purchased. These types of electronic communication and associated product buying decision activities are often known as 'virtual communities' (Flavian and Guinaliu 2005). The characteristics exhibited by these communities include:

1 The members are able to share information and enter into dialogue about topics of interest.
2 The members share common interests and experiences which as they exchange information over time leads to the creation of close relationships within the community.
3 The members feel able to share their hopes, aspirations and problems.
4 The community can provide the basis for assisting members to purchase products or services from sources which they trust and also to exchange views with each other about the suitability of goods both after and before before purchase.

The important aspect of on-line communities is that they represent an important channel for the distribution of both information and the sale of products. In the case of information distribution the critical dimension in many communities is that the consumer, not the supplier, has control over the information being distributed (Pitta and Fowler 2005). In the case of some sites such as eBay the consumer has control over both the distribution of information and also the supply of the majority of products that are sold on-line through the Website. This alternative concept which is becoming known as consumer-to-consumer (or C2C) marketing is estimated to have annual revenue in the region of $5 billion which is equivalent to approximately 5 per cent of the total on-line global sales.

As these various on-line communities continue to grow in size, they are increasingly important as an information distribution channel through which firms can harvest data on topics such as:

• the current level of consumer satisfaction with existing products and services
• gaining understanding of desired and non-desired features for future products
• determination of variances between communities in relation to factors such as brand loyalty and price sensitivity

- identifying unexpected new opportunities and different ways of utilising products
- views about the nature of competitor offerings
- changes in consumer attitudes, values and beliefs over time.

CASE STUDY

Understanding communities

Case aims: To illustrate how on-line communities offer a new promotional medium through which to build consumer awareness.

Bernoff and Li (2008) stress that for entrepreneurs to exploit these new communities there is a need to develop a strategic framework through which the organisation can re-energise their marketing operation to become compatible with the fundamental behaviour shifts associated with C2C marketing. Firms need to go beyond just 'listening' and begin to find creative ways through which they are permitted to 'talk' to communities. In the USA, for example, Chevrolet, which has real problems with building awareness among college students using conventional communication channels, launched the 'Chevy Aveo Livin' Campus Challenge'. This involved recruiting students to live in an Aveo for a week, only leaving to attend classes, and then putting a video record of their experiences on MySpace and Facebook with Chevy awarding prizes for the best video diaries.

Beyond just talking, the next step is to 'energise' the relationship between the company and consumers. The crafts division of Fiskars Corporation in the USA recruited some enthusiastic amateur crafts people to become recruiters and 'lead ambassadors' for the firm's specially created on-line brand community known as 'Fiskateers'. Each ambassador was encouraged to recruit other people they knew within their local craft community to join the site. Within only a few months, the Website has attracted several thousand visitors who regularly participate in on-line discussions about the craft hobbies and the benefits of using Fiskars' products.

In terms of using on-line communities as a distribution channel for information and ultimately as a catalyst for stimulating the distribution of more products through an on-line channel, Bernoff and Li recommend that entrepreneurial companies recognise the existence of the following guidelines in relation to 'best practice':

1 Recognise that the firm will rapidly lose control of what is occurring within the on-line community.
2 Expect that managers within the firm will initially resist the concept because they will receive a much higher level of exposure to criticisms and complaints about the organisation's marketing operation.
3 Start on a very small scale and only expand gradually as understanding is acquired concerning how consumers join the community and wish to utilise the community to achieve their personal day-to-day life objectives.

4   Only expand the concept where it is apparent that the consumer and the company can achieve ongoing benefits from the continued existence of the on-line community.

5   Focus on the information flows being generated and avoid trying to out compete other organisations in terms of the sophistication of the technology being used to support on-line community communication.

CASE STUDY

Exploiting on-line communities

Case aims: To illustrate the entrepreneurial opportunities which exist from exploiting on-line distribution communities.

Given the trust that develops within on-line communities and that participants in some situations share an interest that leads to the purchase of goods, clearly if an entrepreneur is able to create a virtual community this can provide a very effective channel through which to distribute products or services. One of the first individuals to recognise this new distribution opportunity was Gerfried Schuller, a former European snowboarding champion. As one of the earliest participants in this sport he recognised that it provided a potentially huge new market for winter sports equipment (Forscht et al. 2006). He opened a snowboard school in the early 1990s in Schladming, Austria. Alongside the school he created a shop plus a test centre where customers could try out new equipment before making a purchase decision. The first operation was extremely successful and over the next few years he opened similar operations at other ski resorts.

Schuller recognised that the Internet provided a very effective way of becoming an international retailer and in the late 1990s he created the Blue Tomato Website. From the outset the company aim was to develop a strong on-line community where snowboarders could share experiences, comment upon alternative equipment options and interact with the Tomato on-line staff, all of whom are very experienced snowboarders. To ensure that Blue Tomato is perceived as the best option for providing advice, the company invests heavily in both in-house training and sending employees to training programmes offered by key suppliers. The commitment and expertise of the Tomato staff means that among the members of the Tomato on-line community, they are seen not as salespeople, but instead highly knowledgeable individuals whose views are critically important to people who have questions about any aspect of the snowboarding culture.

The Tomato Website offers over 3,000 products, is totally multi-lingual and contains possibly one of the most comprehensive multi-media snowboarding libraries in the world. On average the site attracts over 500,000 visitors every month. Many of these site visitors are seeking information such as news of competitions, snowboard slopes across the world, avalanche guides and partner links to other organisations in the snowboarding industry. Potential customers can also read the views of other snowboarders who have tried out new equipment by visiting one of the company's test centres. The company also now publishes a terrestrial version of its on-line catalogue. This is distributed as an insert in leading snowboard magazines and is also mailed directly to approximately 100,000 snowboarders who are purchasers of products from the company.

SUMMARY LEARNING POINTS

- A common error of both entrepreneurs and conventional small firms is to base their pricing decision on 'cost plus pricing'.
- Successful pricing of an entrepreneurial product or service is determined by customer expectation.
- There is a concurrent need to assess the cost implications associated in supplying goods when determining an optimal price.
- Pricing decisions also have to recognise the influence of macro-environmental factors.
- An alternative to a price reduction is a temporary increase in value by implementing a sales promotion.
- New products often face the hurdle of identifying intermediaries.
- Selection of distribution channels will be influenced by those pathways which can offer the highest level of consumer satisfaction.
- A new distribution concept can offer the basis of launching a completely new entrepreneurial business proposition.
- The Internet is now dominated by major terrestrial companies.
- The Internet has led to the emergence of on-line communities controlled by consumers.

ASSIGNMENTS

1   Select a tangible consumer sector with which you have some familiarity (e.g. cars, consumer electronics) and prepare a report demonstrating how pricing varies in relation to the quality of the products offered and the distribution channel(s) through which the products are marketed.
2   Prepare a report analysing which consumer goods remain extremely important to consumers even during a major recession. Also, on which types of goods are suppliers likely to offer significant price reductions during a recession?
3   Which consumer goods categories have most benefited from the emergence of the Internet as a new channel through which to sell and distribute products and services?

DISCUSSION TOPICS

1   Visit two different major supermarkets and use the data acquired to discuss how these two organisations use pricing policies and sales promotions to maximise store traffic.
2   Visit five Websites operated by different major consumer branded goods companies and use the data acquired to discuss the degree to which each of these organisations are effectively exploiting the potential benefits which are offered by the Internet.
3   Visit social Websites such as YouTube or Facebook and identify three examples of on-line materials which you believe are being supported by major brands as an alternative approach to distributing information to consumers. Discuss the conclusions you have reached having undertaken a comparative assessment of the three different companies' approaches to supporting on-line communities.

Additional information sources

Pricing

Harrigan, K.R. (1980), Strategy formulation in declining industries, *The Academy of Management Review*, Vol. 5, No. 4, pp. 599–619.

Potter, D. (2004), Confronting low-end competition, *Sloan Management Review*, Vol. 45, No. 3, pp. 73–81.

Syam, N.B., Ruan, R. and Hess, J.D. (2005), Customized products: a competitive analysis, *Marketing Science*, Vol. 24, No. 4, pp. 569–588.

Taber, A. and El Bash, H. (2006), Heterogeneity of consumer demand: opportunities for pricing of services, *The Journal of Product and Brand Management*, Vol. 15, No. 5, pp. 331–342.

On-line distribution

Raymond, L. (2001), Determinants of website implementation in small businesses, *Internet Research*, Vol. 11, No. 5, pp. 411–423.

11

Family and Social Entrepreneurship

Chapter objectives

The aims of this chapter are to assist the reader to:

- realise that family firms are a dominant type of business in the small firms sector
- understand that entrepreneurial family firms are a critical source of market innovation
- recognise there is dispute over whether family firms are more successful than their non-family counterparts
- review the critical issue of succession management in family firms
- understand family firms founded by entrepreneurs tend to sustain this orientation into subsequent generations
- realise some entrepreneurs perceive there are significant benefits to society of utilising their skills to assist disadvantaged members of society
- comprehend that social entrepreneurship is perceived as being more effective in developing nations than reliance on the provision of grant aid
- recognise the critical impact of the creation of sources of microfinance.

Family firms

Occurrence and differences

There is some dispute about the exact definition that should be applied to a family firm. Possibly the best solution is to accept one of the simpler definitions; namely that a family firm is one where a single family owns 51–100 per cent of the business. With the exception of partnerships, co-operatives and limited companies in which a number of individuals have purchased shares, virtually all other small business start-ups are founded by a single individual. The implications of this situation are that the majority of small firms are family businesses. Research by Chau et al. (2004), as well as confirming this fact, also showed that the rate of increase in terms of family involvement in the business tends to decline over time and in some cases, may eventually become extremely limited.

In most nations, approximately 70 per cent of small firms can be classified as family businesses (Colli et al. 2003). Across some sectors such as agriculture, and due to the influence of certain values about the importance of families in some countries such as China, this figure can be as high as 85–95 per cent. Not surprisingly, given the dominance of these firms in most economies, the strategies and operational activities of family businesses have generated a significant amount of research about this type of enterprise. One stream of research has focused on finding attributes that distinguish family and non-family enterprises (Ibrahim et al. 2008). Some studies have concluded that family firms exhibit an inward orientation, are less capital intensive, achieve slower growth and participate less in global markets. However, such findings have not always been corroborated in other studies. Research on business attributes has often been accompanied by a comparative assessment of the performance of family firms and their potential to generate new employment opportunities. In some cases, research has concluded that family firms outperform non-family firms and are an important source of new jobs (Anderson and Reeb 2003). Similar conclusions were reached by Lee (2004), about the higher efficiency of family firms and the consequent impact on achieving a higher ROI than non-family firms. This researcher, however, was unable to demonstrate any real difference between family and non-family firms in relation to profitability levels. Westhead and Howorth (2006), in a UK study, found no differences between the performance of family versus non-family and no evidence that family firms had any greater impact on new job creation when compared with their non-family counterparts.

In an attempt to explain why some studies failed to generate evidence about superior financial performance, Castillo and Wakefield (2006) suggested that this reflected the fact that the primary aim of such entities was not that of seeking to maximise profits. Instead, they believe the most important objective within these firms is to ensure the ongoing job security of employees who are family members. To determine the validity of their idea, they reviewed an existing data set of over 1,000 US small family firms. On the basis of their results, it is apparent that in many family firms emphasis on employing family members and seeking to provide these individuals with secure employment is perceived as more important than financial performance.

CASE STUDY

Family firm entrepreneurs

Case aims: To illustrate how very successful entrepreneurial companies started life as family businesses.

Numerous businesses which became large corporations or iconic brands during the twentieth century started life as small family firms in the nineteenth century. Brooke Bond PG Tips, the leading packaged tea brand in the UK was founded by Arthur Brooke in 1845. He opened his first Tea Shop in Piccadilly, Manchester. There was never a 'Mr Bond'; Arthur Brooke chose the name simply because he liked it. Over time the company expanded and moved into supplying tea to retail outlets across the UK. The company's most famous product, PG Tips was first launched in 1930. Similarly, the global chocolate company operation, Cadbury's, was founded by John Cadbury in Birmingham in the 1820s as an outlet selling tea, coffee and drinking chocolate. The manufacture of drinking chocolate and cocoa began in a small rented factory in Crooked Lane, Birmingham. Later in the same century Cadbury's opened a huge factory on their Bournville site to expand the company's range of chocolate confectionery. Although for many years no longer a family enterprise, Cadbury's remains the world's biggest confectionery company holding the number one or number two brand position in 20 of the 50 largest confectionery markets across the world.

Succession

The process

The area of family firm research which has possibly received the greatest attention in the literature is the issue of management succession when the founder hands over the firm to another family member, very typically one of the children. The alternative is to appoint a professional manager either from the existing management team or by bringing in an outsider. The available research suggests that where the succession process is not carefully managed this can give rise to conflict within the family. In some cases, ultimately lead to a closure or sale of the business (Ambrose 1983).

The commonest causes of succession are the founder's decision to retire, ill health or death. Following an announcement of the need to step down, there are a number of factors that can then lead to conflict within the family. In some cases the nominated successor is a child who has never worked in the business and resents having to change their personal circumstances or career plans in order to take on the role. Where there are a number of children, the individuals not selected as the successor, or the respective families of these individuals, may become very resentful about the succession decision. In those cases where these individuals or their families hold a significant proportion of the company shares, their resentment can be reflected in voting decisions that can be a major obstacle for the successful ongoing operation of the business. The ability of family shareholders to disrupt the business may also occur when an outsider such as a professional manager is brought into the firm. This individual may be an extremely competent new leader. Nevertheless this individual is unable to make any progress in implementing new business plans because at every turn he/she is blocked by family shareholders who, to demonstrate their objections to the appointment, vote against any proposals tabled by the new leader (Morris et al. 1996).

In some cases the cause of conflict can be the founder themselves, when having apparently 'handed over the reigns of power', they still wish to remain involved in key decision-making. Examples of troublesome activity can include the founder coming back into the firm and contradicting or reversing instructions issued by the successor. Alternatively the individual may demand that the firm continues to implement their original strategy even when it is apparent that change is demanded to ensure the survival of the business (Rutherford et al. 2006). The scale of conflict is usually most acrimonious when the founder appoints his or her child as the successor and still attempts to behave as a parent, not a business person. Possibly one of the most famous examples of this scenario is provided by Henry Ford. This individual's utilisation of mass production technology to create the world's first affordable car, the Model T, is clear evidence of his entrepreneurial abilities. As he got older, however, he became more fixed in his ways and refused to consider any significant strategic changes despite growing evidence that the Ford Motor Company was losing market share to General Motors. Despite this situation, Henry was not prepared to permit his successor, his oldest son Edsel, to implement needed organisational changes. In fact it was only after Henry's death, that his grandson Henry Ford II was able to introduce the strategies required to revitalise the company (Drozdown and Carroll 1997).

Succession planning

Morris et al. (1996) expressed the view that much of the research on both family firms in general and in relation to the issue of succession is often based on inadequate research designs, limited statistical analysis and heavy reliance on conclusions based on anecdotal evidence. To overcome these criticisms, these researchers carried out a large cross-sectional study of 500 UK small family firms. On the basis of this large data set, they concluded that factors influencing a successful succession outcome include:

1　The heirs are reasonably well prepared in terms of educational background and business experience.
2　Although a formal succession plan is rarely prepared, there has been an extended period of discussion and debate within the family about the best solution to the succession decision and subsequent actions to be implemented.
3　There is an open minded, flexible attitude to the succession process with people being willing to revise and adapt the succession plan on the basis of changes in business circumstances and family dynamics.
4　The most effective successions occur where there is both mutual trust and an affable attitude within the family unit.

A further complication facing the family firm is that in many cases the founder has a very significant shareholding. Unlike a limited company where there are numerous shareholders or the company is a publicly listed corporation, the death of the successor can create very significant tax problems. This is because the shares of the founder are usually included as a component within their personal estate which then attract death duties and/or capital gains taxes. In such cases the scale of the tax bill can lead to the company either having to be sold outside of the family or in extreme situations, the firm can be forced into bankruptcy. Although such outcomes can be avoided by careful estate planning, implementing these actions has to be carefully managed by the firm's professional advisers. To avoid retrospective tax demands, the transfer of shares to other members of the family or the creation of a trust usually needs to have occurred some years before the death of the founder (White et al. 2004).

Even in those cases where careful estate planning has been put in place, second or later generation family members, especially when they are not business employees, often want to diversify their financial holdings to protect their inherited wealth. They tend to be very wary of providing capital to the original business or to trust the new senior management, especially if these individuals are not members of the family. Under these circumstances the subsequent family generations may decide to dispose of their shares in the firm. If timed incorrectly and the shares represent a very significant proportion of the total shares in the business, this can have an extremely adverse impact on the ongoing viability of the firm (Drozdown and Carroll 1997).

In view of all the risks associated with family firm succession, the standard advice which appears in the literature is that there is the need for the development and implementation of a succession plan with this process commencing well before the founder becomes unwilling or unable to continue to manage the business. As many founders do transfer the business to one of their children, it is critical that the potential heir has the values, motivation, skills, experience and capabilities to effectively provide the next generation of effective leadership (Dyer 1986). In preparation for the changeover the founder and successor must work together to reach agreement over future strategies and operational plans for the business. This can only occur if the individuals develop mutual respect and understanding about each other's opinions and values.

In seeking to determine whether differences in the managerial capabilities of the predecessor and successor can influence performance, King (2003) undertook an in-depth study of 31 businesses. The methodology utilised involved both analysing financial performance of the firms over time and undertaking in-depth interviews with the predecessor and successor. The average age of the predecessors who took part in the study was 64 and the average age of successors was 36. As part of the interview process, King measured each respondent's ability to undertake complex mental processing. This is a validated technique for providing a measurement of managerial competence. The primary conclusion she reached was where the successor's managerial competence was higher than the predecessor, the performance of the business tended to improve. In the reverse scenario, however, if the predecessor exhibited a higher level of managerial competence, following the appointment of a successor, the performance in most cases will go into decline. In presenting her conclusions about the critical influence of managerial capability, King noted that her findings should not be interpreted as disputing the results found in other studies. She reiterates that in the management of succession other factors will also impact the ongoing performance of a family firm in the hands of a successor such as commitment, knowledge, business complexity and the relationship which exists with the predecessor.

To gain further insights on the nature of effective relationships between founder and successor, Stavrou et al. (2005) undertook a study to determine the personality characteristics most likely to ensure a smooth and successful transition of power in a family firm. To assess personality, the researchers utilised the Myers-Briggs assessment tool which uses 95 items as the basis for classifying individuals into different types. Their study revealed that transition was most effective in those cases where the founder had a personality which permitted the individual to be an Extrovert-Sensing-Thinking-Perceptive type of person. Additionally they concluded that the success of the transition process will be greatly enhanced where there is a collaborative, participative culture prevailing within the family and the business. Their research also concluded, however, that these factors can be nullified if the founder insists on remaining involved in key decision-making after the handover to the successor.

Although the selection of the best successor is a critically important decision, in those cases where this individual is the founder's child, there is strong evidence that the success of the management changeover can also be heavily influenced by the way this next generation is first introduced into the organisation (Barach et al. 1988). These authors concluded the entry must be carefully managed in order that the potential successor is able to gain acceptance and credibility within the organisation. Achievement of these two aims then provides the basis for establishing the legitimacy of the individual's current and future managerial roles in terms of gaining the respect and confidence of the workforce. Once this occurs the greater is the probability that the transition from the older to the current generation of leadership will be a success.

In assessing the issue of the entry into the family business by the next generation, the two basic options discussed by the researchers was the individual joining the firm straight after completing their education or alternatively, although they may work in the business as a part-time summer job, after college they pursue a career in another larger firm, often in a completely different market sector. Barach et al.'s research confirmed that the most effective way of achieving acceptance and credibility leading on to legitimacy in the eyes of the workforce is for the successor to work in another business for some years before joining the family firm. Additionally, their research findings suggest that achievement of legitimacy and acceptance as the successor is greater if the new entrant spends a few years as a member of the management team in the family business prior to being appointed as the new head of the firm.

CASE STUDY

The Wrigley saga

Case aims: To illustrate the business strategies associated with the successful operation of a multi-generational, entrepreneurial large company.

William Wrigley Jr came to Chicago from Philadelphia in the spring of 1891 at the age of 29. His father was a soap manufacturer, and at the start of his new business in Chicago, Mr Wrigley sold Wrigley's Scouring Soap. As an extra incentive to merchants, Mr Wrigley offered premiums. One of these premiums was baking powder. When baking powder proved to be more popular than soap, he switched to the baking powder business.

Then in 1892, Mr Wrigley got the idea of offering two packages of chewing gum with each can of baking powder. At that time, there were at least a dozen chewing gum companies in the United States, but the industry was relatively undeveloped. Mr Wrigley decided that chewing gum had major potential. His first two brands were Lotta and Vassar. Wrigley's Juicy Fruit gum and Spearmint were introduced a year later. William Wrigley did most of the selling to the trade, but also showed an unusually high level of skill for inspiring enthusiasm in the people who worked with him. He was one of the pioneers in the use of advertising to promote the sale of branded goods, using newspapers, magazine, or outdoor posters to promote the business. The company was also one of the first major firms in the USA to exploit the benefits offered by radio to reach mass market audiences.

As the popularity of Wrigley's gum grew, the company began to expand manufacturing to support company growth. The first factory established outside the United States was in Canada, followed by expansion into Australia (1915), Great Britain (1927) and New Zealand (1939). During the Second World War, the new company president, Philip Wrigley, decided to support US troops but concurrently protect the reputation of the company's brands. Because of wartime rationing, Wrigley could not make enough top-quality gum for everyone. So rather the company took Wrigley's Spearmint, Doublemint and Juicy Fruit off the civilian market and sold the entire output of these brands to the US Armed Forces. During this absence from the consumer market, the company ran the 'Remember this Wrapper' advertising campaign.

William Wrigley succeeded his father, Philip, as president and CEO in 1961. During his 38-year tenure, production facilities were opened in new countries. Currently the company operates 19 production facilities in Australia, Canada, China, France, Great Britain, India, Kenya, the Philippines, Poland, Russia, Spain, Taiwan and the United States and Wrigley is marketed in more than 180 countries. When sugar free gums entered the US market, Wrigley launched their Extra brand which still remains the leading brand in this sector of the market.

When William Wrigley Jr took over as CEO in the late 1990s, his view was that further expansion of the chewing gum business offered limited prospects for sustaining revenue growth. Hence the company embarked on a major acquisition programme of other confectionery companies as a path through which to expand the product line. This decision plus continued growth for chewing gum products resulted in a virtual doubling of total global sales. The company had been the target of numerous takeovers, all of which were successfully resisted by the Wrigley family. Then in 2008 the company was approached by Mars, another privately owned business, whose CEO proposed a merger of the two corporations. After a careful assessment of the bid price for the company, William Wrigley Jr determined the merger offered the best financial prospects for the business in an increasingly competitive global market. Hence he recommended to the Wrigley family that the Mars offer be accepted. On 4 March 2008, the Wrigley company ceased to be the family owned business that had been successfully run for many years by the founder and then his descendants.

Source: www.wrigley.com

Entrepreneurial orientation

Not surprisingly examples of companies such as Cadbury's and Wrigley's have given rise to the perspective that many family firms, especially in the SME sector, are entrepreneurial entities. Although this is a widely held view, in reality very little quantitative research has been undertaken to validate the idea. One of the exceptions is a study undertaken by McCann et al. (2001). These researchers used the typology developed by Miles and Snow (1978) which classifies firms into Prospectors (or innovators), Defenders, Analysers and Reactors. A survey of 231 small US family firms revealed that only 42 per cent could be considered as Prospectors exhibiting an innovative, entrepreneurial orientation. The remaining businesses were more conventionally orientated. This figure of 42 per cent is very similar to the typical figure found in other small business studies where the majority of firms are found to exhibit non-entrepreneurial characteristics. Hence it seems to be reasonable to propose that the mix of entrepreneurial versus non-entrepreneurial firms is similar in both the family and their non-family small business sectors.

As with non-family firms, the level of entrepreneurial orientation within a family business will be heavily influenced by the founder or their successor (Yan and Sorenson 2003). Yan and Sorenson propose the two core competencies which will determine entrepreneurial drive are (1) a recognition/identification of new opportunities and (2) an ability to acquire the resources needed to exploit these opportunities. In their view, however, the unique characteristics of family firms will require that the leader is able to avoid conflict with other family members by exhibiting a collaborative, participative, relationship-based managerial orientation. To assess the validity of their theories the two researchers undertook a survey of small US family firms in which they measured leadership style, organisational conflict and entrepreneurial orientation. The results indicated that if the business leader exhibited a collaborative, participative and relationship-based style, this, positively contributed towards creating and enhancing an entrepreneurial environment within the family firm. A key reason is that this leadership style promotes collaboration within the firm and reduces potential conflict between family members. The study also confirmed earlier research that other family members exhibiting a collective entrepreneurial orientation will contribute greatly to the creativity and the overall success of the business.

CASE STUDY

The Mackintosh and Rowntree sagas

Case aims: To illustrate how succession problems can adversely impact the ongoing survival of a large family business.

John Mackintosh opened a pastry shop in 1890 and then decided to also sell toffees. By 1899 Mackintosh required a larger works so he created a private, limited company. Poor health in 1920 led to the appointment of his son Harold as the new Managing Director (Fitzgerald 2000). Harold was assisted in his new role by his brother Douglas. Together they owned some 93 per cent of the firm. Knighted in 1922, Harold supervised critical changes in ownership, management structure, and labour policies. Greater responsibility was given to his brother Eric. Due to a period of intense price competition, profits fell noticeably in 1924 and did not recover until 1928–9.

The company then sought to extend its product portfolio and in 1932 purchased Caley, a chocolate producer from the Unilver company. Eric Mackintosh was appointed as the Caley chairman and implemented an ambitious plan to create new differentiated products. This led to the launch of 'Quality Street', an innovative mix of mainly toffees covered in chocolate and a chocolate covered toffee called Rolo. After the Second World War, as Britain's fourth largest manufacturer of confectionery, the company was vulnerable to competition from Cadbury, Rowntree, and Mars. This led the company to acquire some smaller companies outside the sweets industry.

The death of Harold Mackintosh exposed the problems between business strategy, marketing, ownership, and management. His brother Douglas was never considered as a replacement, and the job went to the other brother, Eric. The new chairman stated how the company's independence was not endangered, as 'closely knit family interests' were still in control. Nevertheless, blood relations did not prevent the rise of boardroom tensions. Harold's other son, John Mackintosh, was not highly regarded within the company, and Eric was anxious that he should not succeed him as chairman.

By the end of the decade, the long-term implications of commercial difficulties and the problems of succession caused the family in 1969 to decide to accept a merger proposal from Rowntree to create Rowntree Mackintosh. Rowntree was also originally founded as a family business in the nineteenth century by Henry Isaac Rowntree.

By the time of the merger Rowntree was controlled by three family trusts which owned 60 per cent of the company shares. After the merger these trusts held approximately 38 per cent of shares, compared with approximately 10 per cent awarded to the Mackintosh family. Also at this time, Rowntree had a much higher share of the UK market, 16 per cent versus Mackintosh's 6 per cent, and owned very successful brands such as Aero, Smarties and KitKat. Understandably this superior marketing capability meant the Rowntree chairman, Donald Barron, lead the amalgamated operations and over time, the involvement in the day-to-day business operations by members of the Mackintosh family declined. The new larger company enjoyed considerable success but in 1987 was forced to go public to raise more capital. The outcome was the various family trusts could no longer block any takeover bids.

A battle for the company erupted between two major elephants, Nestlé and Jacobs Suchard in 1988. Eventually the larger elephant Nestlé won by offering to acquire Rowntree for $4.6 billion. After the acquisition, it became clear that Nestlé was only really interested in five products; namely KitKat, Aero, Polo, Fruit Pastilles and Quality Street. Hence the rest of the chocolate ranges were re-badged Nestlé-Rowntree except for the fruit pastilles and fruit gums products. The Mackintosh brand disappeared except on the Toffos product.

Sources: www.nestle.co.uk; www.practicallyedible.com

Social entrepreneurship

Motivation

While traditional, 'for profit' enterprises may be established by individuals motivated by the acquisition of personal wealth, those involved in social enterprise are rarely motivated by personal financial achievement. Typically their motivation is to address an unmet social need within a community. Although often thought to be a recent phenomenon, charitable, philanthropic, community orientated entrepreneurs have a long history. In the UK, for example, social entrepreneurship was the bedrock of Victorian private hospitals. Historically, social and community entrepreneurship has its origins in the nineteenth century when philanthropic industrialists demonstrated concern for the welfare of employees by improving their working, education and cultural lives. These industrialists believed that the wealthy had an obligation to give back to society by donating their wealth to good causes (Shaw 2004).

The development of community enterprise in the USA and Europe has taken somewhat different paths. Consequently there is some variation in the definitions currently used on the two sides of the Atlantic (Kerlin 2006). The concept is much broader in the USA and focuses on revenue generation. American academics perceive community enterprise as including organisations which sit along a continuum from socially beneficial activities (e.g. corporate sponsorship) through to dual purpose operations with profit and social goals, and at the extreme other end of the spectrum, non-profit operations. The reason why this development path has arisen in the USA is that in the 1960s the US Government launched the Great Societies programme which funded projects across poverty, education, healthcare, housing and community development. These funds were directed towards non-profit organisations already operating in these areas. Then with the downturn in the US economy in the 1970s, federal funding was drastically reduced. The result was that the non-profits who wished to sustain their community enterprise programmes were forced to look for alternative non-governmental revenue sources.

In Europe academic thought stresses community enterprise in relation to business entities which seek to enhance the social impact of their activities. These are firms which can be fostered as profit or non-profit operations. This leads academics to focus on the concepts such as corporate social responsibility. The alternative view is to perceive community enterprise as the 'third sector' which has a role somewhere between Government social services provision and corporate organisations which have adopted a social mission.

Factors of influence

The label 'social entrepreneurship' has recently emerged as a way of describing the work of community, voluntary and public organisations as well as private firms working for social and community objectives or including such objectives in their mission. The three important reasons for this situation are:

Changing community needs

The traditional providers of social and community products and services have been increasingly criticised as both bureaucratic and slow moving (Mulgan and Landry 1995). Changing demographics, ageing populations, advances in technology, labour market restructuring, plus concerns about drug and alcohol abuse have combined to change the social and health needs of many communities. Unfortunately, the large size and bureaucratic structures of Government agencies and many of the traditional charities has made it difficult for them to respond quickly to these changing social, community and health concerns; thereby failing to address these new needs.

The overstretched welfare state

In most developed economies, the welfare state and provision of government services to address social and community needs has become overstretched and hampered by severe financial resource restrictions (Leadbeater 1997). Consequently the needs of many communities are increasingly unmet by traditional government interventions and social welfare schemes.

Social exclusion

Inequalities have generated spatial concentrations of deprived communities and disadvantaged households. Some communities have responded by developing their own localised activities and initiatives designed to address the social and health needs they face.

McGregor et al. (1997) suggest that social enterprise organisations can be characterised by (1) a 'not for profit' motivation, (2) the capacity to build relationships of trust with their client groups and (3) expertise in dealing with disadvantaged groups and communities. These authors believe that social economy organisations such as community enterprises can play a significant role when (1) the public sector is unable or unwilling to take on the full costs of service delivery and (2) agencies are prepared to make some payment but this is not sufficient to cover the full costs and generate profits.

CASE STUDY

Achieving purpose

Case aims: To illustrate the role of social entrepreneurship in assisting disadvantaged groups within society.

Genesis is a UK community enterprise scheme which was started by Steve Holmes to be run on Christian principles with the aim of making a difference in communities. Based in the East Midlands, the initial Genesis venture was to acquire a chicken farm with an attached residential unit to provide occupational training for 15–25 year olds. Seven years later the operation received a Government grant to buy a large property which was converted into a facility that delivered catering services on a commercial and community basis. This operation generated the revenue to acquire an old church which was converted into a resource centre offering childcare, pre-schooling, post-schooling, breakfast and holiday clubs to a number of villages around the centre. The success of these ventures attracted national attention and support was made available to buy a derelict bus depot. This has been converted into the Genesis Social Enterprise Centre which provides family entertainment (children's play area, sports hall, 10 pin bowling, café, community rooms, a youth centre, business incubators and a conference centre).

Suma is an independent wholesaler of health and whole foods based in a purpose-built warehouse in West Yorkshire, UK. The company distributes 7,000 products to over 2,500 retail outlets. Most of the products are produced to Suma's ethical values in terms of fair trade, wage equality and environmental responsibility. The company started as a one-person business in 1974. In 1977 having employed seven people, the founder sold the business to these seven individuals on the understanding that Suma would be run as a workers' co-operative. All employees own a share in the business, but have to give up this share when they leave. Employees rotate job roles (e.g. office work for two days, truck driving for three). The employees believe their business success is their ability to offer faster, superior service over competition because of their greater commitment to ensuring every-body benefits from the equality which exists within the operation.

KaBoom! was set up in America in 1995 by Darrell Hammond using $25,000 of start-up capital. Darrell was a 30 year old dyslexic who did not finish college, and had been brought up in a children's home. He has a great passion for the idea that every child should be exposed to opportunities for healthy play and he was concerned about the dangers of playing in streets, alleys and disused buildings. His solution was for KaBoom! to focus on the creation of playgrounds for children in inner city areas. The model is simple. A local community group such as the YMCA commits to wanting to create a playground. KaBoom! then works to raise the neces-sary corporate sponsorship to fund the scheme. The role of the community partner is to locate a site and contribute towards the cost of the playground. KaBoom! also provides community volunteers with the training needed to develop their own fund raising skills. By 2002, KaBoom! had worked with 65,000 volunteers to help build 338 playgrounds in urban and low income communities across the USA.

Trade Plus Aid was started by Charlotte Di Vita when she visited Ghana during a severe drought which had ruined thousands of small farmers. She offered money to buy seeds, but the village elders refused her offer. Her counter proposal was that she would give the village £800 to buy seed if they would make her 800 pendant-size carvings. Back in London she set up a stall in a local market and sold the pendants for £6.99. This prompted her to create a seed bank where farmers could borrow seed which they then paid for after selling their crops. She built an interna-tional mail order business which she stocked (1) from sources in Africa and South America and (2) by persuading companies in developed nations to sell her products at cost. Her first seed bank opened in Ghana in 1995. Since then she has diversified into other projects such as establishing a factory in China to make enamel teapots and a wind chime factory in South America. Trade Plus relies mainly on volunteers to run the commercial side of the business and Di Vita only pays herself a very small salary. In less than 15 years she has been able to return over £5 million to producer communities in Africa, South America and the Far East.

Source: Thompson and Doherty 2006

Enhancing overseas aid

There is a growing view that the provision of direct aid such as food to developing nations does little to develop economic independence among the most disadvantaged within local populations (Wheeler et al. 2005). Hence there is growing support for non–governmental organisations (NGOs) and private sector organisations to create community projects specifically aimed at developing communities (or 'networks') to assist a specific economic group within a country. The aims of such projects are to build sustainable businesses, assist local economic development, build economic self-reliance and to enhance the quality of life.

CASE STUDY

Developing nation programmes

Case aims: To illustrate how social entrepreneurship can provide a more effective support system than the more conventional approach of developed economy nations offering Government grants.

Honey Care Africa was launched by a Kenyan entrepreneur Farouk Jiwa and two investors to process and sell high quality honey to the East African and European speciality foods sector. The company sells beehives specifically designed for the Kenyan environment to individuals in rural areas. The company has a relationship with an NGO which supplies the microfinance to fund the purchase of hives. Honey Care guarantees to pay a fixed price in cash to the beekeepers for the honey which they produce. The company has been able to help some 8,000 of Kenya's poorest farmers. Additionally, through their 'bees for trees' scheme the company offers free hives in exchange for farmers who reforest areas of land. As Honey Care has become larger, this has permitted the organisation to also assist 250 community-based organisations, women's groups and self-help associations.

SEKEM, based in Egypt, trains farmers in the use of biodynamic farming which improves the productivity of marginal land. By working with small farmers offering education and micro-financing, the organisation helps rural people become involved in the production of organically produced cotton, other foodstuffs and the manufacture of organically produced textiles.

Balrampur Chini Mills based in Calcutta, India is one of the country's largest sugar producers. The company's four mills are located in one of the poorest regions of the country, Uttar Pradesh. These operations purchase sugar cane from over 180,000 small-scale farmers. Fundamental to the success of the operation is the company policy that all farmers must be paid within seven days of delivering their cane. To minimise the farmers' transportation costs, the company operates 70 local cane collection centres. Additionally within each factory, the company has specialist staff whose role is to provide information and training to local farmers.

Defining social entrepreneurs

While by their very nature community enterprises are community-based organisations, they are typically driven or initiated by individuals motivated to improve the communities in which they live or with which they have an affiliation. A number of academics have identified the importance of the role of the 'community' or 'social entrepreneur' in local economic development (Johannisson and Nilsson, 1989). Like the word entrepreneur, definitions of the social entrepreneur have been debated and contested. Various researchers, development agencies and politicians have, however, sought to identify characteristics common to social entrepreneurs (Leadbeater 1997; Leadbeater and Goss 1998). Early US work in this area described social entrepreneurs as 'good people', who are 'different' as they are willing to take risks on behalf of others to address issues of social concern. In the UK, Leadbeater (1997) has proposed the following, more comprehensive description of those individuals who can be identified as social entrepreneurs:

1   They excel at spotting unmet needs and mobilising under-utilised resources to meet these needs.
2   They are driven and determined, ambitious and charismatic.
3   They are driven by a mission, rather than the pursuit of profit or shareholder value.

In the private sector it is quite possible to be a successful small business owner/ manager without being innovative, whereas it is extremely difficult to establish and create a successful social or community venture without being entrepreneurial. A key reason for this is that social and particularly community enterprises are restricted by the very limited resources of their founders and the excluded communities which they are seeking to help. Faced with such resource restrictions, those founding and involved in community enterprises can only succeed by being creative and innovative in their access to and use of scarce resources (Haugh and Pardy 1999).

Comparisons have been drawn with business and with 'for profit only' entrepreneurs (Drucker, 1989; Leadbeater, 1997). These writers have concluded that many of the traits and behaviours of successful community entrepreneurs mirror those of entrepreneurs working exclusively for profit objectives. These include drive, ambition, leadership, the ability to communicate a vision and inspire others and, maximum utilisation of scarce resources. Nevertheless the social entrepreneur will face certain unique obstacles including:

History of dependence

A history of dependency on a paternalistic government has encouraged a lack of confidence in individual ideas and creativity, restricted capacity building and created a dependency culture within both individuals and entire communities.

Outcomes

As the outcomes of social ventures are not always expressed financially, this can make it difficult to get others to buy in to proposed ventures. Also, because rewards are not always financial, this can make the decision to become involved less clear cut.

Perceptions about social entrepreneurs

For many, when starting up and/or supporting a social venture, challenges can be presented by the perceptions which some have of social entrepreneurs, as they can be regarded as radical, going against the grain and also capable of ruffling feathers.

CASE STUDY

Ecopreneurs

Case aims: To illustrate how support for appropriate agricultural technology can benefit developing nation farmers.

The primary focus of social entrepreneurs in developed nations is to focus on the needs of disadvantaged special groups in a country (e.g. inner city children, ethnic minorities). This can be contrasted with the much broader aims of social entrepreneurs in developing nations. The difference stems from the fact that in these latter countries there are huge numbers of the population such as poor farmers and their families who face poverty, hunger and earn well below their country's level of subsistence income. As a result social entrepreneurs in these countries tend to become involved in projects that can have major impact on a very large number of people. In his review of projects aimed at assisting small farmers in India, Pastakia (1998) has appropriately relabelled the social entrepreneurs involved as 'ecopreneurs'.

One example is Hermangee and Abhay Jambhekar who were teachers at a leadership development centre. They became interested in the non-viability of using expensive Western technology to create a green revolution. Hermangee discovered during her Ph.D. studies, 'vermicomposting'. This is the concept of manufacturing bio-fertiliser with the help of earthworms. The couple persuaded frappe and sugar cane farmers about the benefits of using vermicompost and this resulted in the couple starting to manufacture the product for the farmers. They started a commercial venture which within a short time was producing 2,000 tons per year. In 1993 they realised that expanding the operation was not economically viable so they started selling the technology to local farmers who could then manufacture the product for themselves and also sell their output to other farmers.

P.D. Uplenchwar was a social worker who having taken a post-graduate qualification in agricultural economics decided to return to his village after graduation. He turned to farming but also created community activities such as the creation of a farmer advisory centre. In 1991 he became increasingly concerned about the cost of chemical pesticides and spent his time developing an alternative, herbal pesticide. He decided to ignore the legislation over manufacturing pesticides and started a project in which he sold the recipe to farmers, or if they preferred, he supplied the product by manufacturing the pesticide himself.

Dr W.B. Rahudkar was Dean of an agricultural college who on retirement devoted his time to developing low-cost pest control alternatives for farmers. In 1990 he developed a low-cost, broad spectrum herbal insecticide from extracts of garlic and green chilli. Having validated the formula using farmer friends he then published the recipe in local farming magazines. His next success was to develop a low-cost, broad spectrum fungicide and again after testing, published the formula so that farmers could start making the product for themselves.

Micro-finance

Micro-finance is a concept of making very small loans available to people with no assets that can be offered as collateral, have no credit history or are perceived as a high risk lending proposition when assessed using the conventional lending criteria applied by commercial bankers (Moll 2005). The original thinking behind the micro-finance movement was access to capital is a requirement to support economic growth in agriculture. More recently the thinking on micro-finance has turned more towards how to create and operate micro-finance provision in order to optimise the provision of small loans to local entrepreneurs and communities.

The prevailing view is that subsidies create an artificial market expectation over interest rates among borrowers. Hence most micro-finance organisers charge their client a realistic commercial market rate of interest. Many micro-lenders find their actual operating costs in terms of assessing loans, making contact with people across large areas of geography and managing interest and loan repayments are much higher than those incurred by commercial bankers. Hence many of the micro-finance providers are only able to operate because they received funding from private and public sector sources to cover these higher operating costs (Rallens and Ghazanfar 2006).

The success of micro-finance to alleviate poverty and to create sustainable small enterprises has caused the concept to be widely adopted across both developed and developing nations (Woller 2002). However, recognition of the problems of offering micro-finance facilities to the very poor has resulted in some organisations creating a somewhat different funding model to assist this group in local communities. One such provider is the US-based organisation the Trickle Up Program (TUP) (Maes and Basu 2005). The organisation works in partnership with local organisations in developing nations who have the expertise and knowledge of the cultural and social issues influencing individual and community behaviour patterns. These local agencies select people who meet a poverty assessment score based on criteria such as lack of land ownership, extremely low income, illiteracy and being unable to obtain credit. Individuals who meet these extreme poverty criteria immediately receive a grant of $50. Accompanying the TUP grant, the local organisation provides both training and counselling to assist individuals to acquire basic business skills and to develop a viable business idea. The providers also help individuals to come together to form self-help groups to jointly work on helping each other create effective business propositions. After a few weeks of receiving guidance, the individual is given a second grant of $50. The majority of the TUP-funded, income generating activities are in agriculture (e.g. goat raising, vegetable cultivation).

CASE STUDY

The father of micro-finance

Case aims: To illustrate how one of the founders of the micro-finance movement overcame obstacles by adopting entrepreneurial solutions to encountered problems.

Muhammad Yunus, the founder of the Grameen Bank in Bangladesh has been a leader and innovator in the creation of effective micro-finance systems. His contribution to developing new approaches for helping poor communities has been so significant that he has been awarded the Nobel Prize for his endeavours. His story starts on his return to the newly created independent state Bangladesh in 1971 (Yunus 1998) to teach economics at Chittagong University. Whilst seeking to understand the level of the poverty in the country he observed situations such as

(Cont'd)

that of a woman who was being paid a pittance to make bamboo stools. This person would make more money if she only had the cash to buy the bamboo and to then sell her products in the local market.

He tried to convince a local bank to make micro-loans to people who were unable to offer any collateral on the loan. His request was refused. To demonstrate that this type of lending was commercially viable, he started lending his own money to villagers. Although he was successful, the commercial banks still remained unconvinced. So after seven years of struggle, Yunus was eventually given permission to set up a new independent bank. By the mid-1990s the Grameen Bank was working with 37,000 out of the 68,000 villages in Bangladesh, lending to 2.3 million borrowers, 94 per cent of whom are poor women. The total scale of lending was over $2 billion and the average loan size $175.20. The bank's primary target is the bottom 25 per cent of the population. Any family wishing to borrow funds must demonstrate they own less than half an acre of land and their total wealth does not exceed the equivalent of one acre of land. The most likely borrower within the family will be a woman. This has not been an easy process because the women borrowing funds often face criticism from some people within their village and may also be accused by religious leaders of going against Islamic principles.

The commitment of Yunus to the concept of communities managing profit generating activities that also meet social needs has resulted in the creation of a number of Grameen-sponsored community businesses. One operation is Grameen Cybernet which rents fibre optic cable lines from Bangladeshi Rail. Villagers can use the service to create their own on-line trading operation buying and selling goods. To start these new trading entities, individuals can borrow funds from Grameen Bank. Over time the Internet company will be sold to its customers such that the company is owned by the communities who will determine the longer term future for the operation.

SUMMARY LEARNING POINTS

- Entrepreneurial family firms are a critical source of market innovation.
- There is contradictory evidence about whether family firms are more successful than their non-family counterparts.
- Succession planning is a critical issue in relation to long term success of family firms.
- Succession management problems in family firms can lead to damaging conflict within the business.
- Family firms founded by entrepreneurs tend to sustain this orientation into subsequent generations who take over the running of the business.
- Some entrepreneurs perceive there are significant benefits in utilising their skills to assist disadvantaged members of society.
- Social entrepreneurship is perceived as being more effective than grant aid in many developing nation economies.
- A critical role of social entrepreneurs has been their involvement in the creation of sources of micro-finance.

ASSIGNMENTS

1 Assume that on graduation you have parents who own two small hotels and want you to become the manager of one of the hotels. Define the terms and conditions under which you would be prepared to join the business.
2 What are the problems and conflicts associated with the planning and implementation of a succession plan in a family firm?
3 Why is social enterprise such an important mechanism through which social entrepreneurs can return something to society?

DISCUSSION TOPICS

1 Discuss how you feel your attitudes, values and beliefs would influence your ability to work with parents who have insisted you join the family firm.
2 Identify one or more examples of social enterprise within the immediate area and discuss the purpose and success of the example entity(s).
3 Discuss why social enterprise is so important in assisting people who live in developing nation economies.

Additional information sources

Family firms

Chaganti, R. and Fariboz, D. (1991), Institutional ownership, capital structure, and firm performance, *Strategic Management Journal*, Vol. 12, No. 7, pp. 479–492.
Sharma, P. (2004), An overview of the field of family business studies: current status and directions for the future, *Family Business Review*, Vol. 17, No. 1, pp. 1–37.

Social entrepreneurship

Berkes, F. and Davidson-Hunt, I.J. (2007), Communities and social enterprises in the age of globalization, *Journal of Enterprising Communities*, Vol. 1, No. 3, pp. 209–219.
Dixon, E.A. and Clifford, A. (2007), Ecopreneurship – a new approach to managing the triple bottom line, *Journal of Organizational Change Management*, Vol. 20, No. 3, pp. 326–335.

12
Twenty-first-century Entrepreneurs

Chapter objectives

The aims of this chapter are to assist the reader to:

- understand that only a limited proportion of entrepreneurial successes stem from innovative disruption
- recognise small firm entrepreneurs can often succeed because their large firm competitors are inflexible
- comprehend new technologies offer possibly the greatest opportunities for entrepreneurs during the twenty-first century
- realise the scale of technological success is ultimately determined by market demand from both existing and potential, new customers
- understand innovation success consists of factors such as response of firms using current, dominant sector technology, economic conditions and socio-demographic change
- accept the most significant entrepreneurial opportunities exist by solving major world problems
- realise small firm entrepreneurs are already enjoying success in the field of sustainable energy
- understand developing nation entrepreneurs are already successfully challenging the big pharmaceutical companies in world markets
- realise the human genome project offers the added benefit that much of the data has been retained within the public domain
- accept genetic engineering will permit a diversity of new products across agriculture, numerous industrial sectors and healthcare
- realise the scale of entrepreneurial opportunities available by exploiting nanotechnology to build new products and invent technological processes has yet to be fully understood
- accept as evidenced by YouTube and MySpace there will still remain opportunities during the twenty-first century for entrepreneurs to convert a simple idea into a global business.

The elephant cycle

Disruption theory

Throughout the twentieth century there have been a number of occasions when an entrepreneurial individual had an idea which eventually led to the creation of a major corporation operating on a global scale. Then sometime later along comes another entrepreneur who successfully topples the incumbent elephant business from their leadership position in world markets. Christensen (1997) has proposed that the downfall of the incumbent is not the fault of the management, but instead the blame lies more with the firm's key customers continuing to push for improvements to existing products. As a result the soon-to-fail elephant may be aware of an emerging disruptive technology but is not really in a position to effectively counter the new threat.

There are examples that exist which validate Christensen's hypothesis. Nevertheless, examination of low technology sectors such as the food industry would suggest that only a minority of elephant deaths can be explained by the advent of a disruptive technology (Cravens et al. 2002). Furthermore, the expertise which existed within these major corporations should have permitted reaction to a newly emerging market trend by counter attacking through the establishment of their own operation or alternatively, acquiring the entrepreneurial irritant before the threat could adversely impact their business. For example, when Canon started to make inroads into the photocopier market with their lower price, desk top machine, Xerox clearly had both the technical expertise and dominant market position which would have permitted them to defeat their new enemy. Similarly, it seems inexplicable why the elephants in the branded foods and food service industries did not observe McDonald's early success and immediately open their own chain of fast food outlets. Instead they appear to have not only ignored the threat posed by Ray Kroc, but also just remained on the sidelines as James McLamore and David Edgerton began to expand out from Miami with their Burger King operation.

Loss of entrepreneurial capability

Many examples of entrepreneurs defeating incumbent elephants seem more likely to be explained by the latter organisations having lost the flexibility and proactive culture upon which their global success had originally been based. There appears to be no simple explanation of why a culture shift towards having become a totally conventional, passive and non-innovative organisation has occurred. One reason can be senior management apparently becomes fixated on believing the strategy which was successful in the past will continue to serve the company well in the future; whereas in reality there is an urgent need to shift towards a more entrepreneurial organisational culture (Slevin and Covin 1990). Those leaders whose preference is to avoid implementing change would do well to reflect on Parnell et al.'s (2005 p. 45) review of corporate failure and their observation that leaders 'should resist the notion that today's source of competitive advantage will be eternal'. Regretfully this type of leader, as their organisation moves from growth into market maturity, seems to perceive as totally unacceptable and disruptive, any actions by younger managers to persuade the business to be more innovative. These younger individuals either then learn to accept the status quo to retain their jobs or alternatively, quit and join a more entrepreneurial organisation (Amabile et al. 1996).

Loss of authority

Since the mid-twentieth century, one of the major pressures on senior managers within large organisations is to avoid risk and to build a stable business achieving steady sustained year-on-year profit growth. This is because major investors within the financial community such as the large pension funds want to enjoy ongoing dividend growth and a steady increase in the market value of the company shares. As is all too apparent in the business press, major entities within the financial community now have the power not just to express criticisms about what they perceive as a poorly managed company, but can also orchestrate the immediate removal of the incumbent CEO whose decisions they feel are contrary to their view on how the business should be managed. Most individuals in the world of business want a secure and highly paid career. Hence managers soon learn that to steadily progress up the corporate ladder or to be head-hunted for a senior position in another company, it is extremely important to develop a reputation for being a 'safe pair of hands'. Such individuals can never be expected to exhibit the risks associated with adopting an entrepreneurial orientation. This is why all too often leading elephant brands are overtaken, and sometimes totally disappear, following market entry by a new entrepreneurial upstart (Hill and Hansen 1991).

CASE STUDY

Not prepared to listen

Case aims: To illustrate that occasionally successful entrepreneurs develop an inability to listen to the views of others within the organisation.

In some cases the source of organisational intransigence can be the entrepreneur who originally created the successful business not accepting alternative perspectives proposed by another employee (Anon. 2005). The demise of Wang Laboratories, the company which built word processing into a global industry is one such story. The founder An Wang was an outstanding innovator and entrepreneur. He invented the magnetic pulse memory core essential to the development of computers and was a first mover in areas such as electronic calculators, semi-automated typesetting and computer storage systems. Having achieved market leadership for the first commercial generation of word processors and created a company enjoying over $3 billion in annual sales, Wang became fixated with beating IBM. He launched a hugely expensive head-to-head confrontation with the world's biggest computer firm. Even more disastrously, Wang was blind to the implications of how the PC would alter the word processing market and continued to believe he could convince the world that Wang products were immune to the competitive threat of IBM's entry into the desk top office machines market. As this brand battle progressed, Wang established himself as President, CEO and Director of Research and would not tolerate any dissent over his strategy inside the organisation. The outcome was inevitable. One of the world's most innovative companies was forced to file for bankruptcy in 1992.

Assessing opportunities

Market demand

New technology has been a critical driver in terms of influencing the world economy during the last century. There is no reason to believe that technology will not provide innumerable opportunities for the emergence of new entrepreneurial firms in the twenty-first century. Furthermore some of these new firms can be expected to create entirely new industrial sectors.

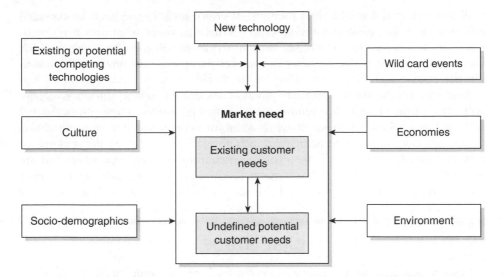

Figure 12.1   *Interaction of technology, market need and influencing variables*

For the next generation of entrepreneurs with the same competencies as Bill Gates, Richard Branson or Steve Jobs, identifying new opportunities will just require an intuitive decision about where to focus their endeavours. For less gifted individuals the task, however, will be more difficult. Hence where insightful intuition is lacking, one approach available to the individual or the organisation is to evaluate the potential opportunities associated with a new technology by assessing the implications of the influencing variables summarised in Figure 12.1.

At the core of the diagram in any size of business will be the customers (Ibrahim et al. 2008). The new technology must usually be capable of effectively satisfying existing customer needs. More importantly, however, in most cases the new technology will offer even greater revenue opportunities by satisfying as yet, unidentified new customer needs. An example of this scenario is provided by the Internet. This technology was initially perceived as an alternative promotional medium and subsequently, a system for supporting customer purchasing. Hence few individuals or organisations, except possibly some of the more perceptive futurists, could have predicted how the Internet would have such a widespread impact on numerous industrial processes across various market systems and would also stimulate customer culture shifts that have led to the emergence of completely new forms of social and buying behaviour.

Demand influencers

To survive most new technologies have to successfully compete with existing technologies (Hoffman 2000). In most cases these existing technologies will be utilised by major corporations who have a vested interest in ensuring the failure of the new market entrant. An example of this outcome is provided by the major pharmaceutical firms who, in the early days of biotechnology, were less than supportive towards this alternative approach to the development of new healthcare treatments.

Another influencing variable is a wild card event. This is a completely unexpected event that acts as a catalyst for increasing the market potential for a new technology. One such example is the sudden rise in world oil prices in 2007–2008 which has acted as a major stimulus over the market acceptance of hybrid and plug-in electric cars.

In many cases the first generation of products or services based on a new technology will be expensive to produce requiring relatively high prices at the time of initial launch. Hence during periods of weak economic conditions potential customers may feel unable to risk purchasing such a high price item and market acceptance may be slow. In some cases poor market penetration means profits generated are insufficient to support the R&D activities necessary to drive down the costs to permit the new technology to become commercially viable. As demonstrated for consumer goods such as the digital camera, the reverse scenario is also a likely outcome; namely during periods of rapid economic growth potential customers are more willing to take the risk of purchasing what currently is a relatively expensive product or service proposition.

Customer acceptance for a new technology will also be influenced by prevailing cultural values. One of the key reasons, for example, for the unexpectedly rapid growth in the consumer market for the first generation of mobile phones was the influence of the product being perceived as a 'must have item' among young people. Market penetration rates for subsequent generations of the product were also greatly assisted by the enthusiasm with which young people then moved into texting and sending pictures.

Societal changes

Socio-demographic change which results in the re-shaping of markets will strongly influence the demand for new products and services. In the Western world, the onset of population ageing has led to people aged 55+ becoming the dominant age group within society (Chaston 2009). Additionally many of these older people are now more financially secure and enjoy a higher standard of living than younger people, especially families with children. The implications of this scenario are that entrepreneurs would be well advised when assessing the potential for a new technology, to give greater attention to the market opportunities among older age groups instead of the traditional primary consumer target group of 18–45 year olds with families

Over the last 20 years there has been a gradual increase with the problems associated with population growth, pollution and the earth's finite supply of key natural resources. Until recently, however, most citizens in developed economies were not too concerned about the impact on their lives of adverse environmental change. Hence other than those entrepreneurs interested in eco-protection, few developers of new technology have worried about the environmental implications of new products and services being created. In the last few years, however, in a large part due to growing awareness of global warming, Governments and their citizens now recognise the need for industries to exhibit greater environmental responsibility. This attitude shift has implications for entrepreneurs in terms of exploiting new opportunities and the expectation of their customers in terms of being supportive of firms exhibiting a higher level of moral and ethical standards.

Global warming

Climate change

Authors such as Canton (2007) and Dicken (2007) have written entire books about the major problems confronting the human race and the opportunities that will emerge in the twenty-first century. Although among these writers there is some degree of disagreement about which are the most difficult problems that will need to be overcome, there is apparent consensus that some of the most important are global warming, healthcare and the highly controversial new technology, nanotechnology.

The idea that burning ever larger amounts of fossil fuels could increase the level of carbon dioxide (or greenhouse gases) in the earth's atmosphere, which in turn would lead to climate change, was first proposed in the late nineteenth century (Dyson 2005). For most of the twentieth century, the theory was ignored until growing concerns about the impact of rising greenhouse gases led to the formation of the international body known as the Intergovernmental Panel on Climate Change (IPCC) in 1988. Successive reports by the panel provided increasingly strong evidence that during the final decades of the twentith century about 75 per cent of the carbon dioxide being released into the atmosphere comes from the burning of fossil fuels. This in turn is leading to a rapid increase in the rate of global warming. Obtaining acceptance for their ideas initially proved extremely difficult for the IPCC. Eventually under the auspices of the United Nations, in 1997 the world leaders met in Kyoto, Japan to discuss proposals about limiting carbon dioxide emissions.

With even countries such as the USA now accepting that global warming is a major potential threat to the human species, an increasing number of offers of entrepreneurs are implementing strategies to exploit the new significant business opportunities that are associated with effectively responding to climate change. For example, with oil perceived as a finite resource and a source of greenhouse gases, entrepreneurs and some large corporations have turned their attention to renewable resources such as the use of solar, wind and wave power (Elliott 1992).

Solar power

In part due to advances achieved by NASA during the development of power sources for the electronic components in space vehicles, the first area of potentially cost effective renewable energy technology which attracted attention is solar power (Caldwell 1994). This technology uses a photovoltaic device to convert sunlight into energy. As well as the benefit that sunlight is a free energy source, the technology has the added attraction that it can be used in remote locations far from utility power grids and as stand alone systems in consumer products, such as outdoor lighting, personal electronics, battery chargers, and solar roof panels.

Like so many new technologies, the initial development of the solar power industry was led by University scientists and individual entrepreneurs because major corporations remained unconvinced about the commercial potential for the technology. From these small players has emerged some of the first generation giants within the renewable energy sector.

CASE STUDY

Solar entrepreneurs

Case aims: To illustrate entrepreneurial activities within the solar energy industry.

One company which is now a large successful corporation is Ausra. This firm started life as a small company, Heat Power & Light Ltd which was formed to exploit a solar cell invented at Sydney University in Australia. Another giant in the game is China's leading photovoltaic cell manufacturer Suntech Power which was founded by Dr Zhengrong Shi in the early 1990s. The success of his venture is demonstrated by the fact that he is now one of China's wealthiest citizens and Suntech is rapidly heading towards becoming one of the top five solar companies in the world.

One of the pioneers in the field of solar energy is the American Stanford R. Ovshinsky. Born into a poor family in Akron, Ohio in 1923, he was a self-taught scientist who led the development of the new science of amorphous and disordered materials. In 1960, along with his wife and collaborator, Iris, he founded Energy Conversion Devices, Inc. to exploit science as a way of solving serious societal problems in the fields of energy and information. He recognised that the key to successful solar power was to minimise the costs of producing photovoltaic devices. Currently there are two primary types of device, crystalline systems where a light-sensitive film is laid on a clear substrate such as glass and the potentially more complex product in terms of ease of manufacturing, thin film photovoltaic material. Initially crystalline systems were more popular because they offered lower manufacturing costs and greater durability upon installation. Ovshinsky was attracted to the idea that thin film technology would eventually offer the benefit of being able to be manufactured like paper which would dramatically reduce production costs and make installation a much easier process. Eventually he developed the needed advances in materials that permitted him to launch ECD Ovonics to manufacture a low-cost thin film product. Having demonstrated the benefits of the material, other leading players in the industry are moving away from manufacturing crystalline systems and building thin film manufacturing plants

Wind power

Exploiting the power of the wind as an energy source is not a new idea. Windmills have existed for hundreds of years for use in tasks such as a method for grinding corn. Probably because of the strong heritage of windmills in Europe, EU countries have tended to favour wind power as the most effective route through which to reduce reliance on fossil fuels (Soderholm and Klaasen 2007). A major drawback to wind energy, however, has been people's adverse reaction to the visual and noise impact of having wind farms built in their area. To overcome this criticism, plans are now in progress to curtail further development of wind farms on-shore and to build the next generation of wind farms out at sea. A number of off-shore wind farms, especially in Western Europe, are either already in operation or expected to come on stream within the next few years. There has, however, been mounting criticism over the efficiency of wind generated energy in terms of the construction and ongoing operating costs relative to electricity generated from more conventional sources such as fossil fuels or natural gas. The counter argument is that wind power may be more expensive but is accompanied by that increasingly important factor of zero carbon emissions.

CASE STUDY

A wind power entrepreneur

Case aims: To illustrate the success of one wind power entrepreneur.

The growing interest in wind energy has already spawned an extremely successful entrepreneurial start-up in Aurich, a small town in Germany. This is Enercon which is a global leader in the industry employing several thousand people. In the early 1980s, the firm's entrepreneurial founder, Aloys Wobben, had the idea of using wind to generate electricity. Wobben's breakthrough came with the development of the gearless wind turbine which still remains the unique selling proposition of the Enercon business offering the benefits of less wear and tear, longer service life and lower maintenance. The company now manufactures a range of models, from the small E-33 for inaccessible locations to the larger, bestselling E-70, E-82 and E-126. These latter products utilise the unique Enercon fin-shaped rotor blades that supply 15 per cent more output than conventional rotors of the same diameter (Orth 2008). How long Enercon is to remain a global leader is a big question because the company faces growing competition from the huge, highly diversified American elephant GE Corporation and two relatively new players in the business, Gold Wind and Sinovel. Both these companies are Chinese and because of their lower manufacturing costs, have the potential to significantly increase the intensity of price-based competition in world markets.

Wave power

The high electricity generation cost associated with wind power has caused some experts to favour the greater use of water as an energy source. Water has been used for many years to power hydro–electric plants and is a critically important economic resource in countries such as Brazil, Canada, Egypt, the USA, Norway and Sweden. Unfortunately, the environmental impact of constructing huge dams and diverting water flow to generate hydro–electricity can be highly adverse. However, given that the majority of the earth's surface is covered by ocean, there is now increasing interest in using the ocean as an energy generation source (Von Jouanne 2006). One approach is to exploit tidal power through the construction of tidal barriers which direct the tidal flow through underwater turbines. The viability of this solution is under some doubt, however, because the idea of creating tidal barriers is now facing increasing resistance from environmentalists concerned about the impact on the marine environment of implementing such large scale alterations in the tidal flow. As a result harnessing the power of the waves is now perceived as a lower cost and environmentally more benign approach to using the oceans as a power generation source.

CASE STUDY

Wave power entrepreneurs

Case aims: To illustrate some of the entrepreneurial ventures engaged in seeking to exploit wave energy as an alternative, sustainable power source.

A leading innovator in the field of wave power is Pelamis, a Scottish company founded in 1998 by Doctors Yemm, Pizer and Retzler (Thilmany 2008). Their idea is to build a wave energy converter that generates electricity from the movement of ocean waves. Each converter is a semi-submerged, articulated structure composed of cylindrical sections linked by hinged joints. Hydraulic rams resist the wave-induced motion of these joints. The force of that resistance is used to pump high-pressure fluid through hydraulic motors via smoothing accumulators, to drive electrical generators that produce energy. Arrays of these interlinked converters are called wave farms. The electricity that they produce is available for utility and electric companies to purchase. A wave farm of 40 converters, covering a square kilometre of ocean surface, can generate enough electricity to power 20,000 homes. The company has three projects under way, two off the coast of the United Kingdom and one near Portugal.

Another power generation approach is to use tethered buoys which have turbines that generate electricity as the buoys rise and fall in response to the passing waves (Von Jouanne 2006). The buoys are connected to a central collection hub on the ocean floor from which the generated electricity is then directed on-shore via an undersea cable. A leading company in this field is the US company, Ocean Power Technologies. Formed by Doctors Taylor and Burns in 1994, the company has developed their own proprietary PowerBuoy™ technology which captures wave energy using large floating buoys anchored to the seabed. Ocean trials commenced in 1997 off the coast of New Jersey and full-scale protoypes capable of generating 40 kW have been installed off Hawaii and New Jersey. The company was floated on the London Stock Exchange's AIM market in October 2003 and completed its US NASDAQ IPO in April 2007. The company has now begun the initial phase of the installation of a 1.39 MW wave farm off the northern coast of Spain. This project is a joint venture with the Spanish utility Iberdrola SA. A full size demonstration plant of up to 5 MW capacity is also being planned for installation in UK waters.

Clean coal

The other even more important solution to the problem of greenhouse gases is to reduce emissions from sources which are burning hydrocarbon fuels such as coal powered fire stations and of course, the ubiquitous human toy, the car. In relation to coal, the primary innovators in this area are the big mining companies because unless a solution can be found to reduce emissions, the world coal industry could face a difficult future. Although advances in power station design and the scrubbing of gases emitted from chimneys are improving air quality, there is still need for chimney emissions to be further reduced. The primary new technology which is being promoted by the energy industry is the capture and under sea storage of carbon dioxide. To date the claims in the numerous industry press releases have been much more positive than the actual technical breakthroughs that have so far been achieved for this new technology. Hence reducing human's reliance upon cars driven by burning hydrocarbon fuels is clearly an important technical and environmental objective.

Alternative car propulsion systems

In the nineteenth century, some early cars were powered by electricity. The weight and poor storage capabilities of electric batteries meant this technology was inferior to the alternative of the internal combustion engine. Although some people believe further developments over the years of the electric car have been blocked due to a conspiracy between the car and oil industry elephants, it is only very recently that the car industry has begun to look at alternative power sources in place of strategies based on reducing oil consumption by improving engine efficiency and exhaust systems (Portney et al. 2003). Given the costs associated with developing a realistically priced vehicle powered by an alternative energy source that can travel a reasonable distance and can compete with the conventional car, not surprisingly most of the R&D in this field has been undertaken by the major car companies.

As has frequently been the case in the past 20 years, the Japanese are ahead of the Americans in this race. Their first innovative solution was to add electric power to augment a petrol powered vehicle. The first hybrid car to use this approach was the Toyota Prius. This vehicle was an immediate marketing success in eco-orientated markets such as California. Other car manufacturers outside of Japan have since raced to regain market share which they appear to be losing to their Pacific Rim competitors. Meanwhile within and alongside the car industry work on developing alternative solutions is in progress, for example, the all-electric car and the use of hydrogen power cells.

CASE STUDY

The Tesla

Case aims: To illustrate the obstacles that can confront the successful execution of a complex entrepreneurial project.

Although most industry observers expect that eventually one or more of the incumbent car manufacturers will dominate the market for zero emission vehicles, there have been a few notable examples of success by small entrepreneurial firms from outside the car industry. One of these small outsiders is Tesla Motors of California (Copeland 2008). The company is named after Nikola Tesla, an eccentric late-nineteenth- and early-twentieth-century inventor. Tesla has developed and commenced manufacturing the first zero emission sports car, the Tesla Roadster. This is currently the only highway capable production electric car of any kind for sale in the United States. With a range of 220 miles per charge and an ability to accelerate from 0 to 60 mph in 3.9 seconds, some of the innovative technology behind the project has come from lessons learned in the computer industry during the development of lighter, more powerful and more efficient batteries for use in mobile devices such as the laptop computer.

The car was conceived by Martin Eberhard, an engineer and serial entrepreneur who was convinced he could create a practical, zero emission vehicle by fitting numerous lithium laptop batteries into an existing sports car chassis. Earlier in his career, he launched a series of start-ups, including an electronic-

(Cont'd)

book company which he co-founded called NuvoMedia. He sold this business to Gemstar for $187 million in 2000. His strategy for minimising the development costs for the project was to build the car by licensing electric-drive-train technology from another company (AC Propulsion) and using an existing carmaker to do the manufacturing. During the development phase of the project Eberhard was responsible for inventing new approaches to battery-cooling, electric motor, and power electronics patents used in the vehicle.

Unable to persuade any venture capital company to fund his ideas, he met with Elon Musk. This individual was the co-founder of PayPal who had been forced out of the on-line-payment company, but still made millions when the company was sold to eBay. Musk agreed to invest $6.3 million into Tesla and was appointed company chairman. The price of his participation, however, was to have major control over strategy. For example, Musk saw the franchise-dealership arrangements in the US car industry as an increasingly expensive, margin-killing business model. His alternative model is that of owning and operating a network of Tesla dealerships.

As the project progressed with Musk injecting more funds into the project disagreements between him and Eberhard increased. In the key area of product design, Musk's viewpoint was influenced by his vision to build the Next Great American Car Company. This caused conflict with Eberhard, who had the more humble dream of rapidly developing and marketing a relatively low-cost, zero emission sports car. By the end of 2006, Musk and other investors such as Google's Larry Page and Sergey Brin who had become involved in the company had injected approximately $150 million into the project. By then, however, major problems began to emerge over the spiralling estimated costs for manufacturing the vehicle and numerous failures by the development team to meet critical project milestones.

To reduce the rate at which the company was burning through cash reserves, plans to build a car plant to produce a zero emission saloon car in 2010 were mothballed by the Board. Eberhard had negotiated with the UK sports car company Lotus to produce the Roadsters. The agreement included financial penalties should production not begin on schedule. When delays occurred Lotus invoked a $4 million penalty clause and this, plus other problems, caused Musk to have Eberhard removed from the Board and to appoint Ze'ev Drori, an operations-focused Silicon Valley veteran as the new CEO. A technical team led by Hal Straubel re-examined every component with the aim of identifying where savings could be made that would permit manufacturing costs to be lower than the launch price. Having achieved this goal, Tesla started production of the Roadster in March 2008.

Source: www.teslamotors.com

Healthcare

Industry evolution

Through natural selection the human body has evolved a capability to survive for approximately 40–50 years. Ongoing advances in medical science have reached the point where this natural life span can probably be doubled for a significant proportion of the human race by the mid–twenty–first century. This achievement comes with very significant added costs. Every time a few more years are added to life spans, there is the emergence of new medical conditions for which identified solutions are extremely expensive. Added to this spiralling in the cost of new treaments is the rapid rise in obesity levels which is already leading to more people developing conditions such as diabetes and requiring replacement surgery for major joints. The combined impact of these two trends is that even the richest nations are finding healthcare is becoming the greatest single area of expenditure. In the UK, the NHS has already been forced to ration care and in the USA, private insurance providers have begun to limit or refuse to fund certain types of treatment (Ahmed and Cadenhead 1988).

The evolution of modern healthcare concepts first emerged in the nineteenth century with the establishment in Europe of medical schools to train doctors in the scientific principles of diagnosis and treatment (Lerer 2005). This event was accompanied by a recognition that diseases such as cholera and typhoid could be controlled by supplying clean water and the construction of sewage systems. A third breakthrough was the work of Jenner and Pasteur who demonstrated that certain diseases such as smallpox could be defeated by using inoculation to develop immunity within an entire population. It was not until the twentieth century that advances in organic chemistry in Europe led to research on the complex organic compounds which provide the foundations for today's global pharmaceutical industry (D'Andrade 1999). One of the first breakthroughs was the discovery in 1932 by a Bayer chemist that a red dye called protosil was found to be active against the bacteria streptococccus. Slightly earlier in 1928 Alexander Fleming in Cambridge discovered that a mould belonging to the genus penicillin was capable of destroying the bacteria staphyloccus.

Commercialisation of these 1930s scientific discoveries was an early demonstration of the vast sums of money which could be made from inventing new drugs. This led to the development of the global pharmaceutical industry which emerged following the Second World War. In the 1950s and 1960s, the focus of the drug companies was to discover new anti-bacterial drugs (or antibiotics) that would treat conditions that did not respond to penicillin. In order to ensure that the vast sums of money invested in R&D could be recovered from the sale of new products, the pharmaceutical companies sought to patent each new discovery to avoid the drug being duplicated by a competitor (Marmor 1998). In their ongoing search for new drugs which would confer a virtual global monopoly for the treatment of a specific illness, the European and American companies have invested vast sums into R&D. Their reward has been a whole range of new drugs such as serotonin inhibitors to treat depression, beta blockers for heart conditions and blood pressure reduction agents. The major drug companies claim that very high prices must be charged for these drugs in order to recover their huge investment in research. The market reality behind the drug industry's success is sales can only occur if funded by a country's welfare state or through private medical insurance. As a consequence over 90 per cent of global branded drug sales are restricted to the world's top 20 economies. There are indications, however, that the share of profits spent on R&D may be much smaller than expenditure by these elephants to retain their domination of global markets (Benner 2004).

The growing healthcare funding crisis now facing Governments has led to the emergence of new opportunities when the patent expires on a new drug for entrepreneurial organisations to enter the market offering generic, low priced versions of the original product. Understandably the global pharmaceutical elephants have been highly resistant to this new threat. However, the healthcare funding crisis has forced Governments to introduce legislation and policies to promote greater adoption of generics by their nation's healthcare providers. The current size of the global generic drug market is estimated to be in excess of $100 billion.

CASE STUDY

India's drug entrepreneurs

Case aims: To illustrate the success of Indian entrepreneurs in successfully challenging the elephants in the world's pharmaceutical industry.

India has been the leading source of new entrepreneurs that have most benefited from the trend towards the increased use of generics. The turning point in the country's pharmaceutical industry came when the Government repealed the Act under which drugs were protected by patents. The explicit purpose of this legislation was to terminate the nation's reliance on imports and to make the country self-reliant through expanding domestic production. To achieve this aim the Indian companies exploited the time lag until international patent law will again apply which will block the use of reverse engineering to discover the formulation of leading patented drugs produced elsewhere in the world (Malhotra and Lofgren 2004). Many of the major companies in the Indian drugs industry share the same development pattern of starting life as a small family business evolving over time into a global player. India's largest company Ranbaxy was founded in 1962 by Ranjit Singh to market pharmaceuticals in Amritsar. Unable to repay funds borrowed from Bhai Mohan Singh, this latter individual took over the company in lieu of the loan repayment and he appointed his son Dr Parvinder Singh to run the business. In 1969 the company began manufacturing Calmpose, a generic version of Valium. As the company product line began to broaden, the company entered key overseas markets in North America and Europe. Now run by Dr Parvinder's son, Malvinder Mohan Singh, in mid 2008 the Singh family announced their intention of accepting a takeover offer in the region of $4 billion from the Japanese corporation Daiichi Sankyo.

The Indian drugs industry achieved worldwide prominence when the firm Cipla offered to supply a triple combination drugs treatment for AIDS to countries in Africa for $350, against the American patent holder's price of $12,000. This company, now India's second largest pharmaceutical company, started life as a small entrepreneurial family business in 1935, when Dr Khwaja Abdul Hamied set up the business in a rented bungalow in Bombay. After the Second World War the company began manufacturing products under licence and also developed their own products such as Rotahaler, the world's first such dry powder inhaler device, the anti-cancer drugs, vinblastine and vincristine, developed in collaboration with the National Chemical Laboratory, and the antiretroviral drug, zidovudine. The expertise acquired in manufacturing drugs under licence and the development of their own products provided the basis for Cipla to successfully enter the global market supplying generic products.

Dr Reddy Laboratories was founded in 1984 by Dr Anji Reddy, the son of a wealthy tumeric farmer, with a $120,000 bank loan. Within only a few years, the company enjoyed success with copies of Bayer's antibiotic ciprofloxacin and AstraZeneca's omeprazole. In the 1990s the company moved into development of new drugs, but lacking the funds to support clinical testing, the company licensed their first product, an insulin sensitiser, to Novo Nordisk in 1997. This was the first ever licensing of an Indian-developed drug to a multi-national pharmaceuticals company. Rapid growth through expansion into numerous overseas markets, a series of acquisitions in America and a merger with Cheminor Drugs made Dr Reddy's India's third largest drugs company in 2001.

Sources: www.cipla.com; www.drreddys.com; www.ranbaxy.com

The human genome

Even with the advent of generics, the richest nations are no longer able to meet the ever rising costs of new drugs that are entering the market. Currently the greatest hope in terms of finding ways of replacing expensive drugs lies in genomic medicine (Benner 2004). This approach is based on exploiting the knowledge which has become available from deciphering the DNA sequencing of the human genome. This new understanding will permit new approaches using molecular biology to treat a diversity of medical conditions. By working at the molecular level, scientists are beginning to understand how to develop new solutions such as blocking molecule synthesis within cancer cells, curing people by introducing missing DNA sequences into their bodies and using recombinant DNA to produce drugs such as human insulin. Genomics also has the potential to more effectively control disease vectors such as the mosquito.

A very important aspect of genomics is the majority of the research is being undertaken in Universities and research institutes. This means the knowledge generated is not locked away within the big pharmaceutical companies, but instead remains in the public domain for exploitation and further development by academics, independent science laboratories and small entrepreneurial technology companies. Although America and the UK are two leading countries in terms of the level of expenditure on genomics research, the knowledge from studies as a result of remaining in the public domain is permitting other countries to enter the field (Katz and Hoffman 2005). To accelerate the involvement of developing nations in this field of medicine, the World Health Organisation is funding collaborative research training programmes between US Universities and scientists from countries such as Thailand, Venezuela and Costa Rica.

Although it is still too early to accurately predict the influence of genomics in the twenty-first century, there are indications that the impact will be even greater than twentieth century discoveries such as vaccines and antibiotics. There is also growing evidence that genomics will provide the basis for the creation of numerous, new entrepreneurial firms across the world which will significantly reduce the probability that the technology will become dominated by a few, huge global corporations (Hammond 2002).

CASE STUDY

The genome entrepreneur

Case aims: To illustrate how the World Genome Project has created new opportunities for one of the world's leading entrepreneurial scientists.

As an unknown researcher at the National Institute of Health, Dr Venter became interested in sequencing human DNA after the first commercial sequencing machines became available (Wade 1999). In 1992, a medical financier, Wallace Steinberg, spotted the significance of Dr Venter's ideas and funded him to create the Institute for Genomic Research. In 1995 he and a colleague successfully decoded the genome of a bacterium. Having joined the PE Corporation, his strategy for the company was to sell the instrument-making operations and to restructure

(Cont'd)

the business as purely a genome company. PE Biosystems would make DNA sequencing machines, and Celera headed up by Dr Venter would focus on genome sequencing research.

Dr Venter then came to prominence by announcing that the world's public sector Human Genome Project research consortium was using a flawed technique and that Celera would be first in decoding the human genome using the faster, but much riskier, 'whole genome shotgun sequencing' technique. To achieve this goal he linked together 300 DNA sequencing machines and one of the world's most powerful computers which provided 20 trillion bytes of disk storage. The funding for Celera's participation in the scientific race was assisted in part by two pharmaceutical companies, Pharmacia and Amgen, each taking out $50 million, five-year subscriptions in Celera's human genome database. President Clinton in America then announced that human genome sequences could not be patented and all results should be made freely available to all researchers. This decision, plus Dr Venter's challenge, spurred the Human Genome Project teams to accelerate their research. The outcome was that in 2001 both they and Celera published full drafts of their results which covered about 83 per cent of the genome.

At that time both groups announced the major aspects of the project were complete, although both continued to publish supplementary research over the next few years. During this period Celera was also engaged in research on sequencing the genomes of three other scientifically important species – the fruitfly, the mouse and rice – to provide the core of a biomedical and an agricultural database. Meanwhile the Human Genome Project licensed their knowledge and technologies to private companies. This acted as a catalyst stimulating significant growth in the multibillion-dollar US biotechnology industry and fostered the development of new medical applications for the science of genomics.

In 2006, Dr Venter abruptly resigned from Celera and used the financial resources he had accumulated to establish the not-for-profit J. Craig Venter Institute (JCVI). The new organisation is involved in a diverse range of genome research. Their ocean sampling expedition uncovered more than six million new genes and thousands of new protein families from organisms found in seawater. Dr Venter believes that this knowledge can be used to reduce global warming by developing an organism capable of accelerating the rate at which carbon dioxide is absorbed by the world's oceans. Work is also underway to sequence the microbial flora found in human environments such as the vagina, oral cavity and intestines. With the aim of alleviating infectious diseases, JCVI has sequenced a variety of important infectious disease agents such as the mosquito species, *Aedes aegypti*, and is seeking to understand the evolution of viral genomes such as influenza and coronavirus.

Source: www.jcvi.org

Nanotechnology

A micro-technology

Nanotechnology is the science which involves using powerful microscopes and advanced chemical techniques to rearrange atoms which permits the creation of new molecular forms (Thomas 2006). The terminology stems from the measurement of one nanometre, which is equal to one-billionth of a metre. Nanotechnology does not refer to any one single area of science because the concept is being applied across a diverse range of activities such as building computer circuits and computer memory storage systems atom by atom, while biotechnologists are manipulating atoms to build new DNA molecules. As all of these activities involve the restructuting of atoms, there is an opportunity for different technologies to be combined in the development of new scientific solutions. Neuroscientists are able to build neurons and with biologists building long strands of DNA to behave like electronic circuits, technological hybridisation means it is now feasible for human brain cells to communicate directly with computers.

The first generation of nanotechnology products are already in use within industry. Nanoparticles are being used in the cosmetics and paint industries to create new colourings and to develop new, more powerful cleaning compounds. In the textile industry, mills are now using nanoparticle compounds to make spill resistant and stain resistant fabrics. Unlike previous coating solutions, the nanoparticles do not alter or coarsen the texture of the fabric. In the world of medicine a number of nanotech-based drugs, new drug delivery systems and diagnostic tests have been developed. Additionally pharmaceutical firms are reformulating existing drugs into a nanoform which both improves performance and permits extension of existing drug patents. In the oil industry, nanoparticles have been used as catalysts to improve extraction of oil from previously uneconomic reserves. The technology is also seen as the path through which to develop more effective alternative energy devices such as solar cell membranes.

Some futurists believe the potential of nanotechnology is such that it will have more impact on the human race than any previously developed form of technology (Kurweil 2006). For example healthcare will be revolutionised by nanochemicals that can pass across cell membranes and be targeted at specific structures within the cell. New nanomaterials will be created that can replace commodities such as rubber, minerals and fibres. Already a product known as quantum wire, constructed from carbon nanoparticles can conduct electricity ten times faster than copper. Possibly one of the most radical applications will be the creation of nanobots that by being linked with our brain cells will permit human memory expansion and permit sensory perceptions that represent a totally virtual reality experience. Additionally because the nanobots can use wireless technology for data transfer, people will be able to link themselves remotely to computers and also communicate telepathically with each other. The implications of such advances, for example, are huge in relation to the entertainment industry because a wide range of visual, auditory and other sensory experiences could be distributed to individual people within an entire society.

Despite huge potential benefits, this technology does come with some very significant risks (Springston 2008). Many chemicals which in their current form are considered to be totally safe can completely change their behaviour when reconstituted as nanoparticles. This is because the small size increases surface area and causes the chemical to become chemically more reactive. Aluminium oxide which has been used in teeth fillings for many years, as a nanoparticle is transformed into becoming a very powerful explosive. Carbon nanoparticles have already been found in the laboratory to cause cancer when inhaled and also may cause damage to brain cells. Another area of risk is the current research in progress to develop new manufacturing systems in which the nanoparticles can grow and self-replicate. The chemicals in these systems will be behaving in exactly the same way as living organisms. The concern must be what happens if there is a spillage and these bio-molecules continue to reproduce, or even worse after escaping into the environment, mutate into an even more deadly form. The world has enough problems dealing with illnesses caused by bacteria and viruses. Nanotechnology offers the potential of creating a huge new range of potentially uncontrollable pandemics.

CASE STUDY

Nanotechnology entrepreneurs

Case aims: To illustrate the activities of some of the ways entrepreneurial scientists are seeking to exploit the commercial opportunities offered by this new technology.

One of early entrepreneurial start-ups is Nanosphere which was founded in 2000 to exploit research at Northwestern University in Evanston, Illinois by Dr Robert Letsinger and Dr Chad Mirkin. One of their commercial applications is a nanoparticle probe which permits ultra-sensitive, multiple detection of proteins in clinical samples. Another application is the enhancement of industrial sensors to permit more rapid and accurate testing for nucleic acid and protein targets in industrial sensors. This type of detection has widespread applications, including drinking water testing, the emergency services sector, such as fire and police departments and in security systems to combat bio-terrorism. Having created a molecular diagnostic testing system the company is now developing tests for cancer, cystic fibrosis gene mutation, herpes viral infection, and cardiovascular disease. The problem is research costs in nanotechnology are very high.

Another entrepreneurial start-up Argonide was founded by Fred Tepper in 1994 to focus the use of nanotechnology in filtration technology and devices. In 2000, Fred, with his associate Dr Leonid Kaledin, invented the nano alumina filter, currently being marketed under the brand name NanoCeram®. The sale of filter cartridges, manufactured by Argonide, is growing rapidly. The original technology that focused on water filtration has been expanded to include other fluids by creation of an activated carbon filter with unusually rapid adsorption capabilities kinetics. Applications include filtration in residential, commercial and industrial sectors for virus and protein separation and for sampling for infectious viruses in water supplies. A current major company thrust is the development of low-cost filter systems for use by people in the third world that are deprived of electric power and clean water. As a result of these ongoing developments, in 2006 Argonide granted a worldwide exclusive license to the global engineering conglomerate Ahlstrom to manufacture and market their patented range of micro-filters.

CALMEC is a high technology company in the molecular electronics industry. Founded in 1997 the company is specialising in the field of molecular electronics using individual molecules to form the components of electronic devices. The reason for this focus is that molecule-sized electronics will eventually lead to the creation of electronic devices hundreds of times smaller and at a cost lower than that possible with semiconductor electronics.

Sources: www.nanosphere.us; www.calmec.com

✎ Conclusions

It can be predicted with certainty that in a garage or laboratory somewhere in the world there are as yet unrecognised individuals working on new entrepreneurial, high technology ideas. Their efforts will eventually lead to the creation of entirely new industries or the introduction of a disruption that will permit these entrepreneurs to create new global corporations. There is a high probability that some of the more alert large companies are concurrently pursuing the same objective in their own much better resourced laboratories. Alternatively these larger firms will gain control of the technology through acquisition of a more successful, smaller firm. One would imagine, for example, that the world's leading microchip company, Intel is already deeply engaged in seeking to exploit nanotechnology as the basis for an entirely new generation of microchips.

In some sectors of industry the large firm may have decided to postpone investment in R&D and instead are satisfied to merely observe and wait. Then should an emerging technology be proven to be commercially viable by a smaller entrepreneur, they can enter the market by exploiting their technology infrastructure and greater resources to develop a competitive response. At the moment, for example, Richard Branson's new enterprise, Virgin Galactic, is working with Burt Rutan's Mojave Aerospace Ventures to create the world's first commercial system capable of taking private citizens into space. Should this venture prove viable, no doubt existing global aerospace corporations, such as Boeing will consider entering the market. The larger aerospace firm's ability to compete would be further enhanced should the world's military decide to start injecting development funds into this sector.

As costs for recently introduced new technology begin to fall and more individuals gain expertise in a sector, it is often the case that only recently established global players fail to appreciate that for a relatively small level of expenditure, new ideas can be converted into successful businesses by individual entrepreneurs. One such example is provided by Facebook, the social networking site which was founded as a new business by Mark Zuckerberg in 2004 while he was still a student at Harvard University.

CASE STUDY

Selling up while the going's good

Case aims: To illustrate that in some cases, the entrepreneurs may decide to accept they cannot refuse an offer from an elephant.

The highly successful social networking site YouTube was founded by Chad Hureley, Steve Chen and Jawed Chen who gained their understanding of the dotcom industry as early employees of PayPal. The initial idea was aimed at assisting local Californian bands and their fans to exchange visual and audio materials through the Internet. It only took a few months to develop the necessary Website software and the business went live in 2005. By mid-2006, YouTube had become the fifth most visited Website in the world. This huge customer base was created mainly on word-of-mouth advertising and by the site

(Cont'd)

providing the conventional media with numerous news stories. The site's success led to the company being sold to Google™ for $1.65 billion just over 12 months after the company was first launched. It remains to be seen whether the price paid will ever provide an acceptable level of return on the investment to Google™ or whether in fact, this acquisition was a 'price to far' scenario similar to those which occurred in the last few months before the dotcom bubble burst in the late 1990s.

For every aspiring entrepreneur in fields such as computing, nanotechnology or renewable energy there are thousands of other individuals striving to succeed in low technology markets and in long established traditional industry sectors. Some, similar to Ben & Jerry's, will identify and exploit a market niche unrecognised by the elephants. Others such as Iverson, the mini-mill entrepreneur, will comprehend the opportunity available through achieving a competitive advantage based upon re-engineering an industrial process to successfully challenge techniques evolved and unquestionably accepted by the elephants. In the service sector a number of entrepreneurs will duplicate Sam Walton's success with Wal-Mart by introducing a different process model which will lead to a fundamental reassessment of the optimal strategic model to be utilised in seeking to retain a dominant market position.

For every one of these future successes, there will also be countless failures. Some entrepreneurs will find their ideas are technically impossible, some will discover there is inadequate market demand, some will exhaust their financial resources before success is achieved and some will lack the managerial skills to move from being a small to a larger business. Others will be destroyed by overwhelming counter-attacks by the elephants. The outcome in some cases will merely be to strengthen the resolve of the individual to try again. Others will conclude that self-employment is no longer of appeal and sadly for some, business failure will be accompanied by major personal and family problems.

Although all potential entrepreneurs should comprehend the risks associated with failure, hopefully some of those who are successful will, similar to Bill Gates' decision to create the Gates Foundation to assist in the fight against disease in poorer nations, want to return to society a significant proportion of the wealth they have enjoyed from their endeavours. The Gates' example and the numerous micro-scale examples provided by entrepreneurs who become involved in social enterprise projects to assist their local communities are evidence that the skills which permit individuals to succeed in business by breaking existing convention are also a vital ingredient in helping the less advantaged peoples around the world to enjoy a more satisfying life through being assisted to begin to enjoy the personal freedom which accompanies self-employment permitting individuals to break free from a life of poverty.

SUMMARY LEARNING POINTS

- Only a limited number of entrepreneurial successes stem from disruptive innovation.
- Small firm entrepreneurs succeed because large firms are slow responders to new market trends.

- New technologies offer possibly the greatest opportunities for entrepreneurs during the twenty-first century.
- Scale of technological success is ultimately determined by market demand.
- Innovation success will be influenced by factors such as alternative technology, economic conditions and socio-demographic change.
- Most significant entrepreneurial opportunities exist by solving major world problems such as global warming.
- Entrepreneurs are already succeeding in areas such as sustainable energy.
- Developing nation entrepreneurs are successfully challenging the major pharmaceutical companies.
- The human genome project and genetic engineering will permit a diversity of new products across agriculture and healthcare.
- Nanotechology's potential to build new products and invent technological processes has yet to be fully comprehended.
- YouTube and MySpace are evidence that there remains numerous opportunities for entrepreneurs to convert a simple idea into a global business.

ASSIGNMENTS

1   Prepare a report comparing the strengths and weaknesses of alternative sources of sustainable energy.
2   Prepare a report examining the strengths and weaknesses of the marketing strategies employed by the world's major pharmaceutical companies.
3   Prepare a report examining the social and economic implications of population ageing in developed nation economies.

DISCUSSION TOPICS

1   Discuss whether you think the UK Government's policy on responding to global warming is appropriate and effective.
2   Should the world turn to atomic power as a major solution for reducing carbon emissions from the electricity generating industry?
3   Many developing nations are concerned about growing GM crops because the EU has threatened to ban all food imports from countries which grow GM crops. Discuss whether you feel this is an appropriate EU policy.

Additional information sources

Disruption and technology

Paap, J. and Katz, R. (2004), Anticipating disruptive innovation, *Research Technology Management*, Vol. 47, No. 5, pp. 13–23.

Global warming

Knapp, K.E. (1999), Exploring energy technology substitution for reducing atmospheric carbon emissions, *The Energy Journal*, Vol. 20, No. 2, pp. 121–144.

Healthcare

Boyatzis, R., Esteves, M.B. and Spencer, L.M. (1992), Entrepreneurial innovation in pharmaceutical research and development, *Human Resource Planning*, Vol. 15, No. 4, pp. 15–30.

Mytelka, L.K. (2006), Pathways and policies to (bio) pharmaceutical innovation systems in developing countries, *Industry and Innovation*, Vol. 13, No. 4, pp. 415–436.

Rothman, H. and Kradt, A. (2006), Downstream and into deep biology: evolving business models in 'top tier' genomics companies, *Journal of Commercial Biotechnology*, Vol. 12, No. 2, pp. 86–99.

Nanotechnology

Kessler, E.H. and Charles, M. (2007) Strategic implications of nanotechnology, *Business Strategy Series*, Vol. 8, No. 6, pp. 401–411.

Thomas, T.C. and Acuna-Narvaez, R.T. (2006), The convergence of biotechnology and nanotechnology: why here, why now?, *Journal of Commercial Biotechnology*, Vol. 12, No. 2, pp. 105–111.

Glossary

advertising   A sponsored paid message that is communicated through a non-personal channel such as the Internet, a magazine, a newspaper, radio or television. The need to ensure that an organisation has selected the correct medium through which to communicate their advertising message means that most advertisers will employ the services of an advertising agency to advise on media selection. The guidance which is provided by an agency will be based on variables such as: the target audience, the nature of the product, the media through which to reach the target audience and the size of the advertising budget.

B2B marketing   Abbreviation used for the phrase 'business-to-business' marketing. It is also used to describe the marketing process between a business and customers in the public or not-for-profit market sectors. A key feature of B2B markets is that the products and services are purchased by a supplier's customers to be incorporated into the output which is then sold to their own customers.

baby boomers   The term, which originated in America, describes those individuals who were born between 1946 and 1964. Boomers have been of great importance to marketers because in many of the developed nations, these individuals have, as both children and subsequently adults, been members of families enjoying increasing wealth and hence exhibiting a high level of consumer spending power. Many boomers have received a college education which has further improved their capability to earn higher salaries. This in turn has meant many have been able to own their own houses and if in a relationship, provide an above average standard of living for their children. Boomers are of great interest to marketing academics because they are the first group of individuals in society who from the day of their birth are likely to have been exposed to mass marketing campaigns involving the use of television advertising. The group continues to cause interest among marketers because factors such as the welfare state, access to free education, remaining for long periods in employment providing high pension payments and the huge gain in house prices over this period has left baby boomers as the richest individuals within most developed countries' consumer societies.

banner advertisement   A paid advertisement inserted on a Website using words, animation, sound and/or visual content so that when the site visitor clicks onto the advertisement, they are taken to the advertiser's own Website. The standard banner advertisement size is 468 × 60 pixels and the commonest size used by advertisers is 125 × 125 pixels.

blog   Originating as a shortened version of the phrase 'web log', this is a hybrid form of Internet communication that combines a column, diary or directory as a way for individuals to implement actions such as communicating their views to others, permitting both amateur and professional journalists to display personalised news stories, customers to complain or compliment the quality of service received from organisations and managers of organisations to communicate their views to their customers or general public. The advent of various improvements in Internet data exchange has led to people now producing *video blogs* (or *vblogs*), *music blogs* (or *MP3 blogs*) and *audio blogs* (or *podcasting*).

brand   A combination of perceived attributes, characteristics and/or benefits which provide an organisation, a company, a product, a line of products, a service or a range of services with a distinct identity which distinguishes the entity in those areas of the private or public sector where the entity is active. This combination of perceived attributes, characteristics and/or benefits which cause a brand to be recognised and therefore memorable can be both tangible and intangible. In many cases the brand has achieved the position of being memorable in the minds of customers and stakeholders through creating a very strong positive recognition for a name, visual logo and/or trademark (e.g. McDonald's globally recognisable Golden Arches visual symbol).

business angels   Wealthy private citizens, who having often previously run their own company, are willing to make a small investment in new firms in return for 10–20 per cent equity stake.

Business Link   UK support agency with regional offices across the country responsible for the provision of Government small business support programmes.

business plan   The totality of analysis, conclusions and proposals which provide the basis for defining what and how an organisation intends to achieve over a defined time period.

cash flow   The flow of money into and out of a business. Cash inflows are usually from sales or by debtors paying their outstanding invoices. Cash outflows are usually paying for inputs such as raw materials, wages and other operating expenses. When cash outflows are greater than cash inflows, the business may need to arrange a loan or a bank overdraft to cover the deficit until cash inflows improve. An inability to pay outstanding invoices because of a cash flow problem is a very common reason why many small businesses fail. This is because smaller businesses tend to have limited cash reserves and find difficulty in persuading lenders such as banks to approve an additional loan. Failure to pay outstanding bills can result in creditors taking legal action to recover the money owed which may lead to the business being put into bankruptcy.

channel conflict   This occurs when there is a disagreement between organisations within or between channels of distribution. *Horizontal conflict* involves disagreement with other organisations at the same level within a distribution channel. This may occur, for example, when one retailer attempts to attract customers from other retailers by offering goods at much lower prices. More common is *vertical conflict* which occurs when there is a disagreement between organisations at different levels within a channel. An example is a disagreement between a supplier and a supermarket chain. The usual cause of the conflict is that one organisation implements an action which breaches a formal or informal agreement that exists within a channel.

channel(s) of distribution   This is the system whereby a producer of goods or services links with the end user customers within a market. The simplest system is *direct distribution* in which the supplier sells and delivers goods direct to the final customer. Direct distribution is most likely to occur where the goods are extremely bulky, there are few customers and the value of purchases by each customer is very high and/or there is need for close, technological interaction between buyer and seller before and during the production of goods being purchases. Such scenarios occur more frequently in industrial markets. In most consumer markets, *indirect distribution* is the more usual system used by suppliers who market their products or services through intermediaries such as national chains or to wholesalers, who in turn then sell the goods on to small retailers. In these situations, the role of the supplier's sales-force is to generate orders from intermediaries and hence they are rarely in contact with the final customer.

chat room   A specific area on a Website where site visitors can interact with each other. Although probably best known for the use by social network sites, company Websites can be an extremely effective medium through which to gain the views of customers as they dialogue with each other and also for company staff to participate in the on-line discussions. High technology firms such as software producers often use chat rooms as the medium whereby their customers can resolve each other's product usage problems and to provide rapid feedback to the company on problems which may exist with a product.

communication   This is the provision of information which in relation to the marketing process is a critically important activity because information is delivered by suppliers to customers. In the case of interactive communication such as that which occurs during personal selling, there is a real-time information exchange between supplier and customer. There is a diverse range of media channels and methods through which communication can occur between supplier and customer. These include adver-tising, press releases, price lists, sales promotion bulletins, annual reports and handling customer complaints. It is also important to recognise that effective communication between staff within an organisation has a critical role in ensuring that all aspects of the marketing process are directed towards maximising customer satisfaction.

communications process   Although there are diverse communications channels and technologies, the actual process of information generation and delivery is common to virtually all scenarios. The *sender* having determined what information is to be provided has to *encode* the message to be delivered. Encoding involves using language, and possibly visual images, which the *receiver* will understand. As most communication scenarios are time or space constrained, encoding will also often involve reducing the information to a length appropriate to the time or space avail-able. The sender now has to select the *communications medium* through which the encoded message will be delivered. On receipt of the message, the receiver will *decode* the information received. This activity involves processing the information and trans-lating this into a form which the receiver can understand. In the case of *one-way* communication such as reading a print advertisement, the receiver may have no way through which to respond to the sender. Some channels such as personal selling or the Internet usually permit *two-way* communications whereby the receiver can provide *feedback* to the sender of the original message.

competition   The interaction which occurs between organisations seeking to achieve the most successful performance results in serving the needs of customers. The nature of competition is a fundamental issue in relation to economic theory and the resultant prices of products or services within a market.

competitive advantage   The aspect(s) of an organisation which is the basis of the ability which provides success in competing successfully with other organisations within the same market sector(s). In terms of the generic competitive advantages available to organisations, Professor Michael Porter has proposed there are two basic types of advantage; namely *cost-based advantage* which permits the organisation to compete on the basis of lower price and *performance-based advantage* which proves an advantage based on superior performance (e.g. higher service quality; more technologically advanced product).

cost leadership A marketing strategy in which an organisation's cost advantage over competition is exploited by offering a lower priced product or service. Sustaining a cost leadership position is often made difficult because other competitors may enter the market who enjoy even lower operating costs.

crossing the chasm This concept was developed by the Californian business expert, Geoffrey Moore, who specialises in providing marketing advice to high technology firms. In his analysis of success and failure, he identified the fact that as a firm moves into the next phase on the product adoption curve, it needs to recognise that the next group of potential customers have different needs and hence the company needs to redefine the benefit proposition being offered. For example, when marketing to *innovators* the company should stress the benefits of the customer gaining access to the latest technology, even though the technology may not yet be completely perfect. In the case of *early adopters* (or 'visionaries') on the other hand, this group of customers want a benefit proposition which promises the technology will provide an entirely new approach to the exploitation of technology. This can be contrasted with the groups who only wish to purchase new technology which has already demonstrated a stable, effective way of improving their personal or business activities. Finally the *laggards* are only interested in one benefit, namely being able to acquire the technology at a very low price.

culture This refers to the attributes, characteristics and values that influence people within a country or a society. The culture within a society is formed through the impact of a multitude of different influences such as the family, education, literacy levels, religion, politics, economic conditions. Culture is critically important in marketing because it will influence consumer acceptance of products, services and other aspects of the promotional mix such as advertising. For example, many of the liberal advertising campaigns showing women dressed in fashionable clothes and using make-up would be perceived as offensive by people living in a country where the culture is deeply influenced by a strong belief in more conservative religious principles.

current assets Assets which are owned by the organisation which are in the form of cash or can be expected to be converted into cash within the next 12 months (e.g. debtors, finished goods inventory).

customer expectations As a result of prior usage experience and/or the information acquired as the customer progresses through the phases associated with reaching a purchase decision, expectations are the assumptions created about the benefits, performance and satisfaction that will be experienced during the next post-purchase usage of the goods. The reason why some organisations are more successful at generating customer satisfaction is because these entities have become extremely effective at using all aspects of the marketing mix to exceed customer expectations.

customer loyalty The concept which recognises that as market conditions are becoming increasingly competitive, only satisfied customers remain long term purchasers of an organisation's products or services. Recent trends, especially in service industries suggest that a growing proportion of customers are prepared to switch to another supplier after only one or two bad experiences when purchasing goods from their current supplier. It is therefore extremely important that every organisation ensures that in all aspects of their interaction with customers, the focus is upon retaining their loyalty. Some organisations have decided that there is benefit in overtly rewarding customer loyalty and have created systems for this to be achieved. Examples include retailers issuing loyalty cards which permit the customers to earn points which can be redeemed against future purchases and airlines giving air miles to passengers that can be used to purchase free or lower cost flights.

customised products   The philosophy of offering a product or service which is specifically designed to meet the needs of an individual or a very small group of customers. The concept has existed in industrial markets for many years in areas such as construction and creating computer systems. For most large consumer goods companies the economies of scale benefits and manufacturing costs have been a barrier to product customisation and hence markets have tended to be dominated by smaller suppliers. This situation is now beginning to change, however, as larger firms are using the Internet to obtain specific data from individual customers and exploiting new technologies such as computer aided manufacturing (CAM) to make very small quantities of a product.

differentiation   A marketing strategy in which the positioning of an organisation's output is based on the product offering some form of superiority over competition. A significant benefit of differentiation is the product can usually command a premium price over competition, thereby generating a higher level of profitability than a marketing strategy based on cost leadership. Sustaining a differentiated position will usually require ongoing investment in innovation.

direct marketing   A range of marketing techniques which involves contact with the final customer without the involvement of an intermediary. Examples of direct marketing include tele-sales, direct mail, on-line marketing and doorstep or in-home selling.

disruptive innovation   The occurrence of significant market change caused by new technology having an adverse impact on revenue flows from an existing technology, product or business process. An example of disruption is that which followed the creation of file sharing via the World Wide Web by firms such as Napster on terrestrial retailing, the major record companies and the film industry. A very critical aspect of disruptive technology is that in many cases the technology is rarely invented by, or recognised as a threat, by existing major firms within an industrial sector. As a consequence in most cases the disruptive technology is first introduced by a smaller, entrepreneurial firm which may eventually become a new dominant player within the sector. An example of this scenario is provided by the development and launch of the Apple PC which ultimately led to a dramatic change in the structure and nature of the world computer industry. An important reason for the myopia of the existing large firms is that in most cases their customers are placing pressure on them to further improve current technology and in many cases this current technology offers higher performance standards than that exhibited by the first generation products which use the new technology.

distribution   This is the key marketing management responsibility, sometimes referred to as the fourth of the 4Ps, 'Place', associated with ensuring that the final end user customer in a market system is successfully provided with access to a supplier's product and services.

distributor   An intermediary which has the role of providing a link between a supplier and the supplier's customers. The term is more commonly used in industrial markets but is also used to describe intermediaries in consumer markets selling high value goods such as boats or specialist electronic equipment.

diversification   A marketing strategy involving expansion into new products and market sectors in those cases where the organisation decides that there are major new opportunities available within another market sector. In some cases implementation of a diversification strategy may require the organisation to become involved in either acquisition or merger activities.

economies of scale   The cost advantages that a business obtains due to being bigger than competitors. Common sources of scale are price discounts from purchasing large quantities of raw materials, operating larger manufacturing plants, lower cost financing when borrowing from financial institutions and in the area of marketing, by being able to obtain volume discounts from the advertising media and being able to spread the costs of promotion over a greater range of products.

entrepreneur   An individual who recognises an unsatisfied market opportunity, develops a new product or creates a new, unconventional approach to business that can provide the basis for launching a new commercial entity.

equity   Funds in a business which have been acquired by individuals or organisations purchasing shares in the company.

equity gap   The difference between the relatively small amount of equity capital being sought by a small firm and the lowest amount of money that a venture capital firm is willing to make available.

experiments   Research process whereby the researcher creates a specific situation to determine the influence of one or more variables on some aspect of the marketing process. The usual way for assessing an experiment is to compare the outcome of changing a variable with data from a control experiment where there has been no change in the variable being studied. For example, changing the price of a product in one group of stores and analysing sales revenue for the product in relation to product sales in another group of control stores where the price has remained unchanged. Experiments can be undertaken in the real world, which is known as 'field experiments' or in a laboratory.

explicit information   Data which are stored in a form accessible to others (e.g. in a written report or computer file).

family business   A firm where a single family owns between 51 and 100 per cent of the business. Approximately 70 per cent of all small firms are family businesses.

family life cycle   A technique based on dividing the life of families into specific life stages. Within each life stage there are different circumstances and levels of disposable income which will influence purchase and consumption patterns. The most widely accepted definition of the phases within the cycle are as follows:

- *Single young persons living at home* These individuals would have few financial commitments and hence are potential opportunities for products and services such as entertainment, fashion, leisure, sports. Their actual purchase patterns will be influenced whether they are in work, on benefits or in full-time education.

- *Newly married couples with no children* These individuals tend to enjoy a higher joint income than single people. The main opportunity they offer marketers is their interest in purchasing their first home, household/consumer durable goods, financial products and vacations.
- *Full nesters stage I* Couples with young children aged under 6. The group is very focused on home purchases but tend to have low levels of disposable income due to commitments such as rent or mortgages. Often a single income family because the wife has ceased work to care for the children. Key target for the marketing of food products, baby items, clothing and toys.
- *Full nesters stage II* Couples with young children aged 6+. If the economy is healthy usually both parents are in work. Children continue to dominate the spending pattern in the household. Target for consumer goods, clothing, bicycles, sports gear and family vacations.
- *Full nesters stage III* Older parents with dependent children still living at home who are in work or in full-time education. Financial position of this group usually continues to improve over time. Both parents are usually working. Main focus of spending is on education for their children and for themselves, new furniture, luxury goods and exotic holidays without the children.
- *Empty nesters stage I* Older couples, both usually working and with no children living at home. Mortgage payments are becoming less onerous, they may be considering downsizing their home and/or acquiring a second home at an overseas location. This group has high incomes and net wealth. Key marketing target for the sale of luxury goods, home improvements, upmarket cars and exotic vacations. Their children are either in education or moving towards the first stage in their own family life cycle.
- *Empty nesters stage II* Older couples, no children at home and the leading income earner has retired. Dependent on pension income the scale of which determines their attitudes to spending and consumption. Tend to spend less on leisure activities and more on healthcare. Couple may be involved in assisting their children's financial position.
- *Solitary survivor stage I* Single individual due to death, separation or divorce who is still working. Income may be adequate but in case of separation or divorce there may have been a dissolution of assets which has reduced their income and level of savings.
- *Solitary survivor stage II* Older retired person whose income has been significantly reduced and increasingly requires healthcare services. Individual may need to be dependent on other family members for financial support or accommodation.

fixed assets   Assets which are owned by the organisation which are expected when initially purchased to remain in use for a period of greater than 12 months. Examples include land, buildings, vehicles and equipment.

focus group   A qualitative market research technique in which a group of potential or actual customers participate in a discussion on a topic which is led by a facilitator. The average size of a focus group is 8–10 individuals. In terms of the number of focus groups undertaken this will be influenced by the depth and breadth of the information being sought. Usually after 3 or 4 focus groups on the same topic, the researcher will perceive that convergence of opinion is emerging and hence decide that scheduling further groups will not provide any additional information.

GDP (gross domestic product)   The total market value of the goods and services produced within a country's borders.

GEM (Global Entrepreneurship Monitor) Research programme created by Babson University and London Business School with the aim of measuring various aspects of small business and entrepreneurship in over 40 countries across the world.

geodemographics Market segmentation technique whereby geographic and demographic variables are combined to produce a more accurate approach to segmenting consumer markets. By utilising data sources such as national census data, consumer surveys and credit card usage patterns it is possible to create a relatively accurate profile of consumers living in a specific street or the same small area within a specific location. The identified geodemographic segments can be exploited through promotional activities such as direct mailings.

global warming The idea that burning ever larger amounts of fossil fuels increases the level of carbon dioxide (or greenhouse gases) in the earth's atmosphere, which in turn leads to adverse changes in the world's climate.

high involvement products These are products or services in which the consumer has a deep interest and hence is willing to acquire detailed information to assist in reaching a purchase decision. Usually high involvement goods are expensive (e.g. a house extension) and/or a subject in which the consumer has a deep interest such as a sporting activity (e.g. golf) or something which enhances personal status (e.g. a sports car).

high-tech (technology) products Term applied to products which utilise the latest technology. Examples include computers, telecoms and consumer electronics goods. The appeal of such products to manufacturers is that innovation can be used to remain ahead of competition and in many cases, the products are able to generate a much higher unit profit than more simple manufactured goods such as clothing or shoes.

HRM (Human Resource Management) All of the personnel aspects associated with managing an organisation's workforce such as planning workforce size, recruitment, training, appraisal, job satisfaction, motivation, conflict resolution and dismissal.

hybrid car An approach to reduce the contribution car emissions make to global warming by creating a vehicle in which electric power is used to augment a petrol or diesel powered engine.

idea generation The first phase in the linear, or stage gate, new product development process in which the aim is to generate as many ideas as possible that could provide the basis for a new product or service.

innovation The process whereby new or improved products and services are created. Innovation is perceived to be critically important at both the individual company and total nation level in terms of sustaining economic growth through the process of remaining ahead of competition. *Continuous* innovation (or 'kaizen') refers to the process where a company seeks to continually introduce minor improvements to existing products. *Discontinuous* innovation occurs where the new product is clearly different from the goods which it seeks to replace. Fundamental innovation occurs in those cases where the new development leads to the creation of a new industry (e.g. the invention of the telephone) or a fundamental shift in the technology used in an existing industry (e.g. the advent of the digital camera).

intermediaries The organisations which act as a link between suppliers and customers in market systems. Examples include distributors in B2B markets and supermarket chains in consumer goods markets. The selection and management of intermediaries plays a crucial role in ensuring the effective distribution of a supplier's products or services.

Internet A global electronic system linked together using a common language protocol, the concept started life as a system created by the US military known as ARPANET designed to maintain communications systems in the event of a nuclear war. The underlying concept is that of data being broken into packets which are reassembled back into a complete message on arrival at the specified destination. The system was then made available to scientists and educational establishments. The World Wide Web and the development of browser technology permitted commercialisation of the technology in the mid-1990s. Early Websites were essentially static due to both the availability of software and the slow download speeds available to consumers. Jeff Bezos' creation of the on-line book store Amazon.com demonstrated the capability of the technology to use the Internet to purchase products. Subsequent further developments in both software and telecoms networks have permitted improved communications capability to be extended to the use of visual data such as video-streaming and transmission of even full length films. Rising Internet usage has been accompanied by more organisations using the channel as an advertising medium with companies such as Google creating successful business models based around the selling of advertising space.

interview Market research technique in which the researcher asks questions of the respondent in a one-to-one situation. Questions can be delivered in a face-to-face situation or via electronic media such as the telephone or the Internet. Data generated can be of a qualitative or quantitative nature.

IPO (Initial Public Offering) The event at which for the first time a private company is listed on a stock exchange and people can purchase shares in the business. This process is often how successful entrepreneurs make their first really significant return on their activities having created a new high growth business.

job creation Processes leading to the generation of new employment opportunities.

large firm sector That component of an economy constituted of large businesses.

lifestyle The mode of living and associated purchasing and consumption behaviour of a consumer which is reflected in dimensions such as where they live, the car they drive, the clothes they wear, their leisure patterns and political opinions.

lifestyle business Small business with which the owner/manager seeks to generate sufficient income to support their desired lifestyle and social activities. The owner/manager has no interest to take on more staff or become involved in growing the business.

low involvement products These are products or services in which the consumer has a little interest and hence is not interested in acquiring detailed information to assist in reaching a purchase decision. Usually low involvement goods are low priced (e.g. a newspaper) and/or a subject in which the consumer has only a limited interest such as buying commodity goods (e.g. sugar) or something which has zero impact over personal status (e.g. a box of matches).

macro-environment   That part of the market system containing generic variables such as economics, culture and technology that have an influence not just on a specific market, but all markets in general.

market   An identifiable group of customers exhibiting similar potential needs or members of the same industrial sector. The defining characteristic of a market is that this is where some form of exchange occurs between the buyer and the seller.

market attractiveness   An analysis of a market to determine the degree to which the supplier can perceive whether the market offers opportunities to be successful. Factors that can influence market attractiveness include variables such as market size, market growth rate and intensity of competition.

market demand   The total customer purchase needs over a defined period of time. There is a wide range of variables influencing market demand. For example macro-environmental influences include economic conditions, financial conditions and the cultural attitudes of a society. Within the core market system demand will be influenced by marketing mix variables such as promotional activity, pricing and product availability (or 'distribution'). A critical aspect of the marketing planning process is to maximise the accuracy of the forecast for future demand. In those cases where a market has moved into maturity or decline, this forecast can be achieved by extrapolating historic and current market demand. Forecasting demand for products in the introduction and growth phases of the product life cycle is more difficult because of the influence of factors such as the nature of the diffusion of innovation influencing initial product trial rates and the speed with which customers become repeat purchasers buying the new product on a regular basis.

market research   All of the activities associated with the acquisition of secondary data, the design and implementation of processes to acquire primary data, the analysis of data acquired and the formulation of conclusions that can be utilised by marketers to enhance the effectiveness and accuracy of their decision-making.

market segmentation   Marketing philosophy which is adopted because suppliers recognise that customers are beginning to exhibit variation in the benefits they are seeking from products. At the stage where it appears there are an adequate number of customers exhibiting different specific benefit requirements, suppliers are able to divide the markets into segments into which more specialised, targeted goods can be sold. An associated benefit of segmentation is that the supplier is often able to shift from prices being defined by the intensity of prevailing market competition for standard goods to achieving higher prices based on the level of added value which is perceived by consumers to be provided by the more targeted products.

market share   An expression of a firm's performance in the form of sales being expressed as a percentage of total market sales. A market leader is usually the firm with the highest market share.

marketing budget   Specification of the funds to be spent on marketing activities over a specified period, most typically over the next 12 months.

marketing mix   All of the elements which constitute the variables utilised by an organisation to influence market performance. The most popular marketing mix model is the 4Ps concept proposed by the academic E.J. McCarthy which is constituted of Product, Promotion, Price and Place (or distribution). More recently this model has been extended in the case of service markets by the addition of the Ps of Physical Facilities, Process and People, which leads to what is known as the 7Ps or 'extended marketing mix' model. Some academics have criticised these two models as being excessively simplistic in that there are other activities both within and external to the organisation which should also be considered as elements capable of influencing an organisation's market performance. Despite such criticisms the 4Ps and 7Ps models have remained as a useful mnemonic both for students being taught marketing and as headings under which to define the more critical actions to be implemented within a marketing plan.

marketing objectives   Specification of the aims to be achieved through the implementation of the proposed marketing plan. Objectives should meet the criteria of being measurable, attainable and realistic. This definition usually infers that the objectives will be of a quantitative nature such as a target for total sales, market share, profitability and/or return on investment (ROI).

marketing strategy   Definition of how the organisation will utilise an identified competitive advantage as the basis for attracting and retaining customers.

mass marketing   This marketing philosophy is based on supplying a standard product to the majority of the market and supporting this activity with heavy promotional spending. The concept was made feasible because firms could exploit the economies of scale associated with mass production to generate high absolute profits which provided the basis to fund the required large promotional budgets that are a critical requirement of successful mass marketing. Validation of the success of the philosophy was first achieved by the major brands in the USA in the period immediately following the Second World War. Many of these brands subsequently used the same concept when expanding into overseas markets and evolving into multi-national corporations. The approach remains effective in any economy where the consumer is satisfied with being offered a single standardised product. In those cases where consumers desire a wider degree of product choice, then mass marketers will be forced to move away from the concept and offer a much broader range of goods.

micro-business   Small business with between 1 and 9 employees.

micro-finance   The provision of very small sums of money to individuals who have no credit record or assets against which to secure a loan. The concept has become increasingly important in developing nations as a mechanism through which to permit many more people to create a small business.

networking   The process whereby an individual such as the owner of a small business interacts with others either socially or for business reasons that results in the individual developing a group of people with whom they exchange information or seek advice. Building a strong network is often critically important because the network can assist in activities such as identifying new customer prospects and to gain additional knowledge about the nature of the potential needs of these customers.

networks   Group of independent organisations who collaborate with each other to achieve a common purpose such as sharing resources to enter a new overseas market.

new market   An opportunity created by the development of a new-to-the-world product or a sector of a market where an organisation has previously not marketed a product or service.

new product   A product or service which has not previously been available in a market.

new product development (NPD)   All of the organisational processes associated with the development and launch of a new product or service. NPD is a high risk activity and a large number of new products fail soon after market introduction. Hence to reduce the risk of failure, many organisations use a linear, sequential development (or 'stage gate') process. The elements in this process are idea generation, idea evaluation, concept development, business planning, product development, test marketing and launch. The purpose and activities associated with each of these process elements are:

- *Idea Generation* The aim at this stage is to maximise the number of ideas for new products. Potential sources of information include customers, intermediaries, competition, the company salesforce, employees, new technology and R&D.
- *Idea Evaluation* The aim at this stage is to ensure that only those ideas which have potential to be commercially viable continue to be progressed. Factors against which each new idea is assessed can include issues such as potential sales, profitability, return on investment and compatibility with the organisation's current products.
- *Concept Development* The aim at this stage is to assess the response of potential customers to the new product. Evaluation will involve market research activities such as running focus groups.
- *Business Planning*. The aim at this stage is to utilise knowledge about potential customer demand as the basis for determining whether the financial forecast for sales, profits and return on investment generate performance figures that are acceptable to the organisation.
- *Product Development* This is the stage at which the first prototypes are created and then assessed using market research techniques such as in-home placement or consumer panels.
- *Test Market* This is the stage where the actual market performance of the new product is evaluated by introducing the product into a geographically restricted area. During the test market the key data to be acquired are the trial and repeat purchase rates for the new product.
- *Launch* This is the final stage in the process during which the new product is introduced into the market.

NGOs (non-governmental organisations)   Organisations which are independent of any specific Government influence which undertake economic and social development especially in underdeveloped nations or following a natural disaster such as an earthquake. In areas such as healthcare and economic development, NGOs can play an important role as both customers and the distribution channel for commercial organisations supplying goods and services.

niche marketing   Marketing strategy based on the supply of a specialist product or service to a small group of customers within a market. This approach is often adopted by small firms which lack the resources to compete with large national brands who usually focus on supplying standard products to the majority of customers within a market. By focusing on the needs of a small group of customers and avoiding confrontations with large national companies, a small organisation can establish a highly profitable business.

operating costs   All of the costs involved in running a business including items such as cost of goods, labour costs, marketing expenditure, administration and depreciation. These costs are critical because their size will determine the level of net profit that is achieved by the organisation.

overdraft   Form of short term bank borrowing utilised for periods when the business is facing an adverse cash flow situation. The banks often refer to this type of funding as 'demand lending' because at any time they are able to either reduce the level of approved borrowing or request that all funds are immediately repaid.

personal selling   An interactive promotional process in which the salesperson and the potential customer exchange information as the basis for assisting the latter to reach a purchase decision. The ability of both parties to pose questions and provide answers to clarify issues raised by the other means that this is the most effective technique for the promotion of a product or service. The extensive time which is required to complete the information exchange, especially in the case of complex products or services, means that personal selling is an extremely expensive process. In some cases, such as in the defence industry or major capital construction projects, the complexity and scale of the purchase may result in the personal selling process taking several years from the initial customer contact through to the final purchase decision being reached. Hence use of personal selling as a promotional technique tends to be restricted to those market scenarios where the customer is purchasing a high value item and the scale of purchase by each customer represents a significant proportion of the supplier's total sales. These constraints usually mean that personal selling is more likely to be utilised in B2B markets than in consumer markets.

political environment   The nature of governments and the prevailing political philosophies which influence the macro-environment surrounding the market system in which the organisation operates. A key issue which firms need to consider when moving into overseas markets is that the political environment in these markets may be different from their domestic market and thereby require significant modifications to one or more aspects of the marketing mix.

population ageing   Structural change in a population caused by people living longer and declining birth rates which combine to result in the average age of the population rising over time. The process has significant implications for those nations where this is occurring because (1) the rising number of older people will place increasing pressure on pension provision and healthcare and (2) to fund an increasingly expensive welfare state the declining number of people in work will be forced to pay a higher level of personal taxation. The implications of higher taxation for the marketer is the important 18–49 year age group will have less disposable income to spend on consumer goods.

positioning   The presentation of the product or service proposition in a market which is designed to maximise customer interest and appeal. The selected positioning will reflect the strategy selected for the product or service. Professor Michael Porter has proposed that there exist four possible basic positioning alternatives. These include offering a superior product at a premium price (*differentiation*), an economy product at a low price (*cost leadership*), presenting a proposition of appeal to the majority of the market (*mass marketing*) or focusing on meeting the needs of a specialist segment within the market (*niche marketing*).

price   The stated amount of money, or another good with an identifiable value, which the supplier requires in order to sell a product or service to a customer.

pricing   All of the marketing activities associated with determining, setting and managing the price to be charged for an organisation's products or services. Pricing decisions are a crucial aspect of the marketing decision process because setting an excessively low price can result in business costs not being covered and hence minimal or no profit is generated. It can also be the case that where price is set too high, customer interest is minimal and little or no sales revenue is generated.

The nature of the market structure will also influence pricing levels. In a monopoly market where there is only one supplier in control of the market, then this organisation is usually able to determine market price. An oligopoly market is one constituted of a limited number of suppliers. In those oligopoly markets where products are undifferentiated then prices from all suppliers will tend to be very similar. However, where opportunity exists for differentiation, then products may be offered at different prices by different suppliers. In a market where there are a large number of suppliers each offering only a small proportion of the standard goods being made available, then no one supplier has the ability to determine price. This scenario, which is known as 'perfect competition' will result in price being determined by the point where the market supply and demand curves intersect.

Another factor influencing prices is the relative quality of the goods being offered. Typically higher quality goods are able to command a higher price. The outcome of this effect is that in most markets there are a number of options available in terms of the price/quality proposition that an organisation may decide to make available. The differing nature of the price/quality options are as follows:

(1) *Premium pricing* where the consumer is offered high quality goods at a high price.
(2) *Penetration pricing* where high quality goods are offered at an average price in order to stimulate higher purchase volumes leading to the supplier achieving greater penetration of the market.
(3) *High value or dumping pricing* will depend on the strategy behind the price level. Where the intention is to permanently offer high quality at well below prevailing prices then this represents a high value price. In those cases where the price is only being offered in an overseas market for a temporary period with the aim of disposing of excess stocks without disturbing the domestic market, then this is known as dumping pricing.
(4) *Skimming* is where the customer is willing to pay an above average price for average goods. This usually applies in those cases where the customer is relatively price insensitive and is willing to pay a price premium in order to obtain the goods ahead of other customers who are prepared to wait until prices decline.
(5) *Average pricing* is the price at which average quality goods are offered to the majority of the market.
(6) *Sale pricing* is where average goods are offered at a reduced price. Typically this low price is a temporary reduction to achieve the effect of increasing sales for a short period of time.

(7) *Single sale pricing* is where the customer having paid a high price for low quality goods will not make a second purchase.

(8) *Limited loyalty pricing* is where the low quality of the goods means the customer will make two or three purchases and then cease to buy the item.

(9) *Economy/value pricing* is the provision of low quality, usually necessity, goods at low prices. This pricing policy is typically used in the lower end of a market to serve the needs of customers with limited spending power.

primary data   New information which is generated by the implementation of a primary research study.

primary research   Any market research activity that has the aim of generating new qualitative or quantitative information. Possible techniques that can be used include experimentation, observation, interviews, focus groups and surveys. This type of research is expensive and hence tends to only be considered where existing secondary data are unable to resolve the questions being posed by the researcher.

process innovation   Entrepreneurial actions directed at achieving operational innovation within the organisation across areas such as the product/service production system, promotion, distribution or logistics. The primary aim of such innovation is typically to improve quality, reduce costs and/or save time.

product life cycle (PLC)   A marketing concept which proposes that all products have a finite life and that this life can be divided into the four phases of introduction, growth, maturity and decline. The events and outcomes associated with each phase of the life cycle are:

(1) *Introduction* during which sales are low as only a small proportion of customers have yet to try the product. During introduction costs usually exceed revenue and for much of this phase the product will generate a loss. The primary marketing objective during introduction is to maximise the magnitude and speed with which potential customers are attracted to purchase the product for the first time. Achievement of a high level of product trial will usually involve using personal selling and/or advertising to build market awareness and to educate potential customers about the new product.

(2) *Growth* during which new customers continue to try the product and existing customers become repeat purchasers. The two marketing objectives during this phase are to maximise the number of new customers trying the product and to maximise the number of customers who become repeat purchasers. These aims will usually require sustaining a relatively high level of expenditure on personal selling and/or advertising. It may also be the case, especially where production costs are declining as output rises, that prices may begin to fall to a limited degree. To further stimulate product adoption, firms may begin to implement a limited degree of sales promotion activity. As customers gain experience and understanding of the product, variations in customer need may emerge. This may cause firms to expand the breadth of their product line and to seek to utilise a market segmentation strategy to enhance customer satisfaction. During this phase revenue tends to grow at a rate much faster than costs and hence towards the end of the phase, product profitability is likely to be maximised. Towards the latter stages of the growth phase an increasing number of competitors may be attracted to enter the market.

(3) *Maturity* is the phase when all the potential customers who are likely to adopt the product are making purchases on a regular basis. As a result there is no further opportunity for sales growth. Early into maturity is usually the point where the maximum number of suppliers are operating in the market. Consequently those companies seeking to achieve further growth will seek to steal customers from competition through activities such as increased advertising expenditure, sales promotions and price competition. Firms may also accelerate the development of line extensions, launch new improved products and seek further opportunities to segment the market. These activities and the need for organisations to protect their sales from competition means with total market sales remaining unchanged and the costs of competing increasing, over time profits will fall. As profits trend downwards, the number of suppliers in the market will tend to decline. This occurs because some firms may leave the market and others may engage in merger and acquisition activities.

(4) *Decline* during which fewer customers are purchasing the product and in many cases even users are reducing their frequency of purchase. The outcome of this trend is that sales will fall and eventually will approach zero. During this period some organisations will seek to sustain sales and will use low price and/or sales promotion activity to support this aim. Falling sales and lower prices will be reflected in an increasingly smaller level of profits being generated as time passes within the decline phase.

productivity   The value of the output of employees which is usually calculated on the basis of productivity per employee by dividing total organisational profit by the number of employees. Organisations which achieve high productivity usually outperform low productivity organisations. Furthermore, a nation's standing in the world economy is influenced by the average productivity achieved by firms within key industrial sectors.

promotion   The marketing process concerned with the provision of information that can influence attitudes, beliefs and behaviours of both potential and existing customers. The marketer has a wide choice of techniques and channels through which to deliver this information. These include advertising, direct mail, the Internet, personal selling, sales promotion, trade exhibitions, collateral materials such as brochures, sponsorship and public relations.

promotional message   Communication between the supplier and the customer providing information designed to build awareness and assist the purchase decision process.

promotional plan   That aspect of the marketing plan concerned with the definition of communication aims, determination of the budget for communication and the selection of promotional vehicles.

promotional process   All of the elements and activities associated with development, transmission and receipt of promotional information.

public relations (PR)   The practice of providing information to the market and the media which has the objective of influencing opinions which are held about a product, service or organisation. Originally evolved as a process used to complement and enhance other promotional activities, over time PR has become an increasingly sophisticated marketing process which is now also used by public sector organisations and politicians as a technique for influencing public opinion. A key aspect of PR is the use of the publishing and broadcast media's willingness to distribute the information made available by organisations in communications such as press (or news) releases. The need for a sophisticated approach and also the intense competition which exists between organisations to gain the attention of the media means that most large operations now employ the services of a public relations agency to manage their PR strategy.

qualitative research   Market research which generates non-quantitative written data or data of a recorded nature concerning topics such as people's feelings, attitudes, beliefs, behaviours and thoughts. Information is acquired through activities such as focus groups and one-to-one interviews. The non-quantitative nature of the information often means that no form of statistical analysis is possible. Consequently, in most cases conclusions should be not assumed to provide a sufficiently accurate assessment of the situation that can be extrapolated as applying to a total population. Generation of qualitative data is usually a lengthy process which means that as market research tends to be a time and personnel resource constrained activity, data will be acquired from much fewer respondents than in a more quantitative study such as a mail survey.

quality   The performance achievement of a product or service acquired and utilised by the customer. During the 1970s many Western organisations responded to rising inflation by reducing the quality of their output in order to reduce the need to further increase prices. In contrast, Japanese firms were moving in the opposite direction by investing in techniques such as Total Quality Management to achieve quality standards exceeding those of competitors elsewhere in the world. The global success of firms such as Honda and Toyota is, to a certain degree, attributable to the superior quality of the products. In the world of service marketing where differentiation between suppliers is difficult to achieve, many leading companies such as Nordstrom and Singapore Airlines have built their strong market position on the basis of offering superior service quality.

quantitative research   Market research which generates numeric data concerning the views and opinions of respondents. Information is acquired through activities such as terrestrial and on-line surveys. The numeric nature of the information usually means that statistical analysis can be applied to the results which can be extrapolated as the basis for making assumptions about the prevailing opinions and behaviour of a total population. The validity of such conclusions is much greater in those cases where the data have been obtained as a result of undertaking a probability survey. The positivist nature of this type of research is often perceived by marketers as being more accurate and reliable in terms of making decisions based on the information acquired.

R&D (research and development)   Activities associated with the development of new products, services and production processes. In some industries such as the pharmaceutical industry where companies are able to patent their products or production process, the level of expenditure on R&D will often be the critical determinant of subsequent market success.

renewable energy   Sources of energy that permit the generation of energy without the accompanying exhaustion of supplies that occurs through the burning of fossil fuels. Examples include solar power, wind power and wave power.

resource-based view of the firm (RBV)   Marketing concept which proposes that in increasingly competitive markets where all firms understand customer needs, differentiation can only be achieved by the development of a superior internal competence.

ROI (return on investment) Quantitative measurement to describe the relationship between the profit being generated by an organisation and the assets being utilised to support the operation. The formula used is ROI = Profit/(Net current assets + fixed assets).

salesforce The generic term to describe all of the individuals within an organisation whose primary role is to generate revenue by involvement in personal selling. Salesforce composition can be somewhat varied. In some cases, the sales staff all operate outside of the organisation calling on customers. Other organisations only operate an inside salesforce with customer communication being via electronic media such as the telephone. It can also be the case that an organisation has a mixed salesforce with some staff based inside the company whilst others are outside calling on customers. These situations can be contrasted with a sales staff in the retail sector where the employees engaged in selling activities are based within a retail outlet.

sales (below line) promotion Tactical promotional technique which seeks to stimulate increased sales over a short period by offering some form of increased value to the customer in B2B markets and the consumer, via the intermediary, in consumer markets. Possible sales promotion techniques include competitions, free goods, price pack, money off coupons, rebates, premiums and product referrals. In the case of the intermediary in consumer goods markets, the ability to feature the supplier's sales promotion in-store may be sufficient reason to participate by passing the offer on to consumers visiting end user outlets. There may be situations, however, where the intermediary requires an additional incentive such as a temporary price discount on all orders during the period when the sales promotion is being offered by the supplier.

SBA (Small Business Administration) US Federal agency responsible for the provision of Government support programmes in the USA.

secondary data Information which already exists and hence can be acquired without the expense of undertaking a market research project such as implementing a consumer survey to generate new data. Existing data is usually much cheaper to acquire than new data. Hence achieving a high cost–benefit relationship from market research is most likely to occur if all or virtually most of any required data can be acquired from existing sources. The advent of the Internet in terms of the breadth and depth of data sources that can be rapidly accessed at extremely low cost has magnified the importance of secondary data searches in market research.

In terms of secondary data sources accessed by terrestrial means or via the Internet, these include an organisation's own employees, existing reports and market research studies inside the organisation, Governments, libraries, trade magazines, trade associations, the media, competition, consultancy firms and market research agencies.

self-employed An individual who works in their own business and is not treated by their Government as an employee for income tax purposes.

self-employment Working for oneself running a business instead of being an employee in an organisation.

service quality An assessment made by the customer concerning the standards of performance achieved by an organisation during the phases of service selection, purchase, delivery and consumption. In those cases where the customer's expectations are exceeded by actual events, the customer's evaluation will be that of having received excellent or superior service.

services   The deeds, processes and performances undertaken by an organisation which are associated with the satisfaction of some form of customer need for an intangible product.

small firm (business)   An organisation employing a limited number of people. The definition over employee size varies by country. In the EU, for example, a small firm is one containing between 1 and 249 employees. This contrasts with the USA where the definition is a firm containing between 1 and 499 employees. Small firms are becoming increasingly important as a potential source of sales in developed economy B2B markets because the number of large organisations has been declining. Small firms are also important to a nation's economy because very often they are the market entry mechanism used by successful entrepreneurs.

small firm sector   That component of an economy constituted of small businesses.

SMEs   Term applied to the small business sector which stands for Small and Medium-Size Enterprises.

social capital   The social resources which are embedded in the relationships which individuals create within both their social and business lives.

social entrepreneurs   These are individuals who undertake a leadership role in social enterprise projects. They are usually driven, determined, ambitious and charismatic individuals who excel at spotting unmet needs and mobilising under-utilised resources to meet these needs.

social entrepreneurship   The activities of individuals and organisations whose primary goal is to implement activities that are of benefit to more disadvantaged members of society. Organisations involved in social entrepreneurship may come from the voluntary, public or private sector. Social enterprise organisations can be characterised by operating a 'not for profit' motivation.

social networks   On-line websites which permit people who share the same interests and/or activities to interact with each other, or individuals who are interested in exploring the interests and activities of others. These web-based services provide a variety of ways for users to interact, such as e-mail, instant messaging and exchanging audio or audio-visual materials. The growing popularity of on-line social networks means these websites provide a major new opportunity for exploiting on-line advertising. Well known examples of on-line networks are Facebook and YouTube.

socio-demographics   Measurable variables such as age, income, wealth, education, occupation, family size and geographic location which can be utilised to identify different customer groups and buyer behaviour. Most developed nation Governments regularly undertake research to measure socio-demographic change as the basis for assisting in the provision of public sector services. Hence these data are easy for marketers to acquire which is why socio-demographics are considered an important tool in determining market opportunities by different socio-demographic groups.

sponsorship   A commercial arrangement to exchange advertising and other promotional activities in return for funding a popular event or organisation. For example, a corporate entity may provide equipment for a famous athlete or sports team in exchange for brand recognition. Many sponsors want their logo featured on sponsored equipment and clothing in return for their financial support. Formula One motor racing teams for many years, for example, relied heavily on the income from tobacco sponsors.

start-up business   The establishment of a new, usually small, commercial operation. Start-ups are important because they provide a route into self-employment for many individuals and can be the source of highly innovative business ideas. Examples of highly successful business start-ups in the IT industry include Apple, Dell and Microsoft.

succession   The process whereby the current leader of a firm is replaced by a successor.

succession planning   The process whereby an organisation manages the identification and appointment of a successor to the current leader with the aim of ensuring the change in leadership has a positive impact on the future business operation.

survey   A questionnaire used to generate primary data.

survey research   A market research technique involving the asking of questions to gather data. The various types of survey research include:

(1) *Street intercept* survey where the researcher stops potential respondents in the street.
(2) *In-home survey* where the researcher visits consumers in their homes.
(3) *Business survey* where the researcher visits the respondent at their place of business.
(4) *Mail survey* where the questionnaire is sent to the respondent in the mail.
(5) *Telephone survey* where the respondent is asked questions over the telephone.
(6) *E-mail survey* where the questionnaire is sent in the form of an e-mail or as an e-mail attachment.
(7) *Online survey* where the questionnaire is displayed on a website and the respondent can either enter their views on screen or download the survey for completion at a later date.

tacit information   Data stored in a person's mind. Providing others with access to such knowledge usually requires a one-to-one interaction between individuals.

Total Quality Management (TQM)   Concept developed and evolved by primarily Japanese manufacturers to produce high quality goods. The concept involves both creation of effective quality management systems not just inside the organisation but also involves gaining the participation of suppliers.

venture capital   Equity made available by venture capital firms in return for an equity stake in a business. The aim of these firms is within only a few years to obtain somewhere in the region of a 40 per cent return on their investment as a result of the firm becoming listed as a public company or by another investor purchasing their shares.

Website   Location on the Internet where specific information is grouped together on one or more web pages. Most major organisations have created Websites to provide on-line visitors with '24/7' access to information about their operations and activities. Many of these sites also provide the facility to reserve, order and purchase products or services.

wild card event   This is a completely unexpected event that acts as a catalyst for increasing the market potential for a new product, service or technology.

References

Adams, J. (1997), Loctite takeover galvanizes Henkel, *Corporate Finance*, London, July, p. 3.

Ahmed, P.K. and Cadenhead, L. (1988), Charting the developments in the NHS, *Health Manpower Management*, Vol. 24, No. 6, pp. 222–236.

Aldrick, P. (2008), Banks which should be lending to businesses more freely are instead raising overdraft rates to crippling levels, *The Sunday Telegraph*, London, 2 November, p. 5.

Allison, C., Chell, E. and Hayes, J. (2000), Intuition and entrepreneurial behaviour, *European Journal of Work and Organisational Psychology*, Vol. 9, pp. 31–42.

Amabile, T.M., Conti, R., Coon, H., Lazenby, J. and Herron, M. (1996), Assessing the work environment for creativity, *Academy of Management Journal*, Vol. 39, No. 5, pp. 1154–1185.

Ambrose, D.M. (1983), Transfer of the family-owned business, *Journal of Small Business Management*, Vol. 21, No. 1, pp. 49–61.

Anderson, A.R. and Atkins, M.H. (2001), Business strategies for entrepreneurial small firms, *Strategic Change*, Vol. 10, No. 6, pp. 311–324.

Anderson, E., Day, G.S. and Rangan, V.K. (1997), Strategic channel design, *Sloan Management Review*, Vol. 38, No. 4, pp. 59–70.

Anderson, M. and Sohal, D. (1999), A study of the relationship between quality management practices and performance in small business, *The International Journal of Quality & Reliability Management*, Vol. 16, No. 9, pp. 859–872.

Anderson, R. and Reeb, D. (2003), Founding family ownership and non-family owned firms, *Family Business Review*, Vol. 9, No. 2, pp. 157–170.

Anon. (1973), Lesson in leadership: Akio Morita of Sony Corp., *Nation's Business*, New York, 1 December, pp. 44–50.

Anon. (1984), Problems tracked in transition from owner to professional management, *Journal of Accountancy*, Vol. 158, No. 4, pp. 38–41.

Anon. (1996), A global case study, *Strategy & Leadership*, Vol. 24, No. 6, pp. 22–23.

Anon. (2002) Transformational leadership @ Apple, *Strategic Direction*, Vol. 18, No. 6, pp. 5–8.

Anon. (2003), News: Budget 2003 – Budget 2003: the response, *Accountancy*, London, p. 16.

Anon. (2004), Strategic partnership to provide users with easy to use XML to PDF publishing capability, *International Journal of Micrographics & Optical Technology*, Vol. 22, No. 2/3, pp. 28–34.

Anon. (2005), Hard cases: life and death lessons from Wang Laboratories, Sno Brands and GM, *Strategic Direction*, Vol. 21, No. 10, pp. 25–28.

Anon. (2006a), The changing life of retired people, *The Daily Telegraph*, London, 20 May, p. 3.

Anon. (2006b), Business: the two kings get together; Google and YouTube, *The Economist*, London, 14 October, p. 82.

Anon. (2006c), Leadership 100, *Quality*, Vol. 45, No. 9, pp. 48–54.

Anon. (2006d), Vertical markets: music industry forced to warm to the Arctic Monkeys, *Precision Marketing*, London, 31 March, pp. 18–19.

Anon. (2007), The Governor's speech in Northern Ireland, *Bank of England Quarterly*, Vol. 47, No. 4, pp. 566–570.

Anon. (2008a), Reflating the dragon, *The Economist*, London, 15 November, pp. 87–88.

Anon. (2008b), A wilting relationship leaves UK business feeling less enamoured of Labour, *Financial Times*, London, January, p. 7.

Ansoff, I. (1965), *Corporate Strategy*, McGraw-Hill, New York.

Apospori, W., Papalexandris, N. and Galanki, E. (2005), Entrepreneurial and professional CEOs: differences in motive and responsibility profile, *Leadership & Organization Development Journal*, Vol. 26, No. 1/2, pp. 141–163.

Araghna, A., Currim, I.S. and Shoemaker, R.W. (1991), Consumer perceptions of promotional activity, *Journal of Marketing*, Vol. 55, No. 2, pp. 4–17.

Aris, S.S., Raghunathan, T.S. and Kunnather, A. (2000), Factors affecting the adoption of advanced manufacturing technology in small firms, *S.A.M. Advanced Management Journal*, Vol. 65, No. 2, pp. 14–23.

Atkinson, C. and Curtis, S. (2004), The impact of employment regulation on the employment relationship in SMEs, *Journal of Small Business and Enterprise Development*, Vol. 11, No. 4, pp. 486–497.

Audretsch, D.B. (2002), The dynamic role of small firms: the evidence from the U.S., *Small Business Economics*, Vol. 18, No. 1/3, pp. 13–24.

Audretsch, D.B. and Lehmann, E.L. (2004), Financing high-tech growth: the role of banks and venture capitalists, *Schmalenbach Business Review*, Vol. 56, No. 4, pp. 340–358.

Aurand, T.W., DeMoranville, C.W., Fredericks, E. and Smith, T.J. (2004), From mass customisation to customisation: an opportunity for entrepreneurial differentiation, *Journal of Small Business Strategy*, Vol. 15, No. 1, pp. 49–61.

Ayyagari, M., Beck, T. and Demirgue-Kunt, A. (2007), Small and medium size enterprises across the globe, *Small Business Economics*, Vol. 29, pp. 415–434.

Bannon, L. (2002), Toy story; three retailers beat one? *The Wall Street Journal*, New York, 14 May, p. B.10.

Barach, J.A., Gantisky, J., Carson, J.A. and Doochin, B.A. (1988), Entry of the next generation: strategic challenges for family business, *Journal of Small Business Management*, Vol. 26, No. 2, pp. 49–56.

Barnes, J.G., Pynn, G.A. and Noonan, A.C. (1982), Marketing research: some basics for small business, *Journal of Small Business Management*, Vol. 20, No. 3, pp. 62–66.

Barrett, R. and Mayson, S. (2007), Human resource management in growing small firms, *Journal of Small Business and Enterprise Development*, Vol. 14, No. 2, pp. 107–116.

Barun, R. (1989), Acer's Stan Shih: against all odds, *Asian Finance*, Hong Kong, 15 November, pp. 17–23.

Bate, J.D. and Johnston, R.E. (2005), Strategic frontiers: the starting-point for innovative growth, *Strategy & Leadership*, Vol. 33, No. 1, pp. 12–19.

Beal, R.M. (2000), Competing effectively: Environmental scanning, competitive strategy, and organizational performance in small manufacturing firms, *Journal of Small Business Management*, Vol. 38, No. 1, pp. 27–48.

Beard, C. and Easingwood, C. (1992), Sources of competitive advantage in the marketing of technology-intensive products and processes, *European Journal of Marketing*, Vol. 26, No. 2, pp. 5–19.

Beaver, G. (2007), The strategy payoff for smaller enterprises, *The Journal of Business Strategy*, Vol. 28, No. 1, pp. 11–20.

Beaver, G. and Jennings, P. (2003), Editorial: small business success and failure, *Strategic Change*, Vol. 12, No. 3, pp. 115–120.

Beaver, G. and Jennings, P. (2005), Competitive advantage and entrepreneurial power: the dark side of entrepreneurship, *Journal of Small Business Enterprise Development*, Vol. 12, No. 1, pp. 9–23.

Becherer, R.C. and Maurer, J. (1999), The proactive personality disposition and entrepreneurial behaviour among small company presidents, *Journal of Small Business Management*, Vol. 37, No. 1, pp. 28–37.

Becherer, R.C., Finch, J.H. and Helms, M.M. (2006), The influences of entrepreneurial motivation and new business acquisition on strategic decision making, *Journal of Small Business Strategy*, Vol. 16, No. 2, pp. 1–14.

Bell, J. (1999), Sam Walton: everyday low prices pay off, *The Journal of Business Strategy*, Vol. 20, No. 5, pp. 36–39.

Bemmaor, A.C. and Lee, J. (2002), The impact of heterogeneity and ill-conditioning on diffusion model parameter estimates, *Marketing Science*, Vol. 21, No. 2, pp. 209–222.

Benner, M. (2004), Catching up in pharmaceuticals: government policies and the rise of genomics, *Australian Health Review*, Vol. 28, No. 2, pp. 161–171.

Bennett, H. (1994), The small firm myth, *California Management Review*, Vol. 36, No. 3, pp. 142–159.

Berman, J.A., Gordon, D.D. and Sussman, G. (1997), A study to determine the benefits small business firms derive from sophisticated planning versus less sophisticated types of planning, *The Journal of Business and Economic Studies*, Vol. 3, No. 3, pp. 1–12.

Bernoff, J. and Li, C. (2008), Harnessing the power of the oh-so-social Web, *Sloan Management Review*, Vol. 49, No. 3, pp. 36–42.

Berry, M. (1998), Strategic planning in small, high-tech companies, *Long Range Planning*, Vol. 31, pp. 455–456.

Besanko, D., Dranove, D. and Stanley, M. (2001), Exploiting a cost advantage and coping with a cost disadvantage, *Management Science*, Vol. 47, No. 2, pp. 221–234.

Beverland, M. and Lockshin, L.S. (2001), Organisational life cycles in small New Zealand wineries, *Journal of Small Business Development*, Vol. 39, No. 4, pp. 354–363.

Beugelssdijk, S. and Noordaven, N. (2005), Personality characteristics of self-employed; an empirical study, *Small Business Economics*, Vol. 24, No. 2, pp. 159–168.

Bigelow, R. and Chan, P.S. (1992), Managing in difficult times: lessons from the most recent recession, *Management Decision*, Vol. 30, No. 8, pp. 34–42.

Biggadike, E.R. (1979), *Corporate Diversification: Entry, Strategy and Performance*, Harvard University Press, Cambridge, MA.

Birch, D.L. (1979), *The Job Generation Process*, MIT Program on Neighbourhood and Regional Change, Cambridge, MA.

Blackburn, R. and Benson, R. (1993), Total quality and human resources management: lessons learned from Baldrige Award-winning companies, *The Academy of Management Executive*, Vol. 7, No. 3, pp 49–67.

Blumentritt, T. (2004), Does small and mature have to mean dull: defying the ho-hum at SMEs, *The Journal of Business Strategy*, Vol. 25, No.1, pp. 27–34.

Boocock, J.G. (1990), An examination of non-bank funding for small and medium-sized enterprises in the UK, *The Service Industries Journal*, Vol. 10, No. 1, pp. 124–148.

Boughton, P.D. (1983), Marketing research and small business, *Journal of Small Business Management*, Vol. 21, No. 3, pp. 38–42.

Brennan, Z. (2007), Plastic; fantastic: from the Queen's breakfast table to gloriously kisch suburban parties, *The Daily Mail*, London, 18 January, p. 49.

Brink, S. (2003), Health on the border, *US News & World Report*, 9 June, p. 3.

Brockhaus, R.H. (1987), Entrepreneurial folklore, *Journal of Small Business Management*, Vol. 25, No. 3, pp. 1–6.

Brown, R. (1990), Encouraging enterprise: Britain's Graduate Enterprise Programme, *Journal of Small Business Management*, Vol. 28, No. 4, pp. 71–78.

Brown, S. (1987), An integrated approach to retail change, *The Service Industries Journal*, Vol. 7, No. 2, pp. 153–164.

Browning, E.S. and Silver, S. (2008), Credit crunch: loan morsels for small firms hurdles to borrowing are emerging, *Wall Street Journal*, New York, 22 January, p. C.1.

Bunn, M.D. (1993), Taxonomy of buying decision approaches, *Journal of Marketing*, Vol. 57, No. 1, pp. 38–57.

Burke, C.I. and Jarratt, D.G. (2004), The influence of information and advice on competitive strategy definition in SMEs, *Qualitative Market Research*, Vol. 7, No. 2, pp. 126–138.

Caldwell, J.H. (1994), Photovoltaic technology and markets, *Contemporary Economic Policy*, Vol. 12, No. 2, pp. 97–112.

Campbell-Kelly, M. (2001), Not only Microsoft: the maturing of the PC software industry 1982–1995, *Business History Review*, Vol. 75, pp. 103–145.

Canavan, O., Henchion, M. and O'Reilly, S. (2007), The use of the internet as a marketing channel for Irish speciality food, *International Journal of Retail & Distribution Management*, Vol. 35, No. 2, pp. 178–187.

Cannon, H. and Morgan, F.W. (1990), A strategic pricing framework, *The Journal of Services Marketing*, Vol. 4, No. 2, pp. 19–31.

Canton, J. (2007), *The Extreme Future: The Top Twenty Trends That Will Reshape The World In The Next 20 Years*, Plume, Penguin Group, London.

Carland, J.W., Carland, J.C. and Busbin, J.W. (1997), Nurturing entrepreneurship: reconsideration for competitive strategy, *Advances in Competitiveness Research*, Vol. 5, No. 1, pp. 85–106.

Carnnes, A. (1997), Levitz files for bankruptcy protection, *The Wall Street Journal*, 8 September, p. A6.

Carson, D. (1985), The evolution of marketing in the small firm, *European Journal of Marketing*, Vol. 19, No. 5, pp. 7–16.

Carson, D. and Coviello, N. (1996), Qualitative research issues at the marketing/entrepreneurship interface, *Marketing Intelligence and Planning*, Vol. 14, No. 6, pp. 51–60.

Carson, D., Gilmore, A. and Rocks, S. (2004), SME marketing networking: a strategic approach, *Strategic Change*, Vol. 13, pp. 369–382.

Case, J. (1996), Corporate culture, Inc, *Boston*, Vol. 18, No. 16, pp. 42–50.

Castillo, J. and Wakefield, M.W. (2006), An exploration of firm performance factors in family businesses: do families value only the 'bottom line'? *Journal of Small Business Strategy*, Vol. 17, No. 2, pp. 37–52.

Cavanagh, R.E. and Clifford, D.K. (1983), Lessons from America's midsized growth companies, *The McKinsey Quarterly*, pp. 2–23.

Cavuto, J. (2002), The market for neurotechnology, *International Journal of Medical Marketing*, Vol. 2, No. 3, pp. 263–274.

Cervantes, M. (1996), Helping industry help itself, *The OECD Observer*, Paris, June/July, pp. 16–20.

Chaffee, E. (1985), Three models of strategy, *Academy of Management Review*, Vol. 10, No. 1, pp. 88–98.

Chaganti, R. and Chaganti, R. (1983), A profile of profitable and not-so-profitable small businesses, *Journal of Small Business Management*, Vol. 21, No. 3, pp. 43–51.

Chaganti, R., Cook, R.G. and Smeltz, W.J. (2002), Effects of styles, strategies, and systems on the growth of small businesses, *Journal of Developmental Entrepreneurship*, Vol. 7, No. 2, pp. 175–194.

Chandler, G. and Hanks, S.H. (1994), Market attractiveness, resource-based capabilities, venture strategies and venture performance, *Journal of Business*, Vol. 9, No. 4, pp. 331–349.

Chaston, I. (1992), Supporting small business start-ups, *Journal of European Training*, Vol. 16, No. 10, pp. 3–9.

Chaston, I. (1996), Critical events and process gaps in the Danish Technological Institute structured networking model, *International Small Business Journal*, Vol. 14, No. 3, pp. 31–42.

Chaston, I. (2000a), *Entrepreneurial Marketing*, Macmillan, London.

Chaston, I. (2000b), *E-Commerce Marketing Management*, McGraw-Hill, London.

Chaston, I. (2002), *Small Business Marketing*, Palgrave, London.

Chaston, I. (2004), *Knowledge-Based Marketing*, Sage, London.

Chaston, I. (2009), *Boomer Marketing: Exploiting Recession Resistant Consumers*, Routledge, Hampshire.

Chaston, I. and Mangles, T. (1997), Competencies for growth in SME sector manufacturing firms, *Journal of Small Business Management*, Vol. 35, No. 1, pp. 23–35.

Chau, H.J., Chrisman, J.J. and Chang, E.O.C. (2004), Are family firms born or made? *Family Business Review*, Vol. 17, No. 1, pp. 38–56.

Chen, L., Harvet, S., Panzich, A., Spigarelli, J. and Jessman, C. (2003), Small business internet commerce, *Information Resources Management Journal*, Vol. 16, No. 3, pp. 17–28.

Christensen, C.M. (1997), *The Innovator's Dilemma*, Harvard Business School Press, Boston, MA.

Christensen, C.M., Verlinden, M. and Westerman, G. (2002), Disruption, disintegration and the dissipation of differentiability, *Industrial and Corporate Change*, Vol. 11, No.5, pp. 955–993.

Chye, K.H., Lin, C. and Leong, G. (2003), Data mining and customer relationship marketing in the banking industry, *Singapore Management Review*, Vol. 24, No. 2, pp. 1–28.

Cochran, A.B. (1981), Small business mortality rates: a review of the literature, *Journal of Small Business Management*, Vol. 19, No. 4, pp. 50–60.

Colli, A., Perez, P.F. and Rose, M.B. (2003), National determinants of family firm development: family firms in Britain, Spain, and Italy in the nineteenth and twentieth centuries, *Enterprise & Society*, Vol. 4, No. 1, pp. 28–39.

Constantinides, E. (2004), Strategies for surviving the Internet meltdown, *Management Decision*, Vol. 42, No.1/2, pp. 89–103.

Copeland, M.V. (2008), Tesla's wild ride, *Fortune*, July, pp. 13–17.

Cooper, R.G., Edgett, S. and Kleinschmidt, E.J. (1997), Portfolio management in new product development: lessons from the leaders-I, *Research Technology Management*, Vol. 40, No. 6, pp. 43–53.

Cosgrove, J. (2001), Cracking the code, *Beverage Industry*, New York, March, pp. 54–55.

Covin, J.G. and Slevin, D.P. (1988), The influence of organisational structure on the utility of an entrepreneurial top management style, *Journal of Management Studies*, Vol. 25, pp. 217–237.

Cravens, D.W., Piercy, N.F. and Low, G.S. (2002), The innovation challenges of proactive cannibalisation and discontinuous technology, *European Business Review*, Vol. 14, No. 4, pp. 257–268.

Cunningham, D. and Hornby, W. (1993), Pricing decision in small firms: theory and practice, *Management Decision*, Vol. 31, No. 7, pp. 46–56.

Curran, J. (2000), What is small business policy in the UK: evaluation and assessing small business policies, *International Small Business Journal*, Vol. 18, No. 2, pp. 32–41.

Curran, J. and Blackburn, R.A. (2000), Policy review section: panacea or white elephant? A critical review of the proposed new small business service and response to the DTI consultancy paper, *Regional Studies*, Vol. 34, No. 2, pp. 181–190.

Curran, J., Jarvis, R., Kitching, J. and Lightfoot, G. (1995), The pricing decision in small firms, Proceedings of the 18th ISBA Conference, Paisley, Scotland, pp. 979–997.

d'Amico, M.F. (1978), Marketing research for small business, *Journal of Small Business Management*, Vol. 16, No. 1, pp. 41–49.

D'Andrade, H.A. (1999), The golden age of medicine, *Viral Speeches of the Day*, New York, 15 December, Vol. 66, No. 5, pp. 142–146.

Dart, J. (1980), The advertising agency selection process for small business, *Journal of Small Business Management*, Vol. 18, No. 2, pp. 1–10.

Davidson, A. (1996), The Davidson interview: Anita Roddick, *Management Today*, March, pp. 42–46.

Davidsson, P. and Henrekson, M. (2002), Determinants of the prevalence of start-ups and high growth firms, *Economics*, Vol. 19, No. 2, pp. 81–104.

Davies, M. (1992), Sales promotions as a competitive strategy, *Management Decision*, Vol. 30, No. 7, pp. 5–11.

Davis, S.J., Haltiwanger, J. and Schuh, S. (1994), Small business and job creation: dissecting the myth and the facts, *Business Economics*, Vol. 29, No. 3, pp. 13–22.

Day, G.S. and Schoemaker, P.J.H. (2005), Scanning the periphery, *Harvard Business Review*, October/November, pp. 135–146.

Demuth, L.G. (2008), A viewpoint on disruptive innovation, *Journal of the American Academy of Business*, Vol. 13, No. 1, pp. 86–94.

Dess, G.G. and Picken, J.C. (1999), Creating competitive (dis)advantage, *The Academy of Management Executive*, Vol. 13, No. 3, pp. 97–112.

De Toni, A. and Nassimbeni, G. (2003), Small and medium district enterprises and the new product development challenge: evidence from Italian eyewear district, *International Journal of Operations and Production Management*, Vol. 23, No. 5/6, pp. 678–698.

Dicken, P. (2007), *Global Shift: Mapping The Changing Contours Of The World Economy*, Sage, London, 5th edn.

Dodge, H.R. and Robbins, J.E. (1992), An empirical investigation of the organisational life cycle, *Journal of Small Business Management*, Vol. 30, No. 1, pp. 27–38.

Drozdown, N. and Carroll, V.P. (1997), Tools for strategy development in family firms, *Sloan Management Review*, Vol. 39, No. 1, pp. 75–88.

Drucker, P. (1999), *Innovation and Entrepreneurship*, Butterworth-Heinemann, Oxford.

Dunn, P. and Cheatham, L. (1993), Fundamentals of small business financial management for start up, survival, growth, and changing economic circumstances, *Managerial Finance*, Vol. 19, No. 8, pp. 1–14.

Dyer, G. (1986), *Cultural Changes In Family Firms*, Jossey-Bass, San Francisco.

Dyson, E. (2005), Bringing society back into the climate debate, *Population and Environment*, Vol. 26, No. 3, pp. 255–266.

Elfring, T. and Hulsink, W. (2003), Networks in entrepreneurship: the case of high-technology firms, *Small Business Economics*, Vol. 21, No. 4, pp. 409–420.

Elliott, S.D. (1992), Golden rules for sustainable resource management, *Environmental Management and Health*, Vol. 68, No. 2, pp. 267–278.

Eun-Jung, K. (2002), The impact of economics and socio-demographics on the decision to eat out, Ohio State University PhD dissertation, UMI-Dissertation Publishers, Michigan.

Evans, J.R. and Mathus, A. (2005), The value of online surveys, *Internet Research*, Vol. 15, No. 2, pp. 195–220.

Feldman, D.C. and Bolino, M.C. (2000), Career patterns of the self-employed, *Journal of Small Business Management*, Vol. 38, No. 3, pp. 53–68.

Fernald, L.W., Solomon, G.T. and Tarabishy, A. (2005), A new paradigm: entrepreneurial leadership, *Southern Business Review*, Vol. 30, No. 2, pp. 1–11.

Fisher, P.S. (1988), State venture capital funds as an economic development strategy, *Journal of American Planning Association*, Vol. 54, No. 2, pp. 166–178.

Fitzgerald, R. (2000), Markets, management, and merger: John Mackintosh & Sons, 1890–2000, *Business History Review*, Vol. 74, No. 4, pp. 55–111.

Flavian, C. and Guinaliu, M. (2005), The influence of virtual communities on distribution strategies in the internet, *International Journal of Retail & Distribution Management*, Vol. 33, No. 6/7, pp. 405–426.

Forscht, T., Swoboda, B. and Morschett, D. (2006), Electronic commerce-based internationalisation of small, niche-oriented retailing companies, *International Journal of Retail & Distribution Management*, Vol. 34, No. 7, pp. 556–567.

Foxall, G. and Goldsmith, R. (1994), *Consumer Psychology for Marketing*, Routledge, London.

Frank, M. (1997), The realities of Web-based electronic commerce, *Strategy & Leadership*, Vol. 25, No. 3, pp. 30–38.

Fraser, J.A. (2004), A return to basics at Kellogg, *Sloan Management Review*, Vol. 45, No. 4, pp. 27–31.

Friel, M. (1999), Marketing practices in small tourism and hospitality firms, *The International Journal of Tourism Research*, Vol. 1, No. 2, pp. 97–106.

Fry, M.J. (1992), *Entrepreneurship: A Planning Approach*, West Publishing, Minneapolis.

Fuchs, P.H., Mifflin, K.E., Miller, D. and Whitney, J.O. (2000), Strategic integration: competing in the age of capabilities, *California Management Review*, Vol. 42, No. 3, pp. 118–148.

Fukugawa, N. (2006), Determining factors in innovation of small firm networks: a case of cross industry groups in Japan, *Small Business Economics*, Vol. 27, No. 2/3, pp. 181–196.

Galbraith, E. Stephens, A.T. and Williams, B. (2006), Forecasts and outcomes for high technology projects, *Research Technology Management*, Vol. 49, No. 3, pp. 27–41.

Gallagher, S., Maher, J. and O'Dwyer, M. (2000), The importance of a distribution strategy within the farmhouse cheese industry, *Irish Marketing Review*, Vol. 13, No. 2, pp. 27–36.

Garnett, T.A. and Wall, H.J. (2006), Creating a policy environment for entrepreneurs, *Cato Journal*, Vol. 26, No. 3, pp. 525–553.

Gartner, W.B. (1988), Who is an entrepreneur is the wrong question, *Entrepreneurship Theory and Practice*, Vol. 13, No.1, pp. 47–64.

Gaskill, L.R., Van Auken, H.E. and Manning, R.A. (1993), A factor analytic study of the perceived causes of small business failure, *Journal of Small Business Management*, Vol. 31, No. 4, pp. 18–32.

Georgelli, Y.P., Joyce, B. and Woods, A. (2000), Entrepreneurial action, innovation, and business performance: the small independent business, *Journal of Small Business and Enterprise Development*, Vol. 7, No. 1, pp. 7–17.

Gilbert, C. (2003), The disruption opportunity, *Sloan Management Review*, Vol. 44, No. 4, pp. 27–34.

Golan, B. (2006), Achieving growth and responsiveness: process management and market orientation in small firms, *Journal of Small Business Management*, Vol. 44, No. 3, pp. 369–388.

Golder, P.N. and Telus, G.J. (1997), Will it ever fly: modelling the takeoff of really new consumer durables, *Marketing Science*, Vol. 16, No. 3, pp. 256–271.

Goodman, M.R.V. (1999), The pursuit of value through qualitative market research, *Qualitative Market Research*, Vol. 2, No. 2, pp. 111–122.

Goodwin, H. and Francis, J. (2003), Ethical and responsible tourism: consumer trends in the UK, *Journal of Tourism Marketing*, Vol. 9, No. 3, pp. 271–284.

Greco, J. (1997), Retailing's rule breakers, *The Journal of Business Strategy*, Vol. 18, No. 2, pp. 28–34.

Greiner, L.E. (1972), Evolution and revolution as organisations grow, *Harvard Business Review*, July/August, pp. 11–19.

Greve, H.R. (2007), Exploration and exploitation in product innovation, *Industrial and Corporate Change*, Vol. 16, No. 5, pp. 945–976.

Gunasekaran, A., Folker, L. and Koby, B. (2000), Improving operations performance in a small company: a case study, *International Journal of Operations of Production Management*, Vol. 20, No. 3, pp. 316–325.

Guthrie, J. (2003), If your cup overfloweth, create a new one, *Financial Times*, London, 17 June, p. 16.

Gywne, P. (1996), 100 years small: managing innovation at Reilly Industries, *Research Technology Management*, Vol. 39, No. 6, pp. 39–44.

Hadjimanolis, A. (2000), A resource-based view of innovation in small firms, *Technology Analysis & Strategic Management*, Vol. 12, No. 2, pp. 263–282.

Hamal, G. and Prahalad, C. (1996), *Competing for the Future*, Harvard Business School Press, Harvard, MA.

Hammond, J.B.W. (2002), Genomic discovery and the medical market: what does the future hold? *International Journal of Medical Marketing*, Vol. 2, No. 2, pp. 167–174.

Hanna, R. (1995), The evil empire, *The New Republic*, Washington, 11 September, pp. 22–26.

Harding, R. and Cowling, M. (2006), Assessing the scale of the equity gap, *Journal of Small Business and Enterprise Development*, Vol. 13, No. 1, pp. 115–133.

Harper, S.C. (1991), Preventing the 'here to-day, gone tomorrow' new venture syndrome, *Business Forum*, Vol. 16, No. 3, pp. 18–26.

Hau, A. and Jiang, L. (2005), Economic growth and Medicare funding systems, *Contemporary Economic Policy*, Vol. 23, No. 1, pp. 17–28.

Haugh, H.M. and Pardy, W. (1999) Community entrepreneurship in North East Scotland, *International Journal of Entrepreneurial Behaviour and Research*, Vol. 5, No. 4, pp. 163–172.

Headd, B. (2003), Redefining business success: distinguishing between closure and failure, *Small Business Economics*, Vol. 21, No. 1, pp. 51–59.

Hellman, T. and Puri, M. (2000), The interaction between product market and financing strategy: the role of venture capital, *The Review of Financial Studies*, Vol. 13, No. 4, pp. 959–974.

Henry, C. (2007), Periscopic media tour, *Strategy & Leadership*, Vol. 35, No. 1, pp. 52–60.

Herbig, P. and Jacobs, L. (1996), Creative problem-solving styles in the USA and Japan, *International Marketing Review*, Vol. 13, No. 2, pp. 63–72.

Hickman, C. and Raia, C. (2002), Incubating innovation, *The Journal of Business Strategy*, Vol. 23, No. 3, pp. 14–19.

Hill, J. and Scott, T. (2004), A consideration of the roles of business intelligence and e-business in management and marketing decision making in knowledge-based and high-tech start-ups, *Qualitative Market Research*, Vol. 7, No. 1, pp. 48–57.

Hill, J., Nancarrow, C. and Wright, L.T. (2002), Lifecycles and crisis points in SMEs, *Marketing Intelligence and Planning*, Vol. 20, No. 6, pp. 361–369.

Hill, W.L. and Hansen, G.S. (1991), A longitudinal study of the cause and consequences of change, *Strategic Management Journal*, Vol. 12, No. 3, pp. 187–200.

Hills, G.E. and LaForge, R.W. (1992), Research at the marketing interface to advance entrepreneurship theory, *Entrepreneurship Theory and Practice*, Spring, pp. 33–59.

Hilpern, K. (2004), Diversity at work, *The Guardian*, London, 21 June, Special Supplement, p. 4.

Hisrich, R.D. and Peters, M.P. (1992), *Entrepreneurship: Starting, Developing, and Managing a New Enterprise*, Irwin, Boston, MA.

Hitt, M.A., Ireland, R.D. and Stadler, G. (1982), Functional importance and company performance: moderating effects of grand strategy and industry type, *Strategic Management Journal*, Vol. 3, No. 4, pp. 315–331.

Hoffman, N.P. (2000), An examination of the sustainable competitive advantage concept: past, present, and future, *Academy of Marketing Science Review*, Vol. 2000, pp. 1–25.

Hogarty, D.B. (1993), Beating the odds: avoid these mistakes at all costs, *Management Review*, Vol. 82, No. 1, pp. 16–22.

Hollander, S.C. (1996), The wheel of retailing, *Marketing Management*, Vol. 5, No. 2, pp. 63–67.

Houston, M.J., Childers, T.L. and Hoeckler, S.E. (1987), Effects of brand awareness on choice for a common, repeat purchase product, *Journal of Marketing Research*, Vol. 14, pp. 404–420.

Huang, C.L. and Sukant, M. (1990), Designing a data system for consumer research, *Agribusiness*, Vol. 6, No. 5, pp. 515–525.

Hunt, J.M. and Handler, W.C. (1999), The practices of effective family firm leaders, *Journal of Developmental Entrepreneurship*, Vol. 4, No. 2, pp. 135–152.

Hussain, J., Millman, C. and Matlay, H. (2006), SME financing in the UK and in China: a comparative perspective, *Journal of Small Business and Enterprise Development*, Vol. 13, No. 4, pp. 584–596.

Hyland, P. and Beckett, R. (2005), Engendering an innovative culture and maintaining operational balance, *Journal of Small Business and Enterprise Development*, Vol. 12, No. 3, pp. 336–352.

Hyrsky, K. (2000), Entrepreneurial metaphors and concepts: an exploratory study, *International Small Business Journal*, Vol. 18, No. 1, pp. 13–34.

Ibrahim, N.A., Angelidis, J.P. and Parsa, F. (2004), The status of planning in small business, *American Business Review*, Vol. 22, No. 2, pp. 52–61.

Ibrahim, N.A., Angelidis, J.P. and Parsa, F. (2008), Strategic management of family businesses: current findings and directions for future research, *International Journal of Management*, Vol. 25, No. 1, pp. 95–116.

Ip, B. and Jacobs, G. (2006), Business succession planning: a review of the evidence, *Journal of Small Business and Enterprise Development*, Vol. 13, No. 3, pp. 326–338.

Jakubovics, J. (1989), Domino's Pizza founder really delivers, *Management Review*, Vol. 78, No. 7, pp. 11–15.

Jelassi, T. and Enders, A. (2005), *Strategies for E-business*, Pearson Education, Harlow, Essex.

Jennings, P. and Beaver, G. (1997), The performance and competitive advantage of small firms: a management perspective, *International Small Business Journal*, Vol. 15, No. 2, pp. 63–75.

Jocumsen, J. (2004), How do small business managers make strategic marketing decisions?, *European Journal of Marketing*, Vol. 38, No. 5/6, pp. 659–674.

Johannisson, B. and Nilsson, A. (1989) Community entrepreneurs: networking for local development, *Entrepreneurship & Regional Development*, Vol. 1, No. 1, pp. 3–19.

Johnson, G. and Scholes, K. (1999), *Exploring Corporate Strategy*, Prentice Hall, Harlow, Essex.

Jolly, V.K. and Bechler, K.A. (1992), Logitech: the mouse that roared, *Planning Review*, Vol. 20, No. 6, pp. 20–34.

Jones, D.B. (1994), Setting promotional goals: a communications' relationship model, *The Journal of Consumer Marketing*, Vol. 11, No. 1, pp. 38–50.

Jones, W. and Chudry, F. (2001), From sophisticates to sceptics: direct and database marketing practice in UK SMEs, *Journal of Database Marketing*, Vol. 8, No. 4, pp. 311–325.

Jun, M. and Peterson, R.T. (1991), Medium and long range forecasts computer vs. paint industry, *The Journal of Business Forecasting Methods & Systems*, Vol. 10, No. 2, pp. 12–18.

Jurek, R.J. (1997), Tools of the trade, *Marketing Research*, Vol. 9, No. 2, pp. 31–34.

Justis, R.T. (1982), Starting a small business: an investigation of the borrowing procedure, *Journal of Small Business Management*, Vol. 20, No. 4, pp. 22–32.

Kale, S. (2004), CRM failure and the seven deadly sins, *Marketing Management*, Vol. 13, No. 5, pp. 42–46.

Kane, J. and Spizman, L. (1988), Self-employment, self-selection, and income distribution, *Review of Business*, Vol. 10, No. 2, pp. 11–17.

Katz, F.N. and Hofman, K.J. (2005), Enabling genetics, *Harvard International Review*, Vol. 27, No. 1, pp. 38–43.

Kaynak, E. and Harcar, T.D. (2005), American consumers' attitudes toward commercial banks: a comparison of local and national bank customers by use of geodemographic segmentation, *The International Journal of Bank Marketing*, Vol. 23, No. 1, pp. 73–90.

Kaynak, E., Ghauri, P.N. and Olofsson-Bredenlow, T. (1987), Export behaviour of small Swedish markets, *Journal of Small Business Management*, Vol. 25, No. 2, pp. 26–33.

Keiningham, T.L., Vavra, T.G. and Aksoy, L. (2006), Managing through rose-colored glasses, *Sloan Management Review*, Vol. 48, No. 1, pp. 15–22.

Kelleher, K. (2005), A site stickier than a barroom floor: Myspace made a business out of social networking, *Business 2.0*, Vol. 6, No. 5, pp. 74–75.

Kerlin, J.A. (2006), Social enterprise in the United States and Europe: understanding and learning from the differences, *Voluntas*, Vol. 17, pp. 247–263.

Kets de Vries, M.J. (1977), The entrepreneurial personality: a person at the crossroads, *Journal of Management Studies*, Vol. 14, No. 1, pp. 34–57.

Khan, A.M. and Manopichetwattan, V. (1989), Innovative and non-innovative small firms and characteristics, *Management Science*, Vol. 35, No. 5, pp. 597–606.

Khandwalla, P.J. (1977), *The Design of Organizations*, Harcourt Brace Jovanovich, New York.

Kickul, J. and Gundry, L.K. (2002), Prospecting for strategic advantage: the proactive entrepreneurial personality and small firm innovation, *Journal of Small Business Management*, Vol. 40, No. 2, pp. 85–98.

King, S. (2003), Organisational performance and conceptual capability: the relationship between organisational performance and successors' capability in a family-owned firm, *Family Business Review*, Vol. 16, No. 3, pp. 173–181.

Kingsley, G. and Malecki, E. (2004), Networking for competitiveness, *Small Business Economics*, Vol. 23, No.1, pp. 71–82.

Kirpalani, V.H. and Macintosh, N.B. (1980), Marketing effectiveness of technology-orientated small firms, *Journal of International Business Studies*, Vol. 11, No. 3, pp. 81–91.

Klassen, A. (2006), Here's a $14 billion print business that's loving the digital revolution, *Advertising Age*, Chicago, 28 August, pp. 3–5.

Klopfenstein, B.C. (1989), Forecasting consumer adoption of information technology and services – lessons from the home video forecasting, *Journal of the American Society for Information Science*, Vol. 40, No. 1, pp. 17–26.

Kornecki, L. (2006), The role of small business development in stimulating output and employment in the Polish economy, *Journal of Problems and Perspectives in Management*, Vol. 1, pp. 32–39.

Kotey, B. and Slade, P. (2005a), Formal human resource management practices in small growing firms, *Journal of Small Business Management*, Vol. 43, No. 1, pp. 16–27.

Kotey, B. and Slade, P. (2005b), Resource management practices in small growing firms, *Journal of Small Business Management*, Vol. 43, No. 1, pp. 16–41.

Kotler, P. (1997), *Marketing Management: Analysis, Planning, Implementation and Control*, Prentice Hall, Upper Saddle River, NJ, 9th edn.

Kotler, P. (2004), *Marketing Management*, Prentice Hall, New York, 10th edn.

Kotler, P. (2006), *Marketing Management*, Prentice Hall, London, 12th edn.

Kotzab, H., Grant, D.B. and Friis, A. (2006), Supply chain management and priority strategies in Danish organisations, *Journal of Business Logistics*, Vol. 27, No. 2, pp. 273–302.

Kroeger, C.V. (1974), Managerial development in the small firm, *California Management Review*, Vol. 17, No. 1, pp. 41–50.

Kuratko, D.F. and Hodgetts, R.M. (1998), *Entrepreneurship: A Contemporary Approach*, The Dryden Press/Harcourt Brace College Publishers, Fort Worth, TX.

Kurweil, R. (2006), Reinventing humanity: the future of machine–human intelligence, *The Futurist*, Vol. 40, No. 2, pp. 39–46.

Laforet, S. and Tann, J. (2006), Innovative characteristics of small manufacturing firms, *Journal of Small Business and Enterprise Development*, Vol. 13, No. 3, pp. 363–375.

Lal, R. and Rao, R. (1997), Supermarket competition: the case of every day low pricing, *Marketing Science*, Vol. 16, No. 1, pp. 60–81.

Lam, K.C. and Postle, P. (2006), Textile and apparel supply chain management in Hong Kong, *International Journal of Clothing Science and Technology*, Vol. 18, No. 4, pp. 26–38.

Lane, S. and Schary, M. (1991), Understanding the business failure rate, *Contemporary Policy Issues*, Vol. 9, No. 4, pp. 93–106.

Lawton, T.C. (1999), Evaluating European competitiveness: measurements and models for a successful business environment, *European Business Journal*, Vol. 11, No. 4, pp. 195–206.

Lazerson, M. and Lorenzoni, G. (1999), Resisting organisational inertia: the evolution of industrial districts, *Journal of Management and Governance*, Vol. 3, pp. 361–377.

Lea, E. and Worsley, T. (2006), Australian's organic food beliefs, demographics and values, *British Food Journal*, Vol. 107, No. 10/11, pp. 855–870.

Leadbeater, C. (1997) *The Rise of the Social Entrepreneur*, Demos, London.

Leadbeater, C. and Goss, S. (1998) *Civic Entrepreneurship*, Demos, London.

Lee, J. (2004), The effects of family ownership and management on firm performance, *S.A.M. Advanced Management Journal*, Vol. 69, No. 4, pp. 46–54.

Lee, P.M. (1990), The micro-marketing revolution, *Small Business Reports*, Vol. 15, No. 2, pp. 71–82.

Lerer, L. (2005), Medicine transformed – implications for medical marketing, *Journal of Medical Marketing*, Vol. 5, No. 2, pp. 167–173.

Levitas, E. and Ndofor, H.A. (2006), What to do with the resource-based view: a few suggestions for what ails the RBV that supporter and opponents might accept, *Journal of Management Inquiry*, Vol. 15, No. 2, pp. 135–145.

Levitt, T. (1965), Exploit the product life cycle, *Harvard Business Review*, November/December, pp. 81–94.

Lewis, K., Massey, C. and Ashby, M. (2007), Business assistance for SMEs: New Zealand owner/ managers make their assessment, *Small Business and Enterprise Development*, Vol. 14, No. 4, pp. 551–566.

Liao, J. and Welsch, H. (2005), Roles of social capital in venture creation: key dimensions and research implications, *Journal of Small Business Management*, Vol. 43, No. 4, pp. 345–363.

Linvol, H. and Razzouk, N.Y. (2006), From market share to customer share: implications to marketing strategies, *The Business Review*, Vol. 5, No. 1, pp. 33–39.

Littunen, H. (2000), Entrepreneurship and the characteristics of entrepreneurial personality, *International Journal of Entrepreneurial Behaviour Research*, Vol. 6, No. 6, pp. 295–303.

Littunen, H. and Tohmo, T. (2003), The high growth in new metal-based manufacturing and business service firms in Finland, *Small Business Economics*, Vol. 21, No. 2, pp. 187–198.

Luger, M.I. and Koo, J. (2005), Defining and tracking business start-ups, *Small Business Economics*, Vol. 24, No. 1, pp. 17–28.

Lyles, M.A., Baird, I.S., Orris, B. and Kuratko, D.F. (1993), Formalised planning in business: increasing strategic choice, *Journal of Small Business Management*, Vol. 31, No. 2, pp. 38–51.

MacKay, R.B. and McKiernan, P. (2004), Exploring strategy context with foresight, *European Management Review*, Vol. 1, No. 1, pp. 69–78.

Madden, C.S. and Caballero, M.J. (1987), Perceptions of the specialty advertising industry implications, *The Journal of Business & Industrial Marketing*, Vol. 2, No. 4, pp. 37–45.

Maes, J. and Basu, M. (2005), Building economic self reliance: Trickle Up's microenterprise seed capital for the extreme poor in rural India, *Journal of Microfinance*, Vol. 7, No. 2, pp. 71–100.

Malhotra, P. and Lofgren, H. (2004), India's pharmaceutical industry: hype or high-tech take-off? *Australian Health Review*, Vol. 28, No. 2, pp. 182–194.

Markely, M.J. and Davis, L. (2007), Exploring future competitive advantage through sustainable supply chains, *International Journal of Physical Distribution & Logistics Management*, Vol. 37, No. 9, pp. 763–778.

Marmor, T.R. (1998), Forecasting American healthcare: how we got here and where we might be going, *Journal of Health Politics*, Vol. 23, No. 3, pp. 521–542.

Marshall, G. and Greenbergronald, E.F. (1983), Lifestyle segmentation by interests, needs, demographics and television viewing, *The American*, Vol. 26, No. 4, pp. 439–459.

Martin, G. and Staines, D. (1994), Managerial competences in small firms, *The Journal of Management Development*, Vol. 13, No. 7, pp. 23–34.

Mason, C.M. and Harrison, R.T. (1996), The UK clearing banks and the informal venture capital market, *The International Journal of Bank Marketing*, Vol. 14, No. 1, pp. 5–16.

Mason, C.M. and Harrison, R.T. (2000), The size of the informal venture capital market in the UK, *Small Business Economics*, Vol. 15, No. 2, pp. 137–149.

Mayhew, K. and Neely, A. (2006), Improving productivity – opening the black box, *Oxford Review of Economic Policy*, Vol. 22, No. 4, pp. 445–461.

McCann, J.E., Leon-Guerrero, A.Y. and Haley, J.D. (2001), Strategic goals and practices of innovative family businesses, *Journal of Small Business Management*, Vol. 39, No. 1, pp. 59–69.

McCarthy, B. (2003), Strategy is personality-driven, strategy is crisis-driven: insights from entrepreneurial firms, *Management Decisions*, Vol. 41, No. 4, pp. 327–340.

McCarthy, B. and Leavy, B. (1998), The entrepreneur, risk-perception and change over time: a typology approach, *Irish Business and Administrative Research*, Vol. 19/20, No. 1, pp. 125–141.

McCrohan, K.F. and Finklemen, J.M. (1981), Social character and the new automobile industry, *California Management Review*, Vol. 24, No. 1, pp. 58–69.

McElwee, G. and Warren, L. (2000), The relationship between total quality management and human resource management in small and medium-sized enterprises, *Strategic Change*, Vol. 9, No. 7, pp. 427–439.

McGregor, A., Clark, S., Ferguson, Z. and Scullion, J. (1997), Valuing the Social Economy and Economic Inclusion in Lowland Scotland, Community Enterprise in Strathclyde, Glasgow.

McIntye, R. (1989), Economic rhetoric and industrial decline, *Journal of Economic Issues*, Vol. 23, No. 2, pp. 483–492.

McKenna, S.D. (1996), The darker side of the entrepreneur, *Leadership and Organisation Development Journal*, Vol. 17, No. 6, pp. 41–49.

McNamara, K. and Watson, J.G. (2005), The development of a team orientated structure in a small business enterprise, *Journal of American Academy*, Vol. 6, No. 2, pp. 184–191.

Mellahi, K. and Johnson, M. (2000), Does it pay to be a first mover in e-commerce, *Management Decision*, Vol. 38, No. 7, pp. 445–462.

Michaelidou, N. and Dibb, S. (2006), Using email questionnaires for research: good practice in tackling non-response, *Journal of Targeting, Measurement and Analysis for Marketing*, Vol. 14, No. 4, pp. 289–297.

Miles, R.E. and Snow, C.C. (1978), *Organizational Strategy, Structure and Process*, McGraw Hill, New York.

Miller, D. (1983), The correlates of entrepreneurship in three types of firm, *Management Science*, Vol. 29, pp. 770–791.

Miller, D. and Friesen, P.H. (1982), Archetypes of strategy formulation, *Management Science*, Vol. 29, pp. 770–791.

Millier, P. and Palmer, R. (2001), Turning innovation into profit, *Strategic Change*, Vol. 10, No. 2, pp. 87–98.

Mintzberg, H. (1990), The Design School: reconsidering the basic premises of strategic management, *Strategic Management Journal*, Vol. 11, pp. 171–195.

Mintzberg, H. and Waters, J.A. (1982), Tracking strategy in an entrepreneurial firm, *Academy of Management Journal*, Vol. 25, No. 3, pp. 463–499.

Mogelonsky, M. (1995), Satisfying senior shoppers, *Marketing Tools*, Vol. 2, No. 2, pp. 4–5.

Mohannak, K. (2007), Innovation networks and capability building in the Australian high-technology SMEs, *European Journal of Innovation Management*, Vol. 10, No. 2, pp. 236–247.

Moll, H.A. (2005), Microfinance and rural development: a long-term perspective, *Journal of Microfinance*, Vol. 7, No. 2, pp. 13–32.

Money, R.B., Gilly, M.C. and Graham, J.L. (1998), Explorations of national culture and word-of-mouth referral behavior in the purchase of industrial services in the United States and Japan, *Journal of Marketing*, Vol. 62, No. 4, pp. 76–88.

Montoya-Weiss, M.M. and Calantone, R.G. (1994), Determinants of new product performance: a review and a meta-analysis, *Journal of Product Innovation Management*, Vol. 11, No. 5, pp. 397–417.

Moore, G.A. (1991), *Crossing The Chasm*, The Free Press, New York.

Moorthy, S. (2005), A general theory of pass-through in channels with category management and retail competition, *Marketing Science*, Vol. 24, No. 1, pp. 110–123.

Morris, M.H., Williams, R. and Deon, N. (1996), Factors influencing family business succession, *International Journal of Entrepreneurial Behaviour & Research*, Vol. 2, No. 3, pp. 68–79.

Morrison, A. and Teixeira, R. (2004), Small business performance: a tourism sector focus, *Journal of Small Business and Enterprise Development*, Vol. 11, No. 2, pp. 166–175.

Mort, G.S. and Weerawardena, J. (2006), Networking capability and international entrepreneurship: how networks function in Australian born global firms, *International Marketing Review*, Vol. 23, No. 5, pp. 549–559.

Mosey, S. (2005), Understanding new-to-market product development in SMEs, *International Journal of Operations and Production Management*, Vol. 25, No. 2, pp. 114–130.

Moss, D., Ashford, R. and Shani, N. (2003), The forgotten sector: uncovering the role of public relations in SMEs, *Journal of Communication Management*, Vol. 8, No. 2, pp. 197–211.

Mulgan, G. and Landry, L. (1995) The other invisible hand: remaking charity for the 21st Century, *Development International*, Vol. 4/3, pp. 140–145.

Mullins, J. (2007), Discovering the 'unk-unks', *Sloan Management Review*, Vol. 48, No. 4, pp. 17–21.

Mukherji, A. (2002), The evolution of information systems: Their impact on organizations and structures, *Management Decision*, Vol. 40, No. 5/6, pp. 497–508.

Munch, A. and Hunt, S.D. (1984), Consumer involvement: definition issues and research directions, in (Kinnear, T., ed.) *Advances in Consumer Research*, Vol. 11, Association for Consumer Research, Provo, UT.

Murphy, M. (2006), Friends Reunited history, www.friendsreunited.co.uk/press/history.htm.

Nagle, T.T. (1993), Managing price competition, *Marketing Management*, Vol. 2, No. 1, pp. 36–46.

Norbert, T. (1990), Innovation management in small and medium-sized firms, *Management International Review*, Vol. 30, No. 2, pp. 181–192.

Oates, D. (1988), Keeping body and soul together, *Director*, Vol. 42, No. 12, pp. 64–68.

Ojala, A. and Tyrvainen, P. (2006), Entry models and market entry mode choice of small software firms, *Journal of International Entrepreneurship*, Vol. 4, pp. 69–81.

Ojasalo, J. (2004), Attractiveness and image of entrepreneurship: an empirical study, *International Journal of Entrepreneurship*, Vol. 8, pp. 73–93.

Olsen, P., Orser, B.J., Hogarth-Scott, P. and Riding, A.L. (2000), Performance, firm size, and management problem solving, *Journal of Small Business Management*, Vol. 38, No. 4, pp. 42–58.

O'Reagan, N. and Ghobadian, A. (2002), Effective strategic planning in small and medium sized firms, *Management Decision*, Vol. 40, No. 7/8, pp. 663–669.

O'Reagan, N. and Ghobdian, A. (2004), Testing the homogeneity of SMEs: the impact on managerial and organisational processes, *European Business Review*, Vol. 18, No. 1, pp. 84–96.

O'Reagan, N. and Ghobadian, A. (2006), Perceptions of generic strategy of SME engineering and electronics manufacturers in the UK, *The Journal of Manufacturing Technology*, Vol. 17, No. 5, pp. 603–614.

O'Regan, N., Ghobadian, A. and Sims, M. (2005), The link between leadership, strategy and performance in manufacturing SMEs, *Journal of Small Business Strategy*, Vol. 15, No. 2, pp. 45–58.

Orth, M. (2008), The power of the wind – the Enercon story, *German Business Review*, April, pp. 11–13.

Ou, C. and Haynes, G.W. (2006), Acquisition of additional equity capital by small firms – findings from the national survey of small business finance, *Small Business Economics*, Vol. 27, pp. 157–168.

Owens, J.D. (2007), Why do some UK SMEs still find the implementation of a new product development process problematical: an exploratory investigation, *Management Decision*, Vol. 45, No. 2, pp. 235–247.

Paap, J. and Katz, R. (2004), Anticipating disruptive innovation, *Research Technology Management*, Vol. 47, No. 5, pp. 13–23.

Parks, G.M. (1977), How to climb the growth curve – eleven hurdles for the entrepreneur manager, *Journal of Small Business Management*, Vol. 15, No. 1, pp. 41–52.

Parnell, J.A., Von Bergen, C.W. and Soper, B. (2005), Profiting from past triumphs and failures: harnessing history for future success, *S.A.M. Advanced Management Journal*, Vol. 70, No. 2, pp. 36–47.

Pascale, C.Q. and Smart, J. (1998), The influence of consumption situation and product involvement over consumers' use of product attribute, *The Journal of Consumer Marketing*, Vol. 15, No. 3, pp. 220–231.

Pastakia, A. (1998), Grassroots ecopreneurs: change agents for a sustainable society, *Journal of Organisational Change Management*, Vol. 11, No. 2, pp. 157–166.

Percy, L. and Rossiter, J.R. (1992), A model of brand awareness and brand attitude advertising strategies, *Psychology & Marketing*, Vol. 9, No. 4, pp. 263–275.

Petersen, R.T. (1988), An analysis of small business ideas in small business, *Journal of Small Business Management*, Vol. 26, No. 2, pp. 25–32.

Petersen, R.T. (1991), Business usage of target marketing, *Journal of Small Business Management*, Vol. 29, No. 4, pp. 79–85.

Petersen, R.T. (2006), Development of useful ideas in the new product development process of small manufacturing firms, *Journal of Applied Management and Entrepreneurship*, Vol. 11, No. 3, pp. 23–40.

Peterson, R.A., Albaum, G. and Kozmetsky, G. (1996), The public's definition of small business, *Journal of Small Business Management*, Vol. 24, No. 3, pp. 63–69.

Piore, M. and Sabel, C. (1984), *The Second Industrial Divide*, Basic Books, New York.

Pitt, L.F., Berthon, P.R. and Morris, M.H. (1997), Entrepreneurial pricing: the Cinderella of marketing strategy, *Management Decisions*, Vol. 35, No. 5, pp. 344–352.

Pitta, D.A. and Fowler, D. (2005), Internet community forums: an untapped resource for consumer marketers, *The Journal of Consumer Marketing*, Vol. 22, No. 4/5, pp. 265–274.

Poutziouris, P., Chittenden, F., Michaeles, N. and Oakey, R. (2000), Taxation and the performance of technology-based firms in the UK, *Small Business Economics*, Vol. 14, No. 1, pp. 11–31.

Porter, M.E. (1980), *Industry and Competitive Analysis*, Free Press, New York.

Portney, P.R., Parry, I.W., Gruenapecht, H.K. and Harrington, W. (2003), The economics of fuel economy standards, *The Journal of Economic Perspectives*, Vol. 17, No. 4, pp. 203–218.

Quader, M.S. (2007), The strategic implications of electronic commerce for small and medium sized enterprises, *Journal of Services Research*, Vol. 6, No. 2, pp. 25–61.

Quinn, J.B. (1980), *Strategies For Change: Logical Incrementalism*, Irwin, Homewood, IL.

Rafferty, E. (2004), Pennywise route to success, *Financial Times*, London, 23 November, p. 13.

Rallens, T. and Ghazanfar, S.M. (2006), Microfinance: recent experience, future possibilities, *The Journal of Social, Political and Economic Studies*, Vol. 31, No. 2, pp. 197–113.

Randall, D.C. (2005), An exploration of the opportunities for growth of the Fair Trade market: three cases of craft organisations, *Journal of Business Ethics*, Vol. 56, pp. 55–67.

Rangone, A. (1999), A resource-based approach to strategy analysis in small–medium sized enterprises, *Small Business Economics*, Vol. 12, No. 3, pp. 233–249.

Raymond, L., Bergeron, F. and Rivard, S. (1988), Determinants of business process reengineering success in small and large enterprises: an empirical study in the Canadian context, *Journal of Small Business Management*, Vol. 36, No. 1, pp. 72–86.

Reichfeld, F.F. and Sasser, W.F. (1990), Zero defections: quality comes to service, *Harvard Business Review*, Sept/Oct., pp. 105–111.

Retkwa, R. (1989), Tri-Seal strives to be the genie in every bottle, *Management Review*, Vol. 78, No. 9, pp. 12–16.

Richardson, B., Nwankwo, S. and Richardson, S. (1994), Understanding the causes of business failure crises: generic failure types: boiled frogs, drowned frogs, bullfrogs and tadpoles, *Management Decision*, Vol. 32, No. 4, pp. 9–23.

Rigby, R. (1998), Tutti-frutti capitalists, *Management Today*, London, February, pp. 54–56.

Rindova, V.P. and Kotha, S. (2001), Continuous 'morphing': competing through dynamic capabilities, form and function, *Academy of Management Journal*, Vol. 44, No. 6, pp. 1263–1280.

Robichaud, Y., McGraw, E. and Roger, A. (2001), Towards development of a measuring instrument for entrepreneurial motivation, *Journal of Developmental Entrepreneurship*, Vol. 5, No. 2, pp. 189–202.

Robinson, R. (1979), Forecasting and small business: a study of the strategic planning process, *Journal of Small Business Management*, Vol. 17, No. 3, pp. 19–28.

Robinson, R.B. and Pearce, J.A. (1984), Research thrusts in small firm strategic planning, *Academy of Management Review*, Vol. 9, No. 1, pp. 128–137.

Robson, P.J. and Bennett, B.J. (1999), Central Government supports to SMEs compared to business link, business connect and business shop and the prospects for the small business service, *Regional Studies*, Vol. 33, No. 8, pp. 779–788.

Rogers, M. (2004), Networks, firm size and innovation, *Small Business Economics*, Vol. 22, No. 2, pp. 141–156.

Rowden, R.W. (2002), High performance and human resource characteristics of successful small manufacturing and processing companies, *Leadership and Organization Development Journal*, Vol. 23, No. 1/2, pp. 79–86.

Rutherford, M.W., Muse, L.A. and Oswald, S.L. (2006), A new perspective on the developmental model for family business, *Family Business Review*, Vol. 19, No. 4, pp. 317–334.

Saemundsson, R. and Dalstrand, A.L. (2005), How business opportunities constrain technology-based firms from growing into medium-size firms, *Small Business Economics*, Vol. 24, pp. 113–129.

Sambrook, S. (2005), Exploring succession planning in small, growing firms, *Journal of Small Business and Enterprise Development*, Vol. 12, No. 4, pp. 579–595.

Sanchez, A.A. and Sanchez, G.M. (2006), Strategic orientation, management characteristics and performance: a study of Spanish SMEs, *Journal of Global Business and Technology*, Vol. 2, No. 2, pp. 1–26.

Sanders, M. (2007), Scientific paradigms, entrepreneurial opportunities and cycles in economic growth, *Small Business Economics*, Vol. 28, No. 4, pp. 333–349.

Sandler-Smith, E., Hampson, Y., Chaston, I. and Badger, B. (2003), Managerial behaviour, entrepreneurial style and small firm performance, *Journal of Small Business Management*, Vol. 42, No. 1, pp. 47–68.

Sanjay, A.A. and Golhar, D.L. (1996), Quality management in large vs small firms, *Strategy of Leadership*, Vol. 34, No. 2, pp. 1–14.

Sanz-Velasco, S.A. (2006), Opportunity development as a learning process for entrepreneurs, *International Journal of Entrepreneurial Behaviour & Research*, Vol. 12, No. 5, pp. 261–270.

Sariona, D.R. and Martinez, J.M.C. (2007), Transmitting the entrepreneurial spirit to the work team in SMEs: the importance of leadership, *Management Decision*, Vol. 27, No. 7, pp. 1102–1114.

Savage, A. and Sales, M. (2008), The anticipatory leader: futurist, strategist and integrator, *Strategy & Leadership*, Vol. 36, No. 6, pp. 28–39.

Schein, E.H. (1996), Career anchors revisited, *The Academy of Management Executive*, Vol. 10, No. 4, pp. 80–89.

Schlesinger, L.A. and Haskett, J.L. (1991), Enfranchisement of service workers, *California Management Review*, Vol. 33, No. 4, pp. 83–97.

Schneider, W. (1985), The paradigm shift in HRM, *Personnel Journal*, Vol. 64, No. 11, pp. 14–17.

Schumpeter, J. (1934), *The Theory of Economic Development*, Harvard University Press, Cambridge, MA.

Schumpeter, J. (1942), *Capitalism, Socialism and Democracy*, Harper & Row, New York.

Sexton, D.L. and Uptan, G. (1987), Small business strategic planning, *Journal of Small Business Management*, Vol. 25, No. 1, pp. 31–40.

Sexton, D.L. and Van Auken, P. (1985), A longitudinal study of small business planning, *Journal of Small Business Management*, Vol. 23, No. 1, pp. 7–10.

Seybold, P.B. (2006), *Outside Innovation*, HarperCollins, New York.

Shane, S. (2000), Prior knowledge and the discovery of entrepreneurial opportunities, *Organization Science*, Vol. 11, No. 4, pp. 448–466.

Shaw, E. (2004), Marketing in the social enterprise context: is it entrepreneurial? *Qualitative Market Research*, Vol. 7, No. 3, pp. 194–203.

Shaw, M. and Cresswell, P. (2002), Standard segments for retail brands, *Journal of Targeting, Measurement and Analysis for Marketing*, Vol. 11, No. 1, pp. 7–24.

Sheshandi, D.V.R. and Henry, J. (2006), Dyson appliances: the never-say-die spirit of entrepreneurship, *South Asian Journal of Management*, Vol. 13, pp. 107–129.

Shoemaker, S. (2003), The future of pricing in services, *Journal of Revenue and Pricing Management*, Vol. 2, No. 3, pp. 271–280.

Shrader, C.B., Mulford, C.L. and Blackburn, V.L. (1989), Strategic and operational planning, uncertainty, and performance in small firms, *Journal of Small Business Management*, Vol. 27, No. 4, pp. 45–60.

Slater, S.F. and Narver, J.C. (1995), Market orientation and the learning organisation, *Journal of Marketing*, Vol. 59, No. 3, pp. 63–75.

Slevin, D.P. and Covin, J. (1990), Juggling entrepreneurial style and organisational culture, *Sloan Management Review*, Vol. 31, No. 2, pp. 43–54.

Slywotzky, A.J. (1996), *Value Migration: How To Think Several Moves Ahead Of The Competition*, Harvard Business School Press, Boston, MA.

Smith, A.J. and Collins, L.A. (2007), Between a rock and a hard place? A case study of the issues facing advisors in introducing IIP to SMEs, *Small Business and Enterprise Development*, Vol. 14, No. 4, pp. 567–581.

Smith, D. (1990), Small is beautiful, but difficult: cost-effective research for small businesses, *Journal of the Market Research Society*, Vol. 32, No. 1, pp. 275–291.

Smith, J.A. (1999), The behaviour and performance of young micro firms: evidence from businesses in Scotland, *Small Business Economics*, Vol. 13, No. 3, pp. 185–197.

Snell, R. and Agnes, L. (1994), Exploring local competences salient for expanding small businesses, *The Journal of Management Development*, Vol. 13, No. 4, pp. 4–16.

Soderholm, P. and Klaasen, G. (2007), Wind power in Europe: a simultaneous innovation-diffusion model, *Environmental and Resource Economics*, Vol. 36, No. 2, pp. 163–185.

Springston, J. (2008), Nanotechnology: understanding the occupational safety and health challenges, *Professional Safety*, Vol. 53, No. 10, pp. 51–58.

Srinivasan, S.S. and Anderson, R.E. (1998), Concepts and strategy guidelines for designing value enhancing sales promotions, *The Journal of Product and Brand Management*, Vol. 7, No. 5, pp. 410–421.

Stanworth, M.J.K. and Gray, C. (1991), *Bolton 20 Years On: Small Business Research Trust*, Paul Chapman Publishing, London.

Stasch, S.F., Lonsdale, R.T., Ward, J.L. and Harris, D.A. (1999), Characteristics of share-gaining marketing strategies for smaller-share firms: literature review and synthesis, *Journal of Marketing Theory and Practice*, Vol. 7, No. 2, pp. 54–67.

Stavrou, E.T., Kleanthous, T. and Anastasiou, T. (2005), Leadership personality and firm culture during hereditary transitions in family firms: model development and empirical investigation, *Journal of Small Business Management*, Vol. 43, No. 2, pp. 187–206.

Steiner, M.P. and Solem, O. (1988), Factors for success in small manufacturing firms, *Journal of Small Business Management*, Vol. 26, No. 1, pp. 51–61.

Sternberg, R. and Wennekers, S. (2005), Determinants and effects of new business creation using Global Entrepreneurship Monitor data, *Small Business Economics*, Vol. 24, No. 3, pp. 193–202.

Stewart, D. and Gallen, B. (1998), The promotional planning process and its impact on consumer franchise building: the case of fast-moving goods companies in New Zealand, *The Journal of Product and Brand Management*, Vol. 7, No. 6, pp. 557–569.

Stewart, W.H., Watson, W.E., Garland, J.C. and Garland, J.W. (1998), A proclivity for entrepreneurship: a comparison of entrepreneurs, small business owners and corporate managers, *Journal of Business Venturing*, Vol. 14, No. 2, pp. 189–214.

Stockport, G.J., Kunnath, G. and Sadick, R. (2001), Boo.com – the path to failure, *Journal of Interactive Marketing*, Vol. 15, No. 4, pp. 56–70.

Stoner, C.R. (1987), Distinctive competence and competitive advantage, *Journal of Small Business Research*, Vol. 25, No. 2, pp. 33–39.

Storey, D. (2002), Methods of evaluating the impact of public sector policies to support small businesses: the 6 steps to heaven, *International Journal of Entrepreneurship Education*, Vol. 1, No. 2, pp. 180–202.

Storey, D.J. and Sykes, N. (1996), Uncertainty, innovation and management, in (Burns, P. and Dewhurst, J., eds), *Small Business and Entrepreneurship*, Macmillan, London, pp. 143–156.

Sudek, R. (2007), Angel investment criteria, *Journal of Small Business Strategy*, Vol. 17, No. 2, pp. 89–104.

Sull, D.N. (2007), Closing the gap between strategy and execution, *Sloan Management Review*, Vol. 48, No. 4, pp. 30–38.

Sullivan, R. (2000), Entrepreneurial learning and mentoring, *International Journal of Entrepreneurial Behaviour and Research*, Vol. 6, No. 3, pp. 160–171.

Sultan, F. and Barzack, G. (1999), Turning marketing research high-tech, *Marketing Management*, Vol. 8, No. 4, pp. 24–31.

Sunday Times, The (2006), Britain's 100 fastest growing private companies, *The Sunday Times*, London, 3 December, Fast Track Supplement, pp. 1–20.

Sweirz, P.M. and Lydon, S.R. (2002), Entrepreneurial leadership in high-tech firms: a field study, *Leadership and Organisation Development Journal*, Vol. 23, No. 7, pp. 380–389.

Takacs, S.J. and Freiden, J.B. (1998), Changes on the electronic frontier, *Journal of Marketing Theory and Practice*, Vol. 6, No. 3, pp. 24–38.

Tanabe, K. and Watanabe, G. (2005), Sources of small and medium enterprises excellent business in a service orientated economy, *Journal of Service Research*, Vol. 5, No. 1, pp. 5–21.

Tay, A.A. and Agrawal, N. (2004), Channel conflict and coordination in the e-Commerce age, *Production and Operations Management*, Vol. 13, No. 1, pp. 93–121.

Taymaz, E. (2005), Are small firms really less productive? *Small Business Economics*, Vol. 25, pp. 429–445.

Tedlow, R.S. and Jones, G. (1993), *The Rise And Fall Of Mass Marketing*, Routledge, London.

Tellis, G.J. and Golder, P.N. (1996), First to market, first to fail: real causes of enduring market leadership, *Sloan Management Review*, Vol. 37, No. 2, pp. 65–75.

Theodosiou, M. and Katsikeas, C. (2001), Factors influencing the degree of international pricing strategy standardization of multinational corporations, *Journal of International Marketing*, Vol. 9, No. 3, pp. 1–19.

Thilmany, J. (2008), Off shore analysis, *Mechanical Engineering*, Vol. 130, No. 5, pp. 32–36.

Thom, N. (1990), Innovation management in small and medium-sized firms, *Management International Review*, Vol. 30, No. 2, pp. 181–193.

Thomas, J. (2006), An introduction to nanotechnology: the next small big thing, *Development*, Vol. 49, No. 4, pp. 39–46.

Thomas, N. (2008), On borrowed time, *Scotland on Sunday*. Edinburgh, 30 November, p. 5.

Thompson, J. and Doherty, C. (2006), A collection of social enterprise stories, *International Journal of Social Economics*, Vol. 33, No. 5/6, pp. 361–376.

Tripsas, M. and Gavetti, G. (2000), Capabilities, emotions and inertia, *Strategic Management Journal*, Vol. 21, No. 10/11, pp. 1147–1161.

Upton, N., Teal, E.J. and Felan, J.T. (2001), Strategic and business planning practices of fast growth family firms, *Journal of Small Business Management*, Vol. 39, No. 1, pp. 60–73.

Utsch, A., Rauch, A. Rothfuss, R. and Frese, M. (1999), Who becomes a small scale entrepreneur in a post-socialist environment: on the differences between entrepreneurs and managers in East Germany, *Journal of Small Business Management*, Vol. 37, No. 3, pp. 31–42.

Van Auken, H.E., Doran, D.M and Rittenberg, T.L. (1992), An empirical analysis of small business advertising, *Journal of Small Business Management*, Vol. 30, No. 2, pp. 87–98.

Van Praag, C.M. and Versloot, P.H. (2007), What is the value of entrepreneurship: a review of recent research, *Small Business Economics*, Vol. 29, pp. 351–382.

Van Stel, A.J. and Storey, D.J. (2004), The link between firm births and job creation, *Regional Studies*, Vol. 38, No. 8, pp. 893–909.

Venkatram, R., Gatigon, H. and Reibstein, D.J. (1994), Competitive marketing behavior in industrial markets, *Journal of Marketing*, Vol. 58, No 2, pp. 45–56.

Vermeulen, P.A.M. (2005), Uncovering barriers to complex incremental product innovation in small and medium-sized financial services firms, *Journal of Small Business Management*, Vol. 43, No. 4, pp. 432–453.

Vermeulen, P.A.M., De Jong, P.J. and O'Shaughnessy, K.C. (2005), Identifying key determinants for new product introductions and firm performance in small service firms, *Service Industries Journal*, Vol. 25, No. 5, pp. 625–640.

Vinson, D.E., Jackson, J.H. and Ray, G.D. (1975), A pragmatic approach to new product planning, *Journal of Small Business Management*, Vol. 13, No. 2, pp. 37–48.

Von Hippel, E. (1986), Lead users: a source of novel product concepts, *Management Science*, Vol. 32, No. 7, pp. 691–714.

Von Jouanne, A. (2006), Harvesting the waves, *Mechanical Engineering*, Vol. 128, No. 12, pp. 24–28.

Wade, N. (1999), The genome's combative entrepreneur, *New York Times*, 18 May, pp. 17–18.

Wagner, E.R. and Hansen, E.N. (2005), Innovation in large versus small companies: insights from the US wood products industry, *Management Decision*, Vol. 43, No. 5/6, pp. 837–851.

Wantuck, M. (1982), Drop by drop, his firm won worldwide success, *Nation's Business*, Vol. 72, No. 7, p. 42–47.

Warner, F. (2006), *The Power Of The Purse*, Pearson Prentice Hall, New Jersey.

Wasserman, T. (2006), YouTube, *Brandweek*, 9 October, pp. M16–M18.

Watson, K., Hogarth-Small, S. and Wilson, N. (1998), Small business start-ups: success factors and support implications, *International Journal of Entrepreneurial Behaviour*, Vol. 4, No. 3, pp. 217–228.

Index

accessibility 44
Acer 150
ACORN 47
actual market size 73
added value 101
advertising 153
Amazon 10, 157–8
Andreesen, M. 80
antibiotics 211
Apple Computers 54
Artic Monkeys 156
assets 59–60
Austrian School 50
Autodesk 174–5
autonomy 13–14

baby boomers 15
bagless cleaner 23
Balance Sheet 60
Ball Barrow 23
bank lending 86
banner advertising 177
Barnes & Noble 158
Baylis, T. 8
Ben & Jerry's 146–7
benefits of planning 24–6
Bezos, J. 157–8
blog mining 39–40
blogs 38
Blue Tomato 179
Boo.com 156–60
Branson, R. 145, 217
Bratz doll 74
break even 59
business angels 69, 87–7
business creation 2
business growth 5–6
business planning 20–1
butterfly planning 31

C2C marketing 180
Cadbury's 184
Canon 201
career anchors 12–13
cash flow 58–9
category pricing 166
changing needs 15
channel access 172–4
channel alternatives 173–4
charismatic entrepreneur 26
chat rooms 38

Christensen, C.M. 126, 201
Cipla 212
clean coal 208
clicks and mortar 158
climate change 205
clockwork radio 8
collaborative innovation 100–2
community enterprise 191
community needs 192
competition 79–80
competitive mapping 79–80
consumer expenditure 82–3
cost factors 163–5
cost leadership 169
cost plus pricing 162–3
crossing chasms 54–5
cultural values 204
culture 88–9
current assets 59–60
current liabilities 59–60
customer personality 152
customer preference 74
customer price expectations 164
customer price sensitivity 168
customer rejection 170

data generation 38–43
DEC (Digital Equipment Corporation) 127
defining strategy 96–7
delivery decision 173
Dell 126, 156
demand influencers 203–4
demand pricing 163
diffusion of innovation 148–9
Direct Line 175–6
direct marketing 154
disruption theory 200–1
disruptive innovation 126–7
distinctive competence 94
distribution assessment 177
distribution communities 178–9
distribution delegation 174
distribution 171–5
DNA sequencing 213
Domino Pizza 62–3
drug entrepreneurs 212
Dyson, J. 23–4

easyJet 10, 169
eBay 178
Eberhard, M. 209–10

Webb, K.L. and Hogan, J.R. (2002), Hybrid channel conflict: Causes and effects on channel performance, *The Journal of Business & Industrial Marketing*, Vol. 17, No. 5, pp. 338–357.

Weiber, R. and Kollman, T. (1998), Competitive advantage in virtual markets – perspectives on information-based marketing, *European Journal of Marketing*, Vol. 32, No. 7, pp. 603–615.

Weinberg, S. and Pruitt, A. (2006), Despite ban, web gamblers pay on, *The Wall Street Journal*, New York, 1 Nov, p. B3D.

Weinrauch, J.D., Mann, O.K., Robinson, P.A. and Pharr, J. (1991), Dealing with limited financial resources: a marketing challenge for small business, *Journal of Small Business Management*, Vol. 29, No. 4, pp. 44–55.

Weinsten, A. (1994), Market definition in technology-based industry: a comparative study of small versus non-small companies, *Journal of Small Business Management*, Vol. 32, No. 4, pp. 28–37.

Westhead, P. and Howorth, C. (2006), Ownership and management issues with family firm performance and company objectives, *Family Business Review*, Vol. 19, No. 4, pp. 301–317.

Wheeler, S., McKague, K., Thomson, J., Davies, R., Medalye, J. and Prada, M. (2005), Creating sustainable local enterprise networks, *Sloan Business Review*, Vol. 47, No. 1, pp. 33–39.

White, W.S., Krinkle, T.D. and Geller, D.L. (2004), Family business succession planning: devising an overall strategy, *Journal of Financial Service Professionals*, Vol. 58, No. 3, pp. 67–87.

Whitlark, D.B., Geurtts, M.D. and Swenson, M.J. (1993), New product forecasting with a purchase intention survey, *The Journal of Business Forecasting Methods and Systems*, Vol. 12, No.3, pp. 18–26.

Widgery, R., Angur, M. and Nataraajan, R. (1997), The impact of status on married women's perceptions, *Journal of Advertising Research*, Vol. 37, No. 1, pp. 54–63.

Wilson, G. (1973), *The Psychology of Conservatism*, Academic Press, London.

Windrum, P. (2001), Late entrant strategies in technological ecologies, *International Studies of Management and Organisation*, Vol. 31, No. 1, pp. 18–106.

Wolff, J.A. and Pett, T. (2006), Small firm performance: modelling the role of product and process improvements, *Journal of Small Business Management*, Vol. 44, No. 2, pp. 268–285.

Woller, G. (2002), From market failure to marketing failure: market orientation as the key to deep outreach in microfinance, *Journal of International Development*, Vol. 14, No. 3, pp. 305–324.

Wong, P.K., Ho, Y.P. and Autio, E. (2005), Entrepreneurship, innovation and economic growth: evidence from the GEM data, *Small Business Economics*, Vol. 24, No. 3, pp. 335–348.

Wood, E. (2001), Marketing information systems in tourism and hospitality SMEs: a study of internet use for market intelligence, *The International Journal of Tourism Research*, Vol. 3, No. 4, pp. 283–298.

Wright, M. (1996), The dubious assumptions of segmentation and targeting, *Management Decision*, Vol. 34, No. 1, pp. 18–31.

Yan, J. and Sorenson, R.L. (2003), Collective entrepreneurship in family firms: the influence of leader attitudes and behaviour, *New England Journal of Entrepreneurship*, Vol. 8, No. 2, pp. 37–52.

Yoffie, D.B. and Kwak, M. (2001), Mastering strategic movement at Palm, *Sloan Management Review*, Vol. 43, No. 1, pp. 55–63.

Young, R. (1988), Future technology trend and related market forecast, *Review of Business*, Vol. 10, No. 1, pp. 19–23.

Yunus, M. (1998), Poverty alleviation: is economics any help? Lessons from the Grameen bank experience, *Journal of International Affairs*, Vol. 52, No. 1, pp. 47–66.

Yusuf, A. and Schindehutte, M. (2000), Exploring entrepreneurship in a declining economy, *Journal of Developmental Entrepreneurship*, Vol. 5, No. 1, pp. 41–57.

Zacharakis, A.L., Meyer, D.G. and DeCastro, J. (1999), Differing perceptions of new venture failure: a matched exploratory study of venture capitalists and entrepreneurs, *Journal of Small Business Management*, Vol. 37, No. 3, pp. 1–15.

economics 81–3
ecopreneurs 196
Edison, T. 26
electric cars 209
Enercon 207
entrepreneurial attitudes 8–10
entrepreneurial creativity 13
entrepreneurial orientation 189
entrepreneurial planning 31–2
entrepreneurial pricing 169–70
entrepreneurial style 9
entrepreneurial success 14–15
entrepreneurial traits 9, 13–14
entrepreneurs 7–8
equity gap 70
equity lending 86
estate planning 186
experiments 41
explicit information 106
export networks 37–8
exporting 77

Facebook 217
failure factors 60–1
failure rates 57–8
Fair Trade 172
family conflict 185
family firms 183–4
finance 85–7
financial resources 98–9
fixed assets 59–60
focus groups 41
Ford, H. 185
forecasting error 75–6
franchise 56, 63
Friends Reunited 76–7
fund raising 68–70

Gates Foundation 218
Gates, B. 11, 80, 218
GEM (Global Entrepreneurship Monitor) 3, 9
generic drugs 211–12
Genesis 192–3
genome entrepreneur 213–14
geodemographics 47–8
Getzs 106–7
giant killers 5–6
global quality 105
global warming 205
Google 6, 33, 218
Government data 38
Government legislation 85
Government policy 1
Grameen Bank 198
greenhouse gases 205, 208
growth opportunities 14

Haji-Innou, S. 10
high-technology start-ups 61–2

Honda 92–3
Honey Care Africa 194
horizontal networks 141
human genome project 214
human genome 213
human resources 102–3
hybrid distribution 175

IBM 127, 202
ice cream 146–7
idea bias 134–5
idea generation 133–4
idea identification 56–7
idea obstacles 133–4
idea relevance 134
inconvenience pricing 165–6
information management 106
initial public offering (IPO)
    70, 86
innovation 7–9, 99
innovation effectiveness 137–8
innovation networks 139–41
innovation process 136–7
intermedaries 171–2
internet 203
Internet Explorer 80–1
internet promotion 157–8
internet research 38–9
interviewing 48–9
interviews 41
intuition 50–1
intuitive segmentation 44
Investors In People (IIP) 64–5
involvement 152
IPCC (Intergovernmental Panel on Climate
    Change) 205
iPod 54
Iverson, K. 130

job creation 2–4
Jobs, S. 26, 54, 176

KaBoom! 193
karmaloop.com 39

Laker, F. 6–7
leadership style 95, 130–1, 189
leadership 93–4
legislation 84
liabilities 59–60
life cycle 3, 53–4
lifestyle firms 5
lifestyle segmentation 48
Logitech 127–9
long term liabilities
    59–60
lottery planning 31

Mackintosh 190–1
macro-environmental factors 167–8
mail survey 41
management responsibilities 65–6
managerial authority 201–2
market demand 202–3
market leadership 92
market potential 73
market research 35
market research benefits 138
market research process 35–7
market segment 44–9
market size 75
mass market 16, 44
Maxwell, R. 96
McDonalds 201
measurability 44
microenterprise 5
micro-finance 196–8
Microsoft 11, 80–1
Morita, A. 168
morphing 66–7
Musk, E. 210
MySpace 29–30

nanobots 215
nanoparticles 215
nanotechnology 214–16
Nestlē 190–1
Netscape 80–1
networked innovation 99–100
networks 37–8
neurotechnology 87–8
new jobs 3
new products 97–8
new technology 203–4
new to the world 49–50
NGOs 194
niche markets 16
Nucor 130

observation 41
on-line communities 178–9
on-line distribution 177
on-line promotion 156–9
on-line surveys 41
opportunity discovery 50–1
overseas aid 194
overtrading 60
Ovskinsky, S.R. 206
owner/manager traits 12

Peerless Saw Company 102
Pelamis 208
personal selling 153
personality promotion 145
PG Tips 184
pharmaceutical industry 211
photovoltaic devices 205–6

planning behaviour 31–2
planning process 21–2
politics 83–4
population ageing 83
potential market size 73
pragmatic entrepreneur 26
price-based competition 169
pricing error 162
primary data 40–3
prior purchase experience 167
process disruption 130
process innovation 100, 129–30
product involvement 152
productivity 101–2
Profit & Loss (P&L) 59–60
promotional affordability 144–5
promotional channels 153–4
promotional chasms 148–9
promotional communication 150–1
promotional planning 147–8
promotional process 147–8
public relations (PR) 154

qualitative research 42–3
quality 104–5
quantitative research 42–3

Ranbaxy 212
recession 15, 82
Reilly Industries 132
resource-based view (RBV) 93
Return On Investment (ROI) 22, 98
reward 13–14
risk 7–8
Roddick, A. 56–7
Rowntree 190–1
Ryanair 169

Saga Ltd 15–16
sales promotion 158, 170–1
sample size 41
Schultz, H. 17
Schumpeter, J. 7–8
scientific management 20
secondary data 38–40
sector importance 1–2
sectoral specialists 5
security 13–14
self employment 12–13
self-identified segment 46–7
simple segmentation 45–6
Sinclair, C. 94–5
Skytrain 6–7
Sloan, A. 20
small firm definition 4–5
social capital 38
social enterprise 191–2
social entrepreneurs 195
social entrepreneurship 191–2

social exclusion 192
social networks 76
societal change 204
socio-demographic change 204
socio-demographics 88
solar entrepreneurs 206
solar power 205
Sony Corporation 168
sources of funds 68–70
Stage Gate Model 135–6
Starbucks 17
Steinberg, S. 27–8
Steinberg's 27–8
strategic plan 20–1
strong network ties 140–1
sub-prime mortgage 83, 86
succession planning 186–8
succession 66, 185
successor capabilities 187
Suma 193
support effectiveness 64–5
support services 63–4
survey design 41
surveys 41–2
SWOT 22

tacit information 106
target audience 148
tax burden 83–4
tax problems 186
Taylor, F. 20
team leadership 131–2
technological disruption 127–9
technology 87
Telsa 209–10
terrestrial data 40
The Body Shop 56–7, 155
The White Company 46
thin film technology 206
tidal power 207
Total Quality Management 106
Toyota 92–3
Toyota Prius 209
trade associations 40

trade magazines 40
Trade Plus Aid 193
Trickle Up Programme 197
Tri-Seal Corporation 103–4
Tupperware 145–6

unconventional promotion 155–6
unk-unks 48–9
US Census Bureau 38

Value Added Resellers 175
value price relationship 164
VCR 78
venture capitalists 25, 70
vertical networks 141
viability 44
Videodisc 78
viral marketing 156
virtual communities 178

Wal-Mart 93
Wang, A. 202
wave power entrepreneurs 208
wave power 207–8
weak network ties 140–1
Web distribution 177
welfare state 192
Whittle, F. 26
wild card event 204
wind power 206–7
word of mouth (WOM) 153
word processors 202
workflow 101
World Wide Web 156, 176
Wrigleys Company 188–9

Xerox 201

Yahoo 66–8
Yellow Pages 153
YouTube 6, 32–3, 217
Yunus, M. 64, 197–8

Zuckerberg, M. 217